Brazil in the Sixties

ATLANTIC OCEAN

RORAIMA
Boa Vista

AMAPÁ
Macapá

Belém

São Luís

AMAZONAS

PARÁ

MARANHÃO

CEARÁ

Fortaleza

RIO GRANDE
DO NORTE
Natal

Manaus

Teresina

PARAÍBA
João
Pessoa

PERNAMBUCO
Recife

ACRE

Pôrto Velho

PIAUÍ

ALAGOAS
Maceió

Rio Branco

RONDÔNIA

MATO GROSSO

GOIÁS

BAHIA

Aracaju
SERGIPE

Salvador

Cuiabá

Brasília
DISTRITO
FEDERAL

Goiânia

MINAS
GERAIS

ESPÍRITO SANTO

Belo Horizonte

Vitória

BRAZIL

SÃO PAULO

RIO DE JANEIRO

São Paulo

Niterói
Rio de Janeiro
GUANABARA

State or Territorial
Boundary ——————

PARANÁ

Federal Capital ●

Curitiba

State or Territorial
Capital ○

SANTA CATARINA

Florianópolis

Pôrto Alegre

RIO GRANDE
DO SUL

BRAZIL
in the Sixties

Edited by
Riordan Roett

VANDERBILT
UNIVERSITY PRESS

Nashville, 1972

Library of Congress Cataloguing-in-Publication Data
Main entry under title:

Brazil in the sixties.

    Includes bibliographical references.
     1. Brazil—Politics and government—1954-
2. Brazil—Economic conditions—1945-   3. Brazil
—Social conditions.   I. Roett, Riordan, 1938-
ed.
F2538.2.B75   320.9'81'06   72-185871

Contents

Brazil in the Sixties—
Significant Dates

1960

April   President Juscelino Kubitschek presides at the formal inauguration of Brasília as the new capital of Brazil.

October   Jânio Quadros elected President with about 45 percent of the popular vote in a three-man race; Vice-President João Goulart re-elected with a plurality of 36 percent in a three-cornered race.

1961

January   Quadros-Goulart ticket inaugurated in Brasília.

March   Government launches an anti-inflation program. The exchange-rate system is reformed; subsidies on essential imports are lowered; government spending is cut; the cruzeiro is effectively devalued by one hundred percent.

August   President Quadros resigns.
             Military ministers attempt to impede the swearing in of Vice-President João Goulart.

September Goulart becomes president under a modified parliamentary system of government which divides executive authority between the president and an appointed prime minister.

November   A stringent law controlling profits repatriation by foreign companies passes the chamber of deputies.
             The first National Peasant Congress is held in Belo Horizonte.

December   The first Master Plan of the Superintendency for the Development of the Northeast (SUDENE) is approved by Congress.

1962

February   Governor Leonel Brizola of Rio Grande do Sul, the president's brother-in-law, expropriates a local telephone company, a subsidiary of the International Telephone and Telegraph Company.

April   President Goulart visits the United States and addresses a joint session of Congress.
             The $131 million United States foreign aid program for the Brazilian Northeast is signed in Washington.

October	Congressional and gubernatorial elections: Jânio Quadros defeated for governor in São Paulo; Miguel Arraes elected governor of Pernambuco; Leonel Brizola wins a seat in the Chamber of Deputies by a large vote.
December	The government's *Plano Trienal* (Three-Year Plan for Social and Economic Development) is announced. It is the work primarily of Celso Furtado, Superintendent of SUDENE, the Northeast Development Agency, who is serving as Extraordinary Minister for Planning.

1963

January	A national plebiscite overwhelmingly returns full presidential power to Goulart.
March	Finance Minister San Tiago Dantas visits Washington and successfully renegotiates the foreign-debt obligations of Brazil. An agrarian reform bill is sent to the congress requiring compensation with government bonds; a constitutional amendment will be required.
May	A Chamber of Deputies committee rejects the agrarian reform proposal by a vote of 7 to 4.
June	The cabinet agrees to a 70 percent salary increase for military personnel and the civil service employees.
	The cabinet is changed and Finance Minister San Tiago Dantas is replaced; fears for the anti-inflationary program of the government are expressed.
July	Two thousand members of the Military Club endorse an ultimatum to Congress demanding the passage of the 70 percent pay increase within ten days.
	Congress passes pay increase bill.
	Finance Minister Carvalho Pinto informs cabinet that the amortization and interest payments scheduled for the 1963-65 period would equal $1.8 billion or about 43 percent of the expected export revenue for that period.
September	General Humberto Castello Branco is appointed chief of staff of the army.
	Noncommissioned officers and enlisted men in the air force, navy, and marines revolt in Brasília; they hold the president of the Chamber of Deputies and a justice of the Supreme Court hostages before surrendering.
December	Admiral Cândido Aragão appointed commandant of the Naval Fusiliers Corps; the Admiral is known as a radical leftist. Finance Minister Carvalho Pinto resigns in what is seen as protest against continuing inflation and the president's unwillingness to work to control it.

December (cont)	The cost of living in the state of Guanabara (Rio de Janeiro) had increased by 55 percent in 1962, it is announced.

1964

February	The government issues decrees creating new agencies to control the pricing of essential consumer goods.
March 13	President Goulart appears at a mass rally in Rio de Janeiro and signs two decrees: the first nationalizes all private oil refineries and the second provides for the expropriation of "under-utilized" properties.
March 20	General Castello Branco circulates a memorandum analyzing the current political situation and reaffirming the nonpolitical role of the armed forces.
March 31	The Armed Forces oust Goulart.
April	An Institutional Act is issued by the military high command which provides a general framework for the governance of the nation.
	General Castello Branco is sworn in as president.
May	Brazil breaks diplomatic relations with Cuba.
June	Former President Kubitschek loses his seat in the federal senate; his political rights are canceled for ten years.
	The SNI is created (National Information Service). It is responsible for collecting information related to national security; the agency reports directly to the president.
July	Congress approves the extension of Castello Branco's term of office until March 15, 1967.
August	The Government's Program of Action (PAEG) to control inflation and promote growth is announced.
November	Brazil's first agrarian reform law is passed by Congress.

1965

February	Ranieri Mazzilli is defeated for the presidency of the Chamber of Deputies by UDN deputy Bilac Pinto; Mazzilli, a São Paulo PSD member, had served as acting president of the republic on a number of occasions.
May	President Castello Branco decides to send Brazilian troops to join the Inter-American Peace Force in the Dominican Republic.
July	The president promulgates the executive's draft of the new electoral code on the grounds that Congress had not taken action in the 30 days allowed by the Institutional Act. On the same day, the president signed the new political party statute reorganizing the nation's party system; the Ineligibilities Law, promulgated at at the same time, established criteria for candidacy in the forthcoming elections.

August	After a trip to Brazil, United States Senator J. William Fulbright announces that the country is working efficiently to stabilize the economy and control inflation.
October	Elections in eleven states for governor; candidates interpreted to be anti-regime are elected in Minas Gerais and Guanabara.
	Second Institutional Act issued: existing political parties are abolished; facilitates federal intervention in the states; determines that the president shall be elected by indirect election.

1966

January	War Minister Arthur da Costa e Silva launches his candidacy for president.
May	ARENA, one of the two recently organized political parties, nominates General Costa e Silva and deputy Pedro Aleixo as their candidates for president and vice-president.
June	The MDB, the opposition party, decides not to participate in the indirect presidential elections.
July	An attempt to assassinate General Costa e Silva fails in Recife.
September	ARENA elects governor in twelve states in indirect elections. Former Presidents Kubitschek and Goulart consulted by Former Governor Carlos Lacerda on the formation of a united opposition front to the government.
	After a series of confrontations with the police, a national student strike is called.
October	Costa e Silva elected the 25th president of the republic in indirect elections.
	President recesses Congress until after the November congressional elections.
November	Congressional and senatorial elections give ARENA a large margin of victory.

1967

January	Congress promulgates, with little change, a new consitution submitted by the executive branch.
March	President Castello Branco decrees a new national security law. General Costa e Silva inaugurated as president.
July	The *Strategic Program of Development* (1968-70) of the Costa e Silva government is approved by the president.
	Former President Castello Branco dies in an air crash.
September	Lacerda and Goulart sign a pact in Montevideo endorsing the formation of a united opposition.
December	Interior Minister General Albuquerque Lima states that the development of the Amazon region is necessary for national security and must be carried out by national organizations.

1968

March   University student Edson Luıs Lima Santos fatally shot in a student encounter with Rio de Janeiro police. Large-scale student demonstrations erupt and continue through August.

October   Military and state officials disrupt the clandestine thirtieth Congress of the National Union of Students (UNE) outside of São Paulo.

December   Governor Carlos Lacerda loses his political rights.

The government issues the Fifth Institutional Act.

The federal congress is recessed indefinitely by the government for its failure to remove deputy Márcio Moreira Alves's parliamentary immunity, allowing him to be prosecuted under the National Security Law.

1969

August   President Costa e Silva is incapacitated; junta of armed forces ministers assume power.

September The United States Ambassador to Brazil is kidnapped by urban guerrillas; his release is gained with the freeing of fifteen political prisoners and their departure from the country.

October   Presidency and vice-presidency declared vacant by the armed forces high command; Vice-President Aleixo prevented from assuming office.

General Emilio Garrastazu Médici elected president by the Congress after his selection by the high command of the armed forces.

Amendment Number 1 to the 1967 constitution is decreed by the military junta; it severely restricts the power of the congress and enhances the role of the president in national decision-making.

November   Former Communist deputy Carlos Marighela, an important leader of the urban terrorist movement, is shot to death by police in São Paulo.

Introduction

BRAZIL IN THE SIXTIES is a collaborative, multidisciplinary effort to explore Brazilian society during a crucial decade. Given the complexity of the changes that have taken place in Brazil between 1960 and 1969, it seemed worthwhile to combine the talents of both the social sciences and the humanities in an attempt to analyze the nature of the changes that are relatively easy to identify but far more difficult to understand.

We are concerned with clarifying some of the important aspects of the "dynamics of modernization" in Brazil. C. E. Black has defined modernization as

the process by which historically evolved institutions are adapted to the rapidly changing functions that reflect the unprecedented increase in man's knowledge, permitting control over his environment, that accompanied the scientific revolution.[1]

The 1960s were the decade in which Brazil grappled with the problems of adaptation in the face of rapidly growing economic and sociopolitical change. It was a decade of transformation, in which the traditional order that had dominated society for centuries felt the surging impact of new groups and new demands. The institutional order, adequate to the relatively uncomplicated Brazil of pre-World War II, was inadequate to cope with these burdens. It collapsed in March of 1964 with the destruction of the constitutional order and the assumption of power by the armed forces.

The Sixties had opened on a Brazil full of promise. The monumental task of constructing a new inland capital city, Brasília, while not completed, had reached a sufficiently advanced stage to merit an inauguration attended by an internationally prominent audience. President Juscelino Kubitschek presided over a political coalition that seemed able and willing to continue the democratic experiment begun

1. *The Dynamics of Modernization* (New York: Harper and Row, 1966), p. 7.

in 1945 with the overthrow of Getúlio Vargas. Social and economic indicators reflected a nation growing rapidly in population and in the process of accelerated urbanization and industrialization. There seemed to the casual observer little to indicate that the Sixties would not bring an expansion of the economy, further social differentiation, and political stability.

Instead, the economy faltered, then seemed to stagger under the burdens of a growing foreign debt and a state of hyperinflation. Agricultural production fell behind consumer needs. The major social groups in society, the armed forces, the Roman Catholic Church, the university students, and political party leadership, grew increasingly antagonistic towards each other; the harmony of the late Fifties disintegrated. There arose a cry for "basic reforms." Positions polarized as the options for dealing with the perceived crises dwindled to two: immediate and perhaps violent radical restructuring of society or a continuation of the hegemony of a preferred few.

The second section of *Brazil in the Sixties* provides a framework within which the major political developments of the decade are evaluated. The editor's article assesses the social mobilization that took place in the 1946 to 1964 period in an effort to explain the eventual intervention of the armed forces in the political system in 1964. The second half of the paper deals with the military in power from 1964 to 1969. Without understanding the relationship between socioeconomic change and political modernization efforts in Brazil, it is difficult to comprehend the emergence of what I have termed a "praetorian army."

Douglas Chalmers's article focuses on political groups and authority in Brazil. Among his conclusions, he states that "the military regime constitutes merely a new form through which elitism has been maintained." Given weaknesses of political groups in Latin American societies generally, and in Brazil specifically, the intervention of the military in 1964 reflects "in a very real sense a logical extension of major trends and characteristics of Brazilian politics."

Commenting on United States-Brazilian relations during the decade, Peter Bell states that "the reflex reaction [of the U.S.] to the perceived threat of communism remained real, and the heady talk of democracy, in the absence of an aid commitment to political development, turned out to be rhetoric." Mr. Bell examines in detail the nature of the relationship between the two nations. The United States, by both its presence and its general policy, provided an important parameter in the modernization efforts underway in Brazil in the 1960s.

The four papers in Section Three constitute an important statement about the Brazilian economy during the decade under examination. Given the spectacular economic growth of the 1950s, and the talk
of "takeoff" that so prominently reflected the optimism of the Brazilian government, the essays offer a sobering review of the complexities
of economic development in a modernizing society.

Werner Baer and Isaac Kerstenetzky state that "the principal
characteristics of the Brazilian economy in the decade of the sixties was
its drifting nature." Characterizing the Fifties as a decade of "economic initiative" and the Sixties as a period of "economic reflex" the
authors probe the adjustments to previous structural changes that
were required for continued growth after the emphasis on import
substitution industrialization in the 1950s.

"For the last twenty years, Brazilian agriculture has appeared to
informed people as living on borrowed time," comments William H.
Nicholls in his essay on the agricultural economy. Analyzing the agricultural performance of the Fifties, he proceeds to consider the lack
of investment in agriculture by the government and the agricultural
needs of the nation faced with "a growing and increasingly prosperous
public."

The public sector has played an increasingly important role in
the Brazilian economy. Andrea Maneschi's article focuses on the fact
that "the very size of the public sector in relation to national income
and the preponderance of public enterprises in several key sectors of
the economy place in the hands of Brazilian policy-makers a powerful
base for effective economic planning." The growing importance of
technocratic planning and decision-making in Brazil under the military
regime, emphasizes the relevance of understanding the role of the public sector and its relationship to Brazilian modernization.

David Goodman's article dealing with industrial development in
the Northeast complements Maneschi's work by examining closely one
public-sector scheme for inducing economic change. The Northeast,
long the most backward of Brazil's regions, acquired new prominence
in the late 1950s and early 1960s. One effort to integrate the area into
the national economy was a tax-credit scheme, referred to as Article
34/18 which served to attract Brazilian corporations to invest in the
Northeast.

While recognizing the contribution to regional development of
the efforts of the regional superintendency, SUDENE, Goodman comments that "the serious resource misallocation arising from 34/18 investment decisions clearly must be recognized. This stems, in great

part, from the absence of carefully formulated priorities in development and industrial policy." Goodman's article, when read in the context of the other three essays in this section, provides some feeling for the barriers to rapid economic development in Brazil.

The social implications of modernization clearly emerge in Section Four. Douglas Graham, in dealing with higher education in Brazil in the 1960s, states that it has become clear that "education in Brazil has now become an area that is considered too important to be left to educators alone. Educated manpower is now a major concern and a top priority to the technocrats responsible for economic planning." After years of neglect, higher education, under the military regime, has slowly begun the transformation process that will adapt it to the needs of Brazil in the decades ahead.

Emilio Willems's article refutes the position of "those who accept the unqualified view that all agricultural resources of Latin America remain in the grip of a few powerful and wealthy feudal barons." Examining the Northern Paraná region, Willems analyzes the emergence of a rural middle class in what remains a frontier society. Given the complexity of change in Brazil during the 1960s, his essay emphasizes the continuing and autonomous social change taking place in Brazil and, indeed, in all developing societies.

Rowan Ireland examines the changing role of the Roman Catholic Church in the Brazilian Northeast in the 1960s. Analyzing both the internal dynamics of the Church as an institution and as a movement, Ireland also inspects the relationship between the Church in Brazil and the international Church. His investigation leads him to summarize by saying that "freedom from the illusions of the early sixties may be the decisive resource of the Brazilian Church in the seventies." One of the most important institutions in Brazil, which has often been identified as one of the most traditional, began to transform itself in the 1960's.

The literature of Brazil serves to reflect the tensions of the modernization process. Earl Thomas's article on protest in the novel and the theater reminds us that "protest in Brazilian literature is as old as the poetry of Gregório de Matos, who left us an unflattering picture of society and government in the colonial Northeast." Analyzing and interpreting the novels and the theater of the 1960s, Thomas offers a fascinating picture of literary and intellectual ferment as writers respond to the discontinuities in their society.

Alexandrino Severino in his study of the short story identifies "the gradual development of Brazilian literature towards maturity and

. . . self-assertion." Using the short-story genre, he explores the major development themes in literature and analyzes their reflection of a changing society.

While each author has written about Brazil in the Sixties from his particular perspective and interest, the common theme of a decade provides a useful framework for uniting the individual efforts. Brazil occupies a unique place in Latin America; its course of modernization is eagerly studied by both students and practitioners of societal change. This collection of essays tries to illuminate some of the complexities of change in Brazil and, simultaneously, to indicate the future course of modernization. If the essays arouse interest in Brazil and inspire others to examine more closely the process of change and adaptation that is characteristic of all the Third World nations, we will have succeeded in our objective of stimulating further thought and reflection about the Sixties and beyond.

Vanderbilt University
January 1972

RIORDAN ROETT

The Political Setting:
From Kubitschek to Médici

1 RIORDAN ROETT

A Praetorian Army in Politics: The Changing Role of the Brazilian Military

THE ARMED forces were inextricably part of the political process in Brazil in the Sixties. As a leading power contender in the political system during the presidency of João Goulart (1961-1964) or as the wielders of national power after the coup d'etat of March 31, 1964—referred to by the military as the Revolution of 1964—it is impossible to explore the vagaries of Brazilian politics without emphasizing the role of the military establishment.

This essay attempts to identify the emergence in the Brazilian political system of a praetorian or politicized/interventionist military. While the focus is the decade from 1960 to 1969, the military in politics can only be understood by the unfolding of the 1946 Republic—the political system created after the overthrow of Getúlio Vargas by the armed forces in 1945. Thus, the first sections of this essay deal with the 1960-1964 period in the context of the 1946 Republic (1946-1964); the final sections concentrate on the politics of the 1964-1969 period during which the military exercised direct control over the political process.

The Brazilian military has intervened in politics since 1889. In that year, a military revolt overthrew the monarchy. Again in 1930, support by young military officers, the *tenentes*, helped Getúlio Vargas topple the Old Republic. In 1945 some of these same officers forced the dictator's retirement. And in 1964 the military high com-

3

mand ousted President João Goulart, the populist and ideological heir of Vargas.

Thus within a general historical framework of continuous intervention in, but rapid withdrawal from, politics, the roots of the more "permanent" 1964 intervention are to be found in the unfolding of the 1946 Republic. Specifically, the military's intervention is an outgrowth of the repercussions of rapid social mobilization and weak political institutionalization: the Brazilian political system confronted a series of modernization "time sequences" and "rates of change" that precluded the political system's successfully coping with growing "loads," given the continuing influence of traditional social and political power contenders.

Definitions

By "social mobilization" we mean, in Karl Deutsch's formulation, "the process in which major clusters of old social, economic and psychological commitments are eroded or broken and people become available for new patterns of socialization and behavior."[1] In discussing political development, Samuel Huntington's focus on institutionalization is relevant to the Brazilian post-1946 experience: "the primary problem of politics is the lag in the development of political institutions behind social and economic change."[2] The stability of a political system will depend on the ratio of institutionalization to political participation in a society.

Increased participation is a basic aspect of the political modernization process. New political organizations must emerge to organize and channel that participation. Praetorian polities are those political systems manifesting low levels of institutionalization and high levels of participation. In these systems, social groups act directly in the political process. Regime authority is weakened and the military is given frequent opportunity to intervene in politics.[3]

Building on this formulation, Amos Perlmutter has identified two types of praetorian army—the arbitrator type and the ruler type. The former "imposes a time limit on army rule" and returns the government to civilian hands while it resumes its role as guardian of the constitution. The ruler-type army challenges the very legitimacy of the

1. Karl W. Deutsch, "Social Mobilization and Political Development," *American Political Science Review*, Vol. LV, No. 3 (September 1961), p. 494.
2. Samuel H. Huntington, *Political Order in Changing Societies* (New Haven: Yale University Press, 1968), p. 5.
3. *Ibid.*, ch. 1.

political system it overthrows; it seeks to remain involved in politics to bring about a transformation of the political process.[4]

The armed forces (and normally the army because of its size and relative pre-eminence in internal security maintenance) become "praetorian" when the political system manifests characteristics of low institutionalization and high rates of social mobilization, leading to the direct involvement of the military in politics. Such a politicized/interventionist army, therefore, reflects the political imbalances of a modernizing state. Military interventions are but one substantive manifestation of a far deeper phenomenon in developing countries: the general and unavoidable politicization of all social forces and institutions.

As Charles Anderson has forcefully argued, the political systems of Latin America are "tentative":

Unlike nations where constitutional provision and the legitimacy of election guarantees a specified life span for any government, in Latin America government is based on a flexible coalition among diverse power contenders which is subject to revision at any time if the terms under which the original government was formed are deemed violated. Revision occurs primarily when an existing holder of an important power capability feels threatened by action of government.[5]

Throughout Latin America, the military possesses one of the most formidable power capabilities. There participation is not a question of whether the military has a role in politics—the question in Latin America is how and when they will participate. Given the existence in many countries of praetorian governments—in which civilian institutions lack legitimacy or are in a position to be dominated by the military—the "military question" is obviously among the most relevant for any examination of politics in Latin America.

A Framework for Analysis

An important consequence of the emergence of a praetorian government is the weakening of regime authority. Using Richard Rose's definition, a political regime is defined as "that set of institutions co-

---

4. Amos Perlmutter, "The Praetorian State and the Praetorian Army: Toward a Taxonomy of Civil-Military Relations," *Comparative Politics*, I, No. 3 (April 1969), 382-404.

5. Charles W. Anderson, *Politics and Economic Change in Latin America* (Princeton, N.J.: D. Van Nostrand Co., 1967), p. 103.

ordinating and controlling the civil administration, the police and the military within a state."[6] This definition explicitly recognizes the unique importance in politics of an organization claiming the monopoly of force within a society. *Authority* is a "universal term to label collectively the different patterns of relationships between regimes and the populations from which they seek obedience and allegiance." The type of authority that a regime exercises can be distinguished "by the degree to which its population acts in accord with regulations concerning the maintenance of the regime and has diffuse cultural orientations approving the regime." The greater the compliance a regime receives and the greater the support from its subjects, the more legitimate it will be—its authority will be exercised without frequent resort to force and/or coercion.

A useful framework within which to analyze the issues of political modernization "loads," the role of the military, and regime authority is that offered by Eric A. Nordlinger.[7] Emphasizing time sequences and rates of change, he calls for a move away from attempts to identify general patterns in political systemic development and urges us to examine various developmental patterns and ask questions about their different consequences. He identifies four political phenomena as crucial, and whose sequence and rates of change constitute independent variables for analyzing political development: national identity, a central government that is institutionalized, the existence of protoparties (as contrasted with mass parties), and mass suffrage. Three dependent variables Nordlinger indicates as correlated to the four independent variables are the presence or absence of widespread violence, an authoritarian government which represses political dissent, and a form of democratic government which is genuinely representative, durable and decisionally effective. With regard to these variables, dependent and independent, Nordlinger cogently argues that

6. Richard Rose, "Dynamic Tendencies in the Authority of Regimes," *World Politics*, XXI, No. 4, July 1969, pp. 602-628.

7. Eric A. Nordlinger, "Political Development: Time Sequences and Rates of Change," *World Politics*, XX, No. 3 (April 1968), 494-520. For purposes of this chapter, I assume that the issue of a national identity in Brazil had been resolved by the mid-twentieth century. For a consideration of the problem of integration in Brazil, which is related to the identity theme, see Alfred C. Stepan, "The Continuing Problem of Brazilian Integration: The Monarchical and Republican Periods," in Frederick B. Pike, ed., *Latin American History: Select Problems* (New York: Harcourt, Brace & World, Inc., 1969) pp. 259-296.

with respect to time sequences, it is argued that the probabilities of a political system's developing in a nonviolent, nonauthoritarian, and eventually democratically stable manner are maximized when a national identity emerged first, followed by the institutionalization of the central government, and then by the emergence of mass parties and a mass electorate. With respect to rates of change, it is argued that if an attempt is made to create a national identity, institutionalize central government, form mass parties and usher in mass electoral participation in a rapid fashion, the outcome is likely to be widespread violence and repressive rule, which make it more difficult to establish a democratic system and, further, assure that if such a system is established, its stability, representativeness, and decisional effectiveness will suffer.

The Challenge of Modernization after 1946

Brazil after 1946 saw the convergence of three potential conflicts of modernization. The first was the drive by the federal government to consolidate its preeminence in national decision-making. Before 1930, Brazil had been decentralized administratively and politically.[8] Vargas's fifteen years in office brought a concerted effort to centralize power in the hands of the national government. With the fall of the dictator, the governments of the 1946 Republic attempted to retain a predominant voice in exercising regime authority without severely limiting the powers of the states in the reconstituted federal system. But the institutions and procedures of national decision-making were new and untried. Strong "private governments" continued to challenge and oppose the pre-eminence of the national government.[9] Douglas

8. A standard history of Brazil remains that by José Maria Bello, *A History of Modern Brazil, 1889-1964* (Stanford: Stanford University Press, 1966). Manual Nunes Dias et al., *Brasil Em Perspectiva*, (São Paulo: Difusão Europeia do Livro, 1969) is an interesting collection of essays on Brazilian historical and political development. Octavio Ianni, *O Colapso do Populismo no Brasil* (Rio de Janeiro: Editôra Civilzação Brazileira, 1968) remains a provocative interpretation of social and political change in Brazil since 1946.

9. To avoid a disciplinary entanglement about modernization versus development, I adopt Dakwart A. Rustow's definition of modernization: "rapidly widening control over nature through closer cooperation among men. It transforms both man and society, but most of all man's mind," in *A World of Nations: Problems of Political Modernization* (Washington: The Brookings Institution, 1967), p. 3. Rustow continues to say that his emphasis is the political strand of the "social tapestry." I have attempted to use modernization here to indicate the societal transformation that Rustow discusses; I have used political modernization or political development to refer to the specifically "political" aspects of that process. Robert E. Scott, "Political Parties and Policy-Making in Latin America," in Joseph LaPalombara & Myron Weiner, *Political Parties and Political Development* (Princeton: Princeton University Press, 1966), p. 332.

Chalmers has described the Brazilian political reality in the following way:

Basically, our proposition is that the fundamental axis for the crystallization of political groupings in Brazil . . . lies not in the shared interests of their members defined in terms of their common occupation or ideology, but in the relationships of authority and interchange between subordinates and superiors. What is involved is the primacy of one or two aspects that are present in all minimally structured groups. They might be considered the organizational aspects and the dimension of shared goals.[10]

Chalmers continues to say that although the two aspects are found in any group, the crucial difference for political behavior is whether groups have crystallized around relationships of authority and domination, which he terms "vertical" groups, or around shared interests, which he calls "horizontal" groups. His conclusion is that vertical groups dominate in Brazil: urban political machines, the followers of a rural *coronel* or patriarch or a governmentally controlled association. Vertical groups emphasize the superior-inferior, dominant-subordinate syndrome of political authority. The horizontal groups, such as independent trade unions, ideological/programmatic political parties, and civic associations, are correspondingly weak and/or nonexistent. These vertical groups are the "private governments" that Robert Scott identifies in the Latin American political process. They are durable, flexible and inexorably related to the distribution and management of power in Brazilian society.

The 1946 Republic witnessed the appearance of a bewildering multi-party system, a second aspect of the modernization process. These were mass parties in that they sought broad electoral strength among the burgeoning urban groups, spoke in terms of mass participation, and shaped their campaign slogans for high emotional appeal.

Suddenly, Brazil had a mass multiparty system without previous experience with any sort of open and competitive party system. The Old Republic had been dominated by the Republican party and its state affiliates, which represented the interests of the local oligarchies. The Vargas period from 1930 to 1937 had seen the rapid rise and decline of fledgling political movements unable to challenge Vargas meaningfully; after the dictatorship had been declared in 1937, no parties were allowed. Thus, 1946 was the first time that the Brazilian

10. Douglas A. Chalmers, "Political Groups and Authority in Brazil," Chapter Two of this volume.

political system had experimented with a competitive party system.

Two of the three major parties of the 1946 Republic were inspired by Vargas himself: the Brazilian Labor party (PTB) and the Social Democratic party (PSD). The former represented the vehicle by which Vargas organized and manipulated the urban following he had created during the 1930 to 1945 period; the latter collected together the state machines and bureaucrats that had played a dominant role in the Vargas years. The two forged a political alliance that would precariously dominate national politics in the postwar years. The third, the National Democratic Union (UDN), was an amorphous group united, at first, by a desire to oust Vargas. It contained the organized opposition to Vargas and the populist politics he represented.[11]

And a third significant manifestation of the modernization process to appear in postwar Brazil was the emergence for the first time of the makings of a mass electorate. In part, this electorate emerged from the struggle for votes and electoral support of the multi-party system. In part, it arose from the continuing agitation for economic growth and social development by populist political leaders. And, in part, it resulted from the rural migration that swelled the urban population and placed new and potentially unmeetable demands on the capacity of the fledgling institutionalized national government.

Social Mobilization in Brazil during the 1946 Republic: Demographic and Economic Data

The Brazilian population grew from 41,236,315 in 1940 to 70,119,071 in 1960 (estimate for 1969: 90,860,000) with an estimated growth rate of 3 percent (the estimated growth rate of the nineteen Latin America Republics being 2.9 percent).[12]

The urban population grew from 31 percent urban in 1940 to 45 percent in 1960. The increase in the urban population between 1950 and 1960 is calculated at 70.3 percent, higher than the 57.4 percent average for all of Latin America. In 1960, 32.3 percent of the total population (71.6 percent of the urban population) lived in urban centers of 10,000 or more. And, as of 1969, Brazil had four cities with

---

11. Fernando Pedreira, *Março 31: Civis e Militares no Processo da Crise Brasileira* (Rio de Janeiro: José Alvaro, Editor, 1964) provides an excellent framework for analyzing the role of parties and the 1946-64 period.

12. The demographic data are taken from *Atualidade Estatística do Brasil* (1969), Fundação IBGE, Rio de Janeiro: *Anuário Estatístico do Brasil* (Rio de Janeiro: Fundação IBGE, 1969); and *Statistical Abstract of Latin America* (Latin American Center, University of California, Los Angeles, December 1969).

populations of more than one million and five other cities with populations of more than half a million people.

The literate population (15 years and over) grew from 10,379,990 in 1940 to 24,321,798 in 1960, the percentages for these years being 43.7 percent and 60.5 percent. In 1940 there were 30,856,325 illiterates; in 1960 there were 45,797,273. The growth rate of the population means that, in absolute terms, Brazil had a larger number of illiterates in the 1960s than in the 1940s.

Douglas Graham has demonstrated that there was a marked increase in the volume of internal migration among the states of Brazil during the decade of the 1950s.[13] In terms of absolute numbers, the grand total for the country as a whole increased 2.7 times its level over the 1940s. In relative terms, the countrywide displacement totals also increased sharply. The countrywide percentages for the period 1950-1960 more than doubled. He documents that the poorer states were net exporters and the wealthier states of the southeast net importers of migrants. Thus, the growing urban population of this era resulted from both migration and natural population increase. The arrival in the cities of waves of migrants meant new and different "loads" for the government as it struggled with the over-all issue of rapid urbanization.

And T. Lynn Smith has indicated that the increases in urban/suburban and rural populations, from 1940 to 1960, indicate a heavy preference for the urban/suburban:[14]

Percent Increase

urban/suburban		rural		urban/suburban increase as a percentage of the total increase
1940-50	1950-60	1940-50	1950-60	1950-60
46.0	70	16.9	17	69

The nature of the Brazilian economy reflects this change. The distribution of the economically active population shifted substantially: in 1940, 71 percent were employed in the primary sector and in 1960, 58 percent were so employed; the shift in the secondary sector was from 9 percent in 1940 to almost 13 percent in 1960; and the share of

13. Douglas H. Graham, "Divergent and Convergent Regional Economic Growth and Internal Migration in Brazil, 1940-1960," *Economic Development and Cultural Change*, 18, No. 3 (April 1970), pp. 362-382.

14. T. Lynn Smith, *Brazil: People and Institutions*, revised edition, (Baton Rouge: Louisiana State University Press, 1963), pp. 597-599.

the population employed in the tertiary sector rose from 20 percent in 1940 to almost 29 percent in 1960.

The structure of the economy shifted (as demonstrated by a percentage distribution of the Gross Domestic Product) from 39.5 percent derived from agriculture in 1940 to 27.6 percent in 1966; the change in industry was from 17.3 percent in 1940 to 35.1 percent in 1966; and in the service sector from 43.2 percent in 1940 down to 37.3 percent in 1966.

While these changes indicate, first, a move away from dependence on the agricultural sector and, second, the population growth in urban areas, the following figures indicate the "dark side" of that change. While the 1950-1960 growth of urban population (average annual rate of growth) was 6.5 percent in Brazil, the growth of industrial employment was only 2.6 percent, indicating the capital-intensive (as opposed to labor-intensive) aspects of the industrial and commercial expansion.

In addition, the annual rate of inflation rose from 20 percent in the 1955 to 1960 period, to 35 percent in 1961, 49 percent in 1962, 72 percent in 1963 and 91 percent in 1964. The increase in the cost of living (state of Guanabara) rose 70 percent between January 1959 and October 1960 and 109.5 percent between January 1963 and February 1964. In addition, the Government deficit rose from 0.7 percent (percent of the Gross National Product) in 1954 to 3.0 percent in 1959 to 5.1 percent in 1963; government expenditures were 30 times larger in 1963 than in 1954 but government receipts increased but 20 times in the same time span.

Perhaps the most time-consuming and deleterious economic issue confronting the Brazilian government was the repayment of the nation's foreign debt. By the early 1960s debt servicing had reached alarming levels. The situation created irreconcilable pressures on Brazil's capacity to meet its external payments. Its international credit standing was at stake—and it required credit to develop. To cut expenses, that is, to reduce imports of scarce resources would also hinder the development effort. The crisis was magnified by the sharp fall in export earnings in the early 1960s which further reduced the government's capacity to meet its obligations. (See Table 1).

By December 1960 Brazil's total external debt amounted to almost $4 billion, and 70 percent of that was scheduled for repayment by the end of 1963. A hasty rescheduling by the Quadros government in early 1961 merely postponed the crisis two or three years. It fell to the Goulart government (1961-1964) to deal with the issue. Given the erratic political orientation of that administration, its efforts in the 1962-

TABLE 1
BRAZIL—EXTERNAL DEBT

Year	Grand Total of Outstanding external debt (millions of dollars)	Total Debt Service repayable in next 3 years	
		Amount	Percent
1956	$2694	1760	65.3
1957	2659	1963	73.8
1958	3069	1905	62.1
1959	3392	2109	62.2
1960	3910	2720	69.6
1961	3773	2167	57.4
1962	4025	2359	58.6
1963	3986	2273	57.0
1964	3874	2104	54.3
1965	4759	2423	50.9
1966	5196	2336	45.0

Source: John T. Donnelly, "External Debt and Economic Development in Postwar Brazil, 1947-1966," unpublished Ph.D. dissertation, Vanderbilt University, 1970.

1963 period to renegotiate payment of its debt with the United States failed. The agreements originally reached between the two countries were unfulfilled and the United States refused to provide further credit. The other creditor nations, United States allies, followed a similar policy. Brazil not only faced an overwhelming foreign debt to repay but was in the situation where her inability to repay precluded further financing required for both repayment and further economic growth.

A continuing problem through the 1950s and 1960s remained the backwardness of the more underdeveloped areas of the nation. The Southeast rose from 79.5 percent of the industrial product in 1955 to 83.2 percent in 1963 while the Northeast (containing about one third of the national population) fell from 6.5 percent in 1955 to 5.2 percent in 1964. The geographic distribution of industrial employment reflects the same gap: in 1955 the Southeast had 70.8 and in 1964 that figure rose to 75.4 percent.

For the same time period, the Northeast fell from 12.6 percent to 8.8 percent. The Northeast remained, during this time, the area in which the population grew more rapidly than the Southeast and in which the general indices of social welfare, such as literacy and infant mortality, were far higher than the average figures for the Southeast region.

These figures indicate some of the social and economic issues that confronted the governments of the 1946 Republic. Rapid urbanization, a slow growth in the availability of industrial employment, a rapidly rising cost of living, and serious inflation all combined to produce heavy strains on the capacity of the regime to satisfy growing demands. The urban-industrial dilemma was accompanied by very slow growth in the agricultural sector as Table 2 indicates. Per capita production remains, in 1969, what it was in the late 1950s with only minor fluctuations. Total production figures indicate uneven growth for the late 1950s and early 1960s.

TABLE 2
INDEX OF TOTAL AGRICULTURAL PRODUCTION—BRAZIL
1957-1959 = 100

Per Capita Production

1961	1962	1963	1964	1965	1967	1968	1969
104	103	91	115	100	104	101	101

Total Production

114	119	109	141	126	135	135	140

Source: *Latin America: Economic Growth Trends* (Washington, D.C.: Agency for International Development, 1969), p. 17.

The Brazilian military were well aware of the implications of the demographic and economic data for political stability. They had participated in the creation of the 1946 Republic and, with some misgiving, had given the political system over to civilian politics. But by the early 1960s important sectors of the military began to believe that the civilians were incompetent. They were unable to manage the economy and they were unable to deal with rising social and economic demands produced by population growth and urbanization. The civilian constitutional regime seemed fragile, bombarded by competing demands, unable to respond. Its capacity to perform, to be "decisionally effective" diminished as the nation moved from crisis to crisis in the early 1960s. The move to institutionalize the central government in terms of effectiveness had not succeeded. The mechanisms for conflict management and the reconciliation of competing demands—the legislature, the electoral system and the party system—appeared as disorganized and ineffectual as the administrative and bureaucratic arms of the regime. Given the large role the armed forces played in fostering the nation's economic growth, they were unwilling to stand by and see their efforts canceled and the nation's progress impeded because of civilian political wrangling.[15]

Electoral Data

The 1946 regime was characterized by what Francisco Weffort, Octavio Ianni, and others have termed "populist" politics.[16] With emphasis on the urban electorate, with little, if any, tendency to institutionalize linkages between voter and government, concerned not about programmatic but pragmatic interests, the populist politician sought votes only to gain public office. Once successful, the populist used his position of influence not in the service of the electorate or the "public good" but in the narrow, parochial sense of satisfying his "clientele" or political following. A populist politician represents clients who are able to "deliver" the popular vote needed for election. The relationship is a "vertical" one as Chalmers describes it. The populist feels no responsibility for socializing his constituency into the prevailing norms of the political system; his contacts with his clients and his voters is intermittent, personalistic, and lacks structure.

The presence of a generation of populist politicians in the political system after 1946 exacerbated the structural duality of Brazilian society. Political debate polarized between the self-seeking urban populists and the lingering but influential representatives of the social and economic elites of the urban areas. The "man in the middle" was the popularly elected president who represented a national constituency which was becoming more and more urban.[17] As "chief bureaucrat" of the national government, he felt more keenly than other national leaders the growing "loads" being placed on the system for higher wages, increased welfare benefits, etc. In his attempts to legislate reform, whether agrarian or tax reform or social welfare measure, the chief executive confronted a strong congressional delegation opposed

15. John D. Wirth, *The Politics of Brazilian Development, 1930-1954* (Stanford: Stanford University Press, 1970) discusses the role of the military in early economic development efforts.

16. The subject of populism has become of increasing interest to Brazilian social scientists recently. See Francisco C. Weffort, "O Populismo na Política Brasileira," in Celso Furtado *et al., Brasil: Tempos Modernos,* (Rio de Janeiro: Editôra Paz e Terra, 1968), pp. 49-75; and *Octavio Ianni, O Colapso do Populismo no Brasil* (Rio de Janeiro: Editôra Civilização Brasileira, 1968).

17. See Jacques Lambert, *Os Dois Brasis*, 2nd ed., (São Paulo: Companhia Editôra Nacional, 1967) for a discussion of the chief executive.

to change, primarily from the underdeveloped regions of the Northeast and North.

The populist politicians exacerbated the political climate by clamoring for drastic reform of the existing social and economic order and blaming the "oligarchy" and its congressional delegation for the nation's lack of progress. Seldom if ever did the "negative" leftists have a meaningful alternative to the aspect of the social or economic order they opposed. Their role was that of gaining personal power by taking advantage of the fears and desires of the urban masses (the ban on illiterates voting effectively precluded populist politics from the rural areas which remained, electorally, under the domination of state and regional elites).[18]

This electoral aspect of the praetorian state can be demonstrated with data from the 1945-1964 period. Table 3 demonstrates the increase in the number of people who voted in Brazil from 1945 to 1963. The presidential vote figure for 1945 and that of 1960 indicated an approximate increase of 100 percent in the number of people voting (from 6 million to 12 million) and approximately 20 percent in the percentage of the population voting (from 13.4 percent to 17.7 percent). Using the 1962 congressional and gubernatorial figures, the rate of in-

TABLE 3
WHO VOTES, BRAZIL, 1945-1963

Year	Population	Registered Voters	% of Pop. Regis.	Actual Vote	% Turnout	% of Pop. Voting
1945 Presidential	46,215,000	7,459,849	16.1	6,200,005	83.1	13.4
1950 Presidential	51,976,000	11,455,149	22.0	8,254,989	72.1	15.9
1954 Legislative	57,098,000	15,104,604	26.5	9,890,475	65.5	17.3
1955 Presidential	58,456,000	15,243,246	26.1	9,097,014	59.7	15.6
1958 Legislative	62,725,000	13,780,244	22.0	12,720,897	92.3	20.3
1960 Presidential	70,967,000	15,543,332	21.9	12,586,354	81.0	17.7
1962 Legislative	75,271,000	18,528,847	24.6	14,747,221	79.6	19.6
1963 Plebiscite	77,521,000	18,565,277	23.9	12,286,173	66.2	15.8

Source: *Brazil: Election Factbook*, No. 2, September 1965 (Washington, D.C.: Institute for the Comparative Study of Political Systems), p. 19.

18. The exception, of course, is the emergence in the Northeast, in and around Recife, Pernambuco, of the Peasant Leagues, led by Francisco Julião and the victory of Miguel Arraes in the race for governor of Pernambuco in October 1962. Both of these related but distinct efforts at political mobilization were eliminated by the March 31, 1964 coup.

crease is even higher: 14.7 million voting in 1962 representing 19.6 percent of the population.

The multi-party system fragmented during this period. The only election for president in which a candidate received a majority of the vote was that of 1945 when General Eurico Dutra received 52.4 percent. In the succeeding elections, the successful presidential candidates received 46.6 percent (Vargas in 1950), 33.8 percent (Kubitschek in 1955) and 44.8 percent (Quadros in 1960). All three presidential elections after that of 1945 (1950, 1955, 1960) had three or more candidates in which a third candidate received 15 percent or more of the total vote.

Far more significant in demonstrating the populist character of the Brazilian praetorian state was the appearance of electoral alliances in the political system after 1946.[19] Formed by any number of the thirteen political parties active after 1946, the alliances existed only for the sake of electing candidates to office under the proportional representation system employed from 1946 to 1964. They offered no true representation, since candidates elected on an alliance ticket assumed their position in congress as party members—the congress was organized along party, not electoral alliance, lines and in no way heeded the ephemeral affiliation the alliance indicated.

The electoral alliance system reflected the populist tendencies of the post-1946 political system. It indicated the fragility and impermanence of the political party system, the one mechanism that might have overcome the vertical patterns of authority and domination, the continuing political influence of the traditional social and economic elites. The alliances allowed candidates to appeal for votes on the basis of a nebulous promise to improve the lot of the voter without any need to worry about specific commitments or returns when office had been gained. The voter, having only the electoral system to turn to in his search for leadership and representation, chose among poorly qualified candidates, bewildered by the "national" political party structure between elections and the sudden emergence of "alliances" when it came time to vote.

In the five congressional elections of the 1946 Republic, the percentage of votes cast for alliances rose from 0 percent in 1945 to 16.7 percent in 1950, to 25.7 percent in 1954, 33.3 percent in 1958 and

19. See Pompeu de Souza, "Eleições de 1962: Decomposição Partidária e Caminhos da Reforma," in Revista Brasileira de Estudos Políticos, No. 16, (January 1964), pp. 7-19.

41.0 percent in 1962 (see Table 4). In some states in 1962 the vote on the alliance tickets went as high as 86.2 percent (Espirito Santo) and 89.1 percent (Rio Grande do Norte). The disintegration of the national political party system seemed imminent. The movement away from party candidates toward alliance choices, and the willingness of the parties to subordinate their identity to an ephemeral alliance, indicated the shallowness of both the`programmatic content and the ideological dedication of Brazilian parties.

TABLE 4

VOTES AND PERCENTAGES OF VOTE OBTAINED BY MAJOR PARTIES IN FIVE CONGRESSIONAL ELECTIONS: 1945, 1950, 1954, 1958, AND 1962

	PSD	UDN	PTB	Other Parties	Party Alliances	Blank Vote	Total Valid
1945	2,531,944	1,575,375	603,500	1,213,797	—	65,840	5,990,456
%	42.3	26.3	10.1	20.3	—	1.1	100
1950	2,068,405	1,301,459	1,262,000	1,467,804	1,552,636	1,656,909	9,309,213
%	22.2	14.0	13.6	15.8	16.7	17.8	100
1954	2,136,220	1,318,101	1,447,784	1,837,177	2,496,501	468,686	9,704,469
%	22.0	13.6	14.9	18.9	25.7	4.8	100
1958	2,296,640	1,644,314	1,830,621	1,606,828	4,140,655	949,410	12,468,468
%	18.4	13.2	14.7	12.9	33.3	7.6	100
1962	2,225,693	1,604,743	1,722,546	723,509	5,855,692	2,149,111	14,281,294
%	15.6	11.2	12.1	5.1	41.0	15.1	100

Source: *Brazil: Election Factbook,* No. 2, September 1965 (Washington, D.C.: Institute for the Comparative Study of Political Systems), p. 60.

The alliances allowed populist politics to flourish. The appeal to the urban masses proceeded in a context of growing demands for social and economic change—the "basic reforms" of President Goulart in 1963-64 represented the climax of that confrontation. Faced with what he termed a recalcitrant and suspecting congress, dominated by conservative elite representatives and cautious constitutional liberals such as the UDN delegation, Goulart felt forced to threaten to reform by decree, to call on the populace for mass support and threaten the discipline and organization of the armed forces in his desperate attempts to satisfy the growing cacophony of demands for radical restructuring of Brazilian society.[20]

20. Thomas E. Skidmore, *Politics in Brazil, 1930-1964* (New York: Oxford University Press, 1967) provides an excellent introduction to the political history of the 1946-64 period.

Thus, the structural duality of Brazilian society, of which S. N. Eisenstadt has written, "the coexistence, under conditions of continuous social change, of different social sectors, especially of a disorganized traditional one and a similarly unbalanced and unintegrated modern one"[21] offered widespread opportunity for "confrontation politics"—mirroring the strains in traditional political relationships that a competitive political system caused.

Politics remained personalist and pragmatic during the 1946 to 1964 period. Neither strong political parties nor effective governmental institutions emerged to meet the growing socioeconomic demands of the urban population brought about as a result of the mobilization process. Weak institutions, self-serving national leadership, continuing residual influence and power in the hands of private governments and regional and state political elites indicated a lack of effectiveness on the part of the regime to incorporate permanently "appropriate mechanisms to originate and to absorb a continuous flow of change while maintaining an appropriate degree of integration."[22] As Chalmers comments, relationships of authority and domination crystallized around vertical groups, which reinforced traditional elite patterns of power distribution and manipulation.

Accompanying the limited institutional capacity of the post-1946 governments and the growing possibility of conflict was the economic question. Brazil experienced higher levels of economic growth than of economic development. Economic growth is "a quantitative process, involving principally the extension of an already established structure, whereas development suggests qualitative changes, the creation of new economic and noneconomic structures."[23]

And, by the early 1960s, economic *growth* had slowed down making it even less probable that the regime would be able to respond to new social and economic demands. Without the political development and the economic growth characteristic of modern societies, the Brazilian government slid into a state of chronic instability. The political immobility and the threat of violence that characterized post-1960 politics led to a series of confrontations that activated the armed forces into intervening on March 31, 1964. Applying the growth/de-

21. S. N. Elsenstadt, *Modernization: Protest and Change* (Englewood Cliffs, N.J.: Prentice Hall Inc., 1966), p. 87.

22. Gino Germani, "Stages of Modernization in Latin America," *Studies in Comparative International Development* (Rutgers University), Vol. V, No. 8, p. 157.

23. Karl de Schweinitz Jr., "Growth, Development, and Political Modernization," *World Politics*, XXII, No. 4 (July 1970), 518.

velopment terminology to politics, Brazil experienced a low level of political growth and insignificant political development.

The emergence of mass parties and a potential mass electorate at the same time that the regime was attempting to consolidate its institutional capacity to govern led to systemic breakdown, the threat of violence, military intervention, and the imposition of an authoritarian military regime. The time sequence had been inappropriate and the rate of change too rapid to produce a nonviolent democratic resolution to the modernization quest followed by Brazil after 1946. Moreover, the lack of strong and effective institutions which reflected the "informal sociopolitical realities" that Martin Needler has discussed precluded the formation of linkages between government and governed that would provide support for the authority of the regime.[24] The low level of compliance received by the regime by 1964 indicated that broad segments of the autonomous groups or private governments that were the structure of the social and political systems questioned the legitimacy of the existing political system.

All through this period the armed forces had become increasingly aware of the weakening authority of the post-1946 governments. Conscious of their traditional role as "guardians of the constitution," the military saw little alternative but to intervene in the political system in 1964 to save Brazilian society from civil war and chaos.

The Military and Politics, 1946-1964

Within the context of the multiparty, competitive system there were military coups in 1954, 1964, an attempted coup in 1961 and the beginnings of a coup in 1955 that brought about a counter-coup in defense of the constitutional regime. During this period, the moderating role of the Brazilian military greatly increased from what it had been in the period from 1889 to 1945. The military, deeply involved in national politics, responded to growing divisions in the praetorian society with increased activism.

The 1955 attempt tried to prevent President-elect Juscelino Kubitschek and Vice-President-elect João Goulart from assuming office. In 1961, the three military ministers unilaterally announced their unwillingness to accept Vice-President Goulart as a successor to President Jânio Quadros who resigned suddenly after eight months in office. Neither coup had the support of a majority of the military high com-

24. Martin C. Needler, *Political Development in Latin America: Instability Violence, and Evolutionary Change* (New York: Random House, 1968), p. 21.

mand nor widespread popular support among the civilian political elite. A small segment of the armed forces favored the coups but without further political justification; the unilateral military decisions were not considered legitimate. The authority of the civilian constitutional order was upheld in spite of the open dissidence of powerful segments of the military establishment.[25]

The 1954 and 1964 coups were political acts with widespread support among the political elite, both civilian and military. These coups also received endorsement from many of the participant sectors of the civilian population. The conduct of President Vargas in 1954 and of President Goulart in 1964 provided sufficient justification for a coalescing of civilian-military opinion in favor of their removal from office through military action.

In 1955 the coup was supported by only one of the political parties, the UDN, but the defeated standard bearers of the party in the election denounced the attempts of their political supporters to subvert the legal order. Such restricted partisan appeals for military force are generally unsuccessful in a praetorian society for fear of a civil war erupting among the major political contenders for power.

The 1961 attempted coup was an immediate reaction by the military ministers which provoked immediate and widespread indignation. They had misjudged the depth of support for the maintenance of the constitutional order by both civilians and military officers. An important factor was the margin of political support provided by the governor of Rio Grande do Sul, Leonel Brizola, the brother-in-law of President Goulart and the anti-coup sentiments expressed by the commander of the Third Army, located in Porto Alegre, the capital of Rio Grande. The civilian-military elite was unwilling to risk bloodshed to impede Goulart from taking office. Without wider popular and institutional support, the coup was doomed.[26]

These two attempts at coups d'etat, 1955 and 1961, indicate the limits of freedom allowed the military establishment. The armed

25. John J. Johnson, *The Military and Society in Latin America* (Stanford: Stanford University Press, 1964), esp. Part III "The Military in Brazil," offers a useful overview. Mario Victor, *Cinco Anos Que Abalaram O Brasil* (Rio de Janeiro: Editôra Civilização Brasileira, 1965) for general background of the years leading to the 1964 military intervention. An excellent study of the military as an institution is that of Alfred Stepan, *Patterns of Civil-Military Relations: The Brazilian Political System* (Princeton: Princeton University Press, 1971). His analysis of the 1945-68 period clarifies many of the issues raised in the literature about Brazilian military intervention in politics.

26. A special issue of *Cadernos Brasileiros*, "Os Militares," Vol. VIII, No. 6, 1966, provides useful background information on the ideas and attitudes of the military.

forces, while the most powerful social institution in Brazil, are not the only actors in possession of a power potential. The military, or a coup-prone segment of it, can be thwarted by widespread opposition if it comes from within the military and/or the civilian sector of society.

The 1954 coup removing Getúlio Vargas from office for the second time (which ended in his suicide) was an example of the military playing its role as moderator in the political system. Vargas had mobilized and manipulated the urban working class throughout his term of office. His populist politics frightened the traditional conservative elites who feared the president would next turn his attention to the social and economic prerogatives they possessed. Their widespread questioning of presidential authority convinced the military that internal peace required the president's removal. In addition, the widespread stories of corruption and maladministration strengthened the argument against Vargas. The postwar concern of the military with economic growth and technological and industrial development, and their basic disapproval of populist politics which seemed to represent a threat to law and order combined to unite the military forces behind Vargas's dismissal.

The Coup of March 31, 1964

The 1964 coup d'etat, the most serious of the military interventions during the 1946 Republic, grew out of the weakened legitimacy of presidential authority. By March 1964 President Goulart had lost the support of a large part of the Left as well as having alienated moderate and conservative civilian and military forces. A feeling grew that the political system might be unworkable, that it could not, as presently constituted, deal with the myriad of problems confronting the nation. The left refused to retreat from its position of calling for immediate and drastic structural changes; the Center and Right, ever loyal to constitutional procedures and the elite conception of political power so long dominant in Brazil, recoiled from the threats of violence and revolution. Immobilism characterized the Goulart years.[27]

Brazilian society of the early 1960s was hyperpoliticized. Beginning with the electoral campaign of October 1960 which brought

27. Two excellent studies of the events surrounding the fall of Goulart are Alberto Dines et al., *Os Idos de Março: e A Queda em Abril* (Rio de Janeiro: José Alvaro, 1964) and José Stacchini, *Março 64: Mobilização da Audácia* (São Paulo: Companhia Editôra Nacional, 1965). For an "insider's" view of the fall, see Abelardo Jurema, *Sexta-Feira, 13: Os Últimos Dias do Govêrno João Goulart* (Rio de Janeiro: Edições O Cruzeiro, 1964).

Quadros to the presidency, the level of political tension remained high. Quadros's resignation in August 1961, the elections for governor and congress in October 1962, the national plebiscite in January 1963 to restore full presidential powers to Goulart, and the drive for "Basic Reforms" in March 1964—all of these political events heightened the tension and the frustration of all groups in the political process.

The Roman Catholic Church, after decades of dormant acceptance of the status quo, awakened to its social responsibilities. Labor unions, long dominated by the federal government, showed signs of independence and active political interest. The university students joined the rising protest against the established order. All groups pressured for change but few had realistic suggestions as to how change might be introduced without destroying the very legitimacy on which the regime rested.

Inexorably, the military were drawn into the center of the growing crisis. For the first time in Brazilian history, the Brazilian Armed Forces found themselves attacked and vilified. Military discipline began to disintegrate as noncommissioned officers defied the orders of their superiors. A revolt of career corporals and sergeants in the air force and marines in Brasília in September 1963 seemed to herald a new phase of military relations. A naval mutiny of noncommissioned officers in Rio de Janeiro in March 1964 confirmed the growing suspicion that the politicization of the military had reached a stage where the structure of heirarchy and command threatened to collapse.

An important element in the growing crisis was the role of President Goulart. His appearance at a giant rally in Rio de Janeiro on Friday, March 13, 1964, seemed to signal the radicalization of national politics as he called for "basic reforms" with or without the endorsement of Congress. A counter-rally in São Paulo on March 19 indicated the fervor of the opposition. Goulart manipulated the commanders of the nation's four armies to suit his own needs. Promotions were more and more a matter of personal loyalty to the President; merit counted for a good deal less.[28]

Goulart himself did not inspire confidence on either the political Left or the Right. The Left, led principally by his brother-in-law, Leonel Brizola, thought him weak and ineffectual in challenging outright the antiquated social and political structures of society. The

28. Four essays that provide a succinct statement of the multiple pressures that converged in 1964 are included in Octavio Ianni et al, *Política e Revolução Social no Brasil* (Rio de Janeiro: Editôra Civilização Brasileira, 1965).

Center-Right part of the political spectrum suspected him of duplicity and incompetence. The president's request for emergency powers from the Congress in 1963—a request to declare a state of seige—met vociferous protest from both the Left and the Right. His attempts to initiate basic reforms without the participation of the requisite constitutional authorities deeply disturbed the legalists in the regime.

Two civilian political manifestos against the Goulart government in March, 1964—one by Governor Magalhães Pinto of Minas Gerais and the other by Governor Adhemar de Barros of São Paulo—indicated the growing solidarity of the civilian political elite against the administration. Military planning increased. The view became widespread that the Goulart government and its supporters had exceeded the well understood boundaries of political conduct that characterized the 1946 regime. The threats of violence and unconstitutional action, the fear of revolutionary reform, the danger of weakening and perhaps fatally undermining military authority—all these provided ample justification for questioning the legitimacy of the government.

With the open support of the civilian political elite, with widespread popular and editorial endorsement, the military forces moved against the Goulart government on March 31, 1964, and within 36 hours resistance collapsed.[29] The 1946 Republic had come to an end; the arbitrator army had once again exercised its moderating power to restore order to the political process.

Thus, social mobilization increased rapidly after 1946. The Brazilian society had to cope with simultaneous "loads": governmental institutionalization, mass parties, and a mass electorate. Given the low level of institutionalization and the increasingly high rates of participation, signifying growing demands for social and economic "payoffs" or "goods," the constitutional system faltered. Confronted with the social and political realities of diffuse power centers in society, the central government remained isolated and removed from the mainstream of political debate even though it remained, in the eyes of the nation, responsible for the resolution of highly conflictful and competitive demands.

As the authority of the regime waned in the early 1960s, it turned to emotional appeals as it sought support from the population. But that population, with no means of providing that support through

29. For a sympathetic examination of the Armed Forces and 1964 see José Américo Almeida *et al. A Revolução de 31 de Março: 2º Aniversario—Colaboração do Exército* (Rio de Janeiro: Biblioteca de Exercito Editôra, 1966).

structured political channels, responded by supporting demagogic candidates and ephemeral electoral party alliances which further weakened the political system. As politics polarized between the "left" and the "right" the threat of violence and massive disorder drew the military deeper and deeper into the political equation. Finally, on March 31, 1964, they opted for intervention and the repression of the "left" and the organization of an authoritarian regime that precludes open, electoral politics. The praetorian army had acted. The question remained whether the Brazilian armed forces would return power to the civilians or retain power and restructure society.

The Military Since 1964

The military regime that seized power in 1964 has experienced three governmental phases: that of Marshal Humberto Castello Branco (1964-1967), Marshal Arthur da Costa e Silva (1967-1969) and General Emílio Garrastazu Médici (1969-present). In each, the supremacy of the armed forces has been clearly evident. The armed forces seem to have opted for the "retain and restrict" option open to interventionist armies: the Brazilian Army has decided to retain power and to restrict political participation.[30]

There are, of course, examples of modernizing armies in the twentieth century. Those of Turkey and Mexico, and perhaps South Korea, are most clearly to be included in this category. Each of these armies decided to retain power but to push toward increased political participation, normally by incorporating the peasantry into the political system and by attacking the antiquated agrarian structure of the society.

In comparison to Brazil in the late twentieth century, these societies, at the time basic reforms were undertaken by the military, were less complex socially and had not experienced the convergence of modernization crises, and at the same rate, that Brazil suffered between 1946 and 1964. The power contenders were fewer and possessed less influential capabilities; private governments were susceptible to neutralization by the concerted efforts of the military regime.

In contrast, the Brazilian military regime has blocked the issue of expanding political mobilization and participation. The regime created and sustained by the armed forces is authoritarian, characterized by the repression of all political dissent. Given the time sequence and rate of change in Brazil, from 1946 to 1964, of the four indepen-

---

30. Huntington, *Political Order in Changing Societies*, p. 235.

dent variables identified by Nordlinger, the dependent variable of an authoritarian government stands as a logical and predictable result.

The primary emphasis of the military regime has been public order and fiscal stability.[31] The political system has been altered in structure and submitted to a series of controls that preclude open, competitive politics. The traditional motto of Brazil, "order and progress," has been reinterpreted to mean "security and development."

Security is defined in terms of repression of dissent; reorganization of the traditional political structures to provide for governmental control; and avoidance of debate about "basic reforms" or the social and economic issues that hastened the end of the 1946 Republic. Development has come to mean economic growth through a program of controlling inflation; a flurry of national development plans; and an emphasis on increasing the gross national product. Social and political development are narrowly interpreted: anything that promises to impede continued military domination is excluded from debate and regime consideration. The military governments define permissible political activity in their interests and judge social policy initiatives in terms of their contribution to continued political stability.

The rule of the Brazilian praetorian army is not opposed by the majority of the urban middle class and the traditional urban and rural elites. No drastic reform programs have threatened their continued hegemony. The successful economic growth emphasis complements middle- and upper-class concern for the continuation of their position of privilege. The controls imposed on the political system insure that the massive threat of rapid and unstructured popular mobilization and participation will not arise to threaten upper- and middle-class status. The military regime has attained de facto legitimacy in the eyes of these groups because it acts as a buffer against the perceived disruption and possible chaos that the entry of the marginal majority of the population into the political system would cause.

Compliance with and support of regime authority exist because the participant citizenry, primarily urban, but including the rural elite, views the military regime as the only alternative to societal disintegration; the passive or subject segment of the population, primarily rural but including the urban lower class or proletariat, accepts regime

31. See, for example, the statement by Planning Minister Helio Beltrão in *Diretrizes de Governo—Programa Estratégico de Desenvolvimento,* Ministerio de Planejamento e Coordenação Geral, July 1967, p. 13; it reflects both the dependence of the Government on planning and the early priorities as seen by the president and his staff.

domination because they have little viable alternative and they fear the threat, real or implied, of force and coercion that noncompliance would bring.

While the 1964-1969 period in Brazil has been one devoted primarily to the amelioration of the consequences of the 1946 Republic, particularly the period from 1961 to 1964, it has witnessed also the emergence of a commitment by the military to retain political power. Contrary to the traditional historical role of the armed forces, they have decided, as an institution, to retain power and restrict participation. In so doing, the military has begun to elaborate a body of doctrine to justify this prolonged participation in and continued domination of the political system. Stemming from the traditional concern of the armed forces with external security, the need for internal order has acquired new significance. Present doctrine does not distinguish between the need for military responsibility internally and externally. The needs of the Brazilian state require the presence of the armed forces at the locus of power for both security and development reasons: to maintain the political climate within which national economic growth can proceed.[32] This is seen as the only sure road to international independence. It is but a small step to the conclusion that the military are best suited to establishing the goals and the priorities for the state without the need for civilian participation through the electoral process.

Thus, the political reforms instituted since 1964 have had two principal rationales: the first to preclude the re-emergence of populist politics with its connotation of social disorder and political instability; and second to provide instrumental and flexible mechanisms through which the military regime's objectives can be implemented. The latter is to be accomplished without violating the letter of the constitution, the mystique of which remains part of the revolutionary rhetoric of the praetorian army in Brazil. Let us turn to a consideration of the major structural changes in the political system and their implications for political modernization in the 1970s.

32. The *Revista Brasileira de Estudos Políticos*, No. 21, July 1966, is devoted to a collection of essays that deal with the theme of National Security. The writers are closely identified with the Superior War College which has emerged as the principal forum for the formulation of development strategy. See General Umberto Peregrino, "O Pensamento da Escola Superior de Guerra," *Cadernos Brasileiros*, No. 38, November/December 1966, pp. 29-38, for a general discussion of the "ESG." Also, Augusto Fragose, "A Escola Superior de Guerra," *Segurança e Desenvolvimento*, XVIII, 132 (1969) 7-40.

The Revolution Defines Itself: the Institutional Acts

There are many ways of dividing the period from 1964 to 1969. For purposes of both coherence and analysis, the divisions I will employ here are those that correspond to the most significant pronouncements of the March 31st Movement: the Institutional Acts. The First Institutional Act appeared on April 9, 1964; the second on October 27, 1965; the fifth on December 13, 1968; and, carrying the same import as these Acts, Constitutional Amendment No. 1 of October 20, 1969 [33] These are the most significant dates of the military regime that has ruled Brazil since the successful coup d'etat of March 31, 1964.

The Institutional Acts are a significant and interesting departure in Brazilian political life. These documents represent the justification for military intervention and also provide a political framework within which major institutional and structural reforms have been made. While not canceling the constitution, whether it be that of 1946 or 1967, the acts supersede and restrict the purview of that document. In so doing, the principle of constitutional rule is brought into focus and the raison d'être of the Movement of March 31st is better comprehended.

It seems clear that the military feel the need to preserve the myth of constitutionalism that has marked Brazilian history in both the 19th and the 20th centuries.[34] It is also clear that the military regime feels little compunction in violating both the spirit and the letter of the constitution when it is deemed necessary in the interests of the Revolution. Thus, the Institutional Acts represent the reality of the 1964 movement in that they are the authoritative statements of the regime's political purpose; the constitution remains a legal exercise that is retained because it signifies so little in reality. It is a juridical statement of intent, not a political document of relevance to the governance of the Brazilian state.

---

33. A recent publication that contains the October 1969 Amendment and the fifth through the seventeenth Institutional Acts is *A Nova Constituição do Brasil* (Rio de Janeiro: Gráfica Auriverde, Ltda., 1970). All of the acts are published in the *Diario Oficial*, as is the 1969 Amendment.

34. For a significant statement on the 1964 Revolution see General Antônio Carlos Muricy, *Os Motivos da Revolução Democrática Brasileira: Palestras Pronunciadas na Televisão Canal 2, nos Dias 19 e 25 de Maio de 1964* (Recife; Imprensa Oficial, n.d.). For an early statement about the military and politics, see General Estevão Leitão de Carvalho, *Dever Militar e Política Partidaria* (São Paulo: Companhia Editôra Nacional, 1959).

Seventeen Institutional Acts and seventy-seven Complementary Acts were issued between 1964 and the end of 1969. The Complementary Acts spelled out the specific intent of the more general principle involved in the Institutional Acts. It is clear from the wording of the acts that they have been decreed by the armed forces acting in a dual role: that of the representatives of the Movement of March 31st, the Revolution, which has a life of its own apart from any institutional or constitutional restraints; and as the executive power of the Brazilian government. The dividing line between the armed forces and the government is at best tenuous; in the area of major legal and juridical innovation it is even more hazy.

The 1967 Constitution emerged, in part, from a feeling that the changes brought about by the early Institutional Acts, and the Complementary Acts, required incorporation into the constitution and that the 1946 document no longer served the needs of the nation. With the First Constitutional Amendment of October 1969, it became clear that the 1967 constitution was an impermanent statement to be ignored when required by the interests of the armed forces.

The violation of both the 1946 and the 1967 constitutions demonstrates the continuing inability to institute rule by law in Brazil. The underlying social and political realities preclude the resolution of societal conflict within legitimated, constitutional means as long as there are social forces, such as the military, willing and able to use force and coercion in the pursuit of their objectives. It is the ambivalence of the praetorian army in Brazil, caught between a tradition of selective intervention in politics and its present direct and prolonged involvement in the nation's political life, that the Institutional Acts make readily apparent. Sworn to defend the constitution, the military have violated and rewritten it to suit their needs; fully aware of their historical role as guardians and defenders of the constitution, the armed forces find themselves challenging and disregarding that document. The Institutional Acts provide both a mechanism and the rationale for this reversal on the part of the military. They further debilitate the tradition of constitutional government, so weakly institutionalized from 1946 to 1964, and make more difficult a return to an open political system in the foreseeable future.

The First Institutional Act

The Presidency of Brazil was declared vacant on the night of April 1, 1964, by the president of the Senate. The president of the Chamber was sworn in as acting president early on April 2. The nation—and the civilian political elite—waited.

After a week of negotiation over the course of the March 31 coup, the armed forces decided to act unilaterally. The political initiative passed to the military; it remained in their hands throughout the remainder of the Sixties. On April 9 the three military ministers issued an Institutional Act; it would become known as the First Institutional Act when others appeared. The act did not rest on any constitutional justification; its authority derived from the moral force of the revolution itself. No further justification was deemed necessary.

The preamble of the act states the reason for its issuance:

The successful revolution invests itself with the exercise of the Constituent Power, which manifests itself by popular election or by revolution. This is the most expressive and radical form of the Constituent Power. Thus, the successful revolution, like the Constituent Power, is legitimized by itself. The Revolution dismisses the former government and is qualified to set up a new one. The Revolution holds in itself the normative strength inherent to the Constituent Power, and establishes judicial norms without being limited by previous norms.

The act vastly strengthened the powers of the chief executive. While the 1946 Constitution remained in force, it was subject to modification by the act. The president received the power to propose amendments to the constitution which the Congress had to consider within 30 days; only a majority vote, as opposed to the 2/3 vote stipulated in the 1946 Constitution, was needed for approval. Only the president could submit expenditure measures to Congress and the Congress could not increase the amount stipulated in the bills. The power to declare a state of seige without congressional approval was given to the president and the executive was granted the power to suppress the political rights of political undesirables for a period of ten years.

The act decreed that the election of the new president, to replace Goulart, and the vice-president would be by an absolute majority of the Congress, to take place within two days of the promulgation of the act. The date for the election of the next president and vice-president, to assume office on January 31, 1966, was set for October 3, 1965. On April 11, 1964, General Humberto Castello Branco, a ringleader of the March 31 coup, was elected president.[35] (See Table 5

35. Two excellent analyses of the Castello Branco government have been written by Candido Mendes, "O Governo Castelo Branco: Paradigma e Prognose," Dados, No. 2/3, 1967, pp. 63-111; and "Sistema Político e Modelos de Poder no Brasil," Dados, No. 1, (1966), pp. 7-41.

TABLE 5
PRESIDENTIAL ELECTIONS, 1946-1969

President	Time in Office	Votes Obtained	Vice-President	Time in Office	Votes Obtained
General Eurico					indirect
Dutra	1946-1951	3,251,507	Nereu Ramos	1946-1951	election
Getúlio Vargas[1]	1951-1954	3,849,040	João Café Filho	1951-1954	2,520,790
João Café Filho[2]	1954-1955	——			
Juscelino Kubitschek	1956-1961	3,077,411	João Goulart	1956-1961	3,591,409
Jânio Quadros[3]	1961	5,636,623	João Goulart	1961	4,547,010
João Goulart[4]	1961-1964	——			
General Humberto		indirect	José Maria		indirect
Castelo Branco	1964-1967	election	Alkmim	1964-1967	election
General Arthur da		indirect			indirect
Costa e Silva[5]	1967-1969	election	Pedro Aleixo	1967-1969	election
General Emílio		indirect	Augusto Hamann		indirect
Garrastazu Médici	1969-present	election	Rademaker Grunewald	1969-present	election

1. Died August 24, 1954; succeeded by Vice-President Café Filho.

2. Incapacitated on November 8, 1955; succeeded by Acting President Carlos Luz, president of the Chamber of Deputies. Acting President Luz was removed by a "preventive" coup on November 11, 1955. He was succeeded by the president of the Senate, Nereu Ramos.

3. Resigned August 25, 1961; succeeded by Vice-President Goulart.

4. Assumed the presidency on September 7, 1961, with the powers of that office shared with the price minister of a new parliamentary system. The full powers of the office were restored after a national plebiscite on January 6, 1963. There were three prime ministers from 1961 to 1963: Tancredo Neves (Sept. 1961 to June 1962); Brochado da Rocha (June 1962-Sept. 1962); and Hermes Lima (Sept. 1962-January 1963).

5. Incapacitated August 1969; executive power exercised by junta of armed forces leaders until October 1969, when General Garrastazu Médici was selected by the military and confirmed by the Congress.

for a list of presidents since 1946.)

Article X of the act, which gave the president the right to revoke legislative mandates and to suspend political rights, was to expire on June 15, 1964. The military government moved quickly to revoke the mandates of those members of Congress identified with the defeated left. By the deadline, three former presidents—Kubitschek, Quadros, and Goulart—as well as six governors and more than forty members of Congress, plus some three hundred individuals active in political life, had had their rights suspended. Under Article VII, which gave the president the power to expel people from the civil service without regard for existing legislation guaranteeing employment, it is estimated that approximately 9,000 people were fired by November 9, the cutoff date stated in the act.

As the military became accustomed to their new political role, it was clear to them that they would not finish their task by January 20, 1966, the date on which the presidential term of Castello Branco would terminate. In July 1964, therefore, a constitutional amendment extended the president's term of office until March 15, 1967; new presidential elections were set for November 1966.

With the decision to extend the president's term, implying a military commitment to retain power for an indefinite period, a number of events in 1965 helped to determine the political strategy of the regime. The first was the election, in the mayoralty race in São Paulo in March, 1965, of a candidate backed by former President Quadros. The victory of a man identified by some as a representative of the populist tradition in Brazilian politics (even though a military officer) provided the impetus required for a move away from the economic emphasis of the Revolution into the political arena.

On July 15, 1965, two laws dealing with elections and political parties were announced. These represented the first substantive revision of the pre-1964 political rules of the game. The Electoral Code reduced the number of parties by increasing the minimum requirement that parties had to meet to achieve or maintain legal status. Electoral alliances were forbidden; candidates were required to reside in the area they sought to represent; voters were required to choose legislators from the same party in order to strengthen party discipline; and the running mates of successful gubernatorial and presidential candidates were automatically elected. These reforms were an attempt to deal with one of the problems perceived by the military as most debilitating in the pre-1964 era: the weak and diffuse multiparty system. It was hoped these reforms would introduce some cohesion into the political system.

The Political Party Statute stipulated stringent procedures for the organization of new political parties. Individuals were forbidden to run for more than one office in any election. Residence and party membership requirements were specified for candidates. It was hoped, with this law, to control the problem of representation, so abused before 1964, when there were few requirements linking a candidate to his constituency.

Also promulgated on July 15, was an Ineligibilities Law. It prevented former ministers in the Goulart government (those appointed after the January 1963 plebiscite) from candidacy. Its primary purpose was to prevent the candidacy of several prominent anti-regime politicians in the upcoming state elections.

Although all three proposals were submitted to Congress for consideration, two became law without final action by that body. The time period for consideration expired, and the president, using the authority granted to him by the Institutional Act, acted unilaterally. The Political Party Statute was passed by the Congress but fourteen items introduced during floor debate were vetoed by the president. It appeared in the form it was originally submitted to the congress.[36]

The gubernatorial elections of October 1965 were a critical event in the unfolding of the military regime. Over the warning and the fears of many members of the armed forces, the Castello Branco government determined to hold open, competitive elections. When the results were counted, candidates identified as opponents of the regime (Israel Pinheiro in Minas Gerais and Negrão de Lima in Guanabara) supported by former President Kubitschek, were victorious.

Immediately, the military hard-liners pressed the government to annul the elections. In order to fulfill his promise to allow the inauguration of all candidates elected, President Castello Branco promulgated a Second Institutional Act.

The Second Institutional Act—October 27, 1965

The October 1965 elections, in retrospect, were a crucial event in determining the unfolding of the Movement of March 31.[37] Before the results were known, it was assumed that direct elections would continue to be the method employed to select new members of the political government elite. With the publication of the Second Act, the military regime made a basic decision to reconstruct national politics to try to insure that the legacy of the 1946 Republic would be effectively neutralized. The elections seem to have been the determining factor in the decision of Castello Branco and the moderate wing of the military that the unity of the armed forces was more important for the future development of Brazil than the constitutional principle of direct elections.[38]

The Second Act determined that only the president could create new positions in the civil service; further restricted the time allowed to Congress to consider legislation before it became law automatically; increased the number of members of the Supreme Court (the Court

36. Three valuable aids for interpreting the electoral complexities of Brazilian politics are *Brazil: Election Factbook*, October 7, 1962; No. 2, September 1965; and No. 2, Supplement, November 1966.

37. James Rowe, *American Universities Field Staff Reports*, provides a good overview of the first years of the military regime: 1964: "Revolution or Counterrevolution in Brazil?", Parts I & II; 1966: "The Revolution and the System," Parts I, II & III; 1967: "Brazil Stops the Clock," Part I & II.

38. For a personal comment on the events leading to the coup and immediately thereafter, see General Joaquim Justino Alves Bastos, *Encontro Com O Tempo* (Porto Alegre: Editôra Globo, 1965). General Bastos was commander of the IV Army in Recife in March 1964.

had been viewed as a last holdout against the more blatantly unconstitutional actions of the Revolutionary government); reserved the right of nomination of all federal judges to the president of the Republic; reorganized the Supreme Military Tribunal; stipulated that civilians accused of crimes against national security were to be submitted to military justice; decreed the indirect election of the president and the vice-president by an absolute majority of the federal Congress; permitted the president to declare a state of seige for 180 days to prevent "the subversion of internal order"; extended the right of the revolution to suspend individual political rights for ten years; established restrictions on the activities of those whose political rights were removed; gave the president the right to intervene in the states of the federation, in addition to the reasons stipulated in the constitution, in order to assure the execution of a federal law and in order to prevent or punish the subversion of order; abolished the existing political parties and canceled their registration; excluded from judicial competence all acts of the Supreme Revolutionary Command and by the federal government in the First and Second Acts and in the Complementary Acts to follow, plus resolutions passed since March 31, 1964, of assemblies canceling the mandates of legislators; and giving the president the power to recess Congress, legislative assemblies and chambers of municipal counselors. The Second Act's jurisdiction was to continue until March 15, 1967, the date of the inauguration of Castello Branco's successor.

The political party situation was further modified by Complementary Act No. 4 of November 20, 1965, which provided for the provisional registration of political organizations sponsored by at least 120 federal deputies and 20 senators. Two parties emerged, replacing the 14-party system of the 1946 Republic; a government sponsored entity, the National Renovating Alliance (ARENA) and the opposition group, the Brazilian Democratic Movement (MDB). ARENA became a UDN stronghold with some PSD support. MDB attracted the remains of the PTB and some PSD elements.

Another Institutional Act, the Third, issued on February 5, 1966, replaced direct election of governors with selection by state legislatures on September 3, 1966, scheduled legislative elections for federal senators and deputies and state deputies for November 15, 1966, and eliminated the election of mayors of major capital cities. They would, henceforth, be selected by the governors of the states.

The Complementary Acts announced through 1965 and 1966 served to implement or elaborate the Institutional Acts. Perhaps the most notorious Complementary Act promulgated during this time was the 23rd, of October 20, 1966; it confirmed the growing centralization of power in the hands of the military and strengthened the determination of the government to allow little, if any, organized opposition to its plans. It was preceded by the cassation of 6 federal deputies on October 12 and a break with the government by the ARENA congressional leadership.

The 23rd Complementary Act decreed the recess of the federal Congress until November 22, 1966—after the scheduled elections. The act stated that there existed in the Congress " a group of counter-revolutionary elements whose objective was to disturb the public peace and upset the coming election of November 15, thus compromising the prestige and the authority of the legislative power." A precedent had been established, allowing the executive power to quiet successfully the legislative branch whenever it suited the government's needs.

Throughout 1966 the administration worked to assure that candidates acceptable to the Revolution would be chosen by the new political parties. It would allow no repetition of the 1965 nominating process. A series of complementary acts further strengthened the government's position vis à vis the political parties. Complementary Act No. 20 of July 19, 1966, for example, made it impossible for an ARENA legislator to switch to or vote for the MDB candidate in either the presidential or gubernatorial elections.

Throughout 1966 a number of challenges to the authority of the regime were confronted and overcome. A manifesto by the bishops of the Northeast brought about a verbal duel between church and state that required presidential mediation. In July 1966, Dominican priests in Belo Horizonte allowed the banned National Student Union to hold its 28th Congress in one of its buildings; in 1967 the same congress met in a building operated by the Benedictine Order.

A growing number of priests were identified as collaborators of the bands of terrorists active in the cities of the south. And a meeting in Salvador, Bahia, brought together laymen who identified themselves as "Political Christians" to discuss their responsibilities in society. In August 1967, 300 priests addressed an open letter to the bishops of Brazil demanding greater involvement in contemporary issues. And in November 1967, the Central Commission of the National Conference of the Bishops of Brazil issued a statement analyzing why it was impossible for the bishops to remain silent on issues affecting the nation.[39]

A large share of the student movement leadership had vociferously supported Goulart before March 31, 1964. In October 1964, the federal Congress, at executive insistence, voted to abolish the National Student Union (UNE) and replaced it with a new organization more directly controlled by the government. A law issued in November 1964, named for Minister of Education Suplicy de Lacerda, was seen as an intolerable interference in the affairs of the university students.

The attempt, finally successful, of UNE to hold its national congress in 1966 and 1967 exacerbated the tension between government and students. A national student strike in September 1966 further raised tensions. The growing strife between the regime and the university students culminated in an armed confrontation in April 1968 which resulted in the death of a student. The government's use of force against the protesting students and the growing intolerance of the regime toward students' demands finally resulted in a breakdown in communication. Some students joined the terrorist groups growingly active in the cities; others became politically apathetic, seeing no possibilities of exercising any restraint on the government.[40]

With the indirect election by the national Congress of Marshal

39. The role of the church in the 1964-69 period deserves special treatment not possible here. For an excellent synthesis of the Church in Brazil since 1964 see Norman Gall, "Latin America: The Church Militant," A *Commentary* Report, New York, 1970, and Emanuel de Kadt, *Catholic Radicals in Brazil* (London & New York: Oxford University Press, 1970). The evidence since 1970 indicates that the Church is more than willing to make its peace with the regime. The protest leadership of Dom Hêlder Câmara, the charismatic Archbishop of Recife, is now marginal in the National Conference of Bishops. In June of 1970 the Primate of Brazil, Cardinal Eugênio Sales, was received with the honors due a chief of state when he arrived in Brasília as the papal legate to a Eucharistic Congress. A few weeks earlier, the Eleventh Assembly of the National Conference of Bishops (May 1970) issued a statement that sought a rapprochement between the spiritual and temporal authorities of the nation. While it is true that a small minority of the religious support and even participate in "illegal" protest, the majority have accepted the guidance of the overwhelming majority of the hierarchy in seeking a modus vivendi to avoid direct confrontation with the regime. In so doing, the church will survive in Brazil as a temporal institution.

40. See Chapter Eight, by Douglas H. Graham, in this volume for a fuller discussior of this theme. The link between the revolutionary clergy and students is close. Both groups feel that there is little hope of weakening the regime by working from within the existing system. Both religious and students, the small minority sufficiently committed to rebel actively, have posed a continuing threat to the regime. But through the use of force and coercion, and the existing legislation, the danger to the regime seems to have been overcome.

Costa e Silva to succeed Castello Branco, the succession issue was settled. Costa e Silva ran unopposed; attempts by the MDB to launch a
rival candidacy had failed. Direct elections on November 15 selected
federal senators and deputies, state deputies, mayors and municipal
councilmen; the ARENA party won overwhelmingly. ARENA elected
senators from 15 states and approximately two thirds of the new deputies (see Tables 6, 7, and 8 for a comparison of the Congress before and
after the 1966 election).

TABLE 6
CONGRESS AT THE TIME OF THE 1964 REVOLUTION

Parties	Senators	Deputies	Total
PSD	22	119	141
PTB	17	119	136
UDN	15	95	110
PSP	2	21	23
PDC	1	18	19
PTN	2	12	14
PR	1	5	6
PL	2	3	5
PRP	0	5	5
PST	0	4	4
MRT	1	3	4
PSB	1	2	3
PRT	0	3	3
Sem legenda	2	0	2
Total	66	409	475

Source: *Revista Brasileira de Estudos Políticos,* No. 23/24, July, 1967/January, 1968.

TABLE 7
1966 CONGRESS—AFTER THE SECOND INSTITUTIONAL ACT

Party	Senators	Deputies	Congressional Total
ARENA	43	254	297
MDB	21	150	171
Sem Legenda	2	5	7
Total	66	409	475

Source: *Revista Brasileira de Estudos Políticos,* No. 23/24, July 1967/January 1968

TABLE 8
BRAZILIAN CONGRESS—1966 VS. 1967

I. Federal Senate			
V Legislature (1966)		VI Legislature (1967)	
ARENA	MDB	ARENA	MDB
43	21	47	19
II. Federal Chamber		VI Legislature (1967)	
V Legislature (1966)		ARENA	MDB
ARENA	MDB	277	132
254	150		

The Fourth Institutional Act of December 7, 1966, convoked an extraordinary meeting of Congress to vote and promulgate a new constitution. The preamble of the Fourth Act stated that it had become necessary to give the country a new constitution that would "represent the institutionalization of the ideas and principles of the Revolution." The constitution was promulgated on January 24, 1967. It further strengthened the executive power and weakened any hope of opposition groups using the constitution to justify opposition to the regime.

The Costa e Silva Government: The Regime Drifts

With the inauguration of President Costa e Silva on March 15, 1967, the Revolution entered a new phase. The early and successful efforts at controlling inflation seemed to be working; the needed structural reforms of the political system had been undertaken; and the crises of confidence within the military seemed to have been overcome with the acceptance by Castello Branco of the Costa e Silva candidacy. The main political event of the first year of the second military government was the discussion about the formation of a united front of opposition forces.

The Failure of the Opposition to Unite

The only significant attempt to organize a united political front against the military regime occurred between 1966 and 1968. Governor Carlos Lacerda of Guanabara, who saw his presidential ambitions destroyed by the military, reassumed his traditional role in Brazilian politics and took the offensive against the regime. Former Presidents Kubitschek and Goulart were contacted and they evinced some interest in a united opposition movement.

In September, Lacerda met with Goulart in Montevideo and

signed a pact with his former political enemy to proceed with the organization of the front. Upon his return, the executive committee of the MDB announced that it would not support the front; President Jânio Quadros let it be known that he would not join the movement. The ex-president of the PTB, Lutero Vargas, attacked the idea in October. And in a speech that received widespread publicity, Interior Minister Albuquerque Lima condemned the front as an attempt to take Brazil back to the days before 1964.

By early 1968 the movement to form a united opposition front appeared badly fragmented. By the end of 1968, Lacerda had his political rights canceled and the moving force behind the front collapsed into silence. The movement was declared illegal and members of Congress supporting it have been expelled from the Congress and banned from political activity for ten years.

The front failed because of the suspicions among the potential leaders over the ambitions of Lacerda. Three former presidents and a principal presidential aspirant would find it difficult, under any circumstances, to form a united front. With the military regime expressing public disapproval and the political parties unwilling to co-operate, the chances of success among the political elite were slim if not nonexistent. The front aroused little popular interest; it did not provide a focus for dramatic civilian protest. It ended where it began—in the ambition of Carlos Lacerda to retain a prominent voice in national political affairs. The military in December 1968 effectively neutralized that ambition for at least a decade.

The Crisis of December 1968

Throughout the last half of 1968 it became apparent that the division within the regime had deepened; between those who supported a moderate, semiconstitutional policy favoring limited civilian participation and the hard line nationalists who argued for military pre-eminence in all matters. The president seemed to favor a more moderate line; the leading proponent of a rigorous, nationalist development policy, carried out by the military, was Interior Minister Afonso Albuquerque Lima.

Albuquerque Lima had a large following among the younger members of the officer corps.[41] He believed in the necessity of pro-

41. For an interesting interview with General Albuquerque Lima, see *Veja* (Rio de Janeiro), October 1, 1969. For a brief statement of his nationalist development thinking, see the brief *Presentation* in the *Relatório Geral das Atvidades*, Ministério do Interior, 1968. Albuquerque Lima's statement contained in the Minutes of the Deliberative Council of the Northeast Development Agency (SUDENE) also reflect his position accurately, especially August 1968.

longed military rule in order to modernize Brazil, a task the civilian politicians of the 1946 to 1964 period had failed miserably in achieving. For him, modernization meant structural reform of such things as the land-tenure system, the development and integration of the Amazon, and the necessity of reducing regional imbalance. The general believed that such a great nation as Brazil could no longer ignore its underdeveloped regions; such a policy of neglect threatened national security and modernization.

The two positions were brought into confrontation over the issue of a speech made on the floor of the Congress by Deputy Marcio Moreira Alves. He had urged Brazilians to boycott military parades on Independence Day and he urged Brazilian parents not to allow their daughters to date military personnel. The nationalists found this address disgraceful and expected that the government would take appropriate action against the deputy. President Costa e Silva attempted to utilize legal channels to convince the Congress to remove Alves's congressional immunity but the Congress balked.

In late October a group of captains of the First Army stationed in Rio de Janeiro issued a manifesto. The document took note of their sacrifices for the revolution including their state of near poverty amidst the plenty enjoyed by some. The message was unmistakable —the government was not responding to the basic needs of the nation. The modernization of the country required firm and decisive leadership; abusive and insolent disregard for national priorities from civilians was not to be tolerated.

On December 12, 1968, the Congress met to consider the insistent request of the government that it lift Alves's immunity. Two hundred and sixteen members of Congress voted against, 141 in favor, and 12 cast blank ballots. The government's demand had been rejected. In the face of this blatant disrespect for military authority, the government moved quickly to regain control of a rapidly deteriorating situation.

The Fifth Institutional Act—December 13, 1968

The Fifth Act stated that the "revolutionary process unfolding could not be detained." The very institutions given to the nation by the revolution for its defense were being used to destroy it, said the preamble of the act. The Fifth Act empowered the president to recess the national Congress, legislative assemblies and municipal councils, by complementary acts. These bodies would again convene only when called by the president. In addition, the president could decree intervention in the states when in the national interests and without regard for the constitutional restrictions on intervention; suspend political rights of any citizen for ten years and cancel elected mandates without regard for constitutional limitations; the national state of seige was prolonged; the confiscation of personal goods illicitly gained was allowed; the right of habeas corpus was suspended in cases of political crimes, crimes against national security and the social and economic order; and the restrictions to be placed on those who lost their political rights were increased and more explicitly designated.

Complementary Act No. 38, of December 13, 1968, decreed the recess of Congress. With the closing of the legislature, the regime had determined the immediate future of the Revolution of March 31, 1964. It would be a period of outright military rule without the inconvenience of elected, civilian interference. The economic planning process, which represented the only significant accomplishment of the regime, would continue unfettered. The possibilities for "humanizing" the revolution gave way to the necessity of internal security, that is, precluding overt opposition from civilian political groups, and development, to be determined by the military regime and its civilian supporters.

The issuance of the act seemed to secure the leadership of the president within the regime. The governing coalition rallied behind the president. Albuquerque Lima's abrupt departure in January 1969 would seem to indicate that the government felt sufficiently in control to no longer need his symbolic presence in the cabinet.

The first eight months of 1969 saw a flurry of revolutionary legislation. The Sixth Institutional Act (February 1, 1969) amended the 1967 constitution (Article 113) and stipulated that the Supreme Court would consist of eleven members nominated by the president. It also said that the Superior Military Court would be responsible for trying all those accused of national security crimes.

The Seventh Institutional Act (February 26, 1969) regulated the functioning of legislative assemblies and municipal councils. It suspended interim elections for executive and legislative positions and decreed government intervention in case of vacancies. The president was empowered to set a new date for elections when he felt it to be useful.

Administrative reform of the states and municipalities, to conform to the model of the federal government, was decreed by the Eighth Institutional Act of April 2, 1969. A constitutional amendment facilitating government expropriation of and compensation for rural lands constituted the Ninth Institutional Act of April 26, 1969. The Tenth Act, of May 18, 1969, further elaborated on the penalties that accompanied the suspension of political rights or the cancellation of elective office.

The Eleventh Institutional Act of August 14, 1969, established dates for the election of municipal officials which had been held in abeyance since the Seventh Act.

All of the institutional acts confirmed the assumption of supreme legislative power by the military regime. Secure in the exercise of the executive powers of government since March 1964, the closing of Congress in December 1968 and the consequent amendments to the constitution, through the acts and the promulgation of political decisions by means of the acts, affirmed the willingness of the regime to pursue its twin themes of security and development.

The President Incapacitated

Two dramatic events in August and September of 1969 demonstrated both the potential vulnerability and the military predominance in the 1964 regime: the incapacitation of President Costa e Silva and the kidnapping of United States Ambassador C. Burke Elbrick in Rio de Janeiro.

A massive stroke incapacitated President Costa e Silva on August 29. By the 1967 Constitution, Vice-President Pedro Aleixo, a civilian from Minas Gerais, an old-line member of the defunct UDN, was next in succession. It was clear that the armed forces would determine whether the constitutional succession would be observed. Within forty-eight hours of the president's illness, the Twelfth Institutional Act (August 31, 1969) was issued. The military had decided against the constitution. The ministers of the navy, the army and the air force "in the name of the President of the Republic . . . temporarily impeded from exercising his functions for reasons of health" promulgated the Act. The document stated that

The situation that the country is experiencing . . . precludes the transfer of the responsibilities of supreme authority and supreme command of the Armed Forces, exercised by his excellency, to other officials, in accordance with the constitutional provision.

As an imperative of National Security, it falls to the ministers of the Navy, of the Army and of the Air Force to assume, for as long as the head of the Nation is incapacitated, the duties given to his excellency by the constitutional documents in force.

The Nation can have confidence in the patriotism of its military
chiefs who, in this hour, as always, will know how to honor the historic
legacy of their predecessors, loyal to the spirit of nationalism, the christian
formation of its people, contrary to extremist ideologies and violent solutions,
in the moments of political or institutional crises.

The act, relatively short in length, stipulated that the military
ministers would act on behalf of the president; that the previously published institutional and complementary acts would remain in
full force; and that all the acts and decisions of the government taken
as a result of the Twelfth Act and its complementary acts would be
beyond judicial purview.

The new act demonstrated the willingness of the armed forces to
violate the constitution they themselves had promulgated in 1967. No
mention was made of the vice-president; none was required, really. It
was clear that the ministers represented the general will of the military
in assuming supreme command of the nation.

The American Ambassador Disappears

On Thursday, September 4, 1969, Ambassador Elbrick was
taken at gunpoint from his limousine in Rio de Janeiro. A note from
his kidnappers identified themselves as members of revolutionary
movements; it demanded the release of fifteen political prisoners held
by the regime in exchange for the life of the ambassador. A note
found in the ambassador's car addressed "to the Brazilian people,"
stated that

With the kidnapping of the Ambassador we want to demonstrate that it is
possible to defeat the dictatorship and the exploitation if we arm and
organize ourselves. We show up where the enemy least expects us and we
disappear immediately, tearing out the dictatorship, bringing terror and
fear to the exploiters, the hope and certainty of victory to the midst of
the exploited.

The demands of the kidnappers were that their manifesto be published
and that the fifteen prisoners be taken to Algeria, Chile, or Mexico
where they would be granted political asylum. A time limit of forty-
eight hours was stated. The manifesto ended with a warning to the
regime from the terrorists: "now it is an eye for an eye, and a tooth
for a tooth."

The government, in the care of the military ministers, responded
immediately. The fifteen political prisoners were rounded up from

their places of detention and placed aboard a plane for Mexico; the manifesto appeared in the Brazilian newspapers. The list of prisoners included some of the leading critics and opponents of the regime. Amidst rumors that members of the officer corps were "unhappy" over the government's decision, the Thirteenth Institutional Act (September 5, 1969) appeared. It empowered the executive to banish from the national territory any Brazilian considered dangerous to national security.

The Fourteenth Institutional Act, issued the same day, stated that "considering that acts of adverse psychological warfare and revolutionary or subversive war that, actually, disturb the life of the country and maintain it in a climate of intranquility and agitation, these deserve more severe repression." The act amended the constitution (Article 150) and established the penalties of death, perpetual imprisonment or confiscation of goods for those guilty of participating in psychological, revolutionary, or subversive war against the state.

The Urban Guerrilla Movement in Brazil

Previously de-emphasized by the regime, the kidnapping of the American ambassador dramatically publicized the existence of a network of guerrilla bands operating in the cities of Brazil. This movement posed a most serious threat to the stability of the regime during the 1967-1969 period. By challenging the authority of the government, the terrorist groups hoped to weaken the support for the military from the middle and upper urban sectors. If the government could not secure public order, what else justified its continuation? The terrorists had begun to have a real impact on the public mind with a series of daring bank robberies—more than 100 by the end of 1969—and public bombings.

The "official" opening of the terrorist war against the government began in early 1967. A bombing attempt aimed at then Minister of War Costa e Silva in the airport of Recife in March was the first evidence of a planned and organized guerrilla opposition. The bombings and bank robberies followed. The kidnapping of the ambassador in September 1969 was a new plateau both in audacity and in challenge to the regime.

The terrorist groups stemmed from dissident elements of the Moscow-oriented Communist Party of Brazil (PCB) led for decades by Luis Carlos Prestes. The first breakoff had been with the formation of the Revolutionary Communist Party of Brazil (PCBR) with a decidedly Maoist or Fidelista orientation. Other fragments represented Trotskyite and Marxist variants.

The most prominent of the groups was the National Liberating Alliance (ALN), founded early in 1967, led by former Communist Party Deputy Carlos Marighella. Committed to terrorist and guerrilla warfare, Marighella became the mastermind of the movement; the ALN combined within its ranks a number of smaller terrorist bands who looked to Marighella for leadership and ideological inspiration.

A group that worked closely with the ALN but maintained its own identity was that led by ex-captain Carlos Lamarca. Called the Popular Revolutionary Vanguard (VPR), it merged with another group called the National Liberation Command (Colina), in June-July 1969 to form the Armed Revolutionary Vanguard (VAR), referred to as VAR-Palmares. Palmares was the site of an unsuccessful slave revolt in the late 19th century in the Brazilian Northeast. The VPR, in turn, had resulted from a fusion of other fragment terrorist groups.

Under Lamarca's daring leadership, the VAR-Palmares became a romantic symbol of protest against the regime and attracted many students to its ranks. Disillusioned by military rule, they accepted Lamarca's leadership in and Marighella's ideological justification for armed insurrection. A pamphlet entitled *The Mini-Manual of the Urban Guerrilla* by Carlos Marighella, which appeared in the middle of 1969, offered a sophisticated and incisive summary of the bankruptness of the regime and the necessity of undermining it by urban revolutionary warfare.

The movement was not a monolithic entity. It was splintered and represented antagonistic views of Brazilian society, ranging from reformist to revolutionary/anarchistic. A congress of VAR-Palmares, held in September, 1969, to debate the future of the organization, resulted in further fragmentation of that group. The murder of Marighella in São Paulo in November 1969 weakened the revolutionary left considerably. The loss of Marighella and the continuing fragmentation of the radical left was accompanied by increasing effectiveness on the part of the regime. In the state of Guanabara, the Center of Operations of Internal Defense (CODI), brought together all the civilian police and armed forces units working on security. A similar movement in São Paulo, Operation Bandeirante (OBAN) united all federal and state police units. OBAN was successful in uncovering clandestine groups of many of the terrorist organizations and by the end of 1969 had made more than 400 arrests.

The terrorist groups scored heavy blows against the regime during the first six months of 1970. A Japanese consul in São Paulo and the West German ambassador in Rio de Janeiro were kidnapped and held hostage until the regime agreed to the release of political prisoners. Both groups of prisoners were flown into exile. An attempted kidnapping of the North American consul general in Porto Alegre was foiled by his personal bravery.

But by the end of 1970 it seemed that this challenge to the regime had been counteracted effectively.[42] The terrorist groups had not weakened the regime in the eyes of its strongest supporters, the middle and upper sectors. On the contrary, those groups interpreted the guerrilla movement as added justification for strong and effective government. The promptness and humaneness with which the government dealt with the kidnappings of foreign diplomats (in contrast to the Guatemalan government which had refused to negotiate with similar terrorists who proceeded to murder the West German ambassador to Guatemala) reassured the international community that the regime was willing and able to release political prisoners without severely undermining its internal support.

One of the most disturbing aspects of the campaign against the terrorists was the reported widespread use of torture by civilian and military authorities. Although the regime declared on numerous occasions that the allegations of torture were exaggerated, sufficient evidence emerged to substantiate the charge. The subject became an internal political issue in 1968 and 1969 as international press coverage dramatically exposed cases of torture. What had been employed originally as a tactic of repression against known guerrillas had been clearly extended to "political" prisoners not charged with terrorism. By the end of 1969 President Médici seemed convinced that the tortures had to be stopped. The question was whether his order would be followed by local and regional civilian and military police units. They justified their tactics in terms of internal security and the need to uproot the serious threat to political order posed by the guerrillas.

42. A series of newspaper reports in July 1970 conveyed the impression that the terrorist movement, especially that segment led by Lamarca, was disintegrating. Members of the group who were arrested publicly confessed their guilt and urged their colleagues not to choose the same route of protest. An interview in the *Jornal do Brasil*, July 20, 1970, with General Antônio Carlos Muricy, chief of staff of the army, disclosed that the Communist terrorist groups were recruiting principally from secondary school students and recent university graduates.

Constitutional Amendment No. 1—October 20, 1969

As the regime surmounted the challenge to its authority that the kidnapping of the American ambassador represented, it became clear that the president's incapacitation was permanent. The country confronted the task of selecting its fifth chief executive in the sixties.

The immediate issue concerned the constitutional succession—would Vice-President Aleixo be allowed to assume the presidency? The answer of the Armed Forces emerged on October 14, 1969, with the announcement of the Sixteenth Institutional Act. The high command of the armed forces, that is, the three service chiefs, promulgated the document:

Considering that the superior interests of the country require the
immediate and permanent filling of the office of President of the
Republic;
. . . considering that Institutional Act No. 12 (of August 31, 1969) . . .
attributes to the military ministers the right to substitute for the President
of the Republic in his temporary incapacitation. . . .
Article 1. The position of President of the Republic is declared vacant. . . .
Article 2. The position of Vice-President of the Republic is also declared
vacant. . . .

By using an institutional act, with Congress in recess, the prerogatives of that body were exercised by the executive power. By precluding the constitutional succession of the civilian vice-president, the military prepared the way for the creation of a more rigidly authoritarian government to succeed Costa e Silva.

The internal dynamics of the selection process for the new chief magistrate are not fully known. It is commonly accepted that the officer corps of the three services was polled. At the time, there were approximately 118 army generals, 60 admirals, and 61 air force brigadiers. These, plus other command officers (an estimated total of about 13,000 men), were asked to nominate those men thought most qualified to replace Costa e Silva. General Emílio Garrastazu Medici, a supporter of the stricken president and commander of the Third Army located in the state of Rio Grande do Sul, ranked highest. He was followed in popularity by General Orlando Geisel and General Afonso Albuquerque Lima, the former interior minister. It is reliably reported that Albuquerque Lima had prepared a program of action which he discussed with the officer corps on trips to the various command posts before the final selection was made by the military ministers. In the end, General Médici, who is reported to have polled the most votes in all four armies, received the military nomination for the presidency. Admiral Augusto Hamman Rademaker Grunewald, then serving as navy minister, received the vice-presidential nomination.

The Sixteenth Act stipulated the elections for president and vice-president would be held by the congress on October 25, 1969; those elected would take office on October 30; their term of office would terminate on March 25, 1974. The act also clearly reserved the right of legislation to the military ministers even though the Congress had been convened.

The political parties were given the right to nominate candidates for the offices. ARENA nominated Médici and Rademaker; the MDB did not offer nominations. The candidates of the revolution were solemnly elected to the vacant positions by the Congress on the 25th of October, 1969.

The Seventeenth Institutional Act of October 14, 1969 gave the president the power to transfer to the reserve any military officer guilty of violating the cohesion of the armed forces. The preamble of the act stated that "the Armed Forces as institutions that serve to sustain the constituted powers of law and order, are organized on a basis of the principles of hierarchy and discipline." The act can be interpreted as a warning to those officers in disagreement with the decision of the military high command in passing over Albuquerque Lima in favor of Médici. Also, the act gave to the new president "legal" means of imposing the military's will on the armed forces without having to resort to other forms of coercion or intimidation.

The Sixteenth and Seventeenth Acts were followed by another unilateral decision of the military commanders: Constitutional Amendment No. 1 of October 17; published in the Official Diary on October 20 and in effect as of October 30. The effect of the amendment has led some political observers to refer to the amendment as the 1969 Constitution, even though 95 percent of the 1967 document remains. The amendment, among other changes, reduced still further the powers of the Congress; the size of the Congress was reduced when the criterion for the number of seats was shifted from population (benefiting the more backward states with a large illiterate population) to registered voters (which benefits the more urban states in the south)—the new chamber of deputies was reduced from 409 to 293; the state assemblies were reduced from 1,076 to 672 seats; the centralized control of the chief executive over the introduction of new legislation, especially money bills, was confirmed.

The amendment represented the determination of the military to insure a presidential succession unmarred by dissent or protest. It provided the new chief executive with all the powers required for governing and controlling the nation. By moving to promulgate these decisions before the election of General Medici, the military high command assumed collectively the responsibility for the political decision to emasculate the 1967 Constitution.

The Military in the Sixties in Perspective

Reacting to the immobilism of the civilian political system in 1964, induced by the rapid increase in social mobilization after 1946, the armed forces once again intervened in the political system. Increasing participation had not been accompanied by the necessary level of political institutionalization; the intervening political mechanisms for mediation, conflict resolution and goal allocation were intermittent and subject to the parochial pressures of a populist political system. As regime authority weakened, the legitimacy of the 1946 Republic became questionable. Given the traditional orientation of the Brazilian military as guardians of the constitution, the crisis of the 1963-1964 period led to the coup d'etat of March 13, 1964.

Having taken the initiative to intervene, the military was confronted with the inevitable choice of returning power to the civilian political elite or retaining it for an indefinite period of time. The first year of the military regime seemed to indicate that no final determination had been made. In part, this was due to the practice of the armed forces to allow the civilians to regain power almost immediately. In part, it was a result of the belief that the reforms required could be implemented in a short period of time.

As it became obvious that the changes desired by the military, in part to preclude their having to intervene again in the near future, required more time; and that the immediate return of power to the civilians would probably result in political breakdown once again; and as the military developed a sense of independent purpose from the assumption of decision-making positions, the determination to retain power and restructure Brazil gained widespread support. The corruption and incompetence of the civilians seemed clear; the stalemate between the supporters of immediate and radical change and the conservative oligarchy seemed impossible to break by normal, constitutional means; the economic slowdown of the early 1960s could not be allowed to continue; and the growing threat of communism and elements on the negative left promised to subvert public order. For these reasons the armed forces, particularly after the state elections of October 1965, opted for the establishment of a military regime.

The traditional role of the Brazilian military is no more. It is a myth that well deserves to be discarded. The armed forces in Brazil have always been an interventionist force, a praetorian institution; the question was really when and how they would participate in politics. With the coup d'etat of March 1964, a basic reinterpretation of their role in Brazilian society appeared. No longer guardians of the constitution, the armed forces were the authors and the interpreters of, and the principal actors in, the constitutional order, as demonstrated by the 1967 document and the 1969 Amendment.

What have been the accomplishments of the military regime since 1964? Certainly they have succeeded in great measure in further centralizing the central government. Decision-making is more efficient, resources are allocated more rationally, and economic growth goals are no longer subverted by the turmoil of the civilian political process. It is the economic record of the regime that stands as its one positive accomplishment. It is that economic record that provides the margin of security in retaining widespread public support among the middle- and upper-class sectors of the population.

The regime has done nothing to deal with the issue of political participation. Illiterates still are not allowed to vote. The political party system is subservient to the whims of the government. Important areas such as social welfare and agrarian reform remain topics of fervent debate and, at times, legislative action—but there is little, if any, attempt to implement these decisions. The question of institutionalization has been dealt with in the most superficial form: administrative and bureaucratic reform, yes; political reform, no.

The legacy of the 1964 Revolution, outside of the narrow area of spectacular economic recovery and planning, is sterile. The three governments of the military regime have become more authoritarian. The eruption of violence, as demonstrated by the activity of the urban terrorists, indicates the alienation of some segments of society. The unwillingness to challenge the continuing hegemony of the traditional, rural oligarchy reflects an all-too-willing acceptance of the status quo if it is characterized by political order.

Moving hesitantly at first, unwilling to tamper with the 1946 Constitution, the military have written and emasculated the 1967 Constitution. They have issued seventeen institutional and more than six dozen complementary acts which derive their authority from the will of the armed forces, not the people. The emphasis on societal change continues to reflect the fears of the early 1960s—the disruption of political stability by growing participation and demands for widespread social and political reform.

With the assumption of President Médici in October 1969, the military regime had survived three leadership changes. The potential challenge posed by student rebellion, the protest of the Roman Catholic Church, and the active opposition of the urban terrorists seemed to have been met and neutralized. The reformist tendencies of the Albuquerque Lima wing of the armed forces, while still active, remained peripheral to the decision-making process. Development remained uppermost in the minds of the regime—that is, rapid economic growth; security dominated the political thinking of the armed forces —the prevention of internal subversion and the maintenance of a strong, united armed forces for both national and international purposes.

The Brazilian military have determined to retain political power and pursue their own version of "A Realidade Brasileira" (The Brazilian Reality). Their vision includes little civilian participation; it precludes basic restructuring of the social order; it opposes an independent political system, free of military domination. There seems little reason to doubt that the armed forces will retain power in Brazil for the immediate future. There is little if any organized opposition; there is widespread acquiesence in continued military rule by the middle and upper sectors; there is cohesiveness among and determination to remodel Brazil within the armed forces.

While the military can retain power, their narrow vision of society precludes political modernization. The praetorian army fears and opposes "politics" which it equates with disorder and subversion. But it fails to see that the ultimate stability and order it seeks is impossible without basic political and social reform. Government without the meaningful, structured participation of the governed remains a sterile exercise in power management. The authority of a regime that must ultimately rely so heavily on a possible resort to coercion can scarcely achieve societal legitimacy. And a regime that fails to create a modicum of legitimacy will, ironically, always confront the possibility of subversion and disorder.

2 DOUGLAS A. CHALMERS

Political Groups and Authority in Brazil: Some Continuities in a Decade of Confusion and Change

Brazilian politics in the 1960s has gone through extraordinary swings in public mood, political institutions, and leadership. The decade began with the euphoria of the early Quadros government, passed through the nationalistic enthusiasm of the Goulart period, and since 1964 has experienced a military government riding the crest of improved economic conditions while restricting liberal-democratic institutions and coming under attack for repression. The various blind men who periodically inspect the Brazilian elephant can find in this history evidence for the most diverse interpretations: some see the decline in democracy and the shadow of fascism; others see the decline in utopian confusion and the rise of stable government supporting the best technical minds in a drive for economic development; still others see the unstable Brazilian giant still thrashing about in a confusion of indecision and rapid change.

Such contradictory testimony is owing superficially, of course, to varied ideological perspectives; more fundamentally, confusion stems from a lack of an acceptable conception of the basic character of the Brazilian political system. Despite the swings of mood and leadership, and despite the rhetoric of Brazil's current leaders, it is clear that no

I am very grateful to Arturo Valenzuela for his assistance in the preparation of this essay.

51

fundamental revolution has taken place. Something is going on very much as usual, and the determination of what that something is is crucial to an understanding of the significance of the military's actions since 1964 and the potentials for the 1970s. Powerful as the military is now, however, merely looking at military intentions—even assuming they were united, which they do not appear to be—would provide only a small clue to the future, since Brazil's leaders, now as before, are confronted by a complex political structure they can change only slowly.

The purpose of this essay is to suggest some of the elements of this basic and enduring political structure. To do so we must start well beneath the level of formal institutions, which in any case exhibit perhaps a higher rate of change than any other aspect of Brazilian politics, and concern ourselves with the basic sociopolitical groupings which link Brazilians with each other and their government, the manner in which these groupings have been brought together to contend for power, and the procedures and authority which have (with limited success) held the system together. Very generally stated, the basic proposition that emerges from this analysis is that Brazil as other Latin American countries has shown a pattern of consistently elitist political groupings of a kind I shall call "vertical," which combine in exceptionally fluid form at the top. Modernization, the military, and the logic of these groupings, furthermore, appear to be pushing Brazil toward a sort of flexible corporate state in which politics takes place essentially within nominally administrative structures.

Brazilian Political Groupings: The Importance of Vertical Relationships

Scholars looking below the façade of formal institutions, whether liberal-democratic or "revolutionary," have in increasing numbers explored the group basis of Brazilian politics. The assumption, whether cast in Marxian or pluralist terms, is that the "real" structure of influence and power can be discovered by examining the manner in which landowners, businessmen, workers, and peasants organize and act to promote their interests. With impressive consistency, such studies have noted aspects of these groups which blur their boundaries, inhibit their independent action, and involve them in entanglements with the government.

Studies of the labor movement, for example, call attention to the importance of patronal relationships in older factories and the extraordinary importance of the Vargas-initiated official syndical and social-

security structures.[1] Discussions of businessmen have drawn attention to heavy reliance on government initiatives and protection and
the patterns of personalist and clientelistic relationships with official
agencies.[2]

Perhaps less surprisingly, analysts exploring the possibility of
collective action among peasants and rural laborers discover that they
are likely to be caught up in (and divided by) special ties with patrons and that the political movements among them in the early
1960s were more like "followings" than class-based movements.[3]
Discussions of the "middle sectors" also emphasize their obvious divisions. The middle classes in Brazil appear to consist largely of employees in public or private bureaucracies. Their specific political action
(as opposed to such diffuse manifestations as the anti-Goulart marches
just before 1964) consists largely of membership in white-collar
unions or corporate-like professional associations whose principal
business is to secure legal rights and privileges from the government.[4]

Such observations as these have stimulated a variety of judg-

1. See, for example, Juárez Rubens Brandão Lopes, *Sociedade industrial no Brasil*,
(São Paulo: Difusão Européia do Livro, 1964); José Albertino Rodrigues, *Sindicato e
desenvolvimento no Brasil*, (São Paulo: Difusão Européia do Livro, 1968) and the unpublished Ph.D. dissertation by Kenneth Erickson, "Labor in the Political Process in
Brazil: Corporatism in a Modernizing Nation" (Columbia University, 1970).

2. See, for example, Fernando Henrique Cardoso, *Empresario industrial e desenvolvimento economico*, (São Paulo: Difusão Européia do Livro, 1964); Luciano Martins,
Industrialização, burguesia nacional e desenvolvimento, (Rio de Janeiro: Editorial Saga,
1968); and particularly the study by Philippe Schmitter *Interest Conflict and Political
Change in Brazil* (Stanford, California: Stanford University Press, 1971).

3. There is a considerable literature on peasant-patron relationships, chiefly from
anthropologists. An article which still appears relevant as a classification and which de-
votes space specifically to various types of political relationships in Brazil is Charles
Wagley and Marvin Harris, "A Typology of Latin American Subcultures," *American
Anthropologist*, LVII (1955), p. 428. For the basic statement of the proposition that
pre-1964 peasant movements were not class movements, see Benno Galjart, "Class and
Following in Rural Brazil" in *America Latina*, July-September 1964.

4. The analysis of the middle sectors in Brazil and elsewhere in Latin America is
very diffuse, in part because of lack of agreement on who is to be included. A summary
of much of the literature can be found in Luis Ratinoff, "The New Urban Groups: The
Middle Classes" in Seymour Martin Lipset and Aldo Solari (editors) *Elites in Latin
America*, (New York: Oxford University Press, 1967). On the importance of establishing the legal status of professional and other associations—and on many of the issues
dealt with in this essay—see Ronald C. Newton, "On 'Functional Groups,' 'Fragmentation,' and 'Pluralism' in Spanish American Political Society." *Hispanic American Historical Review*, Vol. L, No. 1 (February 1970), 1-29.

ments and explanations. Many attribute these features to traditional-ism. Indeed, strong similarities exist between these nominally modern groupings and structures of earlier periods and "backward" rural areas and small towns. In both cases, it has been common to empha-size the links of real and fictive family relationships and the diffuse ties of personal obligation which link patrons and their subordinates. Further, traditional figures such as the rural boss or *coronel* form parts of chains of influence and patronage which involve the local power holders in subtle forms of dependency on state and national govern-ment.[5]

Other interpretations highlight the dependency relationships and find the hidden hand of the oligarchy defending its privileges. One of the more fascinating combinations of this and the traditionalist view is to be found in an article on career patterns by Anthony Leeds.[6] As he portrays the political structures, members of the elite come together in informal groups which cut across conventional interest-group categories and co-operate in maintaining their positions by making use of contacts above to manipulate people and resources below. The discovery of such relationships even in relatively modern sectors has begun to stimulate a line of analysis based on the proposi-tion that "change without development" is occurring in Brazil.[7]

Other scholars suggest that these patterns constitute characteris-tics of "transitional" societies. They call attention to such phenomena as the populism of "charismatic" leaders such as Vargas, Lacerda, or Brizzola and the prominence in politics of such institutions as the military. The latter is sometimes seen as "modernizing," sometimes the tool of classes too weak or disorganized to act for themselves.[8]

5. The classic analysis of *coronelismo*, emphasizing the links upward and down-ward, is Victor Nunes Leal, *Coronelismo, enxada e voto* (Rio de Janeiro: Revista Forense, 1948).
6. Anthony Leeds, "Brazilian Careers and Social Structures: A Case History and a Model," in Dwight B. Heath and Richard N. Adams, *Contemporary Cultures and So-cieties of Latin America* (New York: Random House, 1965), p. 379.
7. Exploring such a proposition would require a major effort to untangle compet-ing definitions and unclarified norms. The basic notion is that economic and other sorts of growth take place without reducing inequality.
8. Belief in the existence of a specific "transitional" type of politics, associated par-ticularly with Lucian Pye's "Non-Western Political Process" and Fred Rigg's "Prismatic Society," seems to be fading as the "traditional" or "modern" end-points are seen to take many forms. The association of "charismatic" leaders with the disorganization of a mass society, or the importance of the "modern" organizations of the army in a so-ciety with relatively weak institutions, still plays a role in much thinking as a sort of transitional feature. On the treatment of populism in this light, see Francisco Weffort "Politica de massas," in Octavio Ianni *et al.*, *Política e revolução social no Brasil* (Rio de Janeiro: Editôra Civilização Brasileira, 1965), p. 161. On the military, see particularly

A further possibility, favored here, combines several elements of these approaches without necessarily drawing the same conclusions— that the process of group formation in Brazil, as in Latin American and other areas, differs in important respects from what we have been led to expect from either Marxian or pluralist approaches. Rather than signifying a passing phase of traditionalism, transitionalism, or the last throes of oligarchical control, this political behavior in Brazil indicates a changing, dynamic, and distinctive style, a distinctive path of development.[9]

Our basic proposition is that the fundamental axis for the crystallization of political groupings in Brazil and Latin America in general lies, not in the shared interests of their members defined in terms of their common occupation or ideology, but in the relationships of authority and interchange of values between subordinates and superiors. What is involved is the primacy of one of two aspects that are present in all minimally structured groups. They might be considered the organizational aspects and the dimension of shared goals. The distinction parallels that which Reinhard Bendix found in Weber between "two attributes of all behavior . . . constellations of interest . . . [and] domination . . ."[10]

Although the two aspects are found in any group, it makes a great deal of difference for political behavior whether groups have crystallized around relationships of authority and domination (which I shall call "vertical" groups) or around shared interests (which I shall call "horizontal" groups). Horizontal groups might include autonomous trade unions, ideological political parties, civic associations, and manufacturers' associations. Vertical groupings on the other hand might include urban political machines, the clientele of, say, defense department purchasing departments in the United States, the fol-

José Nun, "The Middle Class Military Coup," in Claudio Veliz (editor), The Politics of Conformity in Latin America (New York: Oxford University Press, 1967), p. 66.

9. Viewing this as a distinctive path of development is not equivalent to saying that "every country's history is unique." Rather, it is meant to suggest that Brazil belongs to a class of nations (or more accurately, national histories) which can be distinguished from others. Increasingly, however, it appears that there are strong parallels in other cultures. See, for example, the references in John Duncan Powell, "Peasant Society and Clientelistic Politics," American Political Science Review, LXIV, No. 2 (June 1970) 411. Clientelistic politics appears to be a sub-set of vertical relationships as described here. For a provocative essay which argues that distinctive patterns of evolution in Latin America may derive from deepset cultural norms, see Richard Morse, "The Heritage of Latin America," in Louis Hartz (ed) The Founding of New Societies (New York: Harcourt Brace, 1964).

10. Reinhard Bendix, Max Weber, An Intellectual Portrait (New York: Doubleday Anchor Books, 1962), p. 287.

lowers of a rural patriarch, or an officially sponsored professional association. The difference may be expressed along the five following dimensions.[11]

Cross-class Membership

Horizontal groups are composed of members of generally equal status, whereas vertical groups cut through class and status distinctions. Clear examples of vertical groups are the traditional patronal relationships found in rural areas, in which upper-status families or patrons provide the leadership for a diffuse group including large numbers of peasants, rural workers, and occasionally "middle-class" elements connected with small-town economies. A similar cross-class structure may be found in cities, in the populist followings, and clientele of high-status leaders and their intermediary brokers of the middle and lower classes.

Other groups, such as professional associations and trade unions, do not appear at first glance to cut across class and status positions. Yet it is clear that in the early stages of much group formation in Latin America—say, among rural workers and farmers—the leadership seems to come disproportionately from middle- and upper-class backgrounds. More important, such groups do not reinforce solidarity through an emphasis on exclusivity of membership from particular strata but actively seek to identify with higher status groupings. This identification may only be upward, not downward; that is, public employees may find it "beneath their dignity" to associate directly

11. In arriving at the five characteristics listed below, three processes were at work: a loose form of deduction from the basic notion of the primacy of authority relations; rather impressionistic induction, relying on other scholars' descriptions of groups; and an attempt to achieve a particular purpose. That purpose was to recast the common, offhand and often condescending characterizations of Brazilian politics into terms which imply its rationality and its capacity to adapt to "modern" situations. Too often, it seems to me, discussions of the sort of characteristics noted here are cast in terms of the backwardness of Brazilians, or Latin Americans. My objection to this point of view is not based on solicitude for the feelings of "traditional" Brazilians, which would make the effort simply a sentimental distortion. In fact, I personally do not find many of these aspects and practices congenial nor likely to produce much in the way of social justice. They are, however, quite adaptable to situations of high technology, specialization, and other signs of modernity, and in fact may constitute not so much tradition as a wave of the future, as central governments all over the world become more and more powerful. In any case, the multiple methods used to arrive at these characteristics produce a certain eclecticism. I believe, however, that it is more useful at this stage to operate eclectically than to attempt a premature logical or statistical coherence.

with industrial workers or peasants, but a high value is placed on links with upper strata—with those who are capable of moving among the rich, the prestigious, and the powerful. Such links are not only useful in conferring status but are instrumental in satisfying demands which arise from individuals in the group.

Dependency on Higher Authorities

Groups in Brazil, as elsewhere in Latin America, look to the government and political processes for the satisfaction of a wide range of needs. In many fields, such as labor relations, judicial and political institutions play a key role in the resolution of disputes. The effectiveness of particular groups can be severely limited or greatly improved depending upon the degree of support they receive from higher authorities. Resources of every kind are often available only through the national government or sometimes through other national or international organizations. Normative orientations which expect initiatives and resources to come from "above" seem to be combined with the practical reality that resources are mainly available from "above." As a result, the group structures which have emerged place great emphasis on strategies aimed at securing favorable treatment from governmental officials, international economic groupings, and national elites with available resources.

Two consequences of this vertical orientation to the center may be detected: a blurring of any sharp division between the public and the private and between the political and the nonpolitical and the creation of numerous "state-controlled" groups and organizations. These agencies may either be formally and administratively under state jurisdiction, as in the case of official labor syndicates, or they may be informally and "politically" controlled by governmental authorities as in the case of long-standing political machines and the pseudoprivate economic groups dependent upon official favor.

Dependency of this type is not synonymous with political weakness. It is sometimes said that labor syndicates, for example, are powerless *because* they are built into the official structure, a judgment which appears apt in contemporary Brazil. In Brazil, as in the United States, however, dependency is also compatible with power if the groups in question are able to "colonize" the government agencies responsible for their "control" and successfully fight off efforts by other groups to limit their influence.

A concomitant of dependency is a tendency to avoid direct bargaining in the face of conflict and a preference to submit disputes to higher authorities. Intergroup dealings are thus more like confrontations among subordinates in front of the chief (or, in more formalized situations, in a court of law) than direct attempts to solve disputes by compromise or violent conflict.[12]

Emphasis on Demands Intended to Strengthen Group Structure: "Corporate" vs. "Constituency" Demands

The importance of status-ranking and authority relationships both within vertical groupings and in their dealings with the other groups leads to the formation of demands designed to strengthen (or alter) those relationships. For example, these demands take the form of patronage secured and dispensed by the leader in such a fashion as to strengthen the ties between him and his followings. The demand for patronage, therefore, is a demand designed to strengthen the internal authority relations of the groups. Another form of authority-related demand is the demand for official recognition or special legal status of the group endowing it with a strengthened role in the system of national authority relationships.

These might be called "corporate demands," not in the sense that they are made by a depersonalized corporate group, but because they relate to the strength and status of the grouping in its organized or structured aspects. Horizontal groups, on the other hand, emphasize what might be called "constituency demands," which seek to further the interests of the category of individuals or sub-groups that make up the constituency of the group. Rather than making demands which establish the *authority* of the group or leader, horizontal groups seek to establish *identity* with their constituency as a basis for their right to represent them. Vertical groupings make demands only for those members of society in a specific, relatively permanent relationship to group leaders and structures—one in which the authority relationships can play a central role. Horizontal groups, on the other hand, make demands for categories of persons forming a broad constituency, ranging far beyond those individuals with whom they have specific contact.

---

12. This aspect of behavior seems strongly parallel to Michel Crozier's description of the French "*Horreur du face-a-face*," in his *Bureaucratic Phenomenon* (Chicago: University of Chicago Press, 1964). It is also related (negatively) to the "pragmatic bargaining style" which has been suggested as the foundation of Anglo-Saxon pluralism, although scholars tend to forget that acceptance of face-to-face dealings may be just as violent or unjust as submission to higher authority.

The Importance of Particularistic and Diffuse Demands

Since the crystallization of groupings in a vertical pattern involves a focus on authority relationships rather than on specialized interests, there is no sharp restraint on the range and character of the demands being made. Vertical groupings, therefore, are likely to become the channels for a wide variety of particularistic demands ranging from jobs for an individual, schooling for his children, favorable treatment on an application for a pension and a wide variety of "small favors." Leaders—of the traditional coronel type, or less traditional politicians or industrial managers—will satisfy such particularistic demands because they serve to strengthen directly their own authority. In groupings where horizontal ties predominate, toleration of such particularistic demands is likely to be interpreted as corruption unless they are satisfied according to strict egalitarian standards.

Not all vertical groups are dominated by particularistic demands as completely as the traditional patron-client network of the rural boss whose political action is almost entirely devoted to such problems. But the degree of such particularism, and the consequent diffuseness of the demands made by the group as a whole over time, is much greater in vertically structured systems than in others.

Leaders as Brokers and the Blurring of Politics and Administration

In horizontally structured groups, leaders are primarily representatives of the interests embodied in the constituency of the group. Their tasks involve building consensus and bringing pressure to bear on the decision-making centers of government for the interests thus articulated. The leader of a vertically structured grouping also performs these tasks (with the variations in the nature of the demands noted before) but, in addition, serves as a channel or broker through which the benefits secured from government are distributed among his following. In the horizontal groups the leader mobilizes resources and energies to apply the demands and supports which constitute the political inputs of the system. The leader in the vertically structured group must, to maintain his authority, not only play a role in generating inputs but also in channeling the many outputs of the system. He becomes a broker for values flowing both toward and from the government. Patronage is clearly a simple example of downward flows, but so too are official sanctions to control professional activity, exclusive rights to concessions or tariff protection, and other forms of benefits.

In the process, the differentiation of administrative structures from political ones becomes blurred except for the limited case of offices which perform merely routine clerical work. Political parties and interest groups seek to acquire the power to make the many small administrative decisions involved in implementation of policies, and administrative agencies employ their capacity for making such decisions to build politically significant clienteles.

These five related dimensions are presented here as a heuristic framework useful for organizing and rendering meaningful many observations which have often been made about Brazilian and Latin American political behavior. The central factor is the primacy of authority-dependency relations, both within political groups and between groups and political authorities, in such a way that the lines between the two are often difficult to discern.[13] The importance of these vertically structured groups lies not only in understanding the group structure in Brazil but also the conditions and limits which they impose on the national political process based on them.

Elites, Change, and Power Contenders

The first and most general point is that the vertical nature of groups in Brazil constitutes a form of elitism which is very common and very durable, not only in Brazil but elsewhere in Latin America. Inequality is built into the system, although it does not necessarily entail the sharp economic inequalities presently found in Brazil. The socioeconomic elites often overlap with political ones and make use of their high-level status in assuming the key brokerage roles at the top of the various vertical hierarchies. Further, the absence of strongly organized peasant or working-class organizations with substantial autonomy limits potential equalitarian trends.

It is not meaningful to insist, however, that this elitism entails the existence of an oligarchy.[14] In the last century and perhaps in

13. It might be noted that Michels' "Iron Law of Oligarchy" constitutes a hypothesis of the inevitable "verticalization" of horizontally structured groups. Groups, such as Michels' parties, which undergo "bureaucratization" remain essentially horizontal, however, as long as the hierarchy of relations remains internal and up to the point where the leaders seek and exploit official status within the regime, thus blurring the line between the party and the government.

14. See, for example, Francois Bourricaud, "El ocaso de las oligarquias y la sobrevivencia del hombre oligarquico," *Aportes* No. 4 (April 1967), p. 4, for a discussion of a similar point with respect to Peru. See also the same author's *Power and Society in Contemporary Peru* (New York: Frederick A. Praeger, 1970). Bourricaud's criticisms of the theories of inevitable explosions or breakdowns seem very relevant and by no means contradicted by the emergence of a military government in Peru with left-reformist intentions. The traditional "oligarchy" may be in trouble, but the elitism remains.

the Old Republic, it may have made sense to call Brazil an oligarchy because intra-elite conflicts were successfully insulated from inter-class conflicts. In other words, dissident elites were unable or unwilling to mobilize middle- or lower-class support in their competition with other elites.[15] Such an oligarchical situation has not described Brazil since at least 1930.[16] One may suggest several reasons: the weakness of "aristocratic" institutions, the flexibility of the elites, the propensity for co-optation among the middle sectors, and international examples suggesting to the elites the inevitability of oligarchical decline and models for popular mobilization.

Whatever the reasons, the result has been a high level of competition between various factions, many of which have sought to establish their political power by appeals to lower strata and the creation or manipulation of vertical structures capable of mobilizing them.[17] The most obvious examples have been those associated with Vargas and his landowner-rancher protégé João Goulart. They both, with varying success, built organizations including traditional provincial elites and syndicalized workers.

Mobilization of the masses has not resulted in horizontal mass organization because elites have either channeled this mobilization through pre-existing structures or have created new ones of the vertical type.[18] Their success in forestalling more direct threats to their position may be a result of a great variety of relationships around which vertical political groupings have been built. In very

15. This is presumably only one way of defining an oligarchical system. For a different approach which is compatible, see James Payne, "The Oligarchy Muddle," *World Politics*, XX, No. 3 (April 1968), 439. Payne does not, however, consider what is called here the persistence of elitism.

16. 1930 is chosen as a dividing line since the Revolution of that year seemed to mark a rather clear and irreversible step towards the mobilization of mass support. Occasional recourse to mass support can be found much earlier.

17. There is a rather separate problem of what might be called the "circulation of elites," or politico-social mobility. It is clear that major changes in the social backgrounds of the elites has occurred, ranging from the breakin of elites from Rio Grande do Sul with the Vargas era, the rise of new business elites in São Paulo and now, with the rise of military and "tecnico" elites.

18. "Mobilization" is often taken to mean the crossing of a boundary of many people from no contact with the central institutions to some form of involvement. In view of the chains of relations which however indirectly tie a peasant, say, through his patron to national institutions in even very "traditional" situations, it appears more appropriate to define mobilization as a *re*-ordering of relationships rather than the creation of a totally new relationship. Karl Deutsch's classic definition, in fact, emphasizes the breaking or eroding of old commitments and the availability of persons for new ones. Cf. "Social Mobilization and Political Development," *American Political Science Review*, LV, No. 3 (September 1961), 493.

rough order of historical appearance, these have included

1. state political machines built around a coronel or politically prominent families, and later including an element of state-level populism,
2. institutions with nominally nonpolitical functions, as the military and the Church,[19]
3. labor syndicates, professional associations and financial-commercial-industrial groupings,
4. populist movements built around direct contact between leaders and followers, reinforced by media projections of the personalities of the leaders, and
5. government agencies, including financial ones, regional planning agencies (SUDENE), and various politically important "autonomous" institutions such as PETROBRAS and the sugar and coffee institutes.

Not all structures are equal, of course, in terms of relative power. Control over major resources, the ability to survive attacks from hostile factions in control of the governmental apparatus, and the ability to mobilize rapidly in times of crisis vary enormously and are crucial considerations for elites attempting to put together a significant political apparatus for taking or holding power. What is striking in Brazil is the very great variety of structures represented and the multiple levels and axes along which the political universe crystallizes. Brazil's great size and diversity seems to have made the variety greater than in other Latin American countries. Especially in the period from 1945 to 1964, with relatively open electoral competition, expansion of governmental scope, and improvement of communications, there was ample room for political entrepreneurs to build or alter political support structures. Referring only to more dramatic examples, Carlos Lacerda and Lionel Brizzola's use of radio and television; Miguel Arraes' conversion of the political and administrative apparatus of the state of Pernambuco, João Goulart's unsuccessful attempt to create a structure of support among noncommissioned officers, and Celso Furtado's attempts to develop a political as well as

19. Viewing political groupings as either horizontal or vertical suggests a reconsideration of the view of the military as somehow illegitimately involved in politics *because* it is an institution devoted to "other purposes." See, for example, Alfred Stepan, *The Military in Politics: Changing Patterns in Brazil* (Princeton: Princeton University Press, 1971) and Ronald M. Schneider, *The Political System of Brazil: Emergence of a 'Modernizing Authoritarian' Regime, 1964-70* (New York & London: Columbia University Press, 1971).

administrative apparatus in SUDENE all constituted innovative attempts to exploit existing or emerging techniques, channels of communication, and institutions for political purposes.

One of the clearest effects of the military since coming to power in 1964 has been its closing off of many of these opportunities for political experimentation, partly through fear that the new structures with mass bases (or, in reality, mass rhetoric) would lead to radicalization and class polarization.[20] The new governments have sharply limited the significance of elections, weakened the autonomy of the states, moved to prevent the use of the press and other media for political mobilization, exerted greater control over official structures such as lower military ranks and labor syndicates, and, most sensationally, acted directly to prohibit such successful political figures as Quadros, Lacerda, Brizzola, and Kubitschek, from engaging in effective political action.

It is possible that these repressive measures may significantly weaken the flexibility of the political system and threaten the delicate and dynamic balance which maintained elite rule while absorbing wider segments of the population. By clogging the system, so to speak, and inhibiting the sort of pluralism of vertical structures which characterized the pre-1964 situation, the military government may be generating the radical response it was acting to prevent.

Such a development is by no means certain, however. To some extent, the military may by sheer escalation of repression prevent mass involvement. Continued economic boom conditions (and World Cup championships) may forestall discontent. More importantly, the military has cut off many possible avenues for political organization, but not all. In general, political mobilization has been limited to administrative agencies. For the time being at any rate, new political entrepreneurs in Brazil seeking to establish vertical structures, as a basis of support will be found in the ministries, regional developmental agencies, planning and financial agencies. As many scholars have shown, the bureaucracy has long been a focal point of politics.[21]

20. Cf. Stepan, *op. cit.*, for an analysis of the thinking of the military prior to the coup in 1964.

21. Cf. for example, the unfairly neglected work by Raymundo Faoro, *Os donos do poder: formação do patronato político brasileiro* (Porto Alegre: Editôra Globo, 1958) and many of the essays of Helio Jaguaribe. For comments on the Chilean bureaucracy which emphasize their central role in the developing political process, see James Petras, *Politics and Social Forces in Chilean Development* (Berkeley: University of California Press, 1969).

The appreciation of the character of vertical groupings should alert us to avoid the fallacy of assuming that the only significant competitive political support building that goes on is in the public spheres of a free press and free elections. There may be strong normative objections to limiting politics to the intraorganizational maneuvering in the administrative hierarchy, but it cannot be dismissed as a viable possibility.

Distinctions among Power Contenders: Vertically Based Factions

An individual politician may establish his claim to influence through control of a single vertical structure. Gaining political power on the national level, however, requires putting together many of these units. The basis on which such power-contending alliances are held together constitutes a major characteristic of the political system.

In discussions of European politics, one would begin and probably end an inquiry into such alliances with a study of political parties.[22] In Latin American nations, exclusive attention to parties would be highly distorting, since there are powerful groups such as foreigners and the military which are very unlikely to be absorbed into party formations. Indeed, there are relatively few polities—Chile, Colombia, and perhaps Venezuela—in which the analysis of political parties would be a very significant contribution to an understanding of major power contenders. The reasons for party weakness in Latin America are too complex to explore here, particularly since the extreme weakness of parties in Brazil, even in the period during which they were apparently prominent, 1946-1964, is obvious.[23]

Students of Latin American politics have instead established rather ad hoc lists of power contenders, based essentially on socioeconomic categories such as class but adding other obvious elements such

22. Note the underlying assumption in the work of such political sociologists as Seymour Martin Lipset and Stein Rokkan in the introductory chapter of their *Party Systems and Voter Alignments* (New York: The Free Press, 1967) that although there may be blocks to the free expression of social cleavages into political parties, the effectively expressed social cleavages are those which do find expression in parties.

23. See Douglas A. Chalmers, "Parties and Society in Latin America," paper presented to 1968 American Political Science Association meeting. That paper constitutes an earlier version of many of the themes explored here, but deals more specifically with the role of parties. On Brazilian parties in the period 1946-64, cf. Thomas Skidmore, *Politics in Brazil, 1930-1964* (New York: Oxford University Press, 1967).

as the military.[24] Whether class or any other basic cleavage accurately describes the differences between Brazilian power contenders of any period is highly questionable.

As one might expect from the analysis thus far, class categories, however much they might be useful in exploring underlying tensions and long-term trends, are not useful for identifying major organized political blocs. Charles Anderson's recent comment is apropos:

Class analysis is an incredibly blunt instrument for describing or explaining political conflict in Latin America. Most of the interesting things politically in Latin America happen within the conventional classes rather than between them.

He continues, rather pessimistically,

Finding a workable classification scheme for the units of analysis of Latin American politics has become a frustrating task. The more discreet, and in a sense "true to life" we become in identifying the units, the more we are tempted by descriptive journalese ("clique of generals. . . .")[25]

The cross-class character of the vertical groups unquestionably hinders the development of blocs built on class identification. It might still be possible, even with vertically structured bases, to find power contenders conflicting on class issues. While the structure of the group remains cross-class, a (willing or forced) deferential clientele might support the upper-class goals of its leadership, while upper-class elites may assume a populist stance. No such clear-cut alignment seems to have taken place in Brazil. Vargas's populism seems to have been matched

24. Scholars are, in fact, a great deal more likely to refer very loosely and generally to "power contenders" rather than providing lists even for a single country, something that may reflect the significance of the vertical bases described here. Charles W. Anderson provides the following examples in *Politics and Economic Change in Latin America* (Princeton: D. Van Nostrand & Co., 1967): a military "clique," service or unit; a political party, interest group or movement; a group or association identified with a specific economic interest; a community or region; a family, class, or clique. Eldon Kenworthy, in "Coalitions in the Political Development of Latin America," in Sven Groennings, et al., *The Study of Coalition Behavior* (New York: Holt, Rinehart and Winston, 1970) provides this list of "potential actors in the Latin American game": rural elite, church, military, entrepreneurs, middle class, organized labor, and the United States Government (p. 126-127).

25. The quotes are from Anderson's commentary on Markos Mamelakis's "The Theory of Sectoral Clashes," both of which appear in the *Latin American Research Review*, Vol. IV, No. 3 (Fall 1969). The quotation is from page 50.

with solid support from a segment of the upper class, and the same could be said of Goulart, at least until the second half of March 1964.

There are other possible bases for enduring cleavage which do seem more appropriate to a vertically structured system. The fragmentation of national societies into competing blocs based on religious, ethnic, linguistic, or other "primordial" differences might be based on competing sets of institutions. Such cleavages, however, have not been the basis of political blocs in any Latin American society, despite what appears to be very dramatic ethnic differences in, say, the Andean countries, Mexico, and Guatemala.[26] In the Brazil of the nineteenth century and the Old Republic (1889-1930), regional divisions came close to constituting "cultural" divisions politically organized, but these appear to be fading.

Markos Mamelakis's highly interesting suggestion of basic divisions among economic sectors (mining, industry, agricultural, and services) interacting with government and the banking system offers another possibility of major divisions each built on a vertical basis, competing for power or favor.[27] Once again, however, for Brazil, at least, such sectoral division has no obvious applicability to the formation of enduring political groups. The goals of major competing political leaders for the promotion of industry and agriculture seem to have shifted in parallel fashion over the years, rather than in opposition to each other. It would be hard to say that the coalition backing Vargas, for example, was particularly based on agriculture, industry, or services.

Another possible line of division that receives much attention concerns the nationalist-internationalist cleavage. Certainly this cleavage appeared to be ever stronger in shaping political coalitions just before the military coup, and it can be said with some justice that the

26. "The pattern of correlation of social change and intensification of ethnic-linguistic differentiation in Asia and Africa must . . . be matched against the strikingly different sequence in Latin America, where modernization seems to be producing increased cultural (if not always social) integration." Charles Anderson, et al., *Issues of Political Development* (Englewood Cliffs, N.J.: Prentice Hall, 1967). Comparative studies of the bases of politically relevant "cultural pluralism" are not yet available to explain this general difference among areas. It is possible that basic "primordial" cleavages are still in the future in Latin America.

27. Mamelakis, *op. cit.* He uses an "income group" classification to cut through the sectoral one and provide more flexibility. It should be emphasized that he is primarily concerned with interpreting economic development, although the application to politics is relevant since it is through government activity that one or another sector is favored, neglected or suppressed.

military came in as the leadership of an internationalist segment of Brazilian society. The fact is, however, that such a cleavage, while always present in policy problems, does not define the basis of competition between enduring factions. The left can rightfully say that all major power contenders have had strong ties to "imperialism" while others can similarly point to concessions to nationalist sentiment by all governments.

The easy way out of this confusion is simply to suggest that all such divisions are present and that governments (and oppositions) have been built on shifting coalitions among these interests. On the basis of the analysis of groups made previously in this chapter, it may be suggested that a search for enduring cleavages of interest may be misleading. The basic ties which bind power-contending political factions may be relations of authority and dependency, not interest. In other words, the character of the larger coalitions is vertical, as is the case for smaller groups. The binding qualities in Brazil are not provided by *formal* organizational requirements (as one might find in a system with strong parties) but by the exchange of valued commodities throughout the system—among and through the hierarchies—and by loyalties or identifications built around a set of symbols, including a prominent leader (such as Vargas) and/or a central institution such as, in the present situation in Brazil, the military.[28]

Instability and Institutions

Turning to the interaction of these vertically based power contenders, two aspects may be examined: the types of conflict among groups and the procedures or persons who play more or less institutionalized roles in dealing with this conflict. Since Brazilian institutions have been weak and changing, this discussion leads us to an analysis of political instability.

Fluidity versus Rigidity

Within the framework of vertically structured groups and factions, two types of group conflict may place inordinate strains on

28. Although this pattern of ties binding together political factions sounds much like analysis of "backward" conditions, it is also applicable to say "the North American party system." In so far as the elements of coalitions in the United States are the sort of specialized groups which are called horizontal here, however, the symbols, values interchanged and organizational requirements of political parties and Presidentially led "teams" (the principle power contenders) are probably quite different from those found in Brazil.

political institutions and lead to instability. The first is a sort of rigidity which might be called the intransigeance of established groupings, and the second is hyper-fluidity of political support. The first type may be exemplified by Argentina—at least as that nation is portrayed by many scholars. Kalman Silvert traces the weakness of national institutions to the influence of "Mediterranean syndicalism" in which "the Doctrine of the Two Swords is amended to become the Doctrine of the Six or Seven or Eight Swords, depending on the number of institutional pillars created. . . ." The instability and ineffectiveness of the Argentine political system is traced to the lack of commitment to national institutions, and the rigidity and absolutism of the demands made by the "institutional pillars."[29] The situation seems quite the reverse in Brazil. Just as one could find no enduring bases of differentiation according to class, sector, there have been no rigidly drawn lines between power-contending factions. Perhaps the very size and diversity of the country prevents the permanence of such lines much beyond the confines of a state or region—where traditional family-based factions persist. For whatever reason, however, the basic pattern of Brazilian instability appears to be hyperfluidity at the national level, rather than rigidity.

In contrast to Argentina and other Latin American states, Brazil —at least since the expansion of political participation—has not been a country where the president could firmly establish himself with the leaders of a few major segments of the society and be guaranteed a relatively secure tenure. Even in the unique and highly structured area of military support, the securing of a *dispositivo militar* has always been a dynamic process. The president has had to give continued attention to military leaders, supporting them in securing *their* positions within the military organization. This task is far from simple, as João Goulart learned much to his misfortune. The basic characteristic of Brazilian instability appears to have been the evaporation of support for the president and his subleaders rather than the intransigeance of

29. "The Costs of Anti-Nationalism: Argentina" in K. H. Silvert, editor, *Expectant Peoples* (New York: Vintage Books, 1967) p. 347. Systems with relatively rigid "pillars" may find their own form of stability in a kind of classic corporate regime. Newton, in the article cited before, for example, parenthetically suggests, "Argentina stands at the opposite pole from Mexico, a viable 'corporative centralism,' whose institutions have proved adequate until now to maintain the PRI's functional sectors subordinate to the will of the party and national executive." Although this may be too simple a picture of the rather more complex Mexican reality, it does suggest that instability does not have *one* explanation or *one* solution. They vary according to the nature of the system.

the groups making up his coalition.

On the surface, this situation has changed dramatically with the installation of an obvious corporate hierarchy in control of the government—that is, the military. The military's corporate interest, however, is potentially quite different from those which Silvert and others describe. Both its own pretensions at being "above politics" and the limited sorts of demands which the military qua professional military can make on the nation in relatively advanced stages of economic growth *may* make of the military a vessel through which the changing corporate demands of other groups in society play themselves out.

Institutions: Through Legalism to "Planning"?

Turning our attention to the procedures to handle conflict, the most obvious fact concerning Brazil's experience is the rapid changes of constitutional provisions over the last forty years. Congress, the party system, the pattern of elections, executive-legislative relations and the like have often been altered. The "ideal" of firmly established political institutions capable of adapting to socioeconomic changes has obviously not been met in Brazil, nor in much of Latin America. The superficiality of the institutionalization of conventional liberal-democratic institutions during Brazil's "experiment with democracy" from 1946 to 1964 was shown not only by their limitation by the military after 1964 but by the failure of significant segments of the population to offer even token resistance of protest to their virtual abandonment.[30] The search for explanations of the weakness of such institutions has long been a topic of analysis for scholars, and a review of the varied offerings would take more space than is here available.

It is a common mistake, however, to assume that the constitutional provisions concerning legislatures, elections, and party systems are the only significant areas in which regular procedures evolve in a competitive political system. Budgetary procedures, for example, do not cease to become significant instruments for management of conflict when they are taken out of the hands of parliamentarians and put into the hands of bureaucrats. The preparation of investment or developmental plans is not less a significant procedure for dealing with various interests because of the reputed reliance on experts and technicians.

One might postulate that in the evolution of political systems, procedural patterns for resolving conflict and making decisions

30. This point is made in Skidmore, p. 321, for example.

evolved (where not broken by revolution) from the informal adjustments among the very top elite—what in Latin America is sometimes referred to as the informal "acuerdo" among the "oligarchs." In many countries, but in Latin America usually only partially or briefly, the establishment of regular procedures took place in the parliamentary process then expanded to the parliament-cum-parties and electoral process. In Latin America generally, this phase seems to have been omitted in favor of the next phase, the rapid growth of arrangements within the administrative hierarchy for "consultations" with various segments of the population in the decisional process. The bridge between the "acuerdo" phase and the "administrative" phase, provided in some countries by the process of representative government, seems to have been made in Latin America through elaborate legal systems. These sought to regulate and avoid conflict through the strict and highly detailed demarcation of responsibilities, spheres of competence, and rights and duties of entities within the system. Nominally, such legal procedures turn over to jurists many conflicts that might be resolved through face-to-face confrontation and bargaining. For serious conflicts, however, in which juridical solutions by definition will either be unavailable or unacceptable, this legalism appears to be a means of shifting responsibility upward to a person or group in authority. This enables maximum use of hierarchical chains of personal influence adapted to securing favors and concessions from those authorities. These legal procedures for resolving conflicts thus complement the vertical structures of society.[31]

The Authority of Leadership

One of the procedures for resolving conflicts, then, is an appeal to higher authority. In Brazil, as in most Latin American nations, this means the president. Although the presidency is almost always the locus of such final authority, not all presidents are accorded enough authority to make their offices stable sources of conflict resolution. In Brazil, presidential authority is something that has to be continually re-established and reaffirmed.[32]

31. John Leddy Phelan's suggestion that overlapping legal prescriptions in colonial Hispanic America allowed a measure of local adaptability while maintaining royal authority and power may indeed have a parallel in modern Latin American political practice. Cf. Phelan, *The Kingdom of Quito in the Seventeenth Century* (Madison: University of Wisconsin Press, 1967), especially the last chapter.

32. This is of course true for the "personal power" or authority of all presidents. For example, see the analysis of Richard Neustadt in *Presidential Power* (New York: John Wiley & Sons, Inc., 1960). In the United States, however, the need to generate such

The style of authority involved is basically what Gunther Roth calls "personal rulership." It is a type of patrimonialism which does not rely on traditionalist legitimation but is "inextricably linked to material incentives and rewards."[33]

In the recent history of Brazil, the following elements of such personal authority appear to be relevant:

First, the sheer capacity for managing a highly complex system of patronage for a large number of claimants is crucial. The reputation for success in handling a wide range of diffuse and particularistic demands—as in the case of Getúlio Vargas and Juscelino Kubitschek—engenders respect in spite of sarcastic judgments by opposition leaders who allege corruption.

Secondly, an aura of arbitrariness about executive decisions keeps subordinates on edge. At the same time, the president must preserve his legitimacy by adhering to accepted limitations. Since these limitations are not provided by traditional legal norms, they take the form of injunctions against efforts to destroy major power contenders.[34] Getúlio's mastery at maintaining a populist image while steadfastly rejecting any systematic attack on rural, commercial, or industrial power structures is classic. The disastrous consequences of Goulart's attempt to develop support among noncommissioned officers in ways directly threatening military discipline also illustrates this pattern.

A third means lies in the establishment of a popular image which provides the president with the ability to appeal over the heads of brokers, thus holding them in line. The populism of Vargas is an outstanding example, as is the "developmentalism" of Kubitschek. Jânio Quadros's popularity as a reformer with the middle sectors was strong, although it proved to be insufficient to sustain him in a direct challenge with powerful groups in the system. The military presidents also came to power with a general appeal; they claimed to be above politics and sufficiently authoritarian to bring about immediate gains such as the control of inflation.

The fourth strategy for the strengthening of presidential author-

---

power does not seem to be so central to the maintenance of the political system as in Latin America. With increasing conflict, it may become so.

33. Roth, "Personal Rulership, Patrimonialism, and Empire Building in the New States," *World Politics*, XX, No. 2 (January 1968) 194. Roth carefully distinguishes this form of personal rule from "charismatic" types.

34. The image of arbitrariness limited by established norms comes from Weber's description of politics under patrimonial rule. Cf. Bendix, *op. cit.* The injunction against destroying power contenders forms one of the basic "rules of the game" outlined by Anderson as part of the "Latin American political system." See Anderson, *Politics and Economic Change in Latin America* (Princeton: D. Van Nostrand, 1967), chapter 4.

ity involves identification with dramatic large-scale projects which both provide an image and a source of patronage for a support structure which can be clearly identified with the president himself. Vargas, once again, was the master builder. He began his presidency in the early 1930s with the support of a broad coalition of rural oligarchs and urban and military reformers. Later, Vargas saw the need to create programs and organizations aimed at enhancing his personal authority. These included the expanding state structure of the *Estado Novo*, the syndical structure which gave him important leverage among industrial workers, the two political parties simultaneously created in 1945 and further, such projects as the national steel complex and the petroleum authority. Kubitschek's most famous project was Brasília, the new capital, but in the course of actively promoting economic development he created many new agencies and rearranged old ones.

The military governments thus far have not found a significant new project for this type of support-building. The current concern with the Amazon Basin development holds some potential, particularly since the Amazon region holds considerable emotional significance for nationalists, a group to whom the military may find it useful to appeal to discredit the accusations of *entreguismo*.[35] It is in this respect that the possibility of a fairly radical land reform must be very tempting. Land-reform projects are always highly political, not only because they may directly attack the power of the landed elites, but also because successful land reform efforts in Latin America almost always yield a powerful political apparatus for their sponsor. So far the military does not seem to possess the resources and motivation to experiment with far-reaching land reform as a device for building political support. It is possible that in view of military actions against emerging peasant leaders from the pre-1964 period, the military may fear that the political apparatus of a land-reform program would escape its control. If Peru's military regime is successful in its move in this direction, however, one must expect that segments of the Brazilian military would attempt to follow suit.

35. Development of the Amazon, however, may not provide a very significant reinforcement of political support for the military since the remoteness and dispersion of its projects will probably not provide the sort of concentrated patronage which could serve as the basis of solid vertical structure formation. In this way, its value might be as fragile as the jungle road that Peru's President Balaunde was promoting as a dramatic project of his administration—good newspaper copy, but hard to make pay off politically except for the relatively few involved.

Decision-Making and the "Tecnicos"

Many of the factors that have been discussed lead to what might be called "staff" functions in government. It is a commonplace that the increasingly sophisticated technology, the "knowledge explosion" and the pressure for programs to stimulate rapid development, have greatly extended the role of the "expert"—both foreign and domestic —within Latin American political systems. The civil engineer and the lawyer, who were the most prominent professionals in the legalistic political systems of the area, including Brazil, have to some extent been replaced at the highest levels of decision-making a new breed of "tecnicos," by the economist, the planner, the architect, and engineers and managers of more specialized types.

There seems to be a variety of special reasons that the Brazilian system places special emphasis on such figures—which are even more prominent in the current military regime. First, as mentioned earlier, there is the practice of pushing decisions up the political hierarchy. In a more complex society, this requires more elaborate staff work than before. Secondly, the immense pressure which is placed on the president and top leadership for action, and particularly for the development of new programs and structures on which to build their prestige and new political support mechanisms, requires ever more complex planning.

Thirdly, the availability of rapidly expanding technical expertise in other parts of the world encourages the creation of expert channels to transmit and translate new knowledge into local terms.

Finally, the demands which arise through the vertically based system provide a special kind of information. Although it is precise in specifying what is needed for maintaining the structures (such as patronage needs) it is very imprecise concerning needs for and feasibility of major developmental programs, redistribution of resources, and major foreign policy decisions. For example, one scholar, in analyzing a small range of important economic decisions, found that the "autonomy" of planners and bureaucrats at the top level in Brazil is great, a fact which he explained, in part, by the "clientelistic" politics of much of the political structure which failed to promote aggressive policy positions on the part of major economic groups.[36]

Another scholar examining the behavior of organized interests in Brazil suggested that they often behave defensively—that is, rather

36. Nathaniel Leff, *Economic Policy-Making and Development in Brazil 1947-1964* (New York: John Wiley & Sons, Inc., 1968), Chapter 7.

than pressing for general policies in their favor, they react to policies emerging from the government, seeking to turn these policies to collective or individual advantage.[37]

A third study, exploring the making of decisions concerning the droughts of Northeast Brazil, suggested that decisions appear to be made in the absence of any systematic pressure from those directly concerned. Decisions are formulated by a fairly small group of people at the top stimulated by outbreaks of violence or natural disasters and employing some current diagnosis and "final solution" to the problem.[38]

From these studies, a picture emerges of a system in which the vertical structuring of group patterns leads to a situation wherein information relevant to making decisions, and many of the controls and pressures which shape decisions, are not generated directly through the action of political groups, but rather are a product of *técnico*-training, peer-group pressures, and the current dogmas, ideologies and fashions to which they are susceptible.[39]

The emphasis that is placed on the *tecnico* means that the dichotomy which is often posed between the *técnico* and the politician is highly misleading. The *técnico* is expected to produce "solutions" which are not only technically competent, but also politically viable. Political viability in this case is not simply being inoffensive to established interests or public opinion, but in a positive sense creating (or strongly encouraging) the development of structures which will provide the *técnicos* with political support. All politicians are necessarily becoming more technically oriented, and many of the most important *técnicos* are becoming more political. If there is any meaning to the dichotomy between technicians and politicians, it is between the *new* politician-technicians and the *old* politicians.

In most modern societies much of the bargaining over the allocation of resources takes place in an administrative framework. This is only recently being systematically investigated, even in the United

37. Philippe Schmitter, *op. cit.*

38. Albert O. Hirschman, *Journeys Toward Progress* (New York: Twentieth Century Fund, 1963), ch. 1 and ch. 4, where he discusses decision-making styles in Latin America.

39. Leff discusses ideology and "public opinion" (that is of a restricted group of members of the elites and near elites clustered around major cities) as influences on decisions made by authorities. Although Leff uses the term the "autonomy" of government, it is clear that there *are* restraints, but that they do not take the same form as restraints where aggressive interest group activity is found in the legislation stage.

States. Institutions such as planning mechanisms are increasingly recognized as something functionally equivalent to a legislative process,
although the atmosphere, actors, terms of reference, and procedures
are quite different. Systematic study of this administrative politics,
and the varied roles of the experts, the group representatives, the po-
litical-technical innovators still remain to be done in Brazil.[40]

Such analysis will be crucial in interpreting the military government's success or failure in institutionalizing its new regime. The
action of the military in shifting the formation of political groupings
from the open arenas of elections and party formation into the administration parallels similar trends in political systems all over the world.
Building the technician into the political process is not, however, accomplished by "hiring the best mind and backing him to the hilt." It
is by no means clear whether planning and consultative processes
have been established by the military government which can produce
technically and politically realistic policies responsive to the needs of
the Brazilian people.

Conclusions

The military regime in Brazil, as in other Latin American countries, is neither a throwback to the past interventions of ambitious
military leaders in the nineteenth century nor simply an escalation of
arbitrary, dictatorial government—although the incidents of official
repression indicate that the latter is not absent. The military government represents in a very real sense a logical extension of major trends
and characteristics of Brazilian politics. These include the military itself as one of the important vertical structures within the system, the
concentration of both political and administrative tasks within a bureaucracy, an emphasis on patrimonial authority, and the increasing
importance of experts, technicians, and specialists in the modern political process.

There is no reason to believe that the military will fail any more
profoundly than any other set of political leaders. The expectations
generated in some quarters that the "oppressive" military regime will
"inevitably" produce a mass revolutionary response seems to have no
more basis in fact than the endlessly predicted revolutionary situation
in many other countries of the world. The military regime constitutes
merely a new form through which elitism has been maintained. In

40. Cf., however, Robert T. Daland, *Brazilian Planning* (Chapel Hill: University
of North Carolina Press, 1967).

terms of class analysis, the move must be seen as adaptive rather than reactionary.

At the same time, there is no reason to believe that the military will have any greater success than other regimes. The regime gains some political breathing space by eliminating many or most of the public channels through which large numbers of Brazilians can express their judgment of it. It may have also gained some room for maneuver by the selective application of violent repression, although this is open to question. It may have simplified and streamlined the basic political processes through centralization of authority and its contempt for complex liberal-democratic processes. But it is faced with the task of building meaningful and sensitive political indicators into the administrative and political apparatus which it has established. The military's erratic experimentation with the creation of political institutions suggests that Brazil will continue to be marked by institutional instability in the foreseeable future. The earnest declarations concerning the mobilization of all Brazilians for development—also a feature of every regime—will be no substitute for a genuine program.

However one may judge the elitist pattern of vertical groupings that characterizes Brazilian politics and much of the politics in other parts of the continent, it should be noted that it is not the product of underdevelopment or backwardness. Although the verticality of groups is characteristic of traditional patronal relationships, it is also not very far from the model of a modern organizational society. There are no grounds for assuming that Brazil will or must establish a pluralistic, liberal-democratic form of government in order to become more developed. If democratic values of responsiveness to citizen demands, egalitarianism, and provisions for participation in politics are to be achieved, they will not come through copying older democratic institutions appropriate to another sort of politics in another age. They will have to emerge out of efforts to shape new types of vertical groups and new relationships between such groups and the increasingly technical political process. In this respect, the problem of humanizing political institutions, which Brazil faces today, is not essentially different from similar problems facing the United States, Western Europe, and even socialist bloc countries. Understanding these problems will test our capacity for imaginative analysis.

3 PETER D. BELL

Brazilian-American Relations

FROM A Brazilian viewpoint, aid from the United States has always been seen as political, if only because aid concerned vitally important decisions about the economic stability and growth of Brazil. But issues of survival to Brazilian politicians were viewed as financial and technical questions by American policy-makers until Castro's victory in Cuba. From the United States perspective in the 1960s, the victory of Brazil in the struggle against Communism might not determine the fate of Latin America, but the "loss" of the largest, most populous, and most industrialized Latin American country would almost surely mean the eventual communization of the region. This chapter will examine the political aspects of Brazilian-American relations in the 1960s and will be particularly attentive to the use of United States aid for political objectives. My purpose is to convey a sense of the quality of relations, personal and institutional, before and after the Revolution of April 1964 and to identify elements of consistency and variation under the quite different sets of political circumstances.

Of all trips which he made abroad as vice-president, the one

I wish to acknowledge the helpful comments and suggestions on an earlier version of this chapter from Frank Bonilla, Albert Hirschman, Cleantho da Paiva Leite, Simon Schwartzman, and Philippe Schmitter.

Richard Nixon least wanted was his visit to South America in 1958 because he thought "it would be relatively unimportant and uninteresting compared to the assignments I had in Washington at that time."[1] Nixon's reception by hostile mobs in Lima and Caracas aroused widespread concern in the United States about Latin America. It also encouraged President Juscelino Kubitschek of Brazil to come forth with the proposal for Operation Pan America, an effort to reaffirm "sentiments of solidarity and esteem" and to elicit United States participation in a multilateral project for the economic development of Latin America. The idea received a cool and evasive response from Washington, where it was viewed as a "counter-ploy"—"a grandiose scheme to distract us from the financial problems."[2]

The major intervening factor between Kubitschek's proposal of Operation Pan America in May 1958 and Kennedy's scheme for the Alliance for Progress in March 1961 was Castro's victory in Cuba. It transformed Latin America from the "safe backyard" into the "soft underbelly" of the United States. "Here," writes Arthur Schlesinger,

was half of the western hemisphere, which, if it turned against the United States, would mock our leadership before the world and create a hard and lasting threat to our national security, but which, if we could work effectively with its people, might provide the world a model in the processes of democratic development. . . . If the United States were not ready to offer an affirmative program for democratic modernization, new Castros would undoubtedly rise across the continent. [3]

The Alliance for Progress was "the affirmative side of Kennedy's policy"; the other side was "his absolute determination to prevent any new state from going down the Castro road and so giving the Soviet Union a second bridgehead in the hemisphere."[4]

Until the early 1960s United States aid doctrine had assumed that economic growth, social reform, and political democracy were interrelated (perhaps even lineally related) and reinforcing. The Alliance for Progress recognized that these relationships were more com-

1. Richard M. Nixon, *Six Crises* (Garden City: Doubleday & Company, Inc., 1962), p. 183.
2. Interview with Niles Bond, Washington, D.C., January 14, 1970. Bond was Deputy Chief of Mission in the U.S. Embassy, April 1959-March 1963, and Minister Consul General in São Paulo, January 1964-July 1968.
3. Arthur M. Schlesinger Jr., *A Thousand Days: John F. Kennedy in the White House* (Boston: Houghton Mifflin Company, 1965) p. 187.
4. *Ibid.*, p. 773.

plicated. It rejected the easy assumption that social development would flow automatically from economic growth, but it continued to treat political development for the most part as derivative or simply inevitable and even imminent. The political development objectives of the Alliance were expressed as vague ideals over which neither the United States nor Latin Americans had intellectual or practical control. Aside perhaps from covert measures, the principal United States instruments toward these ideals were potentially, first, the proffering or withholding of aid (and occasionally of diplomatic recognition) and, secondly, the aid programs and projects themselves. Such instruments could be used even more easily for short-term political objectives.

If the early political rhetoric of the Alliance now seems excessive, it is partly because such "excess" was judged necessary to signal a break with the past and strike a "new political consciousness and purpose in Latin America"—a counter-myth to the Communist ideology. A second reason for the rhetoric was to mobilize the bureaucracy of the United States government behind the new Latin American policies.[6] But the Kennedy team also misjudged the malleability and movement of politics in Latin America. In his election campaign, Kennedy had cited the decline in the number of dictatorships in Latin America and confidently predicted that three years from then there would not be any. Members of the task force which devised the Alliance proclaimed that within the diversity of the Hemisphere, there was one constant—"the common devotion to democratic instructions and respect for the human individual. Latin America has had its fill of dictatorships."[7]

The Kennedy administration early identified itself with a deeper involvement in the promotion of economic and social development in Latin America and with bolder use of aid as a leverage for institutional and fiscal reforms. The threat inherent in this new concern and activism was tempered by professions of greater tolerance of neutralism and institutional pluralism in underdeveloped countries. So long as countries maintained their national independence, Kennedy professed not to care whether they were "socialist, capitalist, pragmatist,

6. Arthur M. Schlesinger Jr., "The Lowering Hemisphere," *The Atlantic* (January 1970), pp. 80-81.

7. Speech delivered in Rio on October 31, 1961. Lincoln Gordon, *A New Deal for Latin America: The Alliance for Progress* (Cambridge: Harvard University Press, 1963), p. 13.

or whatever."[8] Yet his Task Force on Latin America, led by former Assistant Secretary of State and Ambassador to Brazil Adolf Berle, set out "to develop policies and programs which would *channel* the revolution now going on in Latin America *in the proper direction* and to prevent it from being taken over by the Sino-Soviet bloc."[9] The United States' perception of its security in Latin America in the 1960s carried within it the need for control over and attempts at intervention in the politics of other nations.

Quadros's "Independent" Foreign Policy

In the very month in which the eager and eloquent Kennedy occupied the White House, January 1961, the volatile Quadros took possession of Alvorada Palace in Brasília. The independent former Governor of São Paulo, whose campaign for the presidency was symbolized by a broom, rode to power with a double mission: first, to tidy up the country after the tremendous burst of energy under Kubitschek, to reform the public administration, to eliminate corruption, and to straighten out the economy; and, secondly, to establish for Brazil an "independent" foreign policy, to open new options for the country, to give it greater international maneuverability and at the same time greater moral purpose in the world. In his seven months as president, Quadros was more successful in his foreign than in his domestic policies.

By his foreign policy, Quadros sought to demonstrate Brazil's independence and thereby maintain nationalist support, even as he submitted to greater economic orthodoxy in exchange for assistance. Brazilians felt at once dominated and abandoned by the United States in the postwar period. They noted the United States' "preferential treatment" of Argentina and its failure to make any new loans to Brazil since June 1959, and they concluded that the traditional policy of unquestioning alignment with the United States had failed. An "independent" foreign policy might gain Brazil more attention and greater freedom. It would improve Brazil's bargaining position with the United States, enhance Brazil's role as a mediator and peacemaker, and thrust the country into a place of leadership in the "third world." It would also open up a world beyond the Hemisphere and Western Europe for commercial and cultural relations.

Quadros's position on Cuba dramatized the independence from the United States of the new Brazilian foreign policy. Even as the

8. Schlesinger, "The Lowering Hemisphere," p. 80.
9. Schlesinger, *A Thousand Days*, p. 202. Italics added.

United States was pressing Latin American governments to break relations with Castro's government, Quadros, then a presidential candidate, visited the island, and later, as president, he bestowed on Ché Guevara the Order of the Southern Cross. Quadros aspired to giving up "the subsidiary and innocuous diplomacy of a nation aligned with worthy though alien interests" and to placing Brazil "in the forefront, convinced as we were of our ability to contribute with our own means to the understanding of peoples."[10]

Although relations between the American embassy and the Ministry of Foreign Affairs were cordial, relations with Quadros were taut throughout his short-lived presidency. The embassy was puzzled and annoyed by Quadros, who in turn viewed the United States' attitude as overbearing and oppressive. Ambassador John Moors Cabot recalls that "Quadros spent his time plucking the Eagle's feathers." Within a few weeks after his inauguration, Quadros was visited by Adolf Berle, as a special envoy from President Kennedy, in search of Brazilian backing for the invasion of the Bay of Pigs then scheduled for early April. Ambassador Cabot remembers a "stormy conversation" in which Berle stated the United States had $300 million in reserve for Brazil and in effect "offered it as a bribe" for Brazilian co-operation: "Berle referred to the Cuban menace and the need for solidarity in facing it." Quadros became "visibly irritated" after Berle refused to heed his third "no." No Brazilian official was at the airport the next day to see the envoy off.[11]

10. Jânio Quadros, "Brazil's New Foreign Policy," Foreign Affairs, 40, No. 1 (October 1961), 19. A study by Lloyd A. Free during the Quadros period showed that Cuba actually ranked lowest among ten countries in the esteem of a cross-section of Brazilians. At the same time, neutralism was a highly popular foreign policy at least among educated urbanites. See Free, "Some International Implications of the Political Psychology of Brazilians," (Princeton: Institute for International Social Research, 1961).

11. Interview with John Moors Cabot, Washington, D.C., January 15, 1970. Cabot was American Ambassador to Brazil, July 1959-August 1961. Frank Bonilla recounts how "on the last day of the (Quadros) campaign in Rio . . . a group of students entertained downtown crowds with a series of skits from an improvised stage atop a flatbed truck. The two main characters in the skits who consistently drew applause and laughter from passers-by were Jânio Quadros and a star-spangled and top-hatted United States ambassador. From time to time the ambassador would switch momentarily to the role of Nelson Rockefeller. In his exchanges with the Americans, Quadros usually began feebly defending Brazilian interests only to succumb as the ambassador or Nelson, mouthing some platitude about hemispheric solidarity and mutual co-operation, leeringly stuffed a few greenbacks into one of the candidate's pockets." Bonilla, "Jânio Vem Aí: Brazil Elects a President," American Universities Field Staff Reports Service, East Coast South America Series, Vol. VII, No. 2 (Brazil), October 1960.

Relations with Quadros were further strained by an apparent personality conflict between him and Cabot. The ambassador felt that Quadros was "not sincere about cleaning up the financial mess" and that he was "going to pander to Brazilian nationalism." Cabot recommended that "we shouldn't go all out for Quadros's requirements without getting some 'muffling' of Quadros in return." Quadros should be kept on a "short leash." But the ambassador was overruled by the new administration in Washington, which after the setback at the Bay of Pigs was ready to give Quadros the benefit of the doubt and "to put Brazilian finances on a sound basis."[12] In May 1961 Brazil's international creditors agreed to stretch out its debts, and the United States offered $100 million in new credits, the first such loan in two years.

Cabot hoped that the loan agreement would quiet Quadros's attacks on the United States, but it "only encouraged him."[13] In June, he publicly chastised Cabot for having suggested that Brazil was "committed" to the West as a signatory of the Inter-American Treaty of Reciprocal Assistance in 1948. The next month Cabot was retired as Ambassador. From Berle's visit in February until a visit by Adlai Stevenson in July, no American official of stature, including the ambassador, had been able to see Quadros. He may have agreed to receive Stevenson partly out of their mutual admiration for Lincoln.[14] In any event, they met for more than two hours, and Quadros was reportedly "in good form"—"very forthcoming, lucid, and articulate."[15] A few weeks later Quadros resigned the presidency with cyptic references to forces "foreign" and "terrible," and Vice President João Goulart returned to Brazil from a goodwill mission in Peking.

Goulart's Quest for Power

In foreign policy Goulart adhered to the "independent" approach fostered by Quadros. Brazil was to be culturally a part of the West but no longer committed to any alliance. In November 1961 Goulart renewed diplomatic relations with the Soviet Union, which

12. Interview with Cabot.
13. *Ibid.*
14. In describing Quadros's presidential office, Schlesinger notes, "A steel engraving of Lincoln hung on the wall inscribed by Lincoln himself; it was a gift of Nelson Rockefeller." Schlesinger, *A Thousand Days*, p. 179.
15. Interview with Bond.

had been severed in 1947 after Russian publication of an article criti-
cizing the Brazilian Expeditionary Force of World War II. Brazil established relations with other Eastern European countries as well,
welcomed trade missions from Communist China and sent its own
missions scurrying about the world. Until the Soviet Union agreed in
October 1962 to the withdrawal of its "offensive" missiles without
prior consultation of Castro, the Brazilian position on Cuba continued to epitomize the independence of the new policy. At the Punta
del Este meeting in January 1962, then Foreign Minister Dantas led
the "soft six" nations opposing the ouster of Cuba from the Organization of American States, and as late as September 1962 Brazil continued "to follow the line that Cuba does not presently pose a threat
to the security of the rest of the hemisphere."[17]

The American embassy had been concerned by the election of
Goulart to the vice-presidency in 1960. Even before Quadros's inauguration, the embassy had initiated "a broad and deep appraisal of
the implications of Goulart." When Quadros resigned in August
1961, "a cautious, but perceptible shift in United States-Brazilian relationships inevitably resulted, based upon the conviction of responsible United States officials in Brazil that Goulart would be hard to
work with."[18] Although Goulart was inaugurated on September 7,
Ambassador-designate Lincoln Gordon was withheld from Brazil
until October 13. Niles Bond, the chargé d'affaires, recalls that both
sides of the dispute over Quadros's succession ("especially the anti-
Goulart military") tried to enlist embassy support, that there was a
great deal of "soul-searching as to how the embassy should treat
Goulart," and that "it was decided to give him the benefit of the
doubt, to be friendly or at least proper."[19]

In the four years that he was in Brazil, Gordon was one of those
rare ambassadors with superambassadorial power and influence both
in the United States and Brazil. Even before becoming ambassador,
Gordon had developed a long-term interest in Brazil, was co-author
of a book on United States manufacturing investment in Brazil, and
participated in Kennedy's Task Force on Latin America. He had been

17. Nathan Miller, "Rio Doubts Parley will Act on Cuba," the Baltimore *Sun*,
September 29, 1962.
18. Philip R. Schwab, "United States Policy with Relationship to President Goulart" (Section of unpublished paper written at National War College, 1967), p. 1.
Schwab was a member of the AID Mission in Brazil for most of the period between
1957 and 1967.
19. Interview with Bond.

a major official in the direction of the Marshall Plan and had taught economics and public policy at Harvard. He was well related in the Kennedy administration and the Washington bureaucracy, while being an articulate and persuasive advocate in his own right. Gordon had been involved from the outset in the ideas for the Alliance for Progress, and one reason he accepted the ambassadorship was that "the success or failure of the Alliance depended on the Brazil experience."[20] He "felt" Brazil and had ready-made friends there in and out of government. Brazilians appreciated his scholarly bent (although some resented his lecturing them) and his finesse with the cello. An experienced economist, aid administrator, and Brazilianist, Gordon seemed an ideal ambassador.

Before June 1963, Gordon enjoyed easy access to Goulart, who was reasonable and even accommodating about a number of sensitive issues. Indeed, Gordon was privately asked by the president for his assessment of the "acceptability" of several high-ranking Brazilian officials. When Gordon threatened to invoke the Hickenlooper Amendment after Leonel Brizola's expropriation of the International Telephone and Telegraph subsidiary in Rio Grande do Sul, Goulart agreed to a "just" settlement, partly because the $8 million payment was small relative to the aid leverage and partly because Goulart interpreted the expropriation as an attempt to undermine his own trip to Washington in April 1962. In Washington Goulart addressed the Congress, conversed at length with President Kennedy, completed negotiations for the $131 million Northeast Agreement, and assured "fair treatment" of foreign-owned public utilities in Brazil. In October 1962 Gordon was instructed to read Goulart an advance copy of Kennedy's speech on the Cuban missile crisis, and Goulart reacted unhesitatingly to the revelation of Soviet "offensive" missiles on the island: "That is not just a threat to the United States; it is a threat to all of us."[21] A few days later Brazil voted in the Organization of American States in support of the United States' call for a blockade of Cuba.

But Brazilian-American relations during Goulart's presidency were mixed from the start; after June 1963 their deterioration became precipitant. In November 1961 the Chamber of Deputies passed a strict profit-remittance bill, which provoked a United States Sena-

20. Interview with Lincoln Gordon, Baltimore, November 12, 1969. Gordon was Ambassador to Brazil, October 1961-February 1966, and Assistant Secretary of State for Inter-American Affairs, February 1966-June 1967.

21. Interview with Gordon.

tor to warn that if the bill passed the Brazilian Senate, the Alliance for Progress would be "definitely doomed to failure in Brazil—and the program should be stopped immediately."[23] Goulart managed to delay final congressional passage of the bill. But in September 1962 a milder bill which prohibited remittance in excess of 10 percent of invested capital did become law, and that year foreign investment declined to $18 million from the $120 million average for the six preceding years.

In November 1962 President Kennedy canceled for the third time a trip to Brazil which was to have dramatized the Alliance. In December Kennedy told a press conference that "the Brazilian government is aware of the strong concern that we have for this inflation which eats up aid and which, of course, contributes to a flight of capital."[24] He dispatched his brother Robert to Brasília to tell Goulart that further aid would depend on positive evidence that Brazil was putting "its own house in order." Furtado's new Three-Year Plan and Dantas's diplomacy did achieve the $398.5 million loan agreement of April 1963; however, Brazil failed to qualify for all but $84 million, which was to have been released immediately. Moreover, the Brazilian purchase of the ten American and foreign power subsidiaries, also agreed in April, was indefinitely postponed in the face of nationalist opposition. Inflation soared out of control, and the foreign debt tested the limits of creditors' tolerance.

The Mounting "Threat" of Communism

The United States was even more worried by political than by economic instability in Brazil. The embassy was particularly nettled by the unchecked "agitation" of the stridently anti-imperialist and ultranationalist Brizola, the brother-in-law of the president. And even as Dantas was negotiating the loan agreement with the Kennedy administration in March 1963, Gordon was testifying before the House Foreign Affairs Committee on Communist infiltration of the labor movement, student organizations, and the government itself in Brazil. Assistant Secretary of State Thomas Mann later testified that

23. John M. McClellan et al., Special Report on Latin America: United States Activities in Mexico, Panama, Peru, Chile, Argentina, Brazil and Venezuela, Doc. No. 80, Eighty-seventh Congress, Second Session (Washington: U.S. Government Printing Office, 1962), p. 29.

24. Quoted in Irving L. Horowitz, Revolution in Brazil: Politics and Society in a Developing Nation (New York: E. P. Dutton & Co., Inc.) p. 198.

he was aware in January 1963 "that the erosion toward communism in Brazil was very rapid."[25] Given the importance of Brazil in the Hemisphere, the United States could not afford to admit the failure of the Alliance there. Nor could it afford to do nothing, given its perception of the increasing Communist "threat." But the greater the United States' attempt at intervention, the more virulent became the nationalist reaction in Brazil and the greater the justification for rededicating the United States' effort.

Nothing in Brazil caused the United States greater alarm than the "threat of revolt" in the drought-plagued Northeast. As early as October and November 1960, Tad Szulc's articles in the New York *Times* had aroused Americans to the desperate poverty of the area, the agitation of Francisco Julião, and the menace of the Peasant Leagues, aiming "at a political army of 40 million strong." A municipal official in Recife warned Szulc's readers that "the Northeast will go Communist and you will have a situation ten times worse than in Cuba—if something is not done."[26] Reporting on his visit to Recife with Food for Peace Director George McGovern in February 1961, Schlesinger states that in the 1950s the American embassy had regarded Furtado, the director of the Superintendency for the Development of the Northeast (SUDENE), "with mistrust as a Marxist, even possibly a communist." But in 1961 Furtado's SUDENE represented a new force for developmental change in the Northeast; the presence of "the agitator" Julião symbolized the alternative of violent revolution and strengthened Furtado's hand with the traditional political elite. McGovern and Schlesinger "carried the cause of northeast Brazil . . . back to Washington."[27]

The Northeast, the springboard for victory in North Africa during World War II and the most impoverished and troubled region of Latin America's largest and most important country, became an early test for the Alliance. An American team led by Ambassador Merwin L. Bohan surveyed the Northeast for AID in October 1961 and in February 1962 submitted its report, which recommended both an eighteen-month to two-year "impact program" and a five-year, more fundamental, development program. The $131-million impact pro-

25. Quoted in Carlos F. Diaz-Alejandro, "Some Aspects of the Brazilian Experience with Foreign Aid" (unpublished manuscript), December 1969, p. 11.

26. Tad Szulc, "Northeast Brazil Poverty Breeds Threat of a Revolt," The New York *Times*, October 31, 1960.

27. Schlesinger, *A Thousand Days*, p. 181.

gram, "if promptly carried out," was to improve immediately and conspicuously the living conditions of the Northeast, to convince the masses of the reality of the Alliance for Progress, to allay mass unrest and buy a modicum of time for SUDENE. Most importantly, the aid program was an instrument in the Cold War. As one United States Congressman later concluded upon reading the Bohan report, "At the time we went into the Northeast, it was a decision as to whether President Kennedy or Premier Khruschev was going to go in there in some form or fashion. And it was almost a race to get in there with all the economic and political elements as heavy as possible."[28]

The difficulties between AID and SUDENE began with their differences in perceiving the Communist "threat." SUDENE viewed aid as a means of gaining impetus on its developmental program for the Northeast; AID saw SUDENE as a means of channeling funds into an effort to stop communism. Furtado opposed Julião from the start but recognized his dialectical usefulness. The fact that the United States seemed to regard Julião as more threatening than did Brazil added to the frustration and zeal of the Americans. Furtado and Minister Dantas, who signed the Northeast Agreement in April 1962, understood that the program was to be jointly financed by the United States and Brazil but elaborated and executed only by Brazilian technicians. A former director of AID for the Northeast recalls, however, that "we were in a very serious political situation; we thought that the Communists were going to run all over the place. That was uppermost in our minds. . . . Furtado said that SUDENE only needed capital. They didn't see their problems as clearly as we felt we did." In retrospect, the ex-director admits that "it might have been an honest difference of opinions."[29] The feat of obligating $131 million was accomplished under great pressure from Washington and in spite of the SUDENE of that period.

After examining the two-year crash program in his study of economic assistance and political change in the Northeast, Riordan Roett concludes that the result of the aid was "negative," mainly because of the incompatability of the United States' short-run political

28. Congressman Rosenthal, Hearings Before a Subcommittee on Government Operations, U.S. House of Representatives, Ninetieth Congress, Second Session, U.S. Aid Operations in Latin America Under the Alliance for Progress, February 8, 9, 12, and 13, 1968 (Washington: U.S. Government Printing Office, 1969), p. 681.

29. Interview with Arthur Byrnes, New York, January 12, 1970. Byrnes was deputy director of AID/Northeast, mid-1962-63, and director, 1963-64.

goals and the long-run developmental needs of the region.[30] Roett tells of the spiraling turn of events whereby first, "impact aid" was used (unsuccessfully) to influence the outcome of state elections, and immediate political criteria were given priority over professional or technical judgments; secondly, AID incurred the enmity not only of the politicians whose elections it had opposed but also of SUDENE, whose developmental priorities it had violated and whose regional authority it had undermined; and finally, and more subtly, AID both robbed SUDENE of its moderate constituency and forced it to the left in search of new support. Thereby, the opposition of SU-DENE became associated with the "communist" opposition, and further undermining of SUDENE became a matter of high principle, which in turn vindicated all of the previous events.

The United States' response to "the erratic nature of Brazilian federal policies" was "increasingly to adopt a strategy of co-operation with some individual state governments, autonomous public agencies, and the private sector 'to the extent that this was possible.' "[31] Gordon set forth the elements of this so-called "islands of sanity" policy for Washington in the Country Assistance Program transmittal statement of November 1963. According to an AID informant, the Embassy

begun to seek out those places in the Brazilian political picture where ability, stability, and democratic convictions presented sufficient dimension upon which cooperative ventures could be undertaken. Those places (or persons) represented in Brazil's dark and stormy seas, democratic "Islands of Sanity."[32]

After the failure of the stabilization experiment and the resignation of Dantas in June 1963, the "islands of sanity" policy came to prevail in United States aid relations with Brazil. No new accords were reached with the federal government except for the PL 480 surplus wheat agreements and projects nominally with SUDENE under the Northeast Agreement. Moreover, the World Bank had ceased

30. See Riordan Roett, *The Politics of Foreign Aid in the Brazilian Northeast* (Nashville: Vanderbilt University Press, 1972); also see the Hearings Before a Subcommittee on Government Operations, *U.S. Aid Operations in Latin America*, especially pp. 634-647.

31. Lester B. Pearson, ch., *Partners in Development: Report of the Commission on the International Development* (New York: Praeger, 1969), p. 248.

32. Schwab, "United States Policy in Relationship with President Goulart," pp. 2-3.

making new project loans in 1959, and the IMF had not issued Brazil any new credits since 1961. Assistant Secretary Mann testified that "we did not give any money in balance-of-payments support, budgetary support, things of that kind, which benefit directly the Central Government of Brazil." Instead AID assisted "states which were headed by good governors we think strengthened democracy."[33] Such governors were notably anti-Goulart UDN leaders such as Aluizio Alves in Rio Grande do Norte and Carlos Lacerda in Guanabara, who were seen as "sources of rational behavior" regarding the benefits which the Alliance could bring to Brazil.[34]

The Revolution of April 1964

Beginning in July 1963, it became increasingly evident to Gordon that Goulart's purposes were, in fact, "to overturn the regime himself in the interest of a personalistic dictatorship modeled after Peron in Argentina or Vargas, his mentor in 1945."[35] Gordon thought that Goulart was being "taken in" by the Communists with whom he was allegedly in "active collaboration" by early 1964: "I think he honestly believed he could control these people under any circumstances. He was warned by many people . . . of the dangers of riding a tiger and later being eaten by it. He laughed it off."[36] "During that difficult period," Gordon was "very much preoccupied both with what was happening inside Brazil, and with its implications for Brazilian-American relations, which might have been very much affected by the outcome of this turmoil."[37] Goulart's efforts to reconstitute the political system led only to disorder until the military asserted itself and imposed its authority in the name not of the "old order" but the "Revolution."

Leftist newspapers charged that the 1964 revolt was "planned, paid for, and ordered in Washington." Brazilian students and intellectuals widely believe that the United States played a prominent role

33. Quoted in Carlos F. Diaz-Alejandro, "Some Aspects of the Brazilian Experience with Foreign Aid" (unpublished manuscript), December 1969, p. 11.

34. Ironically, both governors lost their political rights in the months after the coup in April 1964; Lacerda for political "subversion," and Alves for administrative corruption, presumably involving misallocation of AID funds.

35. Hearing Before the Committee on Foreign Relations, U.S. Senate, Eighty-nineth Congress, Second Session, February 7, 1966, *Nomination of Lincoln Gordon to be Assistant Secretary of State for Inter-American Affairs* (Washington: U.S. Government Printing Office, 1966), p. 34.

36. *Ibid.*, p. 41.

37. *Ibid.*, p. 44.

in Goulart's fall, but United States spokesmen, including Gordon and Dean Rusk, have unequivocally denied any part in the coup. In his appendix to *Politics in Brazil*, Skidmore finds that the United States was not a direct sponsor of the military rebels but that the embassy was *"well informed* about the efforts of the conspirators."[38] The most able informant was Colonel Vernon A. Walters, the Army attaché, who had been the assistant to the commander of the Brazilian Expeditionary Force in World War II and the liaison officer between the Brazilian Force and the U.S. Fifth Army.[39] The mutual respect and comradeship between Walters and many of Brazil's senior military officers, forged in the crucible of war, had lasted the twenty-year interim. Walters and Castello Branco, who had shared a tent in Italy, were intimate friends and met frequently before Goulart's overthrow and even after Castello became President. Bond, then consul general in São Paulo, remembers that "our information about what was going on was very good." Bond himself was in the office of Adhemar de Barros as the Governor of São Paulo was fretting over the indecision of General Amaury Kruel and tracking the progress of his co-conspirators in Minas Gerais and Guanabara.[40]

Whereas the United States probably did not participate in the actual planning or execution of the coup, United States complicity, explicit and tacit, did almost certainly occur. First, the "islands of sanity" strategy of aid served to discredit and to undermine the authority of the Goulart government, as did Gordon's statements about Communist infiltration. Secondly, in the months preceding the coup, reliable information itself became an increasingly valued resource for the conspirators and their sympathizers. Whether the CIA actually financed any of the "unofficial, popularly organized groups" which arrayed themselves against the government, the embassy was useful in making disparate but sympathetic civilian and military groups aware of one another and of the government's "treachery."

Thirdly, the "impression" that the rebels could count on the United States for supplies in case of resistance undoubtedly emboldened them. The conspirators, elated by the brevity and blood-

---

38. Skidmore, *Politics in Brazil*, p. 325

39. In the preface to his book on *The Brazilian Expeditionary Force by Its Commander*, Marshal J. B. Mascarenhas de Moraes "gratefully recalls . . . the outstanding service he (then Major Walters) rendered to the Brazilian Division by his flawless command of our language and by his valor and initiative. He served with us and won the esteem of his commanders and comrades, Brazilians and Americans alike."

40. Interview with Bond.

lessness of the coup, never needed the supplies which would have been necessary to sustain a prolonged struggle. But until the evening of March 31 itself, when General Kruel joined the revolt, civil war had seemed a real possibility. Fourthly, the conspirators must have been further emboldened by the obvious sympathy of the embassy and by the understanding, explicit or tacit, that if the coup were successful the new regime would be rewarded with generous diplomatic and financial support. The rebels' implicit confidence in the embassy was demonstrated by their willingness to keep the Americans informed of events before and during the coup. United States officials were in some cases, such as that of Bond, present in the command posts of the Revolution.

The United States made no secret of its delight with the overthrow of Goulart. At Gordon's urging, President Johnson sent a message to Acting President Mazzilli early on April 2 expressing "warmest good wishes" and admiring "the resolute will of the Brazilian community to resolve these difficulties within a framework of constitutional democracy and without civil strife."[41] The following day Secretary Rusk also indicated his satisfaction with the coup and hailed it as "an expression of support for constitutional government."[42] The American recognition arrived even before Goulart had slipped over the Uruguayan border and before the question of the presidential succession or the constitutionality of the transition had been resolved. The unusual rapidity and unbridled enthusiasm of the recognition tended to confirm the widespread suspicion of United States participation in the coup. If Johnson's message was a matter of controversy in Washington, it was applauded by Berle: "Our readiness to send help swiftly will be a major factor, and President Johnson's message was a model of warmth and good sense." "Now," wrote Berle, "it seems the Alliance for Progress may really go forward in Latin America."[43]

Gordon now argues that the early recognition, which he himself had urged on Washington, indicated not the extent of United States complicity but the inadequacy of its information. Gordon believed that Johnson's message would help to avert what "seemed to be a

41. Quoted in Tad Szulc "Washington Sends 'Warmest' Wishes to Brazil's Leaders," the New York *Times*, April 3, 1964.

42. Max Frankel, "Brazil Chief Picks Aides, Rusk Promises U.S. Help," the New York *Times*, April 4, 1964.

43. A.A. Berle, "As the Dust Settles in Brazil," *The Reporter*, April 23, 1964, p. 28.

real danger of civil war," but he overestimated the revolutionary strength of Brizola's Committees of Eleven and Julião's Peasant Leagues. Gordon also believed that the message would buttress the constitutional forces in the coup, but he underestimated the strength of both military and civilian "hardliners." Gordon now confesses that he was "shocked to the core" by the first Institutional Act just a week after the congratulatory statement on the "constitutional" changeover. The idea went through his mind of breaking off relations, but he was reassured by Colonel Walters, who thought that Castello would be "moderate."[44]

The Military Dictatorship

The period of April 1964 through 1969 in Brazilian politics was marked by the initial wavering between liberalization and repression, the effort to control inflation and re-establish economic growth, increasingly closed military rule, and the concomitant use of coercion as a substitute for consensus. In domestic affairs, the early expectation of "redemocratization" gave way to hope for a "political reopening," and all civilian politics paled beside the force of the military dictatorship. International affairs was characterized by reassertion of the traditional alignment with the United States and disavowal of the experiment with an "independent" foreign policy.

The Revolution reversed the "independent" trend of Brazilian foreign policy since the election of Quadros, and fostered a bipolar view of international relations in accordance with the doctrine of the Higher War College. The founders and early commandants of the college, veteran officers from the Italian campaign, identified Brazilian potential with the ideology and technology which they believed to characterize the power of their wartime ally. They had sought the collaboration of United States military in developing the college and more generally in officer-training, and their doctrine for the inculcation of high-ranking officers and civilians had come to reflect the Cold War views of their American advisors. Since the War College ideologies regarded the coup in part as a pre-emptive measure against "Communism" and since they associated Communism with an international movement, they perceived the continuing internal struggle against Communist "subversion" as requiring an external alignment with the United States in the Cold War. Upon his arrival in New York in June 1964, Ambassador Juracy Magalhães, himself a graduate of

44. Interview with Gordon.

the War College like so many of his colleagues in the new government, declared that what was good for the United States was good for Brazil. He later acknowledged the United States as "unquestioned leader of the free world" and "principal guardian of the fundamental values of our civilization."

The military government, headed by Castello Branco, a former director of studies in the War College, immediately severed diplomatic relations with Cuba and then expressed the hope that Cuba would "within the near future free itself from the tyranny of the Communist regime that oppresses it."[45] In August 1964, Foreign Minister Vasco Leitão da Cunha declared that Brazil's preoccupation with the conflict in Southeast Asia was the same as that of the United States and that Brazil would enter the war if it developed into a world struggle.[46] That same month the government repealed the profit-remittance law and made new concessions to foreign companies. In October the government purchased the ten subsidiaries of American and foreign power under terms even more generous than the 1963 "memorandum of understanding." In a message on the achievements of the Revolution in 1964, Castello reported to Congress the "elimination of points of friction" and the "improvement" in Brazilian-American relations, which had been "on the brink of a crisis."[47] Brazilian troops took part in the intervention in the Dominican Republic in 1965, and Foreign Minister Juracy Magalhães visited neighboring capitals in support of an Inter-American Peace Force.

The unbridled enthusiasm with which the United States greeted the coup may not have influenced the immediate course of political events in Brazil. It did signal the beginning of a United States commitment to and identification with the Revolution which would be difficult to alter even as events might put in question the original rationale. The old and intimate personal and professional relations between Walters and Castello and between Gordon and Planning Minister Roberto Campos reinforced the new closeness in political and economic relations between Brazil and the United States. Indeed, Gordon appeared to some Brazilians to enjoy quasi-ministerial status

45. *Boletim Informativo*, Brazilian Embassy, Washington, D.C., No. 29 (July 22, 1964).

46. The Revolutionary Government later sent medical supplies and coffee to South Vietnam as tokens of Brazilian support.

47. Humberto de Alencar Castello Branco, *Summary of the President's Message to the 1965 National Congress* (Brasília: Departamento de Imprensa Nacional, 1965), p. 14.

in the government, occasioning such wall slogans as "Down with intermediaries, Gordon for President." Like Berle and Mann, Gordon became a stalwart defender of the Revolution in the United States. In his public testimony, Gordon systematically overlooked or rationalized away the increasingly arbitrary and repressive political trends. Even if Gordon should admit that Castello's regime was "a transitional regime with some arbitrary powers," he would add that it was "moving very rapidly in the direction of full constitutional normality."[48] And when that "movement" seemed jeopardized, Gordon found himself defending Castello in the councils of Washington on the basis that the only available alternative was a more hard-line military dictatorship which would probably be hostile to the United States.

Gordon initially tried to persuade Castello of the merits of building a broadly based political party in support of the Revolution, but "politics" and "parties" connoted factional divisions and special interests to the marshal. Although Castello seems to have shared Gordon's admiration for constitutional democracy in the abstract, he was more immediately concerned with battling inflation, "subversion," and corruption. Both Castello and Campos, writes an AID official of the time,

considered politics an intrusion on rational decision-making and, given their military backing, saw no need for political accommodation. Finding himself unable to communicate this need to them, Gordon went on to examine their economic stabilization program and concluded, as an expert in the field, that it merited U.S. support.[49]

United States officials had defended the "islands of sanity" policy for supporting "good governors" and not benefiting the Goulart government; yet they now insisted that the decision again to centralize aid was made not for political but for administrative reasons. The administration of AID had become too dispersed and extended and needed revamping. The effect of reinforcing the Revolution was presumably incidental to strengthening AID. Political aspects of Brazilian-American relations appear to have receded and become less explicit, but the deliberate emphasis on nonpolitical, economic, and "technical" criteria was itself a highly political decision.

48. Hearing Before the Committee on Foreign Relations, *Nomination of Lincoln Gordon*, p. 65.
49. Jerome I. Levinson, "Self-Help, Planning and Politics" (Chapter in an unpublished manuscript on the Alliance for Progress) p. 20.

United States assistance to Brazil after the coup was devoted primarily to economic stabilization, especially in support of the balance of payments and repayment of the foreign debt. Both Brazil and the United States wished to soften the choice between high growth rates and inflation, and that objective demanded large amounts of external support. A few days after the coup, the Inter-American Development Bank approved a series of loans for Brazil which the United States' director had earlier been prepared to veto or delay. An emergency loan of $50 million from President Johnson's Contingency Fund, made in June 1964, facilitated the new government's negotiations for rescheduling of its foreign debts. Campos's three-year stabilization and development program earned Brazil its first standby agreement with the IMF in three years and its first new loan from the World Bank in six years. Later, in reviewing the decision for the contingency loan, AID Director Stuart Van Dyke termed it "an expression of confidence in the ability of this technical group Castello Branco had gathered together, to pull the program off, which the United States could support—the program at that time not yet being fully shaped up."[50] But the United States' decision "to support Brazil strongly" during this period was pre-eminently political; Van Dyke himself states that "our support was essential—I should not say 'essential'—our support was desirable in order to prop up—."[51]

Progress in the stabilization program became the measure for affirming the correctness of the Embassy's political judgment, and the program loan became AID's principal instrument for influencing Brazilian monetary and fiscal policies. During the Quadros and Goulart regimes, AID had authorized $625 million in program-type loans to Brazil, of which $525 million was not disbursed until after the coup. From late 1964 through 1968, AID authorized an additional $625 million in new program loans. AID Director William Ellis explained to a congressional hearing that "the United States through its assistance program does not control or direct these situations, but we can support those groups within Brazil . . . who share our common view" as to the definition and approach to the problems.[52] Ellis testified,

50. Hearings Before a Subcommittee on Government Operations, *U.S. Aid Operations in Latin America*, p. 514.

51. *Ibid.*, p. 549.

52. Hearings Before the Subcommittee on Inter-American Affairs of the Committee on Foreign Affairs, U.S. House of Representatives, Ninety-first Congress, First Session, *New Directions for the 1970's: Toward a Strategy of Inter-American Development* (Washington: U.S. Government Printing Office, 1969), p. 577.

In terms of general economic policies, I would say if anything there has
been a net improvement; the Finance Ministry can now do by decree
things that before had to go through Congress; they have been passing out
decrees left and right; and most of them are to the good. Most of them are
very much oriented to strengthening the private sector.[53]

The discrepancies were enormous, however, between the professed
"technical" criteria for United States aid and the political effect of aid
to the military regime.

The Cooling of Relations

After becoming assistant secretary of state for inter-American
affairs in early 1966, Gordon chose as his successor in Brazil John C.
Tuthill, a career foreign service officer and former ambassador to the
OECD. Tuthill did not share Gordon's keen interest and "feel" for
Brazil, but he brought to his post in June 1966 a greater sense of
diplomatic detachment. After the Second Institutional Act in October
1965, Assistant Secretary Jack Vaughn had ordered negotiations
suspended for a new program loan, but Gordon had successfully
countered with the necessity of continued United States support of
Castello against the "hard line" seeking overt military dictatorship.
A year later, after another wave of political repression, now Assistant
Secretary Gordon and his aides reviewed the situation and concluded
that "once inflation was under control, the Brazilian government
could undertake social programs and the political base would fall
into place."[54] The authorization and disbursement of program loans
continued.

But after the presidential inauguration of Costa e Silva in mid-
March 1967, Tuthill felt increasingly "overcommitted" in Brazil in
terms both of American discomfort with the deteriorating political
situation and of Brazilian resentment of American "intervention."
The gloomy political predictions of Tuthill and his chief political officer were initially regarded as "emotional and alarmist" in Washington, but the increasingly blatant assertion of military rule and political coercion made United States identification with the Revolution
more vulnerable to liberal criticism within Congress and the State
Department itself. And for Brazilian nationalists, who were re-emerg-
ing as a legitimate force, especially among the younger officer corps,

53. See Diaz-Alejandro, "Some Aspects of the Brazilian Experience with Foreign
Aid," p. 11.
54. Levinson, "Self-Help, Planning and Politics," p. 23.

after being purged of "Communist" influence by the Revolution, identification with the United States connoted "dependence." In counterpoint to Juracy Magalhães's "General Motors speech," General Albuquerque Lima was now insisting that what was good for Brazilians was good for Brazil.

The partial success of the anti-inflation policy and the concomitant rise in priority of economic growth aroused feelings of "pressure" and "resistance" on either side. The onerous quarterly (semi-annual after 1968) loan reviews, instituted in the pre-April 1964 period to allay mistrust in the United States Congress, often involved thirty people on each side and probed many detailed aspects of Brazilian economic policy. In IMF-like fashion, the reviews concentrated on monetary and fiscal instruments rather than on economic targets.[55] In early 1967, for example, AID suspended payments on its program loan when, in the face of its advice to the contrary, Finance Minister Antonio Delfim Neto eased credit and wage restrictions to combat incipient recession. Only after Delfim revived measures for stabilization, once the rate of inflation (and the rate of growth) appeared to be increasing, did AID resume its disbursements. Such "pushing and pulling" grated both the United States and Brazil. Moreover, the new *dramatis personae* after Tuthill's arrival and Costa e Silva's inauguration felt uncomfortable in the closely collaborative roles which had characterized their predecessors. An AID official recalls that "we were dealing with a new cast of characters, who were less competent."[56]

The former intimacy and indeed identity proved embarrassing for the United States and Brazil; yet each seemed reluctant to renounce it openly for fear of oversteering in the other direction. Gradually the United States sought to reduce its commitment and Brazil to reassert its independence. In order to "lower the profile" of the United States in Brazil (and to placate economy-minded United States Congressmen), Tuthill initiated "Operation Topsy," an effort to reduce substantially the number of embassy personnel, which since the Revolution had "grown like Topsy." During Gordon's tenure, the over-all American staff had increased by 60 percent. AID employees alone had expanded from about 160 in 1961 to more than 400 in 1966; Tuthill reduced the

55. See Diaz-Alejandro, "Some Aspects of the Brazilian Experience with Foreign Aid," p. 11.
56. Interview with Jack Heller, Washington, January 15, 1970. Heller is director of the office of development programs in the Bureau for Latin America.

AID number to 267 by fiscal year 1969. He also phased out such controversial projects as the MEC (Ministry of Education and Culture)-USAID Agreement in educational planning. Costa e Silva's government asserted itself by affirming its opposition to the Nuclear Nonproliferation Treaty, renouncing advocacy of the Inter-American Peace Force, challenging the United States in the soluble-coffee crisis, and joining with other Latin American states in demands for United States trade concessions.

On December 11, 1968, AID Director William Ellis notified Washington that Brazil had met all of the conditions for release of a $50 million loan. Three days later, after the Fifth Institutional Act, Washington placed "under review" (AID's euphemism for "under suspension") $188 million in loans already authorized and all negotiations for new loans. As explained amid security deletions in the Congressional testimony of Ellis and Alliance Co-ordinator James Fowler in February 1969, AID's posture was,

We are reviewing the position. Unfortunately, every time we were
about ready to make a decision, the Brazilian Government would take a
new action. It has been one thing after another. This kept us in the position
of reviewing our program for longer than we thought we would be when
we started back in December. The problem is now placed before the new
administration. This will be looked at by the Secretary when he returns
from Europe.[57]

The suspension, which was the subject of heated debate within AID, State, and Defense in Washington, lasted until May 1969 when it was lifted less because of changes in the Brazilian situation than because of the ineluctable advance of the calender. AID needed to defend its $187 million request for Brazil in the fiscal year beginning July

57. Hearings Before the Subcommittee on Inter-American Affairs, *New Directions for the 1970's*, pp. 588-589. The following exchange *re* the suspension occurs on p. 584 between Congressman Gross and AID Director Ellis:

> Mr. Gross: What actually triggered the suspension of aid? Was there a move toward expropriation? Do we have investments in Brazil?
> Mr. Ellis: We have approximately $1.5 billion in private investment in Brazil. However, they have not been threatened, and that was not the reason for our review of the aid program. The review was triggered by the extraordinary political act which gave power to the President which he used immediately to suspend the Congress and to arrest a large number of people and deprive the leading civilian candidates of their political rights, Kubitschek (sic) and others.

1, and the Rockefeller Mission was to visit Brazil in June. Washington decided for the time being to show its disapproval of political events in Brazil more subtly by being "less than forthcoming" in relation to demands for military assistance. Assistant Secretary of Defense G. Warren Nutter testified in July 1969 that the military assistance program had been "curtailed very markedly in the last year or so as a result of the—."[58] Meanwhile, within the embassy and in Washington, debate and division continued on the future of aid to Brazil in the face of the increased repressiveness of the regime, the rise of urban guerrilla activity, the widespread use of torture by the military, the impressive growth of the Brazilian economy, the swelling dollar reserves of the government, the increasing reluctance in the United States Congress to support aid generally, and the interests of embassy coalitions and Washington agencies in their own survival and prosperity.

In June 1969 Costa e Silva upbraided Governor Rockefeller for the United States' failure to appreciate the "sacrifices" of the Brazilian military and to replace its antiquated equipment with materiel suitable for its strategic mission. Whereas some Brazilian officers may have resented the phasing out of the grant-aid program, virtually all of them resent "the whole policy of our Government in restricting purchase of weapons in which they feel they are spending their own money."[59] Planning Minister Helio Beltrão complained of the annual uncertainty over aid generally: "We know what internal resources we can count upon, but the uncertainty and oscillations of external aid prevent the correct formulation of social and economic development programmes."[60] But most observers failed to note the growing coldness between the two governments. Indeed, the kidnapping and ransoming of newly arrived Ambassador C. Burke Elbrick in September 1969 dramatized the apparent identification of the United States with the new military triumvirate. Early in 1970 the New York Times reported that "perhaps because of press censorship in Brazil, all but the most highly informed Brazilians have apparently been un-

58. Hearings Before the Subcommittee on Western Hemisphere Affairs, Committee on Foreign Relations, U.S. Senate, Ninety-first Congress, First Session, United States Military Policies and Programs in Latin America, July 8, 1969 (Washington: U.S. Government Printing Office, 1969), p. 66.
59. Testimony of General Moore, United States military advisor in Brazil, in Hearings Before a Subcommittee on Government Operations, U.S. Aid Operations in Latin America, p. 492.
60. Quoted in Latin America, June 27, 1969.

aware of a cooling toward Brazil in Washington" since December 1968.[61]

Conclusion

American-Brazilian relations in the 1960s were governed by what Jaguaribe calls "the unchallenged, self-styled concern of the United States, in the name of her own interests and her own security, for the internal development of other countries."[62] The old morality of John Foster Dulles was replaced by the new morality of Kennedy. The adherence to the status quo gave way to the celebration of change, to a new optimism and activism. But the reflex reaction to the perceived threat of communism remained real, and the heady talk of democracy, in the absence of an aid commitment to political development, turned out to be rhetoric. At the outset of the Alliance, Gordon had proclaimed that unless all classes and regions participated in the civil liberties and institutions of representative democracy, the Alliance would become "simply another aid program."[63] By his confirmation as assistant secretary in early 1966, Gordon was less audacious: "Well, I would like to see that the aid programs, in so far as they have this political dimension, are used in such a way as to strengthen . . . fully effective functioning, constitutional, representative democracy. Now, that is the objective."[64]

By the end of the decade, "a mystique of peaceful democratic revolution" had not taken hold in Brazil or Latin America. The "counter-myth" of the Alliance paled before the counter-force of the military in one country after another. The brave political objectives of the Alliance, the "affirmative side" of American policy, were consistently distorted in Brazil, first, by the perceived threat of Communism and the determination to counter it and, after the Revolution, by the "reality" of political events and the unacceptability of alternative courses of action. Ironically, United States spokesmen tried to deny the existence of the military dictatorship or to make it seem more compatible with American idealism, as in Gordon's repeated asser-

61. Joseph Novitski, "Brazil's Military Rulers Lose Look of Caretakers," the New York Times, February 9, 1970.

62. Hélio Jaguaribe, Economic and Political Development: A Theoretical Approach and a Brazilian Case Study (Cambridge: Harvard University Press, 1968), p. 179.

63. Lincoln Gordon, A New Deal for Latin America, p. 111.

64. Hearing Before the Committee on Foreign Relations, "Nomination of Lincoln Gordon," p. 83.

tions that it was "a transitional regime with some exceptional powers." Most astonishing is Berle's contention, as late as 1968, that "there has never been a Brazilian military government—nor is there one today, despite a currently prevailing impression."[65]

The importance to Brazil of American aid, trade, and investment and the fact of its worldwide power made the United States economically and politically preponderant in its relationship with Brazil. At the same time, the highest ranking American policy-makers gave little sustained attention to Brazil or Latin America. Discontinuity prevailed even at the level of the assistant secretary for inter-American affairs, who changed ten times in the 1960s. Particular "crises," short-term objectives, and strong personalities at the ambassadorial level were apt to determine relations between the two nations up to a point and thereby to endow them with an apparently haphazard and zig-zagging course. Throughout the 1960s, however, the United States' inclusive conception of its own security, ranging from prevention of another "Communist" bridgehead in the Hemisphere to protection of its public aid and private investment, underlay the relationship. Perceived threats to that security took precedence over Brazilian development objectives or American democratic ideals.

In a nation as large and diverse as Brazil, it would be difficult to prove that the United States was determinant in any major political change. As ambassador, Gordon was "very aware of the limitations on our influence. Brazil is a very large country with a very active political life of its own, and the American voice although a significant one is in no sense whatsoever a controlling one."[66] The effectiveness of United States attempts to influence particular events in Brazil in the 1960s varied with the specific issues and circumstances. As important as the outcome of American intervention were the modality of United States decision-making and the salience to Brazilians of the issues in which the United States chose to intervene. That the interventions involved vital issues for a purportedly friendly nation and produced apparently negligible gains for the United States makes them the more irresponsible and regrettable.

65. A. A. Berle, "Foreword," in Vladimir Reisky de Dubnic, *Political Trends in Brazil* (Washington: Public Affairs Press, 1968), pp. iii-iv.

66. Hearing Before the Committee on Foreign Relations, "Nomination of Lincoln Gordon," pp. 8-9.

A SELECTED BIBLIOGRAPHY

Bonilla, Frank. "Operational Neutralism." American Universities Field Staff Reports Service, East Coast South America Series, Vol. IX, No. 1 (Brazil), January 1962.

Burns, E. Bradford. *Nationalism in Brazil: A Historical Survey*. New York: Frederick A. Praeger, 1968.

Campos, Roberto Oliveira. *Reflections on Latin American Development*. Austin: University of Texas Press, 1967.

Diaz-Alejandro, Carlos F. "Some Aspects of the Brazilian Experience with Foreign Aid." Unpublished manuscript, December 1969.

Dubnic, Vladimir Reisky de. *Political Trends in Brazil*. Washington: Public Affairs Press, 1968.

Gordon, Lincoln. *A New Deal for Latin America: The Alliance for Progress*. Cambridge: Harvard University Press, 1963.

Lacerda, Carlos. "The United States and Latin America: The Present Bankruptcy of Policy." *The Harvard Review*, Vol. 4, No. 4 (Fourth Quarter, 1968).

Morel, Edmar. *O Golpe Comecou em Washington*. Rio de Janeiro: Editôra Civilização Brasileira S.A., 1965.

Petras, James. "The United States and the New Equilibrium in Latin America." *Public Policy*, Vol. 18, No. 1 (Fall 1969).

Quadros, Jânio. "Brazil's New Foreign Policy." Foreign Affairs, Vol. 40. No. 1 (October 1961).

Roett, Riordan. *The Politics of Foreign Aid in the Brazilian Northeast*. Nashville: Vanderbilt University Press, 1972.

Skidmore, Thomas. *Politics in Brazil, 1930-1964: An Experiment in Democracy*. New York: Oxford University Press, 1967.

Tuthill, John W. "Economic and Political Aspects of Development in Brazil— and U.S. Aid." *Journal of Inter-American Studies*, Vol. XI, No. 2 (April 1969).

U.S. House of Representatives. *New Directions for the 1970's: Toward a Strategy of Inter-American Development*. Hearings Before the Sub-Committee on Inter-American Affairs of the Committee on Foreign Affairs, Ninety-first Congress, First Session, February 25, 1969. Washington: U.S. Government Printing Office, 1969.

U.S. House of Representatives. *U.S. Aid Operations in Latin America Under the Alliance for Progress*. Hearings Before a Subcommittee on Government Operations, Ninetieth Congress, Second Session, February 8, 9, 12, and 13, 1968. Washington: U.S. Government Printing Office, 1969.

U.S. Senate. "Nomination of Lincoln Gordon to be Assistant Secretary of State for Inter-American Affairs." Hearings Before the Committee on Foreign Relations, Eighty-ninth Congress, Second Session, February 7, 1966. Washington: U.S. Government Printing Office, 1966.

The Economy:
Growth versus Development

4 WERNER BAER and ISAAC KERSTENETZKY

The Brazilian Economy

THE PRINCIPAL characteristic of the Brazilian economy in the sixties was its drifting nature. At the opening of the decade the economy was still experiencing the high rates of growth that prevailed throughout most of the fifties. Growth in the fifties largely resulted from the process of import substitution industrialization (ISI) which had been accelerated through various government policies.[1] By 1962, however, the economy lost its dynamism and a prolonged period of stagnation ensued. Only in the last two years of the sixties did growth pick up again, but at this writing it is too early to determine whether this is a renewed period of high growth rates which could prevail throughout most of the seventies.

In the early sixties the Brazilian economy also experienced explosive inflation which was gradually reduced by the regime that took over after April 1964. The governments that determined economic

We wish to thank Claudio M. Castro, Paulo Haddad, Elton Hinshaw, William O. Thweatt, and Annibal Villela for many helpful suggestions.

1. For detailed analyses of the import substitution industrialization of the fifties, see Werner Baer, *Industrialization and Economic Development in Brazil* (Homewood, Illinois: Richard D. Irwin, Inc., 1965); Joel Bergsman and Arthur Candal, "Industrialization: Past Success and Future Problems," *The Economy of Brazil*, edited by Howard S. Ellis (Berkeley and Los Angeles: The University of California Press, 1969), pp. 29-73; and Joel Bergsman, *Brazil's Industrialization and Trade Policies* (New York: Oxford University Press, 1970).

policy in the early sixties made only intermittent and half-hearted efforts to cope with inflation. The Quadros and Goulart governments felt that the intense ISI efforts of the fifties had produced or accentuated structural disequilibria in the society and in the economy. Dealing with these disequilibria was considered as important, perhaps more so, as controlling the inflation inherited from the fifties. For a number of reasons, mostly noneconomic, basic reforms and structural changes were not accomplished, nor was inflation brought under control.

The actions of the post-April 1964 regimes also show a concern with both inflation and reforms. Action on the former, however, received priority. Also, the vision of the reforms needed by the post-1964 governments was somewhat different from that of the overthrown administration.

One thing which seems clear in reviewing the sixties: it was a decade during which succeeding governments had to deal with problems created by the intense ISI process of the fifties. The fifties was a decade of economic initiative in the sense that many deliberate actions were taken to push the economy into an intense industrialization process; the sixties was a decade of "economic reflex"—concerned with adjustments to previous structural changes.

In the pages which follow we shall examine the performance of the economy as evidenced by the statistical data available,[2] review the policy measures taken by succeeding governments during the sixties, and discuss various interpretations of the economy's behavior during the period under examination.

A Statistical Description of the Economy in the Sixties

The growth performance of the Brazilian economy is shown in Table 1. Since the rates of growth attained in 1960 and 1961 were higher than the average of 6.7 percent in the period 1956-62, these years belong to the high ISI growth period. The decline started in 1962 and the average growth rate in the period 1962-67 was not quite 3.5 percent. Preliminary estimates are that the growth rates for 1968

---

2. Unfortunately, at this writing final and complete data for the last two years of the sixties are not available. Results of the 1970 census, which would give some more fundamental data on changes in the structure of the economy, will not be available until about 1973. Thus, the current evaluation has to be based on trends observable in the sixties, which might have to be amended somewhat when the full statistical information on the sixties is available.

The Brazilian Economy

TABLE 1

a. BRAZIL: REAL GROWTH RATES BY SECTORS OF THE ECONOMY

Year	Real Over-all	Product Per Cap.	Agricul- ture	Industry	Total	Com- merce	Services Trans- port & Commu- nication	Other
	(1)	(2)	(3)	(4)	(5)	(6)	(7)	(8)
1957	8.1	5.0	9.3	5.7	9.0	9.6	7.8	8.8
1958	7.7	4.6	2.0	16.2	5.4	7.0	6.1	3.2
1959	5.6	2.5	5.3	11.9	1.2	9.3	9.6	-12.9
1960	9.7	6.5	4.9	9.6	13.0	5.9	17.3	20.0
1961	10.3	6.7	7.6	10.6	11.9	7.0	3.3	18.2
1962	5.3	2.1	5.5	7.8	3.3	5.8	8.4	0.9
1963	1.5	-1.5	1.0	0.2	2.8	0.0	7.8	3.5
1964	2.9	-0.2	1.3	5.2	2.0	1.1	1.6	3.4
1965	2.7	-0.4	13.8	-4.7	1.3	1.6	1.8	0.7
1966	5.1	1.8	-3.2	11.7	5.8	7.7	6.6	3.5
1967	4.8	1.5	5.7	3.0	5.8	4.4	7.8	6.3
1968	8.4	5.0	1.5	13.2	—	8.4	8.8	—
1969	9.0	5.6	6.0	10.8	—	8.7	11.7	—
1970	9.5	6.0	5.6	11.1	—	8.9	14.9	—

Source: Centro de Contas Nacionais, Fundação Getúlio Vargas.

b. BRAZIL: REAL GROWTH RATES OF MACRO-ECONOMIC AGGREGATES

	Personal Consumption	Government Consumption	Gross Capital Formation	Capacity to Import
	(9)	(10)	(11)	(12)
1957	6.2	3.5	13.4	-6.0
1958	9.7	6.5	5.9	-5.6
1959	1.8	6.7	12.9	15.3
1960	12.9	16.6	4.1	2.8
1961	9.1	10.0	5.1	8.2
1962	6.1	0.4	3.1	-14.9
1963	1.4	7.1	-2.8	13.5
1964	3.2	-2.3	2.5	5.2
1965	2.7	-6.9	-2.6	11.8
1966	7.7	6.5	20.1	4.7
1967	5.1	6.8	1.9	-6.2
1968	6.6	5.1	21.6	8.9

Source: Fundação Getúlio Vargas; rates of growth based on aggregates in 1953 prices.

and 1969 were 8.4 and 9.0 percent respectively. Industrial production (see column 4 of Table 1) which was the leading sector in the ISI period of the fifties and grew at average yearly rates of 10 percent between 1950 and 1962, fell to an annual rate of only 3.2 percent in the period 1962-67. After rising to a growth rate of over 13 percent in 1968, it remained at 10.8 and 11.1 percent in 1969 and 1970 respectively. Growth of agricultural production was similar to that observed in the fifties, with average rates somewhat more than 4 percent (population growth stood at almost 3 percent); as can be seen in Table 1 (column 3), however, there were some extremely poor years in the middle sixties, largely because of droughts and/or frosts in various parts of the country. Table 1 (b) also shows that throughout most of the sixties the growth rate of government consumption (column 10) and gross capital formation (column 11) was small in relation to the late fifties and early sixties, while the growth of Brazil's capacity to import (column 12) was quite erratic.

Table 2 shows that developments in the sixties produced scarcely any structural changes if these are measured by the contribution of each functional sector to the Gross Domestic Product. The marked relative gain of industry's contribution to GDP which characterized the period from 1947 to 1960 was not observable in the 1960-67 period. We shall turn to the significance of this trend below.

TABLE 2
CHANGES IN THE FUNCTIONAL DISTRIBUTION OF BRAZIL'S
GROSS DOMESTIC PRODUCTS

	1939	1947	1953	1957	1960	1966	1967	1968
In Current Prices								
Agriculture	25.8	27.6	26.1	22.8	22.6	19.1	19.2	17.9
Industry	19.4	19.8	23.7	24.4	25.2	27.2	26.2	28.0
Other Sectors	54.8	52.6	50.2	52.8	52.2	53.7	54.5	54.1
	100.0	100.0	100.0	100.0	100.0	100.0	100.0	100.0
In 1953 Prices								
Agriculture		30.0	26.1	24.6	22.2	21.9	22.0	20.5
Industry		20.6	23.7	24.5	28.0	28.8	28.3	29.3
Other Sectors		49.4	50.2	50.9	49.8	49.3	49.7	50.2
		100.0	100.0	100.0	100.0	100.0	100.0	100.0

Source: calculated from data of Fundação Getúlio Vargas, Centro de Contas Nacionais and Conjuntura Econômica.

In Table 3(a) we present a number of Brazilian macroeconomic ratios. Column 2 shows a notable decline in the investment ratio, which was principally attributable to a relative decline in private investment (see column 4). It is interesting to observe that the stability of the government investment ratio coupled with the relative decline in the government consumption ratio during the sixties signifies that the decline in government real expenditures fell on current rather than capital items. Many government investment projects were of a long-term nature, financed partially by loans from international agencies and foreign governments, which could not be easily interrupted for stabilization purposes. Although the fifties were characterized by a low marginal capital/output ratio, it would obviously not make much sense to attach significance to the fact that this ratio rose substantially in the sixties. As we shall see further on, much of the economy was working below capacity in the period, and the type of investment that fell the most was that which had shorter gestation periods and had lower marginal capital/output ratios than the investment projects (mainly in public infrastructure projects) which were continued. It would therefore be largely meaningless to conclude from the higher capital/output ratios of the sixties that this represented a long-term trend toward capital deepening and thus a necessity for higher savings rates in order to attain rates of growth similar to those of the fifties.[3]

According to the data presented in Table 3, the private sector continued to be the main source of savings in the economy (see column 7), while the government's savings were in most years substantially below its investment ratio (compare columns 3 and 8). This means that resources were being transferred from the private to the public sector. In most years, this transfer was from the private consumer to the public investment sector. In 1964 and 1965, however, some transfer of resources from private savings to public investment also took place, since in those years the private savings ratio was higher than the private investment ratios. In the early and mid-sixties this transfer was achieved in part through inflation.[4] The con-

3. An interesting recent article called attention to the fact that savings rates have been fairly constant throughout the fifties. It will be noted that there was no tendency for this rate to rise in the sixties. This contradicts the commonly held notion that savings rates should increase as development proceeds. No answer to this phenomenon has yet been found. Of course, the application of savings has changed over the growth process and thus affected growth rates. See N. H. Leff, "Marginal Savings Rates in the Development Process: The Brazilian Experience," *The Economic Journal* (September 1968), pp. 610-623.

4. *Baer*, pp. 103-106.

tribution of foreign savings declined substantially after 1962. Columns 10 and 11 of Table 3 indicate that the government's capacity to marshall resources through the tax mechanism increased by the latter sixties. Especially noticeable is the higher proportion of direct tax collection which reflects a deliberate policy of the post-1964 regime to tighten the mechanism of income-tax collection.

TABLE 3

a. BRAZIL: PRINCIPAL MACRO-ECONOMIC RATIOS
(All variables as a proportion of GDP)

	Total Investment		Government Investment	Gross Private Investment	Consumption	
	With Inventory	Without Inventory			Priv.	Govt.
	(1)	(2)	(3)	(4)	(5)	(6)
1957	16.6	14.2	3.9	10.3	71.5	12.5
1958	17.5	16.2	4.7	11.6	70.7	12.4
1959	21.5	18.5	4.3	14.2	66.9	12.5
1960	18.4	16.9	4.7	12.2	69.6	13.3
1961	19.4	17.2	4.3	12.9	67.8	13.3
1962	20.3	17.9	4.5	13.4	68.6	12.7
1963	18.7	17.6	4.1	13.5	68.4	13.3
1964	18.6	16.5	4.2	12.3	67.6	12.7
1965	18.4	14.7	4.4	10.3	67.6	11.5
1966	15.2	15.3	4.0	11.3	72.3	11.6
1967	15.2	14.4	4.5	10.0	73.0	11.9
1968	13.1	12.5	4.1	12.5	71.8	11.5

	Savings		Bal. of Payments Deficit	Indirect Taxes	Direct Taxes	Exports of Goods & Service	Imports of Goods & Service
	Net Private	Govt.					
	(7)	(8)	(9)	(10)	(11)	(12)	(13)
1957	8.6	1.8	1.2	11.2	5.8	6.1	6.7
1958	6.8	4.5	1.2	13.9	6.0	6.1	6.7
1959	10.3	4.6	1.7	14.8	6.0	6.7	7.7
1960	6.6	4.7	2.1	14.4	5.7	6.1	7.4
1961	12.0	1.3	1.1	12.8	6.0	6.9	7.4
1962	13.1	-0.2	2.6	12.5	5.2	5.1	6.8
1963	12.4	0.3	1.0	12.8	5.2	9.7	10.1
1964	14.3	-0.2	-0.4	13.9	5.4	7.5	6.4
1965	14.1	0.9	-1.5	15.0	6.8	8.8	6.3
1966	7.2	2.9	0.1	16.5	7.6	7.6	6.7
1967	8.5	0.5	1.2	15.3	8.1	6.6	6.7
1968	7.6	3.2	1.6	17.9	8.8	6.9	7.6

Source: Same as Table 2.

TABLE 3-(CONTINUED)

b. FINANCING OF GROSS CAPITAL FORMATION (PERCENTAGE)

	Gross Private Savings	Public Savings	External Financing	Total
1957	81.9	11.1	7.0	100.0
1958	67.0	25.9	7.1	100.0
1959	71.0	21.2	7.8	100.0
1960	62.9	25.7	11.4	100.0
1961	87.3	6.9	5.8	100.0
1962	88.6	-1.2	12.6	100.0
1963	92.9	1.6	5.5	100.0
1964	103.2	-1.0	-2.2	100.0
1965	103.4	4.7	-8.1	100.0
1966	80.0	19.3	0.7	100.0
1967	88.8	3.5	7.7	100.0
1968	72.3	18.4	9.3	100.0

Source: Same as Table 2.

To complete this initial overview of Brazil's economic performance in the sixties, it should be noted that the foreign trade coefficient (taking either exports of goods and services as a proportion of GDP or imports of goods and services) did not display any pronounced trend, as it did in the period from the late forties to the early sixties, when it fell by more than six percentage points (from about 14 to between 7 and 8 percent). We shall comment on the significance of the stability of this coefficient in a later section. Finally, Table 4 shows that the rate of inflation accelerated in the early sixties, reaching a maximum in 1964 (the yearly rate in the middle of that year surpassed 100 percent), and thereafter gradually decreasing, although at the end of the sixties the inflation rate was still higher than at any time in the fifties.

Before interpreting the over-all performance described above, a brief review of the policy measures followed by succeeding governments in the decade is necessary.

Economic Policy in the Sixties

The first year of the decade was the last year of the Kubitschek administration and the high rates of growth in 1960 and 1961 represented the result of the intensified policies of ISI of that administration.[5] They consisted of pushing ISI as far and as deeply as possible (maximizing internal linkages) while neglecting the modernization of other sectors of the economy, especially agriculture, and paying little attention to disruptive forces being produced by government policies, especially rising inflation.

TABLE 4

RATES OF GROWTH

	Cost of Living Guanabara	Wholesale Prices (Excluding Coffee)	Bank Notes	Money Supply Demand Deposits	Total Money Supply	Federal Budget Deficit as % of GDP
1957	16.5	14.3	20.9	40.0	34.1	3.3
1958	14.6	14.4	23.5	20.5	21.3	1.8
1959	13.9	42.9	27.0	47.8	41.9	2.7
1960	29.3	31.5	33.1	39.8	38.1	2.8
1961	33.2	40.3	51.5	50.3	50.6	3.4
1962	51.5	50.1	55.1	65.6	63.1	4.3
1963	70.8	76.4	72.3	61.9	64.3	4.3
1964	91.4	81.3	69.0	91.4	85.9	3.2
1965	65.9	53.6	49.7	82.8	75.4	1.6
1966	41.3	40.7	35.4	10.2	15.0	1.1
1967	30.5	26.6	25.7	47.5	42.6	1.7
1968	22.3	23.1	38.6	44.1	43.0	1.2
1969	22.0	20.0	31.9	32.5	32.4	0.6

Source: Calculated from *Conjuntura Econômica, Boletim* of the Banco Central, and data furnished by the Fundação Getúlio Vargas.

Whether one sympathizes with the development strategy adopted in the fifties, both critics and defenders of that strategy would probably agree that it left a legacy of problems with which policy makers in the sixties would have to come to grips in order to assure continued economic growth and development. First, agriculture

5. For a summary of these policies see: Baer, *op. cit.*; Maria da Conceição Tavares, "The Growth and Decline of Import Substitution in Brazil," ECLA, *Economic Bulletin for Latin America*, Vol. IX, No. 1 (March 1964); Carlos Lessa, "Fifteen Years of Economic Policy in Brazil," ECLA, *Economic Bulletin for Latin America*, Vol. IX, No. 2 (November 1964).

had been neglected.[6] Second, inflation was rising toward rates where any possibility of its contributing to growth through a forced savings mechanism was disappearing; it acted mostly as a distorting force in the allocation of resources. The accentuation of inequalities which industrial growth had brought about—the unequal distribution of the benefits of growth on a regional, sectoral and income group basis—was producing increasing social pressures for remedial actions. Also, there were pressures to deal with the long-neglected and backward educational system, both to supply better trained manpower to the modern industrial sector and to provide greater social mobility, and thus access to the fruits of industrialization to a larger proportion of the population. Finally, there were the mounting balance of payments pressures resulting from the fact that part of the growth in the fifties, especially the second half of the fifties, was financed by a substantial influx of foreign capital, both in the form of direct investment and loans. By the beginning of the sixties Brazil's foreign debt already amounted to more than two billion dollars. A large proportion of which was of a short-term nature, and both the interest payments and amortization, combined with profit remittances of foreign firms, produced increasing balance-of-payments difficulties. The fact that ISI policies had been one sided, that is, that export promotion and/or diversification had been completely neglected, was now coming to be a major problem.

The short-lived Quadros administration was aware of many of these imbalances in the economy and tried to cope with some of them. A determined effort was made to deal with inflation. The multiple-exchange-rate system was simplified and the inflationary subsidies on essential imports, such as wheat and petroleum, were substantially lowered. Although this raised the prices of such consumer items as bread and bus fares, it helped the government to cut its budgetary deficit. In addition, the Quadros government imposed

6. Agriculture had not been completely neglected, since some investment in marketing facilities and extension services occurred at various periods of time. Also, agriculture expanded satisfactorily when compared with the growth of population; however, many experts in the field claim that this was more a result of extensive agriculture than increased productivity in older agricultural areas. There is also substantial agreement that social conditions for most of the agricultural labor force remained precarious (by the early sixties more than 50 percent of the population was still rural). See Julian Chacel, "The Principal Characteristics of the Agrarian Structure and Agricultural Production in Brazil," and Gordon W. Smith, "Brazilian Agricultural Policy, 1950-1967," both in Howard Ellis (ed.), op. cit. See also Chapter Five by William H. Nicholls in this volume.

credit tightening and a wage freeze and began a harsh program of streamlining government operations. By the middle of 1961 some evidence had already developed that the growth of inflation was being slowed and Brazil's foreign creditors were beginning to look at the country in a more sympathetic way. An element which played a role in the latter was also the fact that the first years of the sixties were the beginning of Kennedy's Alliance for Progress which was supposed to favor especially reformist governments. There is little doubt that efforts at structural reforms and the vigorous stabilization effort were among the principal causes for the formidable pressures on Quadros which brought on his early resignation.[7]

The turbulent years from Quadros's resignation in late August 1961 until the overthrow of the Goulart government in April 1964 were devoid of any consistent line of economic policy. This was owing to the lack of leadership shown by President Goulart. In the first half of his tenure this was caused by circumstances not directly of his making. Goulart was allowed to take over the presidency only after it was agreed that he would share power with a newly created parliamentary form of government. This muddled the lines of authority and no clear leadership emerged. After a plebiscite in 1963 which restored full power to the presidency, however, Goulart proved to be a weak man overwhelmed by pressures from many opposing quarters. There were half-hearted attempts at stabilization soon abandoned when Goulart could not resist the demand of labor leaders for rapid wage adjustments, the demand of the business community to refrain from painful credit restrictions, the pressure from many quarters not to abandon inflationary subsidy exchange rates for the importation of petroleum and wheat, and not to readjust public utility and transportation rates in accordance with over-all price increases. The latter created further inflationary pressures through increased public budgetary deficits.[8]

During the Goulart tenure, groups clamoring for basic institutional reforms and for more nationalist policies vis-à-vis foreign capital became increasingly vociferous and had substantial influence over the president. Agitation for land and tax reform grew, institu-

7. For further details on the political situation of the period, see Thomas E. Skidmore, *Politics in Brazil 1930-1964, An Experiment in Democracy* (New York: Oxford University Press, 1967), Chapter VI.

8. Werner Baer, Isaac Kerstenetzky, and Mario H. Simonsen, "Transportation and Inflation: A Study of Irrational Policy-Making in Brazil," *Economic Development and Cultural Change*, January 1965.

tional changes in the country's educational structure and a greater control over foreign capital's activities (and in some cases expropriation) were demanded. Goulart sympathized with these forces for drastic socioeconomic reforms, used their arguments in his pronouncements, but failed to implement concrete programs.

Some actions were taken in the period, such as a severe profit remittance control law passèd by the congress in October 1962, and a Three-Year Plan was formulated early in 1963 which was to control inflation drastically and systematically deal with the economy's principal disequilibria. This plan was soon shelved when it became obvious that the government had neither the means nor the will to impose some of its stabilization measures and reforms. The lack of political control, the continued agitation for reforms and the lip service which Goulart paid to the latter, and the agitation against foreign capital, resulted in increasingly severe economic problems. Budget deficits increased and the rate of inflation grew to levels of 50 percent and finally to yearly rates of more than 100 percent in 1964. With political uncertainties, foreign and domestic investment declined, and the growth rate of the economy steadily declined from its 1961 peak.

Soon after the ousting of Goulart in April 1964, the new Castello Branco government formulated a short-run economic policy program, Programa de Ação Económico do Govêrno (PAEG), aimed at controlling inflation and correcting distortions which had developed in the economic system out of both the one-sided rapid ISI of the fifties and the long period of inflation.[9] These policies were continued without much modification by the government of Costa e Silva which took over in 1967. Classic stabilization measures were used—curtailment of government expenditures, tightening of credit and a squeeze on the wage sector. The new government made special efforts to cut expenditures in a number of sectors and to increase revenues by improving the tax-collection mechanism. As a result real government revenues had increased by about 25 percent by 1965. Wage policy was designed to keep real wages and salaries well within productivity increases. Government policy made wage increases lag behind price increases, causing substantial declines in the real purchasing power of workers. Credit-tightening was such that total real credit available in

9. See *Programa de Ação Económico do Govêrno, 1964-66* (Rio de Janeiro, November 1964); for a description of and rationalization of this program see Mario H. Simonsen, "Brazilian Inflation: Postwar Experience and Outcome of the 1964 Reforms," in *Economic Development Issues: Latin America*, Committee for Economic Development, Supplementary Paper No. 21, August 1967.

the economy during the mid and later sixties was below that of the early part of the decade. Commerce, industry, and credit to individuals bore the brunt of this policy, while the rural sector was better off (see Table 5).

The regimes in control after 1964 introduced a large number of laws and decrees designed both to eliminate distortions inherited from the past and to stimulate economic activity. Subsidies on the importation of petroleum and wheat were eliminated. Public utility rates were raised in a manner commensurate with past inflation rates. Although these measures had an immediate inflationary impact, it was hoped that they would ultimately eliminate the budgetary deficits of the fed-

TABLE 5

BRAZILIAN BANKING SYSTEM—LOANS TO THE PRIVATE SECTOR

(in 1962 prices—1962=100)

	Commerce	Industry	Agri-culture	Livestock	Indi-viduals	Total	
			Monetary Authorities				
1958	107 (7.6)	99 (17.7)	73 (8.4)	63 (3.1)	185 (0.5)	90 (37.4)	
1959	78	86	69	55	56	76	
1960	95	82	71	67	35	79	
1961	109	85	105	61	32	91	
1962	100	100	100	100	100	100	
1963	84	54	112	62	50	76	
1964	67	68	118	56	38	80	
1965	55	55	79	47	41	61	
1966	51	63	97	69	147	72	
1967	60 (4.0)	61 (10.0)	106 (8.4)	83 (3.9)	32 (0.1)	76 (29.4)	
1968						89	
			Commercial Banks				Grand Total
1958	102 (27.3)	83 (22.2)	95 (4.6)	80 (1.2)	97 (7.3)	93 (62.6)	92 (100.0)
1959	100	85	103	70	94	93	86
1960	111	94	109	81	104	103	94
1961	102	95	99	80	99	98	96
1962	100	100	100	100	100	100	100
1963	83	96	112	96	75	90	84
1964	72	94	135	124	74	87	84
1965	77	107	162	149	84	97	83
1966	64	93	145	147	104	88	82
1967	80 (2.0)	116 (28.7)	192 (8.6)	243 (3.5)	139 (9.8)	112 (70.6)	98 (100.0)
1968						143	

Source: Calculated from reports of Banco Centra.
Numbers in parentheses indicate percentage distribution of loans to private sector.

eral government and thus reduce long-term inflationary forces (the inflationary impact of these measures were called "corrective inflation").[10] Efforts were made to modernize financial markets. Special credit institutions were created to help small and medium firms finance the acquisition of capital goods. An important innovation was the creation of financial instruments with values subject to periodic readjustments in accordance with the rate of inflation. The government introduced readjustable bonds, thus eliminating some of the inflationary impact of its deficits (the deficits being financed by bonds sold to the public would be less inflationary than bonds sold to the central bank which amounted to the injection of new money into the economy). Of course, this measure also had a tightening impact on the private credit market; the government was now in effect siphoning off large funds from the capital market. Of great importance was the creation of the National Housing Bank empowered to use debt instruments which could be adjusted to the rate of inflation.[11] After a slow start, the National Housing Bank had a substantial impact on the revival of the construction sector in the latter half of the sixties. It is too early to determine the extent of the success of readjustable debt instruments on the housing sector in the long run. There were nascent signs—delays in payments, defaulting or forced contraction of nonhousing consumer expenditures—in 1969 that the real burden of readjustable debt was too great for many new owners of dwellings.

Numerous measures were also taken to modernize the operations of the stock market. Tax incentive measures were used to increase the flow of savings to the stock market, to increase the flow of investment funds to less favored regions of the country (especially the Northeast, where increasing reliance was placed on articles 34/18 of SUDENE to attract investment funds)[12] and to increase and diversify the country's exports. To help attain the latter, the government established an export credit institution, abolished export taxes, and substantially simplified bureaucratic export procedures. Although

10. For a discussion of the notion of "corrective inflation" see the article by Baer, Kerstenetzky and Simonsen, cited in footnote 8 above.

11. See especially Mario H. Simonsen, "Inflation and the Money and Capital Markets of Brazil," in Howard S. Ellis (ed.), pp. 156-159. It was hoped that the housing bank would not only build up a financial market for construction activities, but that this was the best means to stimulate building activities which would help to eliminate the country's huge housing deficit.

12. Articles 34/18 of SUDENE make it possible for investors to use 50 percent of their federal income-tax liability if within three years it is invested in an industrial establishment of Northeast Brazil.

attempts were made to reduce government expenditures, government infrastructure investments in roadbuilding, hydroelectric projects such as the Boa Esperança dam in the Northeast, the vast hydroelectric Ilha Solteira project in São Paulo were kept up.

The principal aims of the government since 1964 were to reduce gradually the rate of inflation, eliminate the price and other distortions which past inflation had brought along, modernize financial markets, and restore a climate of investor confidence in the economy. Policy-makers thought that, although in the short run these measures would require some painful readjustments by a number of socio-economic groups (during the mid-sixties there was a constant admonition by policy makers to the public of the necessity for "sacrifices" to restore economic order), the ultimate result would be to increase savings available; these would flow into the most remunerative sectors and thus produce long-run satisfactory growth rates. For the policy makers, "the main problem confronting the economy was viewed from the supply side. The return of a price system reflecting relative scarcities and the creation of better institutions to capture the economy's savings were thought to be the royal road to a higher rate of economic growth."[13]

There are two main analytical issues to examine in evaluating the performance of the Brazilian economy in the sixties. First, the effect of and control of inflation and, more importantly, the causes and implications of the lower rates of economic growth that prevailed throughout the period.

Inflation

We already mentioned the explosive inflation of the early sixties Since the change of regime in 1964, the rate of inflation has gradually declined. The decrease in the rate of growth of the price level was brought about by a fairly steady decline in the rate of expansion of the money supply and a steady downward trend in the ratio of the federal government's deficit to the GDP (see Table 4). It is of interest to note when examining Table 5 that real credit extended by both the monetary authorities and private banks declined already from 1962 onward. A possible explanation of this is that in 1962 there was a very large jump in the proportion of the federal government deficit

13. Werner Baer and Andrea Maneschi, "Import-Substitution, Stagnation and Structural Change: An Interpretation of the Brazilian Case," *The Journal of Developing Areas*, January 1971.

to GDP, indicating that much of the real credit was appropriated by the government. Over-all real credit to the private sector by either the monetary authorities or commercial banks had not regained its 1962 level by the end of the decade. Stringencies for individual sectors varied considerably, however. Thus, credit restraint on the industrial sector and on loans to individuals were greater than on the agricultural sector.

A curious phenomenon in the Brazilian economy after 1964 is the continued high rates of inflation. Although the rates were gradually brought down by the various measures mentioned above,[14] the rate of inflation at the end of the decade was still surprisingly high considering the length of time during which one of the prime objectives of the government was price stabilization. This is especially curious since during most of the sixties the Brazilian economy's growth rate was low and, as will be seen below, many sectors were working below capacity.

In Table 6 we have tried to indicate some of the leading and lagging sectors in the rise of both the cost-of-living index and the wholesale price index. This was done by computing a ratio of the rise of individual items in the cost-of-living index to the over-all rise in the cost-of-living index. A similar procedure was followed for the wholesale price index. A ratio of more than 100 indicates that the item was one of the leading price-raising sectors. ("Leading" is used here as indicating relative pressure on the price level rather than as indicating time.) The reader can see that after 1964 food prices were not exerting a leading pressure on the cost of living. The leading sectors were represented by housing and public services (which together represent a weight of more than 18 percent); these pressures represented part of the "corrective inflation"[15] period during which price distortions were being eliminated. Toward the end of the sixties food price increases were no longer lagging behind the general price increase, while manufactured articles such as clothing and household articles were taking the lead. A glance at wholesale prices reveals that chemi-

14. There is a good probability that in the late sixties there existed a substantial amount of suppressed inflation; pressure was placed by government authorities on a number of industrial sectors to keep prices from rising. For example, steel firms (many owned by the government) were not allowed to raise their prices commensurate with costs; other industries were persuaded to refrain from price increases because of the risk of loosing access to government-controlled credits.

15. During the long inflationary period of the fifties and early sixties, prices controlled by the government were not allowed to rise as fast as the general price level. This introduced severe price distortions. Part of the stabilization program of

TABLE 6

a. RATIO OF INDEX OF CHANGE OF INDIVIDUAL CONSUMER COST ITEMS
TO CHANGE OF OVER-ALL COST OF LIVING INDEX—STATE OF
GUANABARA

	Food	Clothing	Housing	House-hold Articles	Health	Personal Services	Public Services
1958	99.8	97.2	101.8	94.1	93.9	93.6	106.3
1959	104.3	99.0	86.0	106.2	107.5	114.0	97.4
1960	100.9	100.3	91.8	108.1	104.9	102.9	101.4
1961	100.8	109.9	87.9	95.6	99.0	110.8	99.1
1962	106.8	98.4	90.2	96.8	88.8	97.1	93.6
1963	97.1	106.0	89.2	112.8	103.6	101.1	112.1
1964	102.4	96.4	78.8	106.0	91.6	107.0	110.7
1965	88.7	99.8	119.4	98.8	109.3	111.0	122.6
1966	98.2	92.5	123.9	87.3	92.7	96.6	107.7
1967	93.8	101.6	152.3	94.5	102.7	105.6	101.6
1968	92.5	103.8	85.8	108.3	105.2	106.0	97.9

Source: Calculated from cost of living date in *Conjuntura Econômica.*

Note: Until July 1966, weights of cost of living index were as follows:

Food	43.0%
Housing	20.0
Clothing	11.0
Household Articles	5.7
Health	4.0
Personal Services	5.8
Public Services	10.5

After that the weights used were as follows:

Food	45.15
Housing	10.57
Clothing	8.48
Household Articles	11.49
Health	5.52
Personal Services	11.12
Public Services	7.67

the government consisted of raising prices of the lagging sectors (food products, fuels, public utilities, rents). This action had a short-term inflationary impact which is called "corrective inflation." See W. Baer, I. Kerstenetzky and M. H. Simonsen, "Transportation and Inflation: A Study of Irrational Policy-Making in Brazil," *Economic Development and Cultural Change,* January 1965; M. H. Simonsen, "Brazilian Inflation: Postwar Experience Outcome of the 1964 Reform," in *Economic Development Issues—Latin America,* Supplementary Paper No. 21 issued by the committee for Economic Development, New York, August 1967; Howard S. Ellis, "Corrective Inflation in Brazil, 1964-1966," in *The Economy of Brazil,* ed. by H. S. Ellis (Berkeley and Los Angeles: The University of California Press, 1969).

TABLE 6 *(CONTINUED)*
b. RATIO OF INDEX OF INDIVIDUAL WHOLESALE PRICES TO
OVER-ALL WHOLESALE PRICE INDEX

	Coffee	Food excl. Coffee	Fuels	Metals & Metal Products	Con- struction Materials	Leather Products	Textiles	Chemical Products
1958	89.1	96.4	107.4	128.3	113.8	92.7	103.8	116.9
1959	76.6	103.3	112.5	104.0	96.1	113.2	96.6	105.9
1960	95.8	104.3	84.5	81.0	86.8	125.8	105.0	102.1
1961	86.9	98.7	121.0	93.6	103.6	91.0	110.4	96.8
1962	97.8	105.0	84.5	101.2	93.3	94.4	92.6	103.1
1963	79.8	98.1	102.2	112.2	115.0	90.9	104.1	120.9
1964	185.2	95.5	103.3	92.7	86.0	84.1	90.7	118.3
1965	87.3	97.3	119.3	112.6	107.6	107.1	101.1	110.2
1966	73.2	109.6	90.9	94.4	101.2	109.9	98.5	ᵛ78.4
1967	89.5	100.3	95.9	95.9	107.0	98.1	101.0	108.5
1968	113.6	93.6	104.0	104.8	108.2	94.3	106.9	98.6

Source: same as part a

Note: Weighting system for wholesale prices:

Food products	57.0
Fuels	3.5
Metal Products	5.9
Construction Materials	6.0
Leather Goods	3.1
Textiles	16.8
Chemical Products	1.8

Since 1969 there have been substantial changes in the weighting system.

cal products, textiles, and construction materials were most frequently the leaders in price increases.

Unfortunately this identification of the greater and lesser pressure points in the continued inflation does not answer the fundamental question of why inflationary forces persisted through a prolonged period of relative stagnation, excess capacity in industry, and, over the entire period, an adequate rate of growth of food supplies. It is true that conditions for continued inflation were present—a continued growth of the money supply and existence of government budgetary deficits. These latter features do not explain, however, the basic causes of the phenomenon.

The most interesting attempt to explain this anomaly was made by Samuel Morley in a recent article.[16] First, on the basis of estimates of quarterly changes in economic activity, Morley found a clear

16. Samuel A. Morley, "Inflation and Stagnation in Brazil," *Economic Development and Cultural Change,* January 1971.

relationship in the rate of change of monetary expansion and real output throughout the sixties. This "suggests that the reason the stabilization program has resulted in so long a period of inflationary stagnation is due to the way it was applied." Monetary constraint "was applied in fits and starts which brought first recession with residual inflation, then recovery with even greater inflation. From the point of view of price stability, the full benefits of each period of constraint were lost in subsequent excessive expansion."[17] What Morley finds is that tight money supply was not maintained for long because of the pressures for ease which were generated. However, since the government's policy of constraint continued, "these temporary reversals of policy only prolonged the period of adjustment to a lower rate of inflation. They also have created the misleading impression of five years of rising prices with constant or declining output. Instead, all the output declines are concentrated in three subperiods while more than half of the inflation comes in different periods of excess monetary expansion."[18]

Although this sheds some light on the phenomenon of coexistence of stagnation and inflation, Morley's analysis says little about the long-term slowness of economic growth in the sixties. Of course, if every few quarters there is a new money restraint which slows down growth, it is hard to know whether growth would have continued without the various short-term monetary restraints. He presents, however, some interesting suggestions about the source of continued inflationary pressures in the sixties.

There is little clear evidence of a prevalence of either classic demand pull or cost-push inflation, or inflation caused by structural rigidities. Food supplies, as we already saw, grew at a satisfactory rate and, except for short periods, did not exert the leading pressure on price indexes. Morley finds that the ratio of raw materials and labor costs to sales in most industries fell in the mid-sixties, which would discount a cost-push explanation. Excess capacity in most industries also discounts a demand-pull explanation.[19] Morley also found that from the mid-fifties to the mid-sixties price increases of the slower

17. *Ibid.*, p. 187.

18. *Ibid.*

19. Although later in this paper we will give some direct evidence of excess capacity in Brazilian industries, Morley shows as evidence the fact that 9 out of 15 of Brazil's main industry groups, representing 65 percent of value added, were operating below 1962 production levels in 1965, Morley pp. 189-91.

growing (more traditional) industries were faster than those of the more dynamic industries. To confound things, it was also found that profits (defined as value of sales less value of inputs) rose in the middle sixties and rose more rapidly in the older, less dynamic industries, although these increased profits failed to stimulate output expansion.[20]

Morley suggests a possible explanation for the phenomenon of inflationary stagnation in the peculiar effect credit restriction has had on Brazilian firms. The latter have relied to a larger extent on outside credit for working capital than firms in more advanced countries. With a drying-up of outside credits, firms had to use internal sources—profits—as working capital. Thus, in order to keep operating in a period when classic stabilization measures are attempted, firms will try to raise prices in order to raise profits. They will tend to use profits for current operations rather than for production and capacity expansion. Thus prices are increased just to increase working capital.[21] Of course, to the extent prices could not be increased in some industries, there has been some pressure on cost-reducing productivity increases in order to generate the necessary working capital.

Alternative Explanation of Slow Growth Rates in the Sixties

Most observers of the Brazilian economy in the sixties would agree that the dynamism it displayed in the fifties disappeared, but there is substantial disagreement about the causes of the economy's sluggishness in the decade. All would agree that the cause of the slowdown of the sixties can be found in the nature of the ISI of the fifties, but there is wide disagreement about the roots of the problem. Let us examine some of these explanations and see what evidence is available to support them.

Import Constraint Explanation

The basic idea behind this explanation is that during the ISI

20. Many of Brazil's traditional industries, such as textiles, are burdened with a large amount of obsolescent equipment. Higher profits due to higher prices might not necessarily induce more investment and output in those industries, since a thorough modernization would only be possible with a large amount of government funds. This possibility was suggested by Annibal Villela.

21. It has also been claimed that the higher per unit costs of lower levels of production have been passed on by the Brazilian producers toward higher prices. Given the oligopolistic structure of the Brazilian industry, higher costs are generally passed on in terms of higher prices rather than being absorbed by firms.

period of the fifties Brazil paid little attention to exports but considered its primary aim to produce domestically products formerly imported to reduce as much as possible the economy's import coefficient. Although the import coefficient was brought down, it cannot be brought much below the present level (about 7 percent) because of the change in the composition of imports. An increasingly large proportion of Brazil's imports are now made up of raw materials and capital goods which are important inputs into the newly established industries. These imported inputs either cannot be substituted at all or only in the long run, with the discovery of new raw materials or with an increased industrial sophistication which would eliminate the requirements for specialized capital goods imports. In the short and medium run, however, these imported inputs are vitally important to keep industrial production going. A decline of such imports resulting from balance-of-payments difficulties would force a contraction or a decline in the rate of growth of industrial production.

Since the outlook for traditional exports is not too favorable and since there is no guarantee that enough private and/or foreign capital inflows would be available in times of falling foreign exchange earnings,[22] it would make sense for Brazil to expand its exports and diversify its export structure in order to avoid import bottleneck situations which could bring on an industrial recession. This has not happened (see Table 7b). There has been little change in Brazil's export structure. Indeed, until the mid-sixties the country had no policy to stimulate both traditional and new exports. As a matter of fact, exporters had to pay export taxes and overcome a complicated bureaucratic barrier to export their products.[23]

One author maintains that the stagnation of the sixties was

22. In another paper we estimated that the growth rates of Brazil's capacity to import between the mid-sixties and the mid-seventies would not be more than 3 percent a year. W. Baer and I. Kerstenetzky, "Patterns of Brazilian Economic Growth," mimeographed; paper presented at Cornell University, April 1966, at a Conference on the Next Decade of Latin American Development.

23. For a description of Brazil's failure to promote exports, see Nathaniel H. Leff, "Export Stagnation and Autarkic Development." *The Quarterly Journal of Economics*, May 1967. In fairness, however, it should be said that in order to stimulate ISI industrialization and attract foreign capital, the Brazilian policy-makers had to hold out the carrot of the large protected internal Brazilian market. Few firms would have made massive investments in Brazil had they been forced from the very beginning to export a large proportion of their output.

brought on by an import bottleneck which made itself felt in 1963.[24] The data do not support this claim. For example, while the quantum of imports of intermediate goods and raw materials fell by 12 percent in 1962, it rose again by 28 percent in 1963; although industrial growth declined in 1962 (see Table 1), it was practically stagnant in 1963.[25] Table 7 indicates that the value of imports declined substantially in the mid-sixties, while the value of exports rose steadily after 1962. While import constraint was not a cause of diminished growth in the sixties, it should not be dismissed as a possible future constraint on Brazilian growth.

Table 8 gives an aggregate view of Brazil's balance of payments in the period 1958-68. Note that except for 1960 and 1962 the merchandise balance was always in surplus, the surplus growing in the mid-sixties and sharply declining in 1968. The favorable merchandise balance of the mid-sixties was clearly a result of the doldrums in which industrial production found itself, since, as noted earlier, an increasing proportion of Brazil's imports over the ISI period consisted of imported inputs for the industrial sector. In the sixties, import bottlenecks were not a cause of the decline of growth, but the decline of industrial growth was a cause of the decline of imports.

Except for a two-year period the current account of the balance of payments has been negative. This is because of the traditional negative balance on services, which has grown over the sixties. While in the early sixties the service deficit amounted to about 400 million dollars, it had risen to more than 500 million dollars in the late sixties. Much of Brazil's service payments consist of transport charges, interest on foreign debt, and remittance of profits by foreign firms. Transport payments have remained at an average of about 125 million dollars throughout the sixties, while interest payments and profit remittance have risen from an average of about 190 million dollars in the early sixties to about 300 million dollars in the late sixties. Brazil is making an effort to build up its merchant marine, increasing the proportion of its exports and imports transported in domestic ships and thus reducing transport payments. The outflow of

24. Nathaniel H. Leff, "Import Constraints and Development: Causes of the Recent Decline of Brazilian Economic Growth," *Review of Economics and Statistics*, November 1967.

25. For rebuttal of the Leff analysis, see Joel Bergsman and Samuel A. Morley, "Import Constraints and Development: Causes of the Recent Decline of Brazilian Economic Growth: A Comment," *Review of Economics and Statistics*, February 1969.

TABLE 7

a. QUANTUM AND VALUE OF BRAZIL'S EXPORTS AND IMPORTS
(1953 = 100)

	Exports				Imports	
	Quantum	Quantum (excluding coffee)	Value	Value (excluding coffee)	Quantum	Value
1957	100	124	90	121	145	113
1958	96	135	81	123	145	103
1959	117	140	83	122	160	104
1960	118	150	82	123	161	111
1961	128	183	91	154	151	111
1962	118	158	79	127	140	112
1963	130	155	91	146	146	113
1964	116	168	93	149	122	96
1965	116	194	104	197	101	83
1966	132	200	113	217	131	113
1967	116	155	107	211	145	126
1968	131	181	126	249	178	162

Source: Conjuntura Econômica

b. BRAZIL'S EXPORT AND IMPORT COMMODITY STRUCTURE
(percentage distribution)

	1950	1960	1965	1967	1968	1969
Exports						
Live Animals						0.1
Raw Materials	23.9	23.6	30.5	28.3	28.0	32.1
Food and Drink	75.0	73.7	61.8	62.4	64.4	59.1
Chemicals & Pharmaceuticals		1.1	1.0	1.7	1.4	1.4
Machines & Transport Materials & Parts	1.1	0.1	1.8	2.6	2.2	2.6
Manufactures		0.5	4.1	4.3	3.4	3.5
Miscellaneous		1.0	0.8	0.7	0.6	1.2
Total	100.0	100.0	100.0	100.0	100.0	100.0
Imports						
Live Animals	0.8		0.1	0.2	0.1	1.5
Raw Materials	28.7	27.6	24.8	19.4	19.7	16.8
Food & Drink	17.1	13.6	19.4	19.6	15.7	13.3
Chemicals & Pharmaceuticals		9.5	15.9	13.8	15.2	14.9
Machines, Transportation Materials & Parts		35.6	22.3	28.5	31.0	33.1
Manufactures	53.4	13.5	17.1	17.7	18.1	20.0
Miscellaneous		0.2	0.4	0.8	0.3	0.4
Total	100.0	100.0	100.0	100.0	100.0	100.0

Source: Anúario Estatístico

TABLE 8

BRAZIL'S BALANCE OF PAYMENTS—1958-68

(in millions of U.S. Dollars)

	1958	1959	1960	1961	1962	1963	1964	1965	1966	1967	1968
Exports (FOB)	1,243	1,282	1,269	1,403	1,214	1,406	1,430	1,596	1,741	1,654	1,881
Imports (FOB)	-1,179	-1,210	-1,203	-1,292	-1,304	-1,294	-1,086	-941	-1,303	-1,441	-1,855
Trade Balance	64	72	-24	111	-90	112	344	655	438	213	26
Current Account Balance	-262	-335	-494	-276	-491	-214	26	208	-112	-354	-525
Net Autonomous Capital Movements	230	248	176	327	244	3	140	79	205	63	498
(Private Direct Investments)	(110)	(124)	(99)	(108)	(9)	(30)	(28)	(70)	(74)	(76)	(61)
(Private Loans)	(223)	(291)	(217)	(346)	(194)	(101)	(61)	(113)	(180)	(304)	(307)
(Official Loans)	(250)	(148)	(130)	(233)	(131)	(149)	(160)	(250)	(328)	(226)	(246)
(Amortization)	(-324)	(-377)	(-410)	(-327)	(-310)	(-364)	(-277)	(-304)	(-350)	(-444)	(-484)
Errors and Omissions	-189	-25	26	49	-138	-76	-217	-31	-19	-31	37
Commercial Arrears				-68	163	4	17	-182	-44	-8	
Compensatory Financing	253	154	430	-47	183	230	-61	-149	-109	253	-32

Source: Boletim, Banco Central, various issues.

interest payments, however, is likely to remain a burden for many years, since the total foreign debt stood at about four billion dollars in 1969 and, given the extensive direct foreign investments (which have often grown in the last few years with a large amount of retained earnings and local borrowing), one should expect profit remittances to grow in the seventies.

Total autonomous capital movement declined substantially in the crisis of the mid-sixties and only in 1968 surpassed levels attained in the late fifties or early sixties. It is interesting to note the drastic decline of private direct investment, which never again rose to the levels of the fifties throughout the decade of the sixties. This slackening of foreign investment resulted partly from a lack of confidence in the political stability of the country. As the sixties progressed, a further aggravating factor was the sluggishness of the Brazilian economy itself. Many of the manufacturing firms established in Brazil in the fifties which expanded their facilities in the sixties relied to a large extent on retained earnings and locally borrowed funds for such expansion.

Official and private loans declined substantially from the early to the mid-sixties, but rose again to levels higher than ever before in the late sixties. Noteworthy also is the rise in amortization payments which absorbed a large proportion of these loans. Considering that Brazil's total foreign debt was about four billion dollars in the late sixties, it is to be expected that in the seventies a large proportion of Brazil's foreign-exchange receipts will be spent on foreign debt servicing.

The data we have presented should clarify the puzzle of substantially higher resources which were placed at the disposal of the Brazilian government by USAID, the IBRD, and other international organs after the change of regime in 1964, which occurred at a time of relative stagnation. Much of the new foreign credit was used to "clean up" the old short-term foreign debt position of the country and did not represent capital used to start massive investments in new sectors, which would have had a cumulative impact on the internal rate of economic activity.[26]

An interesting new policy measure was introduced in 1968. The government instituted what it called a "flexible exchange rate." Before this, the Brazilian government limited its devaluation of the cruzeiro to once or, at most, twice a year. Given the inflation rates, it was obvious that after a certain period of time a devaluation would have to take place, and before such devaluations, substantial speculations against the cruzeiro would occur—exporters tending to keep their money abroad or delay payments, while importers tended to purchase their foreign exchange as fast as possible. Under the new system, changes in the value of the cruzeiro take place at short intervals, but erratically. Theoretically the value could go in both directions, but it is always downward. Given this uncertainty, there is less speculation against the cruzeiro and the exchange rate is kept more in line with the internal rate of inflation; thus exports will not be discouraged and there will be less temptation for speculative import buying. Finally, more frequent devaluations would make the devaluation itself less of a political issue than when it came up only once a year.

Two Opposing Views on Economic Trends in the Sixties.

Although it is generally conceded that in the sixties the Brazilian economy had lost the dynamism of the previous decade, there are two schools of thought about the causes and long-run implica-

---

26. For an interesting analysis of international aid to Brazil in the sixties, see Carlos F. Diaz-Alejandro, "Some Aspects of the Brazilian Experience with Foreign Aid," in *Trade, Balance of Payments, and Growth*, ed. by J. N. Bhagwati et al. (Amsterdam: North Holland Publishing Company, 1971), pp. 443-472. Some of the foreign assistance in the sixties did, of course, help to finance projects such as road-building, the continuation of hydroelectric projects, the building of a new fertilizer plant, etc. But, given the size of the country, none of these projects had a strong enough impact to affect significantly the general level of economic activity.

tion of this loss of dynamism.[27] Let us examine the arguments of each school and the evidence available to support their claims.

The Short-Run School

Writers in this school of thought[28] view the sluggish performance of the economy in the sixties as resulting in part from the political situation in the first half of the decade. The continuation of the economy's stagnation in the middle sixties is attributed to the stabilization policies. The events described above that followed the resignation of Quadros in 1961 created an unfavorable climate for both Brazilian and foreign investors. Political instability and the indecisiveness of the Goulart regime also caused rates of inflation to attain levels counterproductive to growth. These factors explain the decline in the period 1962-64. With the change of regime, the first order of the day was to bring down the rate of growth of the price level. This, as we already explained above, also necessitated the elimination of distortions in prices and resource allocation which had occurred previously. Measures taken to this effect explain the low rate of growth, especially in industry.

The high rates of growth experienced since 1968 are cautiously pointed to by these writers as an indication that the stabilization policies of the sixties are beginning to pay off. The lower rates of inflation, the continued efforts of the government to eradicate budgetary deficits and eliminate price distortions, and the development of incentive systems to invest savings in less favored parts of the economy, in export promotion, and in a modernized financial system have restored confidence in the Brazilian economy to both Brazilian and foreign investors. It is expected that both the private sector's investment activities and the impact of public infrastructure investment activities should lead to a decade of steady and balanced growth in the seventies.

Implicit in the rationalizations of this school of thought is the idea that what happened throughout most of the sixties was inevitable. The industrialization of the fifties was too fast, unplanned, and

27. This dichotomy in viewing the Brazilian stagnation of the sixties was first suggested in a paper by Werner Baer and Andrea Maneschi. See footnote 13 above.
28. Included among the Short-Run School are economists such as Mario H. Simonsen, *op cit.*; and Alexandre Kafka, "The Brazilian Stabilization Program, 1964-66," *The Journal of Political Economy*, August 1967, Supplement—"Issues in Monetary Research."

one-sided to have sustained itself without some readjustments. Thus, the remedial actions of the sixties were really inevitable—a price structure had to be re-established which would indicate relative scarcities; the government had to find noninflationary ways to finance its operations, since the economy had outgrown the capacity to make use of an inflationary mechanism to reallocate resources; a modern financial market had to be established to collect savings for future investment; and through a system of market incentives and tax incentives a way had to be found to diversify exports in order to prevent future import bottlenecks and to counteract the regional disequilibrium which the industrialization of the past had produced.

The Stagnationist School

Like the short-run school, the stagnationists[29] view the slowdown of the sixties as a natural consequence of the ISI industrialization of the fifties. They differ, however, as to the causes of the slowdown and the remedies. Let us examine their arguments systematically.

The process of ISI in the fifties consisted of establishing within Brazil industries which could produce products previously imported. The market for the products already existed, and thus through a series of protective measures, incentives, and subsidies, both domestic and foreign capital were encouraged to build ISI industries. This investment activity accounts for the high growth rates of the fifties. These rates were reinforced through the policies of the Brazilian government to encourage the vertical integration of the newly emerging industrial structure—the building not only of consumer-goods industries, but also capital-goods industries. Implicit was the hope that the implantation of ISI industries would create enough additional in-

29. Representatives of the stagnationist school include Celso Furtado, *Subdesenvolvimento e estagnação na American Latina* (Rio de Janeiro: Editora Civilzação Brasileira 1967). especially Chapter 3; Celso Furtado and Andrea Maneschi, "Um modêlo de simulção de desenvolvimento e estagnação na America Latina," *Revista Brasileira de Economia,* June 1968; Maria da Conceição Tavares, "O processo de substituição de importação como modêlo de desenvolvimento recente na America Latina," and "Auge y declínio del proceso de sustitucion de importaciones en Brasil," *Boletín Econômico de America Latina,* Vol. IX, No. 1 (March 1964); Francisco Lopes, "Subsidios e formulação de um modêlo de desenvolvimento e estagnação no Brasil," *Revista Brasileira de Economia,* June 1969. A more eclectic view of the stagnation problem is contained in Albert O. Hirschman, "The Political Economy of Import-Substitution Industrialization in Latin America," *The Quarterly Journal of Economics,* February 1968. See also the stagnationist model in Baer and Maneschi, *op. cit.*

come, so that when the ISI process would come to an end, that is, when the import/total supply ratio in most industries would have fallen to extremely low levels, enough new incomes would have been generated to continue the process of industrial growth.

This did not come to pass. The technology of the new industries —their high capital/labor ratios—resulted in absorption of a relatively small proportion of the labor force, and a relatively large proportion of the increment in the national income created by ISI went to the nonlabor sector. In other words, the technology of ISI resulted in a greater concentration of Brazil's distribution of income and thus prevented the creation of large new incremental demands for industrial products.[30] Thus, in the sixties, Brazil emerged with a much larger productive capacity than effective demand for that capacity. These trends could have been overcome had the government redistributed incomes between income groups, between regions, and/or between different sectors of the economy. This was not done. Little effort was made to modernize agriculture and increase wages of the agricultural workers. Little redistribution of income among income groups was accomplished through the tax mechanism. And the type of regional income redistribution attempted in the early and mid-sixties did not have much of an impact on aggregate demand.

To sum up, the stagnationists also claim that the exclusive emphasis on ISI in the fifties produced distortions. They are less concerned with the distortions which occurred in the price mechanism, however, than in the neglect of other sectors of the economy and the resulting distributional distortions. The need for investment and reform in agriculture, in less favored regions of Brazil, in education, are all seen as necessary both to maintain social peace and to provide the basis of satisfactory growth rates in the seventies. Policies fol-

---

30. The low rate of labor absorption in industry (approximately 2.5 percent per year) that resulted from the capital intensity of new industries has been blamed by many writers on distortion in the factor remuneration structure, i.e. artificially high wages and low price of capital. Thus, had wages been lower and had there been less subsidization of capital (used to attract it in the first place), more labor-intensive techniques would have been used. In the light of the Brazilian experience this is a questionable hypothesis. In some industries, such as steel, there was little choice of technology. In the automobile industry, the fact that second-hand equipment, less automated than in Detroit or Wolfsburg, was imported would also indicate that a relatively labor-intensive technique was chosen. The well-known ECLA studies of Latin America's textile industry show that production techniques are so old fashioned (and labor intensive) that productivity is extremely low and only some modernization of the production process can save the industry in the long run.

lowed by the regime in the mid and late sixties are seen only as half-way measures. Doing away with distortions in the price mechanism, slowing down inflation rates, modernizing the capital market all work on the supply side. The basic problem of the stagnation in the sixties, however, cannot be solved without parallel measures on the demand side.

The stagnationists are critical of the policy of incentives which the regimes since 1964 have followed. Tax incentives to invest in the Northeast and the Amazon region have led to substantial investments in only two urban centers (Recife and Salvador) where industries are being built which absorb little labor. They have duplicated already under-utilized capacity in the country's Center-South. Also, the new Northeast industries might find themselves in trouble since little has been done in that region to redistribute incomes in the urban and rural centers and thus create a market for the newly built capacity. It is claimed that through these incentives the situation of the fifties for the entire country is being recreated for the Northeast—a regional import-substitution boom which is not producing its long-term raison d'être. Incentives for investing in the stock market, for exporting, etc., are also not thought of as meeting the main problem as seen through stagnationist eyes.

Evaluation of Arguments

Let us examine how well the arguments of both sides are supported by the evidence available. Table 9a indicates that the ISI Process had been rather thoroughly exploited by the sixties. The total ratio of imported goods to total supply stood at 16 percent in 1949. By the mid-fifties a large part of the import-substitution process had already occurred in the consumer-goods industries and by the mid-sixties the ratio for capital goods and intermediate goods had also been brought down to low levels. The fields of activity still largely open to ISI are machinery, chemicals, and specialized transport and communication equipments. In the mid-sixties some investment was being promoted in fertilizer plants and in special steels and aluminum. Thus, some efforts were still being made to lower the ratio still further. It is apparent, however, that the large opportunities for ISI had been made use of by the sixties and thus the country had to look elsewhere for further industrial growth. Part of Table 9b presents more recent estimates of imports and exports as a proportion of total supply of goods and services. This evidence also indicates that

TABLE 9

a. IMPORTS AS A PERCENT OF TOTAL SUPPLY

	1955	1960	1962	1965	1966
Capital Goods	43.2	23.4	12.9	8.2	13.7
Intermediate Goods	17.9	11.9	8.9	6.3	6.8
Durable Consumer Goods	10.0	3.3	2.4	1.6	1.0
Nondurable Consumer Goods	2.2	1.2	1.1	1.2	1.6
Total	11.1	8.1	6.8	3.9	5.0

Source: "A Industrialização Brasileira: Diagnóstico e Perspectivas," Estudo Especial, Programa Estratégico de Desenvolvimento 1968-1970, Ministério do Planejamento e Coordenação Geral, January 1969.

b. IMPORTS AND EXPORTS OF GOODS AND SERVICES AS PERCENTAGE
OF TOTAL SUPPLY OF GOODS AND SERVICES[1]

	Imports	Exports
1957	6.6	5.5
1958	5.8	4.8
1959	6.6	5.2
1960	6.8	4.9
1961	5.8	4.9
1962	5.4	4.0
1963	5.1	4.5
1964	4.4	4.5
1965	4.4	4.9
1966	5.0	4.9
1967	5.3	4.4
1968	5.7	4.4

Source: Calculated from data in Conjuntura Econômica, Vol. 24, No. 6, 1970.
    1. In constant 1953 prices.
Imports: including net income from abroad. Exports: capacity to import.

the import coefficient is hard to drive below the 5 percent level.

Critics of Brazil's industrialization policies have often objected to the very use of the import/total supply ratio as an indicator of how much growth based on ISI is possible. They claim that this represents a complete disregard to current or potential comparative advantage and an utter lack in selectivity as to which sectors merit being promoted. These critics have had the ear of the Brazilian policy-makers in the later sixties, since in March 1967 tariffs were generally reduced. Goods which fell into a special exchange category lost this privilege and the range of tariff protecting them fell from 180 to 220 percent to a range of 60 to 100 percent, while the tariff on other goods was reduced to about 20 percent.[31] The general idea was to increase the efficiency of Brazil's industry through threatened or actual competition. After some industries were beginning to feel this competition, some protectionist measures were again restored, although the general tariff level was left at the new lower levels.

The policy of greater selectivity raises a number of questions. How would policy makers predict where Brazil would have its greatest comparative advantage? Also, selectivity means greater possibilities for exporting manufactured products. Given the past attitudes of more industrialized countries, however, the possibilities of their importing large amounts of manufactured products from such countries as Brazil seemed until recently doubtful. Thus, greater selectivity was not necessarily a road open to Brazil. The question of lessening tariff barriers in order to increase the efficiency of Brazil's industries also raises some questions. Is it wise to do this at the time of a stabilization program, when industrial production is already being hard hit? Also, given the small market, Brazilian industries have little opportunity to benefit from scale economies. Thus, having to share a small market with importers raises their fixed cost per unit and thus not necessarily solves the problem of efficiency. If lower tariffs only are meant as a threat to local industry, forcing them to rationalize their production, then they would make some sense. If high costs of Brazilian industry result in large measure from the lack of scale economies, it could also be argued that redistributive policies, by widening the market, increase the scale of production and thus increase the possibility of lower cost. Finally, many industries were created in the late fifties, and besides the problems of scale they had to go through a certain period in which factors would "learn by doing," gradually. It is still an open question whether one decade is enough for "infants" to grow up, considering the long gestation period of nineteenth-century industries in Germany and the United States.

The evidence available would seem to confirm the stagnationists' claim of a trend toward a concentration in the distribution of income. Table 10 indicates a pronounced decline in the ratio of wages to value added in manufacturing industry from the fifties to the midsixties. This suggests the changing technology in industry—the

31. For a more detailed discussion of changing Brazilian tariff policies see Joel Bergsman, *Brazil's Industrialization and Trade Policies* (New York: Oxford University Press, 1970), Chapter 3.

growth of industries with higher capital/labor ratios in the fifties relative to the capital/labor ratios prevailing in the immediate post-war period. In the mid-sixties the decline of this ratio also reflects the decline of real wages resulting from the government's stabilization policies. In the second part of Table 10, however, it should be noted that the decline in real wages in industry only began after 1963, thus the ratio of wages/value added in industry reflects to a large extent the technology used. Both the figures on wages per worker in manufacturing and the real value of minimum wages leave no doubt that the real income of workers decreased throughout the whole stabilization period. Although the former had risen again by 1968, it was still below real wages in 1965 and the real minimum wage presented in the table show that it was still substantially below the 1964 level in 1969. The last part of Table 10 gives another piece of evidence on trends in the concentration of income. For the industry groups shown and for manufacturing as a whole the rate of growth of productivity was substantially ahead of the growth of real wages in both the second half of the fifties and in most of the sixties.

All evidence also suggests that Brazil faced a substantial amount of capacity underutilization in the sixties. The evidence presented in Table 11 shows substantial excess capacity in the consumer-goods sector and even greater excess capacity in the capital-goods sector.[32] Of course, some of this excess capacity probably results from the lumpiness of many sectors, especially in capital goods industries, which often make it necessary to substantially build ahead of demand. To the extent that this is true, further growth of industrial capacity possibly would require substantially smaller capital expenditures relative to newly desired output. In other words, the existence of excess capacity resulting from the lumpiness of investment might make future investments appear more productive, that is, the marginal output/capital ratio would be substantially higher. In part of Table 11b, for example, it will be noted that the rolling-mill excess capacity is much larger than pig-iron or steel-ingot excess capacity. This means that investment in the latter will substantially increase the capacity for producing final steel products without placing much investment in the rolling mills. Thus, the output/capital ratio of new

32. For an interesting study of excess capacity in Brazil's industrial sector during the sixties, see Ruy Leme, "Capacidade ociosa da industrial Brasileira," *Indústria e Produtividade*, April 1969.

TABLE 10
a. BRAZIL: RATIO OF WAGES TO VALUE ADDED IN MANUFACTURING

1949	29%	1963	26%
1957	32%	1964	25%
1959	27%	1965	23%
1962	28%	1966	24%
		1967	26%

Source: Calculated from IBGE, *Industrial Census; Inqueritos Econômicos.*

b. ANNUAL WAGES BILL PER WORKER IN MANUFACTURING INDUSTRY

(In thousands of 1966 Cruzeiros)

1949	1144	1963	2120
1955	1477	1964	2052
1956	1590	1965	1919
1957	1708	1966	2048
1958	1721	1967	2001
1959	1631	1868	1873
1962	1883		

Source: Same as part (a) above.

c. REAL MINIMUM WAGES IN SÃO PAULO AND RIO DE JANEIRO
(in 1953 prices)

(Monthly wages—NCr$)

	São Paulo	Rio de Janeiro
1958	1.56	1.56
1959	1.17	1.72
1960	1.54	1.58
1961	1.71	1.81
1962	1.43	1.52
1963	1.31	1.39
1964	1.33	1.38
1965	1.32	1.34
1966	1.14	1.20
1967	1.12	1.17
1968	1.09	1.16
1969	1.13	1.13

Source: Calculated from IBGE, *Anúario Estatístico;* and *Conjuntura Econômica.*

TABLE 10 *(CONTINUED)*

d. WORKER PRODUCTIVITY AND REAL WAGE INCREASES IN THE
MANUFACTURING SECTOR
(1955 = 100)

Industry Groups	1956		1958		1962		1963		1964		1965		1966	
	W	P	W	P	W	P	W	P	W	P	W	P	W	P
Group I	110	99	112	125	107	148	117	146	115	152	110	147	100	145
Group II	105	115	109	123	107	152	131	152	131	158	124	158	109	157
Group III	104	117	110	161	111	221	142	216	131	207	125	206	106	231
TOTAL	108	107	113	132	112	173	131	170	129	175	123	173	119	178

Group I: Wood Products, Furniture, Leather Products, Textile Products, Food & Drink, Tobacco, Printing & Publishing.
Group II: Non-Metallic Minerals, Paper Products, Rubber Products, Chemical Products, Metal Products.
Group III: Transport Products, Electrical & Communication Products, Mechanical Products.
W = Real Wages
P = Productivity per worker

Source: Ministerio Do Planejamento e Coordenação Geral, *Programa Estratégico de Desenvolvimento 1969-1970*, Estudo Especial, "A Industrialização Brasileira: Diagnóstico e Perspectivas," Rio de Janeiro, January 1969, p. 146.

steel investment is likely to be much larger in the seventies than in the sixties.[33]

The existence of excess capacity, and of future higher output/ capital ratios in many industries, show up forcefully the necessity for substantial growth in demand. The evidence on income distribution noted above would indicate, however, that the trends observed in the fifties and sixties do not augur well for a substantial demand increase, unless these trends were to be reversed by measures of income redistribution of one kind or another.

Table 12, which contains yearly growth rates of individual industry groups until 1969, shows very low rates of growth for industries catering to mass markets in Brazil—textiles, clothing, leather products, food products. This is especially clear in the doldrums of the sixties, when, for example, in a short recovery period such as 1966 these industries did not rebound as did the transport or pharma-

33. Some of the idle capacity in the mid-sixties was also caused by the shortage of working capital which forced more firms to reduce operations.

TABLE 11
a. CAPACITY UTILIZATION IN SELECTED INDUSTRIES
(Production as a proportion of capacity, 1965)

Mechanical Machinery & Equipment	68% (1 shift)
Electrical Machinery & Equipment	70% (1 shift)
Naval Construction	64% (1 shift) 39% (2 shifts)
Road Equipment	46% (1 shift)
Vehicles	61% (1 shift)
Household Consumer Durables	62% (1 shift)
Total Capital Goods	53% (1 shift)
Total Consumer Goods	65% (1 shift)

Source: Based on unpublished reports of IPEA, BNDE, and Booz, Allen, Hamilton studies for BNDE.

b. CAPACITY UTILIZATION IN THE STEEL INDUSTRY
(Output as a proportion of 1965 capacity)[1]

	1964	1965	1966
Pig iron	54%	50%	65%
Steel Ingot	60%	59%	74%
Flat Products Rolling Mills	15%	17%	23%
Non-Flat Rolling Mills	43%	38%	47%

Source: Werner Baer, The Development of the Brazilian Steel Industry, Nashville, Tennessee: Vanderbilt University Press, 1969.

c. CAPACITY UTILIZATION IN PRODUCT LINES OF BRAZIL'S HEAVY
ENGINEERING INDUSTRY - 1960
(estimated demand as % of capacity)

Pressure Vessels, Cyclones, Large Diameter Tubes	43%
Steam Generators, Direct-Fired (upright) Furnaces	26%
Metal Structures & Direct-Fired (horizontal) Furnaces	21%
Electrical Turbines	20%
Electrical Generators	48%
Step-up Transformers	21%

Source: Nathaniel H. Leff, The Brazilian Capital Goods Industry, Cambridge, Mass.: Harvard University Press, 1968.

1. Only 1965 estimates of capacity were available.

ceutical/chemical sectors. Given the long-term trends in Brazil's distribution of income and the falling of the absolute real-wage levels of the working classes in the sixties, it is not surprising that industries catering to those classes (just looking at the weight of the consumer price index, we find that almost 54 percent of the worker's wage is spent on food and clothing) experienced the lower growth rates.

Given the lack of disaggregative information at this writing on the high growth rate which the Brazilian economy experienced after 1968, we can only use some partial evidence to evaluate the meaning of these trends at the end of the decade. Do they mean that the economy was getting back on a new long-term high-growth path and thus vindicating the short-run school of thought, or was this a temporary phenomenon?

From preliminary information, the high growth rate of the industrial sector in 1968 and 1969 was led by the automobile sector, construction, construction materials, and steel. The rate of growth of passenger vehicle production from 1967 to 1968 was more than 22 percent. Growth of construction in 1968 was reflected by a 15 percent growth rate in the average monthly cement production over 1967. Ingot steel production in the same period grew by more than 20 percent, which is probably a response to increased construction activity, automobile production, and government investment programs in such areas as hydroelectric projects and road construction.

The boom in automobile production is mainly attributed to the rise of *consorcios*. This is an ingenious device invented in the sixties to create credit for buying cars. Under a typical scheme, a group of, say, twenty-four people get together to buy a Volkswagen. Each member of the *consorcio* agrees to pay every month 1/24th of a price of a Volkswagen into a kitty and every month one Volkswagen is bought. Payments are readjustable for inflationary rates. Thus, each month one member gets a Volkswagen, but everyone continues to pay for twenty-four months, until everyone has received his Volkswagen. This has enabled the sale of many models of cars to rise in Brazil. And the rise of automobile production has certainly increased the production of steel and also affected other sectors. The doubt which can be raised about this source of growth is whether the resulting opportunity cost of the economy is not too great. People buying cars will forego the buying of many other goods, often foregoing rent payments or defaulting on other debts, and many will forego saving. Thus, one could question the *consorcio* as a basis of growth. It uses purchasing power to increase automobile production at the cost of the production of other goods and at the cost of saving and thus the building of new productive capacity in the economy.

As we stated previously, the rise in the rate of construction ac-

TABLE 12
a. RATES OF GROWTH OF BRAZIL'S INDUSTRY

	1949	1953	1955-64	1957	1958	1959	1960	1961	1962	1963	1964	1965	1966	1967	1968	1969
Nonmetallic Minerals	9.8	20.3	4.9	-0.4	2.2	2.5	14.5	6.8	4.0	-0.1	5.8	-9.5	8.9	8.6	12.8	5.9
Metal Products	19.2	14.2	10.4	-7.8	19.6	18.1	11.3	9.3	20.4	3.4	6.1	-3.8	23.5	-2.5	8.7	14.4
Mechanical Products			10.5	-4.1	8.1	13.2	27.4	24.2	10.7	2.6	1.4	-12.0	1.7	-5.3	33.0	8.5
Electric Machines and Equipment			20.7	-1.9	67.6	13.2	47.3	24.2	10.7	-3.8	9.4	10.6	25.4	9.6	23.6	5.4
Transport Equipment			25.1	121.1	46.0	35.7	28.4	-0.4	28.9	-10.7	3.4	-0.7	23.9	0.2	26.8	34.5
Wood Products			8.1	-2.1	7.4	7.6	11.6	11.1	18.3	2.5	2.9	-20.9	-8.6	2.1		
Paper Products	15.9	11.2	7.6	-4.7	14.9	5.6	7.8	5.8	11.6	7.8	6.5	-2.3	9.7	15.9	14.6	3.5
Rubber and Products	13.9	11.7	8.9	2.9	15.0	20.0	22.4	4.8	16.1	0.9	6.6	-5.9	27.0	8.2	10.3	5.9
Leather and Products	2.6	6.1	2.1	3.2	10.3	-1.3	-6.4	1.7	-0.6	-7.2	10.0	29.7	-16.0	9.0		
Chemical and Pharmaceutical Products	8.3	19.2	14.4	1.9	16.6	7.5	15.5	21.3	23.2	3.6	9.9	-3.7	15.4	3.4	13.3	11.6
Textiles	7.0	5.2	3.5	-12.0	17.9	7.3	3.9	11.3	4.3	-2.7	4.4	-16.1	-4.8	-1.9	19.3	2.5
Clothing, Shoes			1.4	1.0	21.8					0.8	12.1	-10.9	14.0	-5.7	19.6	-25.6
Food Products	13.8	6.4	5.0	21.7	9.7	9.7	5.6	7.0	5.6	-0.8	1.4	-4.8	4.8	7.3	-4.6	13.8
Beverages	2.0	3.9	0.5	7.4	8.9	0.0	-0.6	16.2	-2.6	2.0	-10.5	8.6	20.1	-12.4	3.7	19.1
Tobacco	15.6	4.1	2.5	-1.4	2.7	7.0	2.8	11.2	9.6	0.5	-1.3	-4.7	2.5	9.6	12.9	7.3
Printing & Publishing	-1.9	2.0	26.6		-8.2											
Miscellaneous				-8.7	-0.8											
TOTAL MANUFACTURING	11.0	9.3	8.3	5.6	16.7	12.8	10.6	11.1	8.2	-0.3	5.1	-4.7	12.3	2.4	13.2	10.8
Mineral Extraction	0.9	7.9	12.3	3.4	18.1	25.2	17.4	5.9	1.5	18.4	12.0	21.4	7.7	5.6	16.2	
Construction	6.5	6.7	4.4	4.0	14.9	-1.0	-4.0	9.8	0.6	1.3	2.3	-24.0	6.0	9.3	16.2	7.3

Source: Instituto Brasileiro de Economia, Fundação Getúlio Vargas.

TABLE 12-(CONTINUED)

b. CHANGES IN THE STRUCTURE OF BRAZIL'S MANUFACTURING INDUSTRY(Proportion of Value Added)

	1949	1952	1953	1954	1955	1956	1957	1958	1959	1962	1963	1964	1966	1967
Nonmetallic Minerals	7.4	8.9	7.4	8.0	6.0	6.1	6.9	6.7	6.7	5.0	5.2	5.0	5.0	5.6
Metal Products	9.4	10.8	9.6	9.9	10.5	11.7	11.1	11.5	11.9	12.4	12.0	11.4	11.6	11.1
Mechanical Products	2.2	2.3	2.4	2.6	2.7	2.9	2.8	3.0	3.5	3.2	3.2	3.3	4.3	5.2
Electric Machinery	1.7	2.4	3.0	3.4	3.8	3.9	4.1	4.3	3.9	5.5	6.1	6.4	5.5	6.2
Transport Equipment	2.3	4.1	2.0	2.3	2.9	2.9	5.2	7.0	7.6	10.2	10.5	10.5	8.1	8.0
Wood Products	6.1	6.0	6.6	6.0	6.3	5.9	5.5	5.4	5.5	4.5	4.0	3.8	4.0	3.8
Paper Products	2.1	2.3	2.7	3.0	2.8	2.4	2.2	2.4	3.1	2.9	2.9	2.5	2.0	3.3
Rubber & Products	2.0	2.2	2.2	2.0	2.5	2.1	2.4	1.9	2.3	2.0	1.9	2.2	2.4	2.0
Leather & Products	1.3	1.4	1.3	1.4	1.2	1.2	1.2	1.2	1.1	1.0	0.7	0.8	0.7	0.8
Chemical and Pharm. Products	9.4	10.3	11.0	12.3	12.3	12.1	13.2	13.1	13.4	14.0	15.5	17.3	20.0	18.8
Textiles	20.1	16.2	17.6	18.4	17.2	16.8	14.1	13.4	12.0	13.8	11.6	11.7	10.5	9.7
Clothing, shoes	4.3	4.6	4.9	4.2	4.4	4.4	4.3	4.0	3.6	3.4	3.6	3.1	3.1	3.0
Food Products	19.7	17.0	17.6	16.1	16.7	17.5	16.5	15.8	16.6	13.3	14.1	14.6	14.3	13.4
Beverages	4.3	3.4	3.5	3.6	3.5	3.0	2.9	2.8	2.9	2.6	3.2	2.7	2.4	2.4
Tobacco	1.6	1.8	2.3	1.6	1.5	1.6	1.8	1.6	1.3	1.9	1.6	1.4	1.4	1.7
Printing & Publishing	4.2	3.7	3.5	2.8	3.4	3.1	3.4	3.3	3.0	2.5	2.5	2.1	2.6	3.0
Miscellaneous	1.9	2.6	2.4	2.4	2.3	2.4	2.4	2.6	1.6	1.8	1.4	1.2	2.1	2.0
TOTAL MANUFACTURING	100.0	100.0	100.0	100.0	100.0	100.0	100.0	100.0	100.0	100.0	100.0	100.0	100.0	100.0

Source: Same as Part a

141

tivity in the late sixties was largely a result of the functioning of the National Housing Bank, which could operate with financial instruments readjustable to the rate of inflation. This channeled substantial amounts of credits into that sector. Construction is a labor-intensive industry, which could become a long-term source of growth in Brazil, given the country's huge housing deficit. It remains to be seen, however, to what extent low-income families can incur a debt which will not diminish in weight until it is paid.

Is the Brazilian Economy in a Structural Lock?

The latter development is related to an important question Georgescu-Roegen has asked in recent years in connection with Latin American inflations.[34] The industrial structures built up in Latin American countries through ISI reflected the demand profiles existing in these economies at the time. Suppose that after a decade or two of ISI, governments decide to undertake measures which redistribute incomes—either for the sake of equity or for reasons of demand creation. It is then entirely possible that the new demand profile created by the new distribution of income does not synchronize with the industrial structure. In Georgescu-Roegen's original reasoning, the inflations of Latin America have partially acted to redistribute income to the rich and thus once again resynchronize the demand and the production capacity profile. Within this same spirit, it could be argued that the *consorcios* are redistributing the expenditure structure of the economy, so that idle capacity in the automobile industry will not develop.

Georgescu-Roegen reasons that once a heavy commitment has been made in a certain industrial structure, it is very hard, if not impossible, for the economy to retrace its steps. The vast amounts of capital sunk into a certain structure will determine or at least limit the choices of future growth paths.

Although many assumptions behind Georgescu-Roegen's theory

34. Nicholas Georgescu-Roegen first raised this question in an article published in Brazil, "Inflação Estrutural e o Crescimento Economico," *Revista Brasileira de Economia*, March 1968; since then he has written an expanded version in English, "Structural Inflation-Lock and Balanced Growth," *Economies et Sociétés*, Cahier de l'I.S.E.A., Tome IV, No. 3, Librairie Droz, Geneve, March 1970. An interesting model of growth and stagnation based on Georgescu-Roegen's original idea is contained in Francisco Lopes, "Subsidios a formulação de um modêlo de desenvolvimento e estagnação no Brasil," *Revista Brasileira de Economia*, June 1969.

are open to question, they certainly deserve to be tested. How rigid are the industrial structures which were built in the past? How much could they be adapted to new demand profiles? If there is rigidity, should the development path be fashioned so as to occupy fully existing capacity, or is the opportunity cost involved in having idle capacity worth the returns involved in the development of entirely new sectors? These are important questions for Brazil and other developing countries as they face the post-ISI phase.

Brazil might also find itself in another type of structural dilemma because of its continued high rate of population growth. Because of this growth, government expenditures must grow rapidly, since a growing population necessitates increasing infrastructure expenditures. But the rate of expansion of the economically active population lags behind. This means that government tax receipts will lag behind government expenditure increases. The result is a growing government budget deficit and inflationary pressures. Periodic stabilization attempts will slow down the growth of the economy. Long-term growth rates, however, will also be slowed because of the changing structure of total investments. Government infrastructure investment will probably have higher marginal capital-output ratios than directly productive investment. Given a certain savings capacity of the economy and the necessity for government infrastructure investments, which means that the participation of government investment in total investment will increase, the over-all marginal capital/output ratio will rise and the growth rate obtained by total savings will decline. To make things worse, a proportionately growing, economically inactive population means that the savings ratio of the economy will decline. In sum, high population growth rates could imply lower economic growth rates since the inflationary tendencies produced will imply periodic stabilization programs accompanied by stagnation and since these population growth rates result in rising capital output ratios and declining savings ratios. Thus, Brazil in the seventies might not be able to continue to ignore the implications of high rates of population growth in making its future development plans.

Outlook for the Seventies

The decade of the seventies opened for Brazil after two years of high rates of growth. What are the possibilities for maintaining such rates?

We have estimated that maintaining the average savings ratio of the sixties, the real annual growth rate of the Gross Domestic Product in the seventies could reach 5.6 percent.[35] If, however, the savings ratio were to increase to 18.5 percent with a capital/output ratio of 3 (slightly higher than in the sixties), a 6.2 percent real growth rate per annum could be obtained. This assumes that savings of the private sector could be increased through various types of incentives from 13 to 15 percent and that government savings could reach 3.5 percent. Thus, according to the savings constraint analysis, the growth experience of 1970-71 does not seem feasible for the seventies.

We also considered the possible constraints of foreign exchange earnings on Brazilian growth. We believe that it would be unrealistic to expect the import coefficient to fall below the 5 percent level which was reached in the sixties. If Brazil were to maintain the commodity export structure of the late sixties, total receipts from exports would rise at an annual rate of 3.9 percent. This projection is based on studies of long-term trends in world trade.[36] Our balance of payments constraint analysis showed that the required growth rate of exports would be 6.6 percent per year in order to obtain a real product growth rate of 6.2 percent. Thus, unless there is a drastic change in the structure of Brazil's exports, or an inflow of the necessary foreign savings, growth rates in the seventies would be substantially below 6.2 percent per year.

It is interesting to note that under our most favorable projection Brazil could reach a per capita income of about US$490 in 1980, 40 percent above the US$350 per capita income of 1969. It should be stressed, however, that these projections only give us a framework of aggregate feasibility. They say nothing about the composition of the GDP or the demand side of the picture. They also say nothing about possible changes of the country's demand profile and its productive capacity profile.

In his first major speech after accepting the presidency in late 1969, president Emílio Garrastazu Médici pointed to agriculture and

35. Our projections are based on a two-gap model presented in the paper mentioned in footnote 22 above.

36. It is our impression that the extremely high growth rates of exports in the late sixties result from special circumstances. They reflect partially a more realistic exchange rate adopted by the government which made it possible for the country to recapture some of the world market share lost through former unrealistic exchange policies. They also reflect an unusual expansion of world trade which hardly seem sustainable, given trends over the last two decades.

education as the priority sectors in his government's effort to modernize the economy. He also stated that it would be his aim to insure
that Brazil's masses would at last be able to participate in the fruits
of the country's industrial growth. According to the magazine *Visão*,
Médici's minister of planning, J. P. Velloso, was already drawing up
policy actions which would go a long way to meet the aims of the
president. Thus, it was reported that it would be the government's
policy to "insure the full use of the economy's capacity, while at the
same time the government will promote the expansion of the internal
market and the regional and social redistribution of income."[37]

In the early seventies, Brazil's leaders appear more preoccupied
with structural and growth problems than with stability and efficiency.
This might imply either the recognition of the validity of some of the
structuralist diagnoses or the feeling that the country has achieved as
much efficiency and stability as could be expected under the present
circumstances.

37. *Visão*, 7 November 1969, pp. 24-25.

5 WILLIAM H. NICHOLLS

The Brazilian Agricultural Economy: Recent Performance and Policy

Ah! o sertão do Brasil . . . que os que
vivem nas cidades grandes asfaltadas,
furadas de arranha-céus,
nem sequer imaginam que exista.
> —Paulo Setúbal, *Confiteor*

Brazilian Agriculture at the Threshold of the 1960s

BRAZILIAN AGRICULTURE entered the 1960s after a decade of marked expansion in its physical output. Between 1948-52 and 1958-62, crop production (including coffee) had grown by 57 percent (Table 1), almost entirely attributable to a 56-percent increase in cropland, there being virtually no over-all change in per-hectare crop yields (Table 3). During the same period, the output of livestock and livestock products[1] had also increased by 54 percent (Table 1), far above the increase of only 12 percent in total pastureland, with a modest increase in the percentage planted. With a total population increase of only 34 percent, crop and livestock output per capita had grown at average rates per annum of 1.7 and 1.5 percent, respectively, while per capita real income was growing annually at 4.5

I am indebted to my long-time Brazilian research partner, Ruy Miller Paiva, for his well-informed comments and criticisms of this paper.

1. It should be emphasized that the best available data on Brazilian agricultural output, as reported by the Ministry of Agriculture, are generally recognized as unreliable, the data on livestock numbers and production of livestock products being beclouded by even stronger doubts as to accuracy than are the crop data. (Cf. U.S. Department of Agriculture, *Brazil's Position in World Agricultural Trade*, ERS-Foreign 190, Washington, October 1967, p. 28, and Table 25, p. 108).

TABLE 1
INDEXES OF TOTAL OUTPUT OF PRINCIPAL CROPS AND ANIMAL
PRODUCTS, TOTAL LIVESTOCK NUMBERS, AND LIVESTOCK SLAUGHTER,
BRAZIL, 1948-69 [a]

(1948-52 = 100)

Crop or Animal Product	1948-52	1953-57	1958-62	1963-67	1968-69[b]
Beans	100	122	135	180	199
Corn	100	118	146	193	221
Rice	100	122	163	222	224
Wheat	100	177	128	117	203
Manioc	100	118	139	197	236
Potatoes	100	130	153	185	222
Peanuts	100	127	336	504	540
Cotton	100	102	135	159	178
Bananas	100	130	162	219	272
Oranges	100	109	137	185	225
Sugar Cane	100	129	173	219	237
Tobacco	100	126	144	202	225
Cocoa	100	127	130	133	130
Coffee	100	110	191	132	109
All 14 Crops[c]	100	118	157	182	n.a.
Milk	100	154	194	252	278
Eggs	100	152	192	248	286
Wool	100	137	138	144	157
Honey	100	103	129	136	122
4 Animal Products[c]	100	152	189	240	n.a.
No. Cattle	100	120	142	165	177
No. Swine	100	146	184	229	249
No. Sheep	100	123	131	151	167
No. Goats	100	117	132	164	175
All Herds[c]	100	125	148	174	n.a.
Cattle Slaughter	100	106	121	124	144[b]
Swine Slaughter	100	119	140	166	191[b]
Sheep Slaughter	100	117	116	148	167[b]
Goat Slaughter	100	113	122	144	147[b]
All Slaughter[c]	100	110	126	136	n.a.
All Animals and Products[c]	100	129	154	180	n.a.

a. These annual data on crop production, livestock numbers, livestock slaughter, and animal-product production are those estimated by the Serviço de Estatística da Produção (SEP) of the Ministry of Agriculture. For 1947-67, these data were summarized in *21 Anos de Evolução da Agricultura, 1947 a 1967*, Vargas Foundation (IBRE), Rio de Janeiro, janeiro 1969; to these we added the data for 1968 and 1969 (and, where later revised, the revised data for 1966 and 1967) from the percent. Despite substantial population growth and rapidly rising per capita incomes, Brazilian agriculture had responded sufficiently well to hold over-all food prices (excluding coffee) at virtually constant real prices during the 1950s (Table 4). Indeed, the expansion in crop production had been great enough to *lower* the average real prices of foods of vegetable origin (excluding coffee) by 9 percent, but, with rising incomes turning consumer preferences heavily toward meats, livestock production had lagged well behind burgeoning demand, the real prices of foods of animal origin *rising* by 27 percent during the 1950s.

While the real prices of milk and eggs had not shown marked changes, the rapid rise in the price of beef cattle was by 1958-62 signaling that the most serious lag in the livestock sector was in beef production, the still substantial but considerably lower increase in swine prices clearly indicating that swine production had made the greatest relative progress in meeting demand during the previous decade (Table 2). Of the major staple food crops, potatoes, cotton, and peanuts (major sources of vegetable oils), and sugar-cane—all having enjoyed major increases in per-hectare yields—had shown the greatest declines (15-22 percent) in real prices; beans, wheat, bananas, and oranges, and rice—all but rice having experienced some decline in crop yields—had actually shown some increase in real prices. By far the most serious rise (fully 45 percent) in real price was found in beans, other price increases being limited to only 3 to 7 percent with rice and orange prices at least being substantially below their peak prices of the mid-1950s. Thus, the principal production lags in Brazilian agriculture at the turn of the 1960s were to be found in meat (especially beef) and beans, and, to a much lesser extent, in wheat (for which high price supports had not been yet very success-

---

Anuário Estatístico do Brasil for 1969 and 1970. The data were then converted to index numbers, with the 1948-52 average taken as 100. While these production data are the best available for Brazil as a whole, they are generally considered to be very unreliable, especially the livestock data. For example, the SEP data indicated that during 1950-60 cattle numbers expanded by 40 percent and cattle slaughter by 21 percent. On the other hand, the Census enumerations of 1950 and 1960 produced cattle numbers which were respectively 16 and 29 percent lower than the SEP estimates, indicating an increase of only 19 percent in cattle numbers during 1950-60.

b. Animal slaughter data are for 1968 only.

c. Production indexes computed from the individual SEP production series (see above) by the Vargas Foundation in *21 Anos de Evolução da Agricultura.*

TABLE 2

INDEXES OF REAL PRICES OF PRINCIPAL CROPS, ANIMAL PRODUCTS, AND ANIMALS, BRAZIL, 1948-69[a]

(1948-52 = 100)

Crop or Animal Products	1948-52	1953-57	1958-62	1963-67	1968-69
Beans	100	122	145	105	102
Corn	100	103	91	74	67
Rice	100	127	103	90	86
Wheat	100	103	107	110	108
Manioc	100	92	99	78	81
Potatoes	100	93	78	77	66
Peanuts	100	93	89	95	95
Cotton	100	73	80	63	58
Bananas	100	101	104	105	103
Oranges	100	124	103	103	117
Sugar Cane	100	96	85	100	102
Tobacco	100	90	100	80	93
Cocoa	100	124	107	93	172
Coffee[b]	100	106	77	79	88
All 14 Crops[c]	100	103	92	84	n.a.
Foods of vegetable origin (excl. coffee)[d]	100	103	91	89	84
Milk	100	96	97	101	96
Eggs	100	101	104	100	100
Wool	100	97	108	104	55
Honey	100	102	107	155	199
4 Animal Products[c]	100	97	101	101	n.a.
Cattle, per head	100	116	143	165	132
Swine, per head	100	108	117	134	107
Sheep, per head	100	118	156	167	120
Goats, per head	100	110	143	173	152
All animals[c]	100	114	138	159	n.a.
All animals and animal products[c]	100	105	119	128	n.a.
Foods of animal origin[d]	100	117	127	136	129
All foods (excl. coffee)[d]	100	103	99	101	98

a. Same sources as for Table I, the prices having been derived by dividing total value of production by physical output, both as estimated by SEP. It is not clear whether the unit prices used were those received by producers or were wholesale prices. In any case, the prices in current cruzeiros were *deflated* by the Vargas Foundation index of all wholesale prices (excluding coffee) before the index numbers (1948-52 = 100) were computed.

ful in expanding domestic production), bananas and oranges, and rice.

Despite these problem areas, Brazil entered the 1960s with an agriculture which, while still technologically backward and unstable, had shown a practical performance far better than might reasonably have been expected in view of the continuing official neglect of the domestic food sector during the previous decade. The principal public policies contributing to the expansion of Brazilian agriculture had been largely related to improvements in the infra-structure—primarily in the form of highway development, expansion of storage facilities, and the establishment and expansion of agricultural extension services—and to subsidized exchange rates on imports of fertilizers, petroleum products, and tractors and trucks and, late in the decade, some increase in agricultural credit.[2] It is doubtful, however, that any of these public policies, with the exception of the development of highways and truck transportation, could have accounted for more than a small part of the excellent performance of Brazilian agriculture during 1950-60.

Indeed, the principal objective of public policy during that decade had been the exploitation of its exportable agricultural surplus (coffee, cotton, and cocoa) to finance *industrial* development through an elaborate system of multiple-exchange rates which discriminated against the traditional exports while favoring imports of industrial machinery and producer goods. The intent, begun at a

2. For an excellent review of Brazilian agricultural policy during the 1950s and early 1960s, see Gordon W. Smith, "Agricultural Policy, 1950-67," *in* Howard S. Ellis, Editor, *The Economy of Brazil*, (Berkeley: University of California Press, 1969), pp. 213-265.

---

b. Changes in the coffee prices (unbeneficiated) used by SEP do not appear even to approximate those from other sources. They are included here only because the overall index of the prices of all 14 crops, as computed by the Vargas Foundation (cf. footnote c), include coffee priced at these particular levels. According to the Vargas Foundation index of wholesale coffee prices (Table IV), as regularly published in *Conjuntura Econômica* until late 1969, these index numbers (reading across) would have become 100, 109, 56, 49, and 46. According to data from the Divisão de Economia Rural, coffee prices received by São Paulo coffee producers would have been 100, 114, 55, 59, and 52. The last two series would presumably be for beneficiated coffee.

c. Price indexes computed from the individual SEP price series (as shown above) by the Vargas Foundation in *21 Anos de Evolução da Agricultura*.

d. For details, see Table IV below.

TABLE 3
INDEXES OF PHYSICAL YIELDS PER HECTARE, PRINCIPAL CROPS, BRAZIL,
1948-69

Crop	1948-52	1953-57	1958-62	1963-67	1968-69
Beans	100	99	98	98	96
Corn	100	96	102	104	105
Rice	100	93	101	98	91
Wheat	100	114	82	102	123
Manioc	100	99	101	108	114
Potatoes	100	107	116	131	146
Peanuts	100	112	137	127	122
Cotton	100	101	117	110	115
Bananas	100	94	96	100	111
Oranges	100	105	95	94	99
Sugar Cane	100	101	109	115	117
Tobacco	100	103	102	114	128
Cocoa	100	96	76	77	82
Coffee	100	89	115	104	84

Sources: Same as Table I.

time of war-depleted commodity stocks and high world prices, was
to capture a large part of Brazil's exchange earnings, diverting them
through selective public credit to industrial development under a
policy of strong protectionism. This objective was largely thwarted
by the near doubling during the 1950s of coffee production, associated with the development of the North of Paraná, despite artificially
low domestic prices which netted farmers only about half of the
foreign-exchange earnings from coffee. By 1960, with coffee production nearly double current demand, the costs of government stock-
piling of coffee had exceeded the amounts syphoned off by the low
"coffee dollar."[3] Even worse, the consequent benefits to agriculture
continued to accrue to the coffee sector, to the serious neglect of the
increasingly important nonexport (domestic food) sector of agriculture. A significant publicly financed expansion in commodity storage
facilities, primarily state operated, during 1956-60 failed to bring the
expected benefits to cereal-producers, in part because it had been
poorly located, since truck transportation was displacing the rail-
roads, and in part because of a failure to facilitate the discounting of
warehouse receipts through the banking system. A minimum-price
program for staple crops dating from 1951 had never been effectively

3. Cf. Werner Baer, *Industrialization and Economic Development in Brazil* (Homewood, Illinois: Richard D. Irwin, 1965), pp. 48-58, 117-118.

TABLE 4

INDEXES OF REAL PRICES OF AGRICULTURAL PRODUCTS AND FOOD PRODUCTS, BRAZIL, 1948-69[a]

Year	Wholesale Prices					Retail Prices[a]	
	Coffee	All Agri. Products (excluding coffee)	All Food Products (excluding coffee)	Foods of Vegetable Origin (excluding coffee)	Foods of Animal Origin	Rio de Janeiro	São Paulo
1948-52	100	100	100	100	100	100	100
1953-57	109	103	103	102	117	106	113
1957	86	100	102	101	110	106	108
1958	76	97	97	94	109	106	105
1959	56	96	97	100	96	111	110
1960	54	104	100	88	137	112	118
1961	46	102	97	80	144	113	125
1962	46	107	105	91	147	121	119
1963	36	103	101	91	131	117	115
1964	70	102	101	93	128	119	120
1965	61	95	98	84	128	106	111
1966	42	103	103	88	147	104	112
1967	38	104	103	89	145	97	107
1968	44	96	98	83	133	90	105
1969[c]	47	93	98	85	124	90	103
1958-62	56	101	99	91	127	113	115
1963-67	49	101	101	89	136	109	113
1968-69	46	95	98	84	129	90	104

a. These are the price series regularly published in *Conjuntura Econômica* (Vargas Foundation) until late 1969—when an entirely new set of price series was introduced—with 1953 as the base year (= 100) but here converted to the base period 1948-52 after *deflating* all wholesale price series with the Vargas index (old Index No. 45) of wholesale prices of all products (excluding coffee). Reading across, the indexes of this table had the following old Vargas Foundation numbers: Wholesale Price Indexes No. 47, 48, 57, 59, and 60; retail price indexes from the old cost-of-living indexes for São Paulo and Rio de Janeiro (cf. footnote b).

b. The indexes of the food component in the cost-of-living index, divided (deflated) by the corresponding indexes of the overall (all-products) cost-of-living index, for the two cities.

c. First eight months only, after which all of these old series were abandoned in favor of an entirely new set of index numbers.

implemented as a means of guiding production decisions and, except for cotton following the bumper crop of 1952, government commodity purchases (excluding coffee) were never large enough to raise farm prices or use much public storage capacity.[4]

4. Smith, pp. 224-225.

On the other hand, as a partial offset to the unfavorable effect
of multiple exchange rates on the prices they received for export
crops, Brazilian farmers did for a time benefit from favorable exchange rates on fertilizers, petroleum products, and tractors and
trucks. Fertilizer import subsidies, which cut domestic fertilizer
prices (relative to crop prices) by nearly half during 1950-59, had
helped to increase Brazilian consumption of plant nutrients more
than fourfold, the principal beneficiaries probably being potatoes,
tomatoes, cotton, sugar cane, coffee, and irrigated (but not the more
typical upland) rice.[5] Although agricultural production credit (in
real terms) extended by the Bank of Brazil and commercial banks had
expanded by 31 percent between 1954-56 and 1958-59, that part
supplied for crop production credit by the Bank of Brazil was in
1957-59 still heavily concentrated on coffee (40 percent), rice (18 percent), sugar cane (13 percent), and wheat (13 percent), with little attention to corn, beans, and other important domestic food crops.
Furthermore, of all agricultural credit conceded by the Bank of Brazil
during 1955-59, only 20 percent was allocated to livestock production.[6] In São Paulo, the major beneficiaries of 1958 crop production
credit from the Bank of Brazil and the State Bank were cotton, coffee,
rice, sugar cane, and peanuts. Once again, coffee was being officially
favored to an undue extent although the upward trends in the per-
hectare yields of peanuts, cotton, and sugar cane were undoubtedly
attributable in considerable part to the combination of low fertilizer
prices and official credit preferences.

Brazilian agriculture had also benefitted during the 1950s from
favorable exchange rates on the import of trucks, tractors, and motor
fuel. Heavy truck imports during 1955-60 had increased the number
of trucks in Brazil to a level more than five times that of 1946 and, in
conjunction with the expanding highway network and concomitant
growth of the independent trucking industry, were giving farmers
quicker, easier, and cheaper access to product markets and manufactured inputs. With domestic truck manufactures growing rapidly,

5. *Ibid.*, pp. 227-228, 230-231. For fertilizer and crop-yield data for São Paulo, cf.
Oscar J. Thomazini Ettori, "Produtividade Física da Agricultura em São Paulo," *Agricultura em São Paulo*, Ano XI (July 1964), pp. 45-48.

6. Judith Tendler, *Agricultural Credit in Brazil*, U.S. Agency for International Development, Washington, October 1969 (mimeographed). This is the most competent
and comprehensive study of Brazilian agricultural credit yet undertaken.

however, truck imports were to be reduced by 1962 to a negligible level. The number of farm tractors had meanwhile increased nearly eightfold during 1950-60 (80 percent concentrated in the four southernmost states), largely through 1955-60 imports, but tractor imports were soon to be largely displaced by domestic manufactures. Thus, the mechanization of both transportation and farm production which had been further encouraged by subsidized motor fuels was soon to lose much of the stimulus of these import subsidies as truck and tractor prices moved up with the shift to highly protected domestic manufactures, reinforced by the subsequent abandonment of subsidies on fuel imports.

Finally, by 1960 the idea of agricultural extension had become firmly rooted in Brazil. Well before 1950, a number of Brazilian states had established agricultural promotion (fomento) agencies which furnished gratuitous technical services and subsidized farm inputs. It was only with the founding in 1948, however—as a Rockefeller family philanthropy with some financial participation by the state and federal governments and United States foreign aid—of the Rural Credit and Assistance Association (ACAR) of Minas Gerais that a genuine agricultural extension service can be said to have been established in Brazil. Initially conceived as an instrument for offering supervised credit to small low-income farmers, ACAR soon found this approach too expensive per client served. Hence, by 1956, ACAR had evolved into a more traditional form of extension service, seeking to accelerate the adoption of new practices by furnishing technical orientation and (although on a much reduced scale) credit to innovation leaders. As a consequence, technical assistance was increasingly extended to the larger farmers as higher productivity displaced social welfare as ACAR's primary objective. Most important, the success of the ACAR experience had encouraged other states to demand similar programs. Stimulated by the creation in 1956 of a national organization (ABCAR), with rapidly increasing federal support as private external financing ended, ACAR-type programs had been established in twelve states by 1960. São Paulo had also responded by establishing its own state extension service, whose 400 local offices and 900 technicians alone dwarfed the national effort. Even in 1960, ABCAR's 582 technicians were still reaching only 11.5 percent of the 2,351 counties (excluding São Paulo's) in Brazil, supplemented only by the 425 technicians in the Ministry of Agriculture's own ineffective extension activities.[7]

Favorable though the development of the ACAR idea was during the 1950s, it can hardly receive much of the credit for the substantial growth in Brazil's agricultural output during the 1950s. But at least it had gained strong popular and political acceptance for a Brazilian agricultural extension service; had upgraded the quality of agricultural technicians through higher salaries for full-time, politics-free, service-oriented personnel; and had provided a more effective channel for stimulating revision of the excessively theoretical curricula of the faculties of agronomy and the development and institutionalization of a more problem-oriented type of agricultural research, whose paucity was its biggest handicap.

Whatever net contributions these various public policies may have made directly or indirectly to the agricultural development of the 1950s, their value was dwarfed by the agricultural benefits derived as a major by-product of Brazilian highway construction during the same decade. In the eight years 1952-60, the federal highway system increased from 12.3 to 32.4 thousand kilometers (27 percent paved) and the state highway systems from 51.0 to 75.9 thousand kilometers. While still grossly inadequate for so vast a nation, this expansion in the federal and state highway networks was accompanied during the 1950s by a fourfold increase in the volume of commodities transported by truck, the share of all commodity transport carried by highway having increased from 37 to 62 percent during 1950-60. Initially, the principal beneficiary of these highway developments was the South of Brazil, centering on the city of São Paulo, as the extension of highways brought an ever-widening circle of towns and rural areas into an increasingly integrated regional economy. Even in the Northeast (which also had far less extensive a railway network), highways and trucks had created at least the beginnings of an integrated Northeastern economy. This development was also considerably stimulated by the creation (1956-60) of Brasília, whose major by-product was the imperative of initiating arterial highways to link the new federal capital with the rest of Brazil. The completion of the Brasília-Belém highway, followed by rapid progress on other projected highways to the major cities of the Northeast, was by 1960 demonstrating that this highway network was becoming a major na-

7. G. Edward Schuh, *The Agricultural Development of Brazil*, (New York: Praeger, 1970); recent volumes of *Anuário Estatístico do Brasil*; and Associação de Crédito e Assistência Rural (ACAR), *ACAR: Dez Anos à Serviço do Povo de Minas Gerais*, Belo Horizonte, 1960.

tional integrating force which would surely become a landmark in Brazilian economic (and particularly agricultural) development.[8]

Indeed, most of the rapid growth of agricultural output during 1950-60 must be attributed to the stimulus which highway development gave to the commercialization and intensification of agriculture in the more remote older areas and to the settlement and rapid growth of Brazil's many remaining agricultural frontiers. Since nearly all of the increased crop output had come from the increased area of cropland, it is significant that the agricultural frontiers of the State of Paraná alone accounted for 20 percent of the new cropland and for 23 percent of the increment of rural population during the 1950s. Thanks largely to improvements in transportation, spontaneous internal migration of several million people had taken place, much of it rural-to-urban but increasingly rural-to-rural as Paraná gained in a decade 1,350,000 net in-migrants, Goiás 542,000, and Mato Grosso 257,000 (my estimates), with Maranhão also a major recipient.[9]

To sum up, Brazil's public policy of the 1950s had for the most part been more concerned with exploiting agriculture for financing industrial growth than with promoting agricultural output and rural welfare. Yet, somehow, millions of Brazilian farmers had kept crop output expanding at a rate well ahead of population growth in an environment of unstable prices, little technical orientation, weak public agricultural research, and shameful neglect of rural education and migration and colonization policies. The relatively favorable picture in over-all crop production, however, was allowed to conceal such important problem areas as bean and fruit production and more general problems of supply and price instability. Furthermore, there was a serious lag in the production of livestock, the demand for which was much more stimulated by rising per-capita incomes. That the livestock sector required higher managerial skills and greater dependence on purchased inputs, hence much more effective public research and extension services, had received virtually no official attention. Hence,

8. Various volumes of *Anuário Estatístico do Brasil;* Smith, p. 223; and William H. Nicholls, "The Changing Structure of Farm Product and Input Markets in Brazil," in Kurt R. Anschel, *et al.* (editors), *Agricultural Cooperatives and Markets in Developing Countries,* (New York: Praeger, 1969), pp. 63-78.

9. William H. Nicholls and Ruy Miller Paiva, *Ninety-Nine Fazendas: The Structure and Productivity of Brazilian Agriculture, 1963,* Chap. VI, *The North of Paraná,* Graduate Center for Latin American Studies, Vanderbilt University, Nashville, Tennessee, September 1969, pp. 40-51.

as the early 1960s were soon to reveal, the Brazilian food situation was far less rosy than it appeared as the decade of the 1950s ended.

Agricultural Performance in the 1960s

The decade of the 1960s began with an upward surge of food prices in the major cities which had considerable political repercussions (Table 4). This fact was largely concealed within the five-year average for 1958-62 which we used in our previous comparisons. Thus, at the wholesale level, the real prices of all foods (excluding coffee) averaged in 1958-62, 1 percent less (Table 2) and the real prices of all agricultural prices only 1 percent more than their 1948-52 levels. In São Paulo, the index of real prices received by farmers was also down by 3 percent excluding (21 percent including) coffee. At the retail level, however, food prices (relative to the total cost-of-living index) had nonetheless increased by 15 percent in the city of São Paulo and 13 percent in the city of Rio de Janeiro during the same period, reflecting increasing urban distribution costs. Much more serious, real wholesale and retail food prices reached a temporary low point during 1957-59, after which they increased rapidly in 1961 and 1962 as general inflation began to accelerate rapidly. Thus, however measured, real food prices were in 1961-62 at or near their peak levels for the entire period 1948-69, following relatively low levels a few years earlier. For example, relative retail food prices in São Paulo rose by 14 percent during 1958-62, and in Rio by 19 percent during 1958-61. Wholesale prices rose somewhat less sharply but still significantly, the index for all agricultural products except coffee rising by 11 percent during 1959-62 and the index for all food products (also excluding coffee) by 8 percent during 1961-62. Except for a temporary but severe upsurge in rice and bean prices during 1962—apparently more a problem of distribution and price controls than of production—the principal feature of this food crisis was a shortage of livestock marketings which boosted the real prices of foods of animal origin by 53 percent within the three-year period 1959-62. The index of real prices received by São Paulo farmers (coffee excluded) also jumped by 18 percent during 1959-62, following a decade of gradually declining prices, restoring this index to a level only 2 percent below its postwar high of 1953.

Thus, after a decade of relatively good agricultural performance, especially in the crop sector, Brazil entered the 1960s with a food crisis which—exacerbated by the distortions of increasingly runaway inflation and clumsy efforts to combat rising food prices by administrative controls—clearly indicated the need for renewed political attention to agriculture, first by the Goulart government and then, after ever-growing political and economic turmoil, by the military regime which displaced President Goulart in March 1964. Before looking at the public agricultural policies which were to follow, let us first consider the performance of Brazilian agriculture after 1960 and the major problems which that performance was to present.

Between 1958-62 and 1963-67, Brazilian crop production grew by an additional 15.9 percent (Table 1), not quite keeping pace with the 16.8 percent increase in population. Just as the doubling of coffee production had inflated the rate of increase in the index of total crop output during the 1950's, however, so the sharp decline in coffee production in the 1960s significantly depressed the growth in that index. Thus, coffee production in 1963-67 averaged 31 percent less than in 1958-62 and by 1968-69 was 43 percent below its 1958-62 peak and only 9 percent above even its low 1948-52 level. In large part, this decline was attributable to two severe freezes which greatly reduced the coffee harvests of 1963 and 1964 and, to a lesser extent, reflected the public coffee-eradication program of 1962-67 which subsidized the removal of 1.4 billion trees. In real terms, prices received by São Paulo coffee producers during 1960-68 averaged only 50 percent of their 1953-57 peak, rising from 45 to 79 percent during 1960-64, dropping to a low of 35 percent in 1966, then increasing to 45 percent in 1968. Thus, substantial strides were made during 1960-69, at on-the-whole relatively moderate levels of producer price supports, in reducing coffee production and stocks to more realistic levels.

The new freeze of 1969 in Paraná however,—the most severe and general in its history—has raised anew the question that this now dominant state is as ecologically suited for coffee production as originally believed. Even if it is, Brazilian coffee production—with the prospect of sharply lower harvests during 1970-72 which might completely exhaust present stocks by mid-1973—again faces the need for stimulating expansion of its coffee production if it is not soon to fall short of meeting export needs. In this expansion, São Paulo (usually frost-free) may perhaps again assume a more important role but, insofar as replantings in Paraná still appear to be appropriate, a larger "normal" level of national buffer stocks will be required to offset its greater year-to-year instability. To achieve such an expansion without a new wave of excessive planting and subsequent overproduction and unduly large stocks will require much skill in formulating public coffee policy and considerable cooperation from the weather. Meanwhile, the recent appearance and spread of coffee rust—a plant disease of great potential seriousness—in Bahia, Espírito Santo, and Minas Gerais has added another important element of uncertainty to the already cloudy Brazilian coffee situation.

Of the 13 other major crops (Table 1), only cocoa failed to keep pace with the 30 percent increase in population between 1958-62 and 1968-69. The 32-37 percent expansion in the production of cotton (about one third exported), sugar cane, and (though down significantly from its 1965 peak) rice slightly exceeded population growth, with bean and potato production up by 45 to 47 percent and corn by 52 percent. Tobacco and wheat production had increased by 59 percent each, wheat output in 1969—85 percent above its 1967 mark after a decade of low-level stagnation—having slightly exceeded its previous all-time peak of 1955. Production of peanuts—Brazil's major source of vegetable oils—was down from its 1966 peak but was still 60 percent above its 1958-62 level. Orange and banana output had enjoyed very marked increases of 65 and 68 percent while manioc (much of it used as livestock feed) led all crops with a 70 percent increase since 1958-62.

This performance in crop production had been sufficient to reduce the index of real wholesale prices of food products (excluding coffee) of vegetable origin (Table 4) by an additional 6 percent between 1958-62 and 1968-69, making a total decline since 1948-52 of 16 percent in real terms—a very satisfactory record. Bean prices (Table 2) had shown by 1968-69 the greatest decline (30 percent) from their high level of 1958-62, the problem of scarcities in this important staple food having found at least a temporary solution in Brazil's still-expanding agricultural frontiers. (Thus, in 1966 Paraná supplied 66 percent, and Goiás, the Minas Triangle, and Mato Grosso an additional 21 percent, of the bean requirements of the city of São Paulo.[10] Cotton prices had also resumed their downward trend, declining 27 percent between 1958-62 and 1968-69. Real corn prices in 1968-69 stood 26 percent below their 1958-62 level. This continuing sharp downward trend in corn prices again reflected expanding agricultural frontiers (Paraná, Goiás, and Minas Gerais in 1966 supplied 50 percent of São Paulo city's requirements for corn as food) as well as the increasing use of hybrid seed and better cultural practices, also stimulating the accelerated growth of swine production, particularly in the newer regions of Paraná.

10. For sources of staple foods for the city of São Paulo, see Pérsio de Carvalho Junqueira, et al., "Comercialização de Produtos Agrícolas no Estado de São Paulo," *Agricultura em São Paulo*, Ano XV (March/April 1968).

The real prices of manioc, rice, and potatoes also dropped by 15 to 18 percent between 1958-62 and 1968-69. Tobacco prices were down 7 percent from both 1958-62 and 1948-52. In real terms, the 1968-69 prices of bananas and wheat were essentially unchanged from 1958-62. Peanut prices, following their substantial decline during the 1950s, rose 7 percent during the 1960s. Orange prices showed an irregular upward trend during the 1960s, in 1968-69 standing 14 percent above their 1958-62 level (a period of sharply declining prices), exhibiting a renewed tendency for their supply to lag behind a rapidly increasing demand. Sugar cane prices had reversed their downward trend of the 1950s, reaching an all-time peak in 1963-65 but in 1968-69 still 20 percent above their 1958-62 low. Finally, cocoa prices soared to an all-time peak in 1968-69, when they were fully 61 percent above their 1958-62 average.

In summary, after the crisis of 1962-64 which saw manioc, beans, corn, rice, oranges, bananas, wheat, peanuts, sugar cane, and coffee reach their highest real prices of the 1960s, most of the staple food crops—notably beans, cotton, corn, manioc, rice, potatoes, and bananas—had experienced declining prices thereafter, with wheat, peanuts, and oranges the major exceptions. Thus, the latter half of the 1960s was a period of generally favorable downward trends in the real prices of Brazil's principal crops. In the longer-run perspective which a comparison of 1968-69 and 1948-52 prices permits (Table II), the net effect of changing supply and demand factors—including special public price and production programs for sugar cane and wheat—had been a *reduction* since 1948-52 of 42 percent in (real) cotton prices, of 33-34 percent in potato and corn prices, of 19 percent in manioc prices, of 14 percent in rice prices, and of 5 to 7 percent in tobacco and peanut prices. On the other hand, there had been an *increase* since 1948-52 of 2 to 3 percent in the (real) prices of beans, sugar cane, and bananas; of 8 percent in wheat prices, of 17 percent in orange prices, and of (thanks to their doubling during 1967-69) 72 percent in cocoa prices.

While crop production of the late 1960s helped to reverse the tendency of the early years of the decade toward rising relative prices of most of the leading staple foods, this accomplishment was temporarily facilitated by low economic growth rates during much of the 1960s. Thus, while the increase in the production of the major food crops exceeded population growth, the need for production increases was reduced by a sustained period of low or even negative growth rates in per capita income, which averaged only 0.5 percent per year during 1962-67 as compared with 5.1 percent in 1957-61, 3.2 percent in 1952-56, and 4.0 percent in 1948-51. Thus, as growth rates returned to much higher levels in 1968-69, those foods most responsive to rising incomes[11]—particularly oranges, bananas, vegetable oils, and potatoes—were again beginning to face stronger tests on the supply side if real prices were not to face renewed upward pressures. Furthermore, as we shall see later, the substantial increases in the prices of modern agricultural inputs during the late 1960s, by seriously reducing agriculture's terms of trade, were creating the danger of an adverse production response in some of the technically most improved crops such as cotton, potatoes, rice, peanuts, corn, and sugar cane which are now most dependent on purchased inputs. Finally, despite their sharp price decrease during the 1960s, beans could easily become once more a major problem commodity as the recently settled agricultural frontiers have begun to draw down their initial fertility and original freedom from yield-cutting plant diseases.

Turning to the livestock sector, we find that the serious problems already evident in the early 1960s had by the end of the decade been ameliorated but, particularly given the prospect of burgeoning demand as per capita incomes move to higher levels, was far from resolved. In reaching such a conclusion, however, we must depend upon real price trends more than upon livestock-production data, which in Brazil continued during the 1960s to be highly suspect. According to the Vargas Foundation index of animal production (all animals and animal products in Table 1), based on highly unreliable Ministry of Agriculture data, total livestock output increased by 16.9 percent, virtually the same as the rate of population growth, between 1958-62 and 1963-67. Of the major components of this index, milk and egg production were up by 29 to 30 percent, cattle numbers (probably overestimated) were up by 16 percent and swine numbers up by 24 percent, and slaughter numbers (probably substantially underestimated) were up by only 2 percent for cattle and 19 percent

11. According to the estimates of the Getulio Vargas Foundation (*Projections of Supply and Demand for Agricultural Products of Brazil*, July 1968, published for the U.S. Dept. of Agriculture, p. 47), a 1 percent increase in per capita income (at constant relative prices of 1962-63) would lead to increased consumption of 1 percent or more for poultry, fresh pork, and milk products; of 0.70-0.74 percent for oranges, fresh beef, and eggs; of 0.55-0.64 percent for bananas, vegetable oils, and all foods; of 0.36-0.48 percent for potatoes, margarine, and wheat products; of 0.21-0.24 percent for mutton and goat meat, sugar, and rice; and from −0.08 percent to 0.04 percent for beans, lard, manioc (human consumption only), and corn meal.

for swine. For the later period 1968-69, the corresponding increases since 1958-62 were as follows: milk production up by 43 percent, egg production up by 49 percent, cattle numbers up by 25 percent, swine numbers up by 35 percent, cattle slaughter up by 19 percent, and swine slaughter up by 36 percent. If these figures are to be taken seriously, they indicate that milk, eggs, and swine more than kept pace with the 30-percent increase in population during the same period while cattle fell substantially short of the growth in population.

To what extent did changing relative prices of animal products (Table 2) confirm or conflict with these apparent differences in production trends? Real (presumably producer) prices of all animals and animal products were 8.3 percent higher (meat animals up 14.8 percent and animal products unchanged) in 1963-67 than in 1958-62 and 28.4 percent above their 1948-52 average. Real wholesale prices of foods of animal origin in 1963-67 were 7.3 percent higher than in 1958-62 and 35.3 percent above 1948-52. In 1968-69, however, the latter index dropped 2.3 percent below 1958-62 although still 29 percent higher than its 1948-52 average. For the decade as a whole, this index (1948-52 = 100) was characterized by two cycles, reaching a high (from a 1957-59 low of 105) of 146 in 1961-62 and an equal high (from a 1963-65 low of 129) of 146 in 1966-67, again declining to a low of 129 in 1968-69. Returning to the first index (Vargas Foundation, based on Ministry of Agriculture data), the trends in real prices by individual product (cf. Table 2) were as follows. Relative to their 1964 highs, (real) cattle prices in 1968-69 were down by 30 percent, swine prices down by 32 percent, sheep prices down by 36 percent, goat prices down by 18 percent, and milk prices down by 13 percent. Relative to their lows of 1957, 1958, or 1959, however, cattle prices in 1968-69 were still up by 20 percent, swine prices 2 percent higher, sheep prices 10 percent higher, goat prices 33 percent higher, and milk prices 11 percent higher. Egg prices behaved rather differently, moving within a rather narrow range, with a gradual decline during 1958-63 when most other animal products were reaching major peaks, then recovering during 1965-69 to essentially their 1960-62 level. Over the longer period since 1948-52, average real prices in 1968-69 had shown the following changes: milk prices down by 4 percent, egg prices unchanged, goat prices up by 52 percent, cattle prices up by 32 percent, sheep prices up by 20 percent, and swine prices up by only 7 percent.

Despite these unreliable and often inconsistent data on livestock production, marketings, and prices, it would appear that, as the 1960s came to an end, Brazil had weathered reasonably well the serious crisis in meat-animal prices which had afflicted the country during the first years of the decade, with substantial price reductions during 1967-69. Considerable price instability remained, however, in part reflecting the vagaries of public anti-inflation price controls as they affected livestock deliveries. Furthermore, producer prices of cattle and goats in 1967-69 still stood 22 to 24 percent higher than their average levels of 1957-59 compared with 11 percent higher for sheep, 2 percent higher for milk and swine, a 4-percent decline for eggs, and a 33-percent decline for wool. The corresponding change for the wholesale price index for foods of animal origin was a 28-percent increase, although by 1969 (first 8 months) the latter was only 19 percent above its 1957-59 level. There was still no room for complacency, however, particularly for beef cattle, and—since the resumption of higher growth rates in per capita incomes in 1968 and 1969—the combination of high population growth and higher incomes is sure to put heavy pressure not only on beef prices but also substantially increased pressure even on swine, milk, and egg prices unless production and marketings of these consumer-favored products expand more rapidly than in the recent past.

The over-all effect of these various trends (Table 4) was that the real wholesale price index for all agricultural (crop and livestock) products, excluding coffee, in 1967-69 was unchanged from 1957-59 and 5.7 percent below its 1960-64 average, and the index for all food products, again excluding coffee, was only 1.0 percent higher than in 1957-59 and 1.1 percent lower than in 1960-64. For 1969 (first 8 months) only, the two indexes were 13 and 7 percent below their 1962 peaks, 3.6 percent below and 1.0 percent above their 1958-59 lows, and 7 and 2 percent below their 1948-52 lows. Indeed, in 1969, the first index was lower than in any year during 1948-68 and the second index during the same period was lower only in 1950-51 and in three of the four years 1958-61. Relative to the prices of all products in the cost-of-living index, retail food prices in 1967-69 were 21 percent lower in Rio de Janeiro, and 12 percent lower in São Paulo, than their 1960-64 averages; even relative to 1957-59, these two indexes had by 1967-69 declined by 14 and 3 percent, respectively. For 1969 (first 8 months), relative retail food prices in Rio were 26 percent below their 1962 peak and those in São Paulo were 18 percent below their highest level of 1961. Relative to 1958, their 1969 levels were 15 and 2 percent lower; and relative to their 1948-52 averages, 10 percent lower and 3 percent higher.

Thus, Brazilian over-all food prices ended the 1960s on a relatively favorable note. In order to put the performance of Brazilian agriculture in better perspective, however—the great year-to-year fluctuations in food production, marketings, and prices makes the choice of meaningful time periods for shortrun comparisons difficult—let us complete this examination of food-price trends by a longer-run comparison, that between the averages for 1960-69 and 1950-59. Surprisingly, despite the food crisis of 1960-64, the average level of the wholesale price index of all agricultural products (excluding coffee) was the same in 1960-69 as in 1950-59. The same was true for the wholesale price index of all food products (again excluding coffee) although there had been a slight rise (2.1 percent in Rio, 5.2 percent in São Paulo) in relative retail food prices. The principal change had been in the two main components of food products, with relative wholesale prices of food products (excluding coffee) of vegetable origin having fallen by 11 percent while those of food products of animal origin had increased by 22 percent. That the former decline had been sufficient to offset the latter marked increase, with no net increase for the two combined, was no mean achievement given a 36 percent increase in average population and about a one-third increase in per capita income.

Brazilians should consider themselves exceedingly fortunate that expanding agricultural frontiers, highway improvements, and the increasing use of modern purchased farm inputs have thus far permitted such a remarkable performance. The recent resumption of rising per-capita incomes, however, compounding the effects of a continuing very high rate of population growth; the filling up of Brazil's best remaining agricultural frontiers; the recent decline in agriculture's terms of trade with the manufacturing sector, from which most modern farm inputs must be purchased; and the continued public neglect of agricultural research, accurate production and market statistics, and effective agricultural extension and commodity-storage facilities—all of these point toward potential future food crises, particularly in the livestock sector, if not promptly corrected.

Infrastructure Development in the 1960s

The most tangible benefit to Brazilian agriculture during 1960-69 was the continued extension and improvement of the highway system.[12] Between 1960 and 1969, the total road network in Brazil more

---

12. Recent volumes of *Anuário Estatístico do Brasil*; Smith, pp. 222-223; and draft report of International Bank of Reconstruction and Development, Brazil: *Agricultural Sector Survey*, Annex 13, *Rural Roads and Electrification*, March 31, 1970.

than doubled, the federal system increasing from 32,402 kilometers (27 percent paved) to 50,101 kilometers (44 percent paved), and the state system from 75,875 km. (5 percent paved) to 131,316 km. (16 percent paved). During the same period, the poor *municipal* (county) road system increased much more rapidly and, although only 0.4 percent paved in 1969, this system's share of all roads increased from 77 to 83 percent as the extension of the agricultural frontiers quickened. Most significantly, the total extent of all *paved* roads in Brazil increased more than threefold during the nine-year period. Nearly three fourths of this increase was located in Minas Gerais, Espírito Santo, and the six states to their south, notably Paraná, although São Paulo alone accounted for more than half of the eight-state total in 1969. The remaining states and territories received more than one fourth of the new paved roads and 68 percent of the increase in all federal and state roads, unpaved or paved. During 1960-68, the concomitant increase in number of trucks was from 397,000 to 588,000, or 48 percent, virtually all of the new trucks being of domestic manufacture. With the total ton-kilometers of commodities transported in Brazil increasing by 51 percent during 1960-65, the share contributed by highway transport increased from 62 to 69 percent. This continued gain—at the expense of coastal shipping (whose share fell from 21 to 13 percent) as highways were gradually being extended from the South to the Northeast and North—was made in the face of substantially higher equipment and fuel costs as domestic manufactures displaced cheaper imports and as subsidies on fuel imports ended.

Local feeder roads have lagged far behind arterial highway development, many farmers still facing impassable roads for several months a year. Nonetheless, the much greater flexibility, speed, and reliability of private truck transportation have brought its rapidly expanding use in preference to the nominally less costly but highly inefficient public railway and coastal-shipping systems, although the government was putting considerable resources into the improvement of docks, port facilities, and harbors as the decade ended. Trucking has also introduced an important new competitive element into the local assembling, transportation, and distribution of agricultural products, reducing significantly the marketing margins between farmer and consumer. Settlement and development of the remaining agricultural frontiers has been much stimulated with the improved access to farm-product markets, to farm-production goods, to the surplus rural labor of the older regions, and to the greater variety of consumer goods. Thus, highway and trucking developments have finally turned that part of Brazil south of Brasília and Salvador into a well-integrated regional economy for both food products and agricultural inputs. The large and backward Northeast region is also feeling the beginnings of the same integrating force, both internally and in its interregional trade with the South. Trucks have become the major means of moving the products (especially manufactures) of the South to the northeastern and northern regions and of moving the largely primary goods and the human out-migrants of the latter regions southward and westward. Thus, the settlement, expansion, monetization, and commercialization of the agriculture of the more remote regions received strong impetus from the highway development of 1960-69.

The 1960s also saw a substantial expansion of the nation's agricultural extension services and some revival of agricultural research activities. During 1960-69, ABCAR—which had become Brazil's official extension service in 1966—increased its number of regional offices from 26 to 138 and its number of local *(município)* offices from 193 to 1,025; the number of *municípios* served rose from 272 to 1,393 (about 41 percent of all *municípios*, excluding those of São Paulo which was outside of the federal system); and the number of technicians employed from 582 to 2,423 (2,103 in the field). Under the Strategic Program of Development 1968-70, the goal for 1970 was fixed at 1,410 local offices, with 3,280 technicians reaching 1,903 *municípios*, but this goal was apparently far from realized, Brazil's agricultural colleges complaining in mid-1970 that their considerably increased output of agronomists had recently been confronting a severe shortage of employment opportunities and very low salaries. In 1966, extension activities received 40 percent of the Ministry of Agriculture budget and 29 percent of the budgets of all federal agricultural programs. (During the 1960s, São Paulo's separate extension service was maintained at a relatively constant level, with 873 technicians in 1966.) By 1969, ABCAR was orienting some 220,000 families (215 per local office), not more than 3 percent of all rural families in the relevant states but these undoubtedly including many of the most progressive and influential leaders of their local communities. The latter were also increasingly benefiting from the expanding technical orientation programs of the various private firms selling such modern agricultural inputs as fertilizers, hybrid seed, livestock rations, and insecticides. Most of the gains from these structural developments, given their long gestation period, still remain largely in the future. However, since they represent an essential step toward the progress and modernization of Brazilian agriculture, they deserve the renewed and sustained commitment of the government.[13]

Meanwhile, the expansion of agricultural extension services has placed in bold relief the need for an effective research base in agriculture.[14] Agricultural research, which had languished seriously during the 1950s under public budgetary neglect, was somewhat revived after 1960 but has continued to be a serious bottleneck in Brazilian agricultural development. The Ministry of Agriculture had in 1970 eight regional research institutes and 63 associated experiment stations, employing a total of 700 technicians, of which 70 percent have had some university training. Except for the Southern Institute (in Pelotas, Rio Grande do Sul), the ministry's research institutes are weak and suffer from serious deficiencies in both quality of personnel and budgetary support. In the 1969 national budget, the Ministry of Agriculture received an allocation of only 2.3 percent (all agricultural programs, including colonization and agrarian reform, raised the share to only 3.0 percent) compared with 5.9 percent in 1960. Meanwhile, the total federal budget having increased nearly threefold in real terms during 1960-69, the ministry's real budget was virtually unchanged. The 1970 federal budget allocates only $7.4 million to all agricultural research activities—only 0.2 percent of agriculture's contribution to the Gross Domestic Product. Little wonder that Brazil's myriad needs for agricultural research have continued to be so much neglected!

The State of São Paulo—in whose Department of Agriculture are found what are probably Latin America's best centers of agronomic research (the Instituto Agronômico of Campinas and sixteen associated experiment stations) and agricultural economic research (the Instituto de Economia Rural)—continued to support agricultural research activities on a much more adequate scale after 1960. In 1966, for example, the budget of São Paulo's Department of Agriculture was virtually the same as that of the Ministry of Agriculture, supporting 547 professional research workers compared with the ministry's 430. In 1965, the real budget of the Department of Agriculture was nearly four times its level of 1959 and its share of the total state budget had increased from 4.3 to 7.8 percent, with a peak of 10.4 percent in the previous year (1964). From 1965 on, however, the Department of Agriculture

13. G. Edward Schuh, op. cit.; recent volumes of Anuário Estatístico do Brasil; and Ministério do Planejamento e Coordenação Geral, Programa Estratégico de Desenvolvimento, 1968-70: Agricultura e Abastecimento, September 1969, pp. 271-283.

14. G. Edward Schuh, op. cit.; and IBRD Agricultural Sector Survey, Annex 9, Agricultural Research; Divisão de Economia Rural, "Diagnóstico da Agricultura Paulista," Agricultura em São Paulo, Ano XIV (May/June 1967), pp. 32-33.

suffered a substantial reduction in both absolute and relative support, all agricultural and natural resource programs of the state (whether in the department or elsewhere) being allocated only 2.5 percent of the State budget in 1969, with total real budgets for such uses less than half of the 1962 budget of the department alone. Nonetheless, relative to the federal government, the state of São Paulo (currently spending 8 to 10 million dollars for agricultural research) has continued to be a paragon of virtue in the provision of effective research services. Some other states, particularly Pernambuco and Rio Grande do Sul, have been putting considerable resources (currently about $1 million each) into state agricultural research, the Instituto de Pesquisas Agronômicas of Recife having a relatively strong research staff and program. All other states together provide about $1.5 million for agricultural research. Finally, two private organizations—IRI (formerly the IBEC Research Institute) and the Anderson Clayton Company—have made significant contributions to agricultural research. IRI, founded by the Rockefeller brothers and later supported for a time from United States foreign-aid funds and other public sources, has done outstanding work on fertilizer use (particularly as related to Brazil's difficult *cerrado* soils) and, perhaps more important, on pasture improvement and animal nutrition. IRI also helped to stimulate the State of São Paulo to extend since 1960 its research interests to problems of animal nutrition (including pasture improvement and forage crops) and animal husbandry, previously seriously neglected fields, although these efforts are still in a sadly rudimentary stage.

The food crises of 1960-64 gave strong impetus to the Brazilian government's support of agricultural credit.[15] Between 1960-62 and 1966-68, while agriculture's share of the GNP was falling from 28 to 24 percent, its share of the total credit which the Bank of Brazil and the commercial banks were extending to the private sector increased from 20 to 30 percent, most of the increase coming before 1965. Total agricultural production credit (working and investment capital) from these sources (in real terms) increased by 65 percent (or, including agricultural marketing credit, by 76 percent) while the corresponding increase in total credit to the private sector rose by only 16 percent, indicating the sharp shift in favor of the agricultural sector during the 1960s. During the 1960s, the Bank of Brazil also sharply reallocated the total credit resources available for working capital in crop production,

---

15. Tendler, *op. cit.*; and draft report of IBRD Agricultural Sector Survey, Annex 6, *Agricultural Credit*.

which had doubled in real terms between 1957-59 and 1966-68. In the interim, coffee's share had dropped from 40 to 10 percent, sugar cane from 13 to 7 percent, and wheat from 13 to 5 percent. The principal beneficiaries were rice (from 18 to 27 percent), corn (5 to 19 percent), and cotton (6 to 13 percent). While still underfinanced, beans increased their share from 1 to 3 percent, a variety of other crops (notably soybeans, peanuts, potatoes, and manioc) also receiving significant financing by the end of the 1960s.

Livestock production, as in 1955-59, received during 1960-62 only about 20 percent of total Bank of Brazil agricultural credit but its share was allowed to drop to only 13 percent during 1963-65. By 1969, the livestock sector's share was back to 21 percent, its highest level since 1962 after an average of only 17.6 percent for 1966-68. Between 1957-59 and 1967-69, the Bank of Brazil's total livestock and crop loans (in real terms) had both doubled but the increase during 1965-69 was only twofold for crops and was nearly fourfold for livestock. In recent years, about two thirds of total Bank of Brazil agricultural credit has been allocated to seasonal production credit (mostly for crops) and one third to credit for agricultural investment in buildings, machinery and equipment, irrigation facilities, acquisition of improved breeding stock, pasture improvement, and other productive uses. The number and value of loans to small farmers has been growing steadily, while absorbing an increasing proportion of the time of bank personnel in processing loans. Nonetheless, probably less than 15 percent of all Brazilian farms even now receive any Bank of Brazil credit. The regional distribution of total agricultural credit in recent years has closely approached the regional distribution of the value of agricultural product, the Bank of the Northeast and state banks of that area providing enough resources to offset the much stronger financial advantages of the South, particularly in private banking resources.

Throughout the 1960s, the interest rates on Brazilian bank credit for agriculture were *negative* in real terms. Current legal maximum annual rates (with no monetary correction for inflation) are 14 percent for loans up to about $2,000; 18 percent for higher loans; and 12 to 18 percent for loans to co-operatives (depending on the size of loan to individual members). Commercial banks may charge below these rates but few do—the official rate for industrial and commercial loans is 22 percent and the real rate is said to be more than 30 percent—and that portion (10 percent) of their deposits required to be allocated to agricultural credit is made to preferred well-secured customers at the expense of less wealthy (often smaller) farmers who could nonetheless make very productive uses of such funds. The latter must pay as much as 25 percent *in real terms* outside of official credit channels. Nonetheless, in early 1969, the Bank of Brazil reduced its own rates to agricultural borrowers to 9 percent for loans of up to $2,000; to 15 percent for loans from $2,000 to $20,000; and to 18 percent only on those loans about $20,000, the average rate for its production credit now averaging about 13.5 percent. Other special public agricultural funds have special rates—nil on fertilizer loans, 14 percent on tractor loans, and 14 percent (plus monetary correction to yield 8 percent in real terms) for the International Bank's livestock loan fund. With an inflation rate still exceeding 20 percent per year, all but the IBRD fund charge interest rates which are still substantially negative in real terms —though much less so than in 1963-64 at the height of Brazil's inflation —and there has been virtually no borrowing from the IBRD fund.

While these low nominal interest rates have been sincerely justified as a subsidy for agricultural development, they have had many undesirable effects. They have artificially stimulated the demand for agricultural credit while drying up the supply from private commercial sources, requiring banks to ration the available credit with regressive effects on smaller farmers and placing a premium on personal and political influence. Most important, negative real interest rates make it profitable for farmers to borrow for relatively low-yielding uses and to divert their own financial resources to land purchases and other speculative activities and weaken financial intermediaries by reducing their incentive to promote developmental credit in agriculture. With sufficient supervision, lending agencies could direct scarce credit resources to only higher-yielding uses but, in practice, they lack both the quantity and quality of personnel to do more than determine the commercial credit-worthiness of the borrower.

Until Brazil's agricultural research and extension services are more adequately developed and more effectively co-ordinated with public agricultural-credit institutions, much of Brazil's now relatively substantial credit resources will be largely wasted in terms of their potential for modernizing agriculture, all the more so if subsidized interest rates continue to make credit "cheap" with its use virtually uncontrolled. While an element of subsidy in interest rates to agriculture may be justified when tied to a specific desirable use of credit (such as increased application of fertilizers), it is a very dull tool for trying to offset the increasing handicap which Brazilian farmers have faced as industrial protection of new domestic manufactures substantially raised the cost of important agricultural production goods. Here, a direct attack aimed at improving the scale and efficiency of those domestic industries of importance to agriculture would clearly appear to offer the more rational solution.

The 1960s saw much talk but little effective action in altering the agrarian structure in terms of land tenure and the distribution of land ownership. The rise of radical movements demanding "agrarian reform," particularly in the sugar zone of the Northeast, had the overt but cynical support of President Goulart—who was himself meanwhile buying up large tracts of land—during 1963-64. But these movements, accompanied by invasion of the land and threats of armed conflict, were in fact highly localized and their scope and significance as a mass movement were very much exaggerated by both the foreign and Brazilian press. Goulart's attempts to push an adamant Congress into passing laws expropriating land for redistribution, even with the full compensation in cash required under the Brazilian constitution, met a predictable rebuff which he surely expected but needed to support his cry for "constitutional reform." Nonetheless, the military regime which took over in March 1964 was sensitive enough to the issue to persuade Congress to pass a land-reform law soon thereafter.[16]

Through the Institute of Agrarian Reform (IBRA), a comprehensive cadastral survey was made in 1965, initially embracing 3.4 million properties holding 829 million acres of land and increased in 1967 to 3.8 million with 889 million acres (average size 234 acres). While serious problems of comparability exist between this cadastre and the Census of 1960, the latter had counted 3.3 million agricultural "establishments" with 656 million acres of land (average size 199 acres per farm). While farmers were asked to declare the value of their land, IBRA had the final word, fixing initial minimum values in late 1964 for the different areas of the various states. While IBRA attempted to update these values in 1966 and 1967 to correct for inflation, it did so timidly and in 1969 made no monetary correction. The principal purpose of these efforts was the collection of the Rural Land Tax which before 1960 had rested within the jurisdiction of the state governments. However, shortly after São Paulo passed an Agrarian Revision Act (providing for progressive taxation by size of land-holding with offsetting credits for approved practices), Congress transferred this tax to the jurisdiction of the *municipios*, which were dominated by large landholders. In 1966, assessment and collection responsibilities appro-

16. The following paragraphs are based on the excellent Annex 4 *(Taxation of Agriculture)* of the recent IBRD Agricultural Sector Survey.

priately passed to the federal government (IBRA) with the objective of promoting agrarian reform through the tax system, IBRA retaining 20 percent and returning 80 percent to the local governments.

The basic tax rate of 0.2 percent on the value of unimproved land is multiplied by four coefficients reflecting property size, location, on-farm social conditions, and quality of management which together could make the actual rate range from 0.024 to 3.456 percent. The formula for fixing this actual rate is a "lawyer's nightmare" and, while the basic principles were highly commendable, compliance during the first three years 1966-68 was both low and deteriorating, with wide-spread evasion by the largest landowners. The present government has also been much less successful in applying its income-tax laws to agriculture than to the urban sector but in 1969 substituted the concept of actual net income for presumed income (a haven for tax evasion). The new laws require more accurate record-keeping while providing that up to 80 percent of net income can be used as a deduction against tax-able income by applying different multiples (indicating official priori-ties) to actual investment expenditures during the tax year, with a three-year carryover privilege of any excess "investment allowances." If enforcement procedures for the federal income tax can be as much improved in agriculture (at least against medium to large landholders) as was recently achieved in the nonagricultural sector, they should not only facilitate greater compliance with the Rural Land Tax but should encourage productive agricultural outlays and reduce the present heavy reliance (92 percent of all tax revenues from agriculture) on the value-added tax (at current rates of 15 to 18 percent) levied against agricultural and other products at each stage of the marketing process.

While IBRA has also had the power to purchase or expropriate large landholdings in long-settled areas for redistribution, it has thus far limited this type of activity to a few socially critical areas such as the sugar zone of Pernambuco, the coastal plain of Rio de Janeiro, and the colonial areas of Rio Grande do Sul. Thus, it has ignored (in my opinion wisely) the counsel of the heavily biased CIDA report of 1966 on land tenure in Brazil[17]—which would have been welcome grist

---

17. Inter-American Committee for Agricultural Development (CIDA), *Land Tenure Conditions and Socio-Economic Development of the Agricultural Sector: BRA-ZIL*, Pan American Union (OAS), Washington, D.C., 1966. While containing many valu-able data, this large volume was written with such an extreme agrarian-reformist bias as to distort severely the picture which it presents of Brazilian agriculture. If the Brazilian situation were as black as painted in the CIDA report, the relatively dynamic agricultural performance here reported could hardly have taken place since 1950.

to President Goulart's mill—and has concentrated most of its attention on how best to develop colonization projects on public lands in previously unsettled areas. To date, however, IBRA's accomplishments in this field have been modest, with the resettlement of only 5,000 families on some 494,000 acres of land. But at least IBRA has recognized that the major problems of "land hunger"—especially acute in the Northeast—require assisting landless people to move to the more productive lands of the remaining agricultural frontiers rather than trying to keep them through land redistribution in their present agriculturally less promising environs. (In their hasty and probably ill-conceived launching of the Trans-Amazon Highway in mid-1970, the Brazilian military regime clearly had in mind such a population redistribution from the currently drought-ridden Northeast.) With or without such public assistance, however, spontaneous rural-to-rural migration will continue to be the major force for accomplishing this end.

While general internal migration data for the 1960s are not yet available, the rate undoubtedly continued to be high. For example, on the basis of preliminary population projections, I have estimated that the State of Parana—which had already received from other states some 1,900,000 people, largely attracted to its northern region, during 1940-60—gained net an additional 812,000 in-migrants during 1960-65 as its sparsely settled Western region began to fill rapidly.[18] In other largely rural-to-rural migration, the states of Mato Grosso, Goiás, Maranhão, and other labor-scarce frontier states must also have gained many in-migrants after 1960 as stagnating industrial-commercial activities in the major cities made these a less attractive destination. In general, such migrants must certainly have improved their socioeconomic status despite the many hardships which, like the world's immigrants throughout history, they have often faced.

In recent years, Brazil's urban newspapers (for example, the *Jornal do Brasil* in July 1968) have at times waxed indignant over the abuses which migrants from the Northeast have suffered at the hands of both interregional truckers in the guise of labor recruiters and the large landholders at their destination who pay their transport and lodging costs en route and in effect place them under indenture while they work off the landlord's advances. It is true that a well-developed system of truckers, boarding houses, and would-be agricultural em-

18. William H. Nicholls, "The Agricultural Frontier in Modern Brazilian History: The Case of Paraná, 1920-65," in Merrill Rippy (ed.), *Cultural Change in Brazil*, Ball State University, Muncie, Indiana, 1970, pp. 36-64.

ployers has spontaneously developed between the low-income Northeast and the better agricultural areas of Central and Southern Brazil in order to meet the joint needs of underemployed *nordestinos* and labor-short landowners. Such a wholly private market mechanism undoubtedly is at times abused—by false or misleading forms of solicitation by recruiters and through harsh treatment by employers—but I am convinced from extensive field experience that such abuses are extremely rare. Hence, to attack this system as "Motorized Slavery"—journalese reminiscent of the CIDA report—ignores the significant contribution which it makes to a desirable reallocation of human resources in the absence of better alternatives.

To be sure, it would be desirable if the Brazilian government or a private organization could develop an employment service where the migrant could obtain more objective information about employment opportunities, rural and urban, while regulating the present system to prevent abuses at major points of both origin and destination. Furthermore, the government could gradually ameliorate the problem (apart from present largely abortive efforts to industrialize the Northeast) by more attention to the still woefully neglected area of rural primary education and to the closely related area of developing a rational population policy. Official government attitudes continue to oppose family planning and population control, in part because of recent papal doctrine but, in larger part, because most Brazilians are mesmerized by the large unsettled areas of their vast country, including the huge Amazon whose developmental possibilities are as yet virtually unknown. What they and their government have not yet recognized is that population growth has a *temporal* as well as a *space* dimension. Accepting the view that Brazil's optimum population is twice or three times its present level, an annual population growth rate of 1.5 percent would permit Brazil to expand its private employment and essential public services (for education, sewerage and public utilities, research and extension activities, etc.) sufficiently to improve steadily the quality of its population. Continuation of the present annual growth rate (2.9 percent) on the other hand, can mean only more unemployment and underemployment, increasing illiteracy and continued low productivity for the masses (particularly in the Northeast), and greater concentration of wealth in the hands of the rich who *do* practice family limitation.[19]

19. Cf. the excellent economic analysis of the Brazilian population problem by Herman Daly in *Economic Development and Cultural Change*, July 1970.

Agricultural Price Policy, 1960-69

As we noted earlier, the authorization for minimum prices for agricultural products dated from 1951 but was little used during the 1950s. The food crises of 1960-64 were met primarily by a rapid expansion of agricultural credit, but the Goulart government also activated the minimum-price program[20] to stimulate staple food production. Relatively high minimum prices for 1963 were set for rice, corn, and beans in September 1962, in advance of planting, and were to be made effective if need be largely by government purchases rather than by loans. In general, such minimum prices for 1963-66 proved to be well below the inflated prices prevailing at and following the subsequent harvest, reducing the extent of their favorable influence on the output of the supported crops. To be sure, of the corn harvests of 1963 and 1965, 6.3 and 3.5 percent was purchased or put under loan by the government; of the 1963 peanut harvest, 11.4 percent was so treated; of the 1965 rice crop, 22.4 percent was purchased or under loan; and of the 1964 and 1965 bean harvests, 3.3 and 4.0 percent was purchased. Even in these cases, however, producer prices were usually well below official minimum prices, further undermining the influence of price supports on production decisions. For the 1965 and 1966 crops, the Castello Branco government sought to correct for the problem of inflation by fixing minimum prices for a two-year period with periodic monetary corrections but soon reversed this policy when it threatened to price Brazil out of the world market in exporting part of its bumper rice harvest of 1965.

Although the government's increased rice stocks of 1965 were disposed of at a considerable profit in 1966, a poor rice harvest having followed the largest in Brazilian history, the government thereafter retreated substantially to much lower price-support levels, having given much more credit than warranted to the effects of its relatively high price supports in 1965. Beginning in 1967 loans rather than purchases became the principal instrument for making official minimum farm prices effective, with the Bank of Brazil given the responsibility for making commodity loans and purchases, while arms of the National Superintendency of Supply (SUNAB) were put in charge of storage, sales and distribution. Minimum prices, which had previously been

20. The information on the Brazilian minimum-price and storage programs is largely based on Ruy Miller Paiva, "Apreciação Geral sôbre o Comportamento de Agricultura Brasileira," *Revista Brasileira de Economia*, January/June 1969, pp. 88-89 and 114; Smith, pp. 243-248; and Annex 18 *(Pricing and Marketing Farm Products)* of the recent IBRD Agricultural Sector Survey.

fixed only at a few large urban centers, were also thereafter announced at various interior points as well. Nonetheless, given the erratic policies followed in fixing levels of minimum prices and their monetary correction, Smith's recent econometric analysis found little evidence that—apart from two industrial crops, peanuts and probably cotton—the Brazilian price-support program has had a significant influence on the amount of acreage planted or the use of fertilizers and other modern inputs. With a serious "credibility gap" continuing between producers and public agencies, minimum prices have done little to guide crop production through a reduction of producer risk and uncertainty about future prices. As a result, year-to-year fluctuations in output have remained largely a function of weather-determined crop yields and producer adjustment of acreage to unstable market-price guidelines.

Nevertheless, in the long view, it is perhaps fortunate that Brazil has not become generally involved in price-support programs which raise domestic agricultural prices above world market levels. Of course, on coffee, its dominant export crop, Brazil has long imposed various production and marketing controls aimed at *raising* the world market price while returning to coffee-producers only that smaller part calculated to equalize supply and demand. Only for wheat has Brazil been supporting domestic prices *above* (in 1969 at twice) world levels in a drive to reduce significantly its heavy wheat imports through expanded domestic production. In addition, the government has stabilized domestic sugar prices by a system of production quotas whose main purpose is to protect the inefficient sugar industry of the Northeast from São Paulo's much more modern sugar producers. Otherwise, most Brazilian price supports have usually not been above world price levels (on those occasions in which short-run domestic prices have risen above world prices, however, price-reducing imports have normally been excluded), subjecting agriculture to the considerable competitive pressures needed to assure that any modest exportable farm surpluses (such as rice and corn) can without "dumping" readily find foreign markets. As a largely unprotected industry, however, Brazilian agriculture's terms of trade have been seriously affected by the highly protected domestic manufactures upon which it depends for much of its modernization and by the lack of adequate public services in technical orientation.

Thus far, the Brazilian government has not defined the objectives of its minimum-price program for agriculture within a sufficiently longrun context, tending to react sharply to particular shortrun food crises while losing interest soon after these crises subside. While an effective price-support program aimed merely at stabilizing agricultural prices at their competitive equilibrium levels can promote greater agricultural efficiency and modernization by reduced price uncertainty, perhaps a wiser course would be to achieve a similar goal indirectly by greater stabilization of physical supplies through public storage programs. After all, the principal price problem faced by farmers and consumers alike is wide short-term (seasonal and year-to-year) swings in food supplies and prices. Furthermore, the most pernicious effects of periodic urban food prices have been the fixing of maximum retail prices on staple foods by SUNAB which quickly dried up marketings and with some time-lag production, particularly in products most heavily dependent upon purchased inputs whose prices were uncontrolled. In such crisis-born policies, far too much emphasis has been put on the machinations of middlemen and too little on the more basic longrun marketing and production problems which are their underlying cause.

In 1965, the Central South region of Brazil had about 15,000,000 tons of storage capacity of which about 33 percent was government-owned. Privately-owned storage facilities were much more fully utilized, being subject to less bureaucratic "red tape," more flexible, and often better designed and (particularly in view of the sharp shift toward truck transportation) better located. Even for that favored region, a recent study estimated a 1970 deficit of 4,000,000 tons in storage capacity for grains and potatoes. That a serious problem still exists was shown in late 1969 when a bumper crop of wheat in Rio Grande do Sul so overtaxed storage and transport facilities that it had to be stored in the open, even the supply of tarpaulins for temporary protection being quickly exhausted. Thus, there is clearly a renewed need for a co-ordinated expansion of Brazilian food-storage capacity, both private and public, and related handling and transport facilities. Only thus can SUNAB or other government agencies have at their command sufficient supplies to check occasional extreme seasonal consumer price increases and to reduce significantly the range of year-to-year price fluctuations related to largely weather-determined variations in crop yields.

During the 1960s, most crop yields in Brazil showed modest upward trends (Table 3). Relative to the 1958-62 average, crop yields for 1968-69 were as follows: Wheat yields were up by 50 percent, having recovered to near their peak levels of the mid-1950s; potato yields were up by 26 percent, having continued their sharp rise of the 1950s, reflecting heavy use of fertilizers and imported selected seed potatoes.[21] Tobacco yields were up by 25 percent and banana yields up by 16 percent, the latter (after a decline during 1950-60) standing at a new high. Cocoa yields, which had declined during the 1950s, were up by 8 percent; and manioc yields, after a negligible increase during the 1950s, were up by 13 percent. Sugar cane yields were up by 7 percent, continuing their upward trend of the previous decade. For Brazil as a whole, corn yields were only 3 percent higher; but in São Paulo (1966-68) they were up fully 27 percent, having continued their previous favorable trend, in large part because of the rapid increase (from 39 to 65 percent between 1959-63 and 1965) in the use of high-yielding hybrid seed furnished by both private and public sources and favorable treatment by public-credit agencies. Orange yields, while 5 percent higher, were still well below their peak yields of the mid-1950s. Bean yields for all of Brazil had not quite held their own (down by 2 percent) but in São Paulo, after a very severe drop during the 1950s, were up by 12 percent (1966-68) thanks to a somewhat wider use of selected seeds.

For Brazil as a whole, cotton yields fell by 2 percent, partially off-setting their previous upward trend; in São Paulo, however, cotton yields (1966-68)—after nearly doubling during the 1950s—were up by another 39 percent under heavy credit support by the federal government as the State continued to make mandatory the use of selected seeds and improved varieties, while the use of insecticides was doubling. The 1960s also saw a decline in rice yields (10 percent for Brazil and 19 percent for São Paulo), the decline in São Paulo taking place despite very favored treatment by public-credit agencies and a moderate increase in the use of selected seeds and (in the irrigated rice which constituted a relatively small proportion of total rice production) substantial application of fertilizers. On the other hand, peanut yields, after burgeoning during the 1950s, were down by 11 percent in Brazil and by 4 percent (1966-68) even in São Paulo. Reflecting the erratic effects of the several freezes of the 1960s, Brazilian coffee yields were down by 27 percent although (apart from weather) were still holding most of their gains of the 1950s as higher-bearing tree varieties came into production.

The extent to which improved seeds were used in 1965-67 in the

21. The data on the extent of use of modern agricultural inputs here presented are from the following sources: "Diagnóstico da Agricultura Paulista," loc. cit.; Programa Estratégico de Desenvolvimento, 1968-70, pp. 135-136, 147-149; Annex 6 (Agricultural Credit) and Annex 15 (Fertilizer and Farm Machinery) of the IBRD Agricultural Sector Survey; and Smith, pp. 227-231.

whole Central South region of Brazil was as follows: cotton 90 percent (but only 20 percent for all major producing states, including the Northeast), wheat 65 percent, corn 43 percent, soybeans 16 percent, peanuts 10 percent, rice 4 percent, and beans negligible. During 1960-67, the use of pesticides in Brazil was somewhat erratic but did show an upward trend, averaging about 35 percent higher in 1965-67 than in 1958-60 as domestic production doubled absolutely and increased its share of total consumption from 15 to 17 percent. In São Paulo, pesticide consumption trebled between 1958-60 and 1961 and in 1963-65 was still about double its 1958-60 level. The number of tractors in Brazil increased only about 23 percent (from 63,500 to 78,500, of which 70 percent were in São Paulo and Rio Grande do Sul) during 1960-67, as domestic production almost completely displaced imports but remained at levels (a peak of 11,500 in 1964 and averaging only 8,640 during 1965-69) scarcely more than sufficient to replace wornout equipment. With the Brazilian tractor industry operating at less than half of its one-shift plant capacity, domestic tractor prices in 1969 were double those of the United Kingdom although, for certain tractor and animal-drawn implements, Brazilian prices are more favorable.

Finally, the consumption of fertilizers in Brazil continued to expand somewhat erratically during the 1960s. The sharp increase in fertilizer use during the 1950s, as we saw earlier, had been attributable to highly favorable exchange-rate treatment up to 1961, with the bulk of (unmixed) fertilizer imports remaining tariff-exempt even under the highly protectionist Tariff Act of 1957. Furthermore, fertilizers had been exempt from federal and state sales taxes and had been given highly preferential rail freight rates and port fees. By 1961-62, however, the price of fertilizer (relative to crop prices) in São Paulo was 65 percent above its low of 1959, resulting in a substantial setback in fertilizer consumption from its 1960 high. Despite a continuing rise in relative fertilizer prices, consumption in 1963 again approached its 1960 volume and then held to fairly high levels in 1964-65 even though relative fertilizer prices in São Paulo had by 1965 reached nearly three times their 1959 low. In 1966, Brazil's physical consumption of nitrogen was 7 percent higher, and its consumption of potassium and phosphates 12 and 11 percent lower, than in 1960.

In 1966, however, the government introduced a special fund for promoting fertilizer use by interest-free loans which were apparently a major factor accounting for a doubling of nitrogen and potassium consumption and more than a doubling of phosphate consumption between 1966 and 1968. As in the use of other modern agricultural inputs,

São Paulo agriculture dominated Brazilian fertilizer consumption, alone accounting for 60 percent with the South and Central West regions using more than 90 percent. In 1968, domestic phosphate production supplied 45 percent of total consumption, but the corresponding figure for nitrogen was only 6.4 percent, while all potassium was still imported. The primary product of the domestic fertilizer industry has been single superphosphate, with prices' far above those at which they could be imported. With the projected creation by 1973 of a domestic production capacity of 116,000 tons (80 percent of total consumption in 1968) of nitrogen, based on imported naphtha, there is a similar danger that this basic plant nutrient will also be priced far above world markets. Even though high fertilizer prices have recently been reduced by their exemption from the 17-percent value-added sales tax and loans for fertilizer use have been heavily subsidized, fertilizer consumption in *Brazil* remains at extremely *low* levels. It can reach desirable levels only if relative fertilizer prices are also reduced considerably, a goal to which the current import-substitution drive may easily become an even more serious barrier in the near future.

Relative to the index of prices received (for coffee, 19 other crops, and 4 animal products), the index of prices paid by São Paulo farmers (1948-52 = 100) averaged 134 percent in 1956-61, 118 percent in 1962-64, and 139 percent in 1965-67.[22] (Inversely, relative to prices paid, São Paulo prices received by farmers were 75, 85, and 72 percent respectively, reflecting a longrun tendency toward less favorable terms of trade for agriculture). In 1960, relative to their 1948-52 levels, machinery and equipment and work animals had shown the greatest price rises and vaccines, medicines, and fertilizers the smallest; the prices of animal feeds and construction materials rose less than average, the prices of tools, purchased services, and fuels increasing at about the average rate. During 1960-65, however, it was chemical, petroleum, and drug products (fertilizers, insecticides, fuels and lubricants, and vaccines and medicines) whose relative prices increased most relative to all farm prices paid, fertilizer prices rising at more than twice the average rate. The prices of animal feeds and purchased services also significantly exceeded the average rate. Tool prices showed an average rate of increase, with prices of machinery, construction materials, and work animals rising less than average. By 1964-66 a 60-kilogram sack of rice, beans, or corn in São Paulo would buy only about 50 percent

22. The São Paulo data on changing prices paid by farmers are from "Diagnóstico da Agricultura Paulista," pp. 24-29; and Paiva, p. 112.

as much nitrate or phosphate fertilizer, and about 42 percent as much potassium fertilizer, as in 1958-60. Potatoes and cotton were only moderately better off, even relative coffee and sugar cane prices being less favorable to fertilizer use than in the earlier period.

In 1965, with real agricultural prices received by São Paulo farmers down by 9 percent (and real prices paid down by less than 3 percent) from 1960, the prices paid for different agricultural inputs relative to prices received showed the following changes during 1960-65: fertilizer up by 136 percent, insecticides up by 93 percent, fuels up by 47 percent, and vaccines up by 43 percent; feeds and purchased services up 26 to 29 percent; tools up by 7 percent; and machinery, construction materials, and work animals down by 3 to 11 percent. Comparable data are not available for Brazil as a whole but, relative to wholesale prices of all agricultural prices (including coffee), wholesale prices of all chemical products increased by 104 percent, construction materials by 71 percent, and metallurgical products and fuels by 56 to 59 percent, between 1959-61 and 1967-69. These latter data suggest that Brazilian agriculture still faced high relative manufactured input prices (much of the increase coming during 1967-69) as the decade ended. Subsidized interest rates on credit for fertilizer and tractor purchases and exemption from the general sales tax on such agricultural inputs would appear to be an inadequate offset to the high prices of Brazil's tariff-protected domestic industries insofar as they were agricultural suppliers.

While Brazilian agricultural output was surprisingly well maintained in the last half of the 1960s despite an unfavorable turn in its terms of trade, much of that output was from new areas whose initial high fertility permitted high crop yields with a minimum of purchased agricultural inputs. Such a situation cannot be counted on indefinitely. Hence, if Brazilian agriculture's first timid steps toward a more conservative and more modern technology are not to prove abortive, public policy must become much more concerned than ever before with bringing the costs of productivity-increasing manufactured farm inputs more closely in line with present moderate levels of farm-product prices.

Conclusion

There can be no doubt that, whether judged for the entire period since 1950 or only for the decade 1960-70, Brazilian agriculture has performed remarkably well. That it did so is far more attributable to the enterprise and energy of Brazilian farmers than to the sporadic and crisis-oriented agricultural policies of the government. Somehow—largely spontaneously in the absence of well-conceived longrun public agricultural policies—Brazil's farmers and rural people have filled up the remaining agricultural frontiers, which in a few years have been converted from forests to productive farming areas; have kept crop and livestock output expanding apace with a high rate of population growth and rising per-capita incomes; and, in the process, have even managed against all odds to raise their productivity at least modestly by adopting better practices and techniques. Given the extent to which the Brazilian government has failed to provide agriculture's most fundamental needs in terms of adequate agricultural research and extension services, modern agricultural inputs at prices which farmers can afford to pay, less unstable markets and prices, and accurate production and market information, Brazilian urban consumers have fared far better in meeting their food needs than they deserved.

This does not mean to say that Brazilian public policy has been completely lacking in concern for agriculture. Particularly in highway development, government has made a major contribution to the expansion and improvement of agricultural output and productivity. Nor has public agricultural-credit policy lacked for resources, although the failure to find effective ways for using credit as a direct incentive for raising agricultural productivity has been a serious fault of that well-financed system. The continued expansion of the federal agricultural extension service during most of the 1960s was also a favorable sign, although under its recent public sponsorship this extension service appears to have been running out of steam as budgetary restrictions prevent the utilization of a much-needed new surplus of graduate agronomists in the further expansion of this program. Furthermore, with agricultural research continuing to languish at an inexcusably low level, extension workers still lack the firm research base which is essential to making their efforts far more effective. While the present government has, in its approach to agrarian reforms, been slow to engage in land redistribution—appropriately so in view of the importance of the nation's large farmers in assuming the risks of agricultural innovation—its failure to date in enforcing compliance with the wholly justifiable alternatives of a Rural Land Tax and (in the agricultural sector) the federal income tax clearly require immediate correction.

During the 1960s, the Brazilian government also gave much attention to a minimum-price program for agriculture, but this policy was erratic and largely ineffective, suffering strongly from the absence of well-defined objectives within a longrun context. Had the government placed greater emphasis upon an indirect stabilization of prices through a more adequate program of public storage—which would help to reduce wide short-term (seasonal and year-to-year) swings in food supplies and prices, thereby avoiding the pressure to apply counterproductive consumer price controls—both farmers and consumers would have been much better off. While such a policy would have required a substantial public investment in additional storage facilities, there is no reason why such facilities would not have been profitable if adequate attention were given to appropriate location, efficient design, and flexibility of management within the limits of a single-minded objective of stabilizing physical supplies of staple food products. Finally, whether judged by its effectiveness in producing modern agricultural inputs at prices favorable to greater agricultural use or its contribution to the absorption of a significant part of agriculture's substantial surplus of underemployed people, the public-sponsored program of domestic import-substituting industrialization has not yet served well the rural sector. Insofar as industrialization continues to dominate the objectives of public policy, more attention to increasing the efficiency of both farm-input manufactures and the less capital-intensive agricultural processing industries will be needed if it is to become a milestone rather than a millstone for Brazilian agriculture and rural people.

For the last twenty years, Brazilian agriculture has appeared to informed people as living on borrowed time if the quantity and quality of the national diet are to match the needs of a rapidly growing and increasingly prosperous urban population. That it has thus far met these needs so well is a near miracle, given the relative public neglect which it has traditionally faced. Such a favorable outcome cannot much longer continue, however, especially in the livestock sector. Unless the government at long last offers on a sustained basis much fuller financial assistance and technical orientation than Brazilian agriculture has yet had—as it faces the imminent necessity of making the transition from its present exploitative and intensive practices—agricultural performance during the next two decades probably will finally be found to be seriously wanting.

6 ANDREA MANESCHI

The Brazilian Public Sector

WHAT ARE the economic functions of the public sector in a developing country such as Brazil? How, and with what efficiency, were they carried out in Brazil during the 1960s?

The public sector, whether intentionally or not, affects a country's allocation of economic resources, income redistribution, stabilization of cyclical fluctuations and of the price level, and economic growth.[1] The allocative functions of the government are both direct and indirect; the first include the various forms of public expenditure, on both current and capital account, which result in the appropriation by the government of a certain fraction of the country's Gross Domestic Product (GDP). This type of public expenditure is carried out in such areas as national defense or infrastructural projects which normally fall outside the sphere of competence of the private sector. In addition to purchasing goods and services in the market, the government indirectly influences the allocation of resources in the private sector by granting tax, credit and other types of incentive to promote certain socially desirable ends.

Secondly, the government's spending and taxing powers can be used to alter the market-determined distribution of income in accord-

1. A normative framework of analysis for the public sector incorporating the first three of these objectives is discussed in Richard A. Musgrave, *The Theory of Public Finance*, (New York: McGraw-Hill, 1959), chapters 1-3.

185

ance with the society's (or the governing elite's) consensus as to what constitutes an optimum degree of income inequality. Some economists (such as Musgrave) believe that the most efficient way to accomplish this so as to minimize undesired interference with resource allocation is to tax the wealthier members of the community and transfer the proceeds to the poorer ones. Such government transfers are an important part of public expenditure but do not represent a claim by the government on part of the national income since the beneficiaries of these transfers are the ones who decide on their allocation.

Since the depression of the 1930s and especially since the Second World War, a third area of public sector concern has been added to the two preceding ones, namely the stabilization of output, employment and price-level fluctuations. Such fluctuations can be prevented or at least greatly reduced by the use of fiscal, monetary, and other types of compensatory policy. In accordance with Keynesian economics, the government can combat a cyclical downturn by running a budgetary deficit and can rid the economy of inflationary pressure by engendering a budgetary surplus. This rather simple framework of analysis must of course be modified in the case of an economy such as Brazil's between 1963 and 1966, in which a high rate of inflation coexists with a widespread underutilization of industrial capacity.

In a low-income country such as Brazil, the government can influence decisively a fourth objective—a satisfactory rate of economic growth. This objective inevitably conditions its actions in the fields of allocation, distribution, and stabilization, which must be made consistent with it. Thus the government may tolerate a highly unequal distribution of income if it generates a high rate of saving and of economic growth and may avoid a "shock treatment" of runaway inflation for fear that it will be accompanied by the stagnation of economic activity.

After this necessarily cursory and rather general discussion of the objectives of the public sector in a developing economy, we come to the second question posed above: what do the available data reveal about the way in which successive Brazilian governments carried them out during the sixties?

The direct allocative functions of the public sector are reflected in aggregative national income accounting terms by the items "government consumption" and "government investment," the first of these being subdivided into expenditure on public employees and on other goods and services.[2] The ratios of these four variables to GDP during

2. In this section the term "government" is used to designate the public sector as a whole, which includes federal, state, and municipal governments and the federal and state *autarquias* but excludes firms which are wholly or partially owned by federal, state, or municipal governments.

the years 1960 to 1968, all variables being expressed in terms of current prices, are given in Table 1. Their trends over time show whether these types of public purchases have tended to grow faster or slower than economic activity as a whole as measured by the GDP.[3]

In order to first gain a historical perspective on the participation of the government in economic activity during the sixties, these ratios are shown in Figure 1 over as long a period of time as data allow; namely, the year 1939 and the years since 1947.[4] Their time paths are also summarized in Table 1 which gives their values in 1939 and their simple averages over the periods 1947-1950, 1951-55, 1956-60, 1961-63, 1964-66, and 1967-68, which roughly correspond to the administrations of Dutra, Vargas-Café Filho, Kubitschek, Quadros-Goulart, Castello Branco, and Costa e Silva.[5]

The ratios of government consumption, salaries of government employees, and public investment to GDP all show a tendency to rise over the thirty-year period under examination. The ratio of "other purchases" (that part of government consumption other than employee salaries) to GDP rose until the first half of the fifties and has tended to fall ever since, so that at the end of the sixties it was lower than in 1939. Since the consumption-GDP ratio has risen over these thirty years in spite of the fall in its "other purchases" component, this implies that its other component (employee salaries-GDP ratio) has risen even faster.

The foregoing remarks relate to trends observable during the thirty-year period. If we now examine the sixties, a somewhat different pattern emerges. The ratios to GDP of public consumption and of "other purchases" have both fallen significantly, that of public investment has remained roughly constant, and that of public employee salaries has, on the average, continued to rise, with a slight drop toward

3. Gross Domestic Product seems a more relevant index of economic activity than Gross National Product, since it measures the total production and tax base of the country, whereas GNP excludes the net income which accrues to nonresidents but can nevertheless be subject to taxation.

4. Public sector data for the years 1939 and 1947-66 were calculated by the Centro de Estudos Fiscais of the Fundação Getúlio Vargas and published in *Conjuntura Econômica*, Vol. 23, No. 12, 1969. I wish to thank Dr. Margaret Costa, director of the CEF, for supplying me with revised data for 1967 and preliminary estimates for 1968, as well as for her helpfulness in interpreting the Brazilian public sector accounts. The national income accounts data are revised estimates calculated by the Centro de Contas Nacionais of the FGV and published in *Conjuntura Econômica*, Vol. 24, No. 6, 1970.

5. This correspondence is only approximate for two reasons: because data are available only for calendar years, whereas the tenure of office of each administration usually began at the end of January or of March, and because the pattern of expenditures and receipts at the start of any administration was inevitably affected by decisions made towards the end of the preceding one.

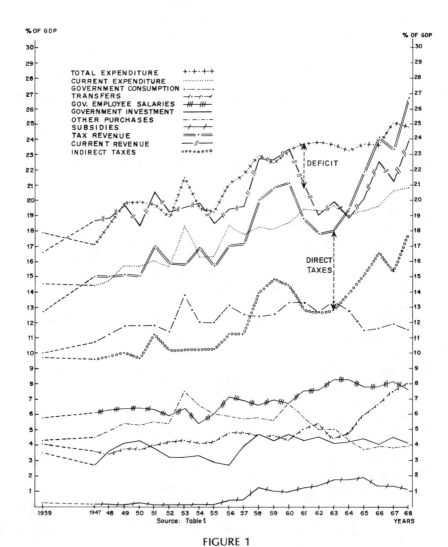

FIGURE 1

PUBLIC SECTOR EXPENDITURES AND RECEIPTS AS PERCENTAGES
OF GROSS DOMESTIC PRODUCT: 1939 AND 1947-1968

TABLE 1
BRAZILIAN PUBLIC SECTOR'S EXPENDITURE AND REVENUE FLOWS AS
PERCENTAGES OF GROSS DOMESTIC PRODUCT, 1939 AND 1947-1968

Years	Gov. Consumption/GDP (1) = (2) + (3)	Gov. Employee Salaries/GDP (2)	Other Purchases/GDP (3)	Transfers/GDP (4)	Subsidies/GDP (5)	Current Expenditure/GDP (6) = (1) + (4) + (5)	Gov. Investment/GDP (7)	Total Gov. Purchases/GDP (8) = (1) + (7)	Total Gov. Expenditure/GDP (9) = (6) + (7)	Tax Revenue/GDP (10) = (11) + (12)	Indirect Taxes/GDP (11)	Direct Taxes/GDP (12)	Other Current Receipts/GDP (13)	Total Current Revenue/GDP (14) = (10) + (13)	Gov. Savings/GDP (15) = (14) - (6)	Deficit/GDP (16) = (7) - (15) = (9) - (14)	Indirect Taxes/Total Taxes (17)
1939	10.2	5.8	4.3	4.1	0.2	14.5	3.5	13.6	17.9	12.7	9.7	3.0	3.9	16.6	2.2	1.3	76
1947-50	11.4	6.3	5.0	3.6	0.1	15.1	3.7	15.0	18.8	15.0	9.8	5.2	3.8	18.8	3.7	0.0	65.2
1951-55	12.2	6.0	6.2	4.2	0.1	16.5	3.3	15.5	19.7	16.3	10.7	5.5	3.2	19.5	3.0	0.3	65.9
1956-60	12.8	6.9	5.9	4.6	0.8	18.2	4.1	16.8	22.2	19.0	13.1	5.9	2.5	21.5	3.4	0.7	68.9
1961-63	13.1	7.8	5.3	4.9	1.4	19.4	4.3	17.4	23.7	18.2	12.7	5.5	1.7	19.9	0.5	3.8	69.9
1964-66	11.9	8.0	4.0	5.8	1.6	19.3	4.2	16.1	23.5	21.8	15.2	6.6	-1.3	20.5	1.2	3.0	69.8
1967-68[1]	11.7	7.8	3.8	7.7	1.2	20.7	4.3	16.0	25.0	25.0	16.6	8.4	-2.5	22.5	1.9	2.4	66.2
1960	13.3	6.7	6.7	4.3	0.9	18.5	4.7	18.1	23.3	20.1	14.4	5.7	3.1	23.3	4.7	0.0	71.7
1961	13.3	7.5	5.8	5.0	1.2	19.4	4.3	17.5	23.7	18.8	12.8	6.0	2.0	20.8	1.4	2.9	68.2
1962	12.7	7.6	5.0	5.3	1.3	19.3	4.5	17.2	23.8	17.8	12.6	5.2	1.2	19.0	-0.3	4.8	70.6
1963	13.4	8.3	5.0	4.5	1.7	19.6	4.1	17.4	23.6	18.0	12.8	5.2	1.9	19.9	0.3	3.8	71.0
1964	12.7	8.3	4.3	4.7	1.7	19.0	4.2	16.9	23.2	19.4	13.9	5.4	-0.5	18.8	-0.2	4.4	72.1
1965	11.5	7.8	3.7	5.9	1.9	19.3	4.4	15.9	23.7	21.8	15.0	6.8	-1.7	20.1	0.9	3.5	69.0
1966	11.6	7.8	3.9	6.6	1.3	19.6	4.0	15.6	23.6	24.1	16.5	7.6	-1.6	22.5	2.9	1.0	68.4
1967	11.9	8.1	3.8	7.5	1.3	20.6	4.5	16.3	25.1	23.3	15.3	8.1	-2.2	21.2	0.5	3.9	65.4
1968[a]	11.5	7.6	3.9	8.0	1.1	20.7	4.1	15.6	24.8	26.7	17.9	8.8	-2.8	23.9	3.2	0.9	67.1

a. preliminary estimates

Source: See footnote 4.

the end of the decade. Far from achieving the decrease in the share of public consumption in GDP by reducing its wage bill, the government maintained the share of the latter in GDP and introduced drastic economies in all other consumption expenditures. The swelling of public-sector *funcionalismo* at the expense of other types of purchases on current account has probably represented a misallocation of resources; if this policy is not reversed in the near future, it may result in severe inefficiencies within the public sector.

One can only speculate on factors responsible for the decline in the government consumption ratio at a time that the private consumption ratio (to GDP) was increasing. A probable contributing factor was the sizable increase in government spending other than that resulting in the purchase of goods and services, namely transfers and subsidies. In order to offset this increase at a time the government was under pressure to control its total spending for anti-inflationary reasons, public consumption was allowed to shrink in relative terms.

Resource allocation in the public sector has been discussed thus far in very aggregative terms. In order to make any appraisal regarding the efficiency of this allocation given the government's objectives, it becomes necessary to disaggregate public spending in accordance with the functions it is meant to serve, such as defense, health, education. Unfortunately, such data for the public sector as a whole are not yet available in Brazil. The data calculated for 1964 by the Ministry of Planning relate only to the federal government and the "decentralized administration," which consists of federal *autarquias* and the wholly or partially federally owned enterprises.[6] These data, however, apart from excluding state and municipal expenditures, lump together both purchases and transfers; therefore, even within their limited sphere of applicability, they do not give a true picture of resource allocation.[7] The expenditures of the federal government are presently available for the sixties only classified by the type of ministry and the various legislative and judiciary entities which effected them. They are not even approximately indicative of a functional breakdown of public spending because of the diversity of purposes which the expenditure in each ministry has served.

The trend of government investment discussed above relates to investment of the traditional kind in infrastructural projects, schools, hospitals, and public buildings. In an economy such as Brazil's another important category of investment over which the government has direct control is that carried out by public and mixed public-private enterprises.

To complement our picture of resource allocation in the public sector, we summarize in Table 2 the available data covering the period 1947-1965 and relating to the investment carried out by the enterprises of the federal government (thus excluding the numerous state-owned and municipally owned enterprises). This table shows the proportion of total gross fixed investment carried out by the "government" in the national accounts sense of the term (GI/TI), by government enterprises (GEI/TI) and private enterprises (PEI/TI), where PEI equals TEI (total enterprise investment) minus GEI; in addition

6. Ministério do Planejamento e Coordenação Econômica, *Balanço Orçamentário Consolidado do Govêrno Federal-1964*, Rio de Janeiro, September 1965.

7. The omission of state government expenditure in any functional breakdown of public sector expenditures is especially serious in such fields as education, where it is known that state spending exceeds that by the federal government.

TABLE 2
PUBLIC AND PRIVATE INVESTMENT SHARES AND SECTORAL
PARTICIPATION IN GOVERNMENT ENTERPRISE INVESTMENT, 1947-1965
(percentages)

Years	$\frac{GI}{TI}$	$\frac{GEI}{TI}$	$\frac{PEI}{TI}$	Sectoral Participation in GEI					
				Mining	Iron & Steel	Chemi-cals	Power	Trans-port	Other
1947-50	23.3	2.6	74.1	17.5	23.1	0.8	7.1	13.7	37.8
1951-55	20.2	3.0	76.8	4.0	34.1	24.2	11.9	5.2	20.7
1956-60	25.5	7.8	66.7	4.5	9.0	36.9	11.5	26.2	11.9
1961-63	24.4	13.1	62.5	3.9	40.3	17.3	12.7	17.2	8.7
1964-65	27.6	12.9	59.5	5.2	38.0	21.7	16.7	10.7	7.7
1960	27.1	11.6	61.3	6.3	15.3	38.2	13.0	13.3	13.9
1961	24.8	14.4	60.7	3.1	42.1	17.1	8.9	16.3	12.4
1962	25.2	13.5	61.3	3.6	49.9	14.5	9.5	16.4	6.2
1963	23.3	11.4	65.4	5.3	26.2	20.8	21.4	19.2	7.1
1964	25.4	9.4	65.3	4.6	24.8	24.3	23.8	13.5	9.0
1965	29.9	16.5	53.6	5.6	45.7	20.2	12.6	9.0	6.9

Symbols: TI= total gross fixed investment
                        GI= government gross fixed investment
                        GEI= government enterprise gross fixed investment
                        PEI= private enterprise gross fixed investment

Source: see footnote 8.

it gives the sectoral participation in GEI.[8]

Government enterprise investment began assuming quantitative importance in 1957 and gathered momentum during the remaining years of the Kubitschek era until it amounted to 14.4 percent of total investment in 1961. Its average share in total investment over the peri-

8. The data of public enterprise investment for the period 1947-65 are taken from Arnaldo de Oliveira Werneck, "As Atividades Empresariais do Govêrno Federal no Brasil," *Revista Brasileira de Economia,* vol. 23, No. 3, July-September 1969; and those of government and total enterprise investment (the latter being equivalent to *formação bruta de capital fixo das emprêsas)* from *Conjuntura Econômica,* vol. 23, No. 10, 1969.

Our nomenclature is slightly misleading to the extent that the above-defined residual private-enterprise sector contains state and municipally owned enterprises as well as certain federally owned enterprises which have not been included under that category.

The percentages shown in Table 2 for various groups of years since 1947, which correspond to those given in Table 1, are obtained by deflating all variables by the implicit deflator of gross fixed capital formation, taking the sums of the numerator and denominator variables over the years in question and dividing the first sum by the second.

od 1961-65 was approximately 13 percent, a maximum recorded level of 16.5 percent being reached in 1965. The share of total investment under public control, (GI + GEI)/TI, rose continuously during the successive governments of the fifties and sixties, attaining an average value of 37.5 percent in 1961-63 and 40.5 percent in 1964-65, a dramatic increase over the corresponding value of 23.2 percent in the years 1951-55. In 1965, the last year for which data are available, the government was responsible for about one half of total investment.[9]

During the sixties the entrepreneurial activities of the government concentrated on the iron and steel industry (represented mainly by Companhia Siderúrgica Nacional, Companhia Siderúrgica Paulista, and Usinas Siderúrgicas de Minas Gerais) and the chemical industry (mainly Petrobrás), these two sectors together receiving more than one half of government enterprise investment.

As mentioned above, in addition to its direct allocational functions the government has influenced resource allocation in the private sector through various types of fiscal, credit, and other incentives, as will be shown later in this chapter.

We now turn to income redistribution. A rough measure of the government's direct redistributional activity is given by the ratio of consumer transfers to gross domestic product (Table 1, col. 4).[10] This ratio has shown a continuous tendency to increase throughout the postwar period. A large fraction of its over-all increase was registered during the sixties, its value in 1968 being almost double that of 1960. The vastly expanded scope of social security benefits, which constitute the bulk of transfers to consumers, is analogous to that observed in presently advanced countries at earlier stages of their development.[11]

Subsidies also rose at a much faster rate than GDP, at least until 1965 (col. 5). They have a redistributional objective since they allow consumers to purchase certain services at a lower price. Since in Brazil the transport sector has been the main beneficiary of subsidies, it is safe to assert that the lower income groups have benefited more from them than those of higher income. The ratio to GDP of government current expenditure, defined as the sum of public consumption plus

9. It should be recalled that the figures for GEI/TI given in Table 2 are underestimates because of incomplete coverage.

10. Note that the government's allocational expenditures on current and capital account also have distributional implications which should be taken into account in any detailed analysis of the incidence of public expenditure.

11. Cf. Richard A. Musgrave, *Fiscal Systems*, (New Haven: Yale University Press 1969), chapter 4.

transfers plus subsidies, has tended to rise ever since 1939, exceeding 20 percent by the end of the sixties (col. 6).

As well as acting through the pattern of its expenditures, the government has influenced the state of income distribution through the structure of taxation. Cols. 10, 11, and 12 of Table 1 show the trends in the ratios to GDP of tax revenue and of its two component parts, indirect taxes and direct taxes. The ratio between indirect and total taxes is given in col. 17: it tended to increase from 1947 to 1964 and subsequently to decrease. Since indirect taxes are usually considered regressive in nature and direct taxes progressive, one may be tempted to argue that during the second half of the sixties the tax pattern grew slightly more equitable.

Such a conclusion, however, is not warranted. In the first place, social security contributions rather than income taxes were chiefly responsible for the relatively greater rise in direct taxes (Table 3). Secondly, indirect taxes have been levied with respect to different and changing bases such as turnover and value added, and at rates which, in the case of the federal consumption tax, have varied from commodity to commodity and have also been subject to frequent changes. It is therefore impossible to assert, in the absence of a detailed investigation, that the increase in the proportion of direct to indirect taxes has either improved or worsened the distribution of income. Furthermore, the government influenced the latter not only by varying the tax structure but also by acting on people's income before taxes, chiefly through its wage policy. I present below evidence that the real values of both the minimum wage and the average industrial wage have declined between 1964 and 1968 as a result of the revolutionary governments' stabilization program. Hence, even had the tax mix turned more progressive since 1964, this effect would probably have been more than offset by the regressive impact on income before taxes of the government's wage policy.[12]

12. To derive a measure of the distributional impact of the government's expenditure, tax, and wage policies, aggregative analysis must be substituted by a study of the incidence of these policies by income class and, if possible, for different regions of the country and different sectors of the economy. Two studies along these lines (which, however, omit the impact of wage policy) are Henry Aaron, "Estimates of the Distributional Impact of Brazilian Taxes and Expenditures," written for the Council for International Progress in Management (USA), Inc., under contract with A.I.D., mimeo, 1968; and Gian S. Sahota, The Distribution of Tax Burden in Brazil, mimeo, 1968. Aaron concludes that in Brazil as a whole "estimated tax burdens follow a hump-shaped pattern, rising sharply over income classes to income five to eight times the minimum wage and diminishing thereafter" and that "the estimated expenditure pat-

While the changing structure of budgetary policy is an important factor in the government's impact on economic activity and the price level—the stabilization of which constitutes the third economic function of the public sector—it must be considered jointly with other policies of similar impact—monetary, credit, price and wage policies. These various facets of public policy (with the exception of price policy) are analyzed below, where an appraisal is made of the revolutionary governments' stabilization efforts since 1964. For the present we restrict our attention to the spending and revenue flows in the public sector as a whole and to the deficit given by the difference between them. As shown in Table 1, to calculate the deficit (taking all variables in proportion to GDP), tax revenue (col. 10) is first added to other current receipts (col. 13), obtaining total current revenue (col. 14).[13] Secondly, current expenditure (col. 6) is added to public investment (col. 7), giving total expenditure (col. 9). Finally, total current revenue is subtracted from total expenditure, yielding the deficit (col. 16).[14]

Total government spending (col. 9) has tended to rise with re-

tern is progressive through the lower five (of nine) income classes" (op. cit., p. 1). Interestingly enough, he finds that the incidence of social security benefits is regressive over the lowest five income classes, in spite of the over-all progressivity of total government expenditures.

13. In the Brazilian government account, total current revenue is underestimated since its component "other current receipts," instead of representing nontax revenue only, is the difference between this and transfers other than those to consumers. Such transfers are those between different levels of government (which are zero since we are here dealing with the consolidated government account) and transfers to certain public and mixed enterprises and nonprofit organizations in the private sector. Since 1964 these transfers have exceeded nontax revenue, causing "other current receipts" to turn negative. Similarly, current expenditure and total expenditure are underestimated since they omit the transfer expenditures which appear, with negative sign, in "other current receipts."

14. An equivalent way of calculating the deficit is to subtract current expenditure from total current revenue, yielding public saving (col. 15). The deficit is then found by subtracting public saving from public investment.

Note that this deficit is different from the déficit de caixa discussed earlier for two reasons. The déficit de caixa refers to the union government only (that is, the federal government and the federal autarquias) instead of to the entire public sector, and the deficit discussed in this section is of the national income accounts type, that is, it registers the way that fiscal transactions affect the income stream. The déficit de caixa is instead analogous to the consolidated cash budget deficit in the United States since it records payments and receipts on a cash rather than an accrual basis. Moreover, it includes loan transactions and purchases and sales of existing assets, none of which directly affects national income.

spect to GDP ever since 1939, the proportion between them reaching approximately one quarter by the end of the sixties. Government revenue (col. 14) has also increased, but in a more irregular manner. After rising throughout the fifties, its ratio to GDP remained between 1961 and 1965 below the average level attained during the second half of the fifties, exceeding this level only in 1966, with a significant further jump in 1968. The difference in the trends of expenditures and receipts is reflected in the deficit-GDP ratio (col. 16) which, after slowly rising in the fifties and maintaining an average value of 0.7 percent in the Kubitschek years, more than quintupled during the Quadros and Goulart administrations. It decreased somewhat during the Castello Branco regime and a further sizable fall was achieved in 1968.

It is no coincidence that the widening of the deficit-GDP ratio in the early sixties was accompanied by a rapidly accelerating inflation, nor that, with the decline of this ratio in the second half of the decade, the rate of inflation also decreased. The huge deficits recorded in the early sixties were not so much the result of excessive public spending since, as shown by col. 9, the ratio between total spending and GDP merely conformed to its "secularly" rising trend. The cause was rather a breakdown in the government's tax-collection mechanism, which was such that taxes remained practically constant in real value.

The Performance of Budget Policy in the Sixties

I now take a more detailed look at the changes in expenditure and revenue flows during the successive administrations that have governed Brazil since 1961. This analysis of different time periods is needed to complement that of different categories of expenditures and receipts over time offered in the previous section. In addition, I discuss how changes in tax revenue were determined by those in the most important taxes levied at the federal, state, and municipal levels, whose trends in real terms are shown in Table 3.

Quadros and Goulart

Between 1961 and 1963, the trends of all broad categories of expenditure with respect to GDP were similar to those registered during the Kubitschek administration (Table 1). The government wage bill continued rising in relative terms, other consumption expenditures fell, and consumption as a whole increased slightly. Transfers also rose slowly with respect to GDP, as did public investment. The most noticeable change occurred in the ratio of subsidies to GDP: after

rising substantially in the Kubitschek years, this ratio gave another
sizable jump, as a reflection mainly of the deficits in the public transport system. Current and total expenditure increased, on the average,
by 1.2 percent and 1.5 percent of GDP respectively over the ratios
reached under the previous administration.

While all classes of expenditure (with the exception of nonwage
consumption) increased their participation in GDP, taxes (both direct
and indirect) and other current receipts decreased theirs, as is ap-

TABLE 3
REAL TAX REVENUE BY LEVEL OF GOVERNMENT AND MAJOR
TYPES OF TAX, 1960-1968
(millions of 1953 NCr$)

	1960	1961	1962	1963	1964	1965	1966	1967	1968[a]
Federal Government									
Taxes: Total	70.3	60.2	61.3	64.4	70.1	80.2	91.3	78.9	102.7
Consumption Tax	23.3	25.7	27.5	30.8	35.7	34.3	41.6	42.1	58.4
Income Tax	17.9	18.3	16.3	18.3	19.6	26.8	25.2	23.0	26.0
Import Duties	6.1	7.5	7.9	6.5	5.0	5.5	6.4	5.5	9.4
Stamp Tax	7.1	7.6	8.6	8.1	7.6	9.1	10.1	-	-
Net Premiums on									
Imports	14.6	-	-	-	-	-	-	-	-
Other	1.2	1.2	1.0	0.7	2.1	4.5	8.0	8.4	9.0
Federal Autarquia									
Taxes: Total	28.6	39.2	36.0	35.2	38.5	53.6	65.6	74.0	87.5
Social Security									
Contrib. (employer and									
employee)	16.1	22.0	21.5	20.9	23.5	29.8	38.3	40.3	46.8
Fuel Tax	7.7	11.3	9.1	9.1	9.7	17.7	16.8	15.4	18.4
Other	4.9	5.9	5.5	5.2	5.3	6.1	10.5	18.3	22.3
State Taxes: Total	48.4	52.5	53.2	52.4	63.1	64.9	73.5	85.7	103.7
Sales Tax	37.3	41.2	44.5	43.8	53.9	57.5	64.5	81.1	97.5
Other	11.1	11.3	8.7	8.5	9.1	7.4	9.0	4.7	6.2
Municipal Taxes: Total	7.3	7.7	7.9	9.9	9.3	11.8	13.3	8.6	10.7
Public Sector Taxes:									
Total	154.7	159.6	158.3	161.8	180.9	210.6	243.7	247.2	304.6

a. Preliminary estimates

Source: *Conjuntura Econômica*, Vol. 23, No 12, 1969; revised data for 1967 and preliminary estimates for 1968 were supplied by the Centro de Estudos Fiscais of the
Fundação Getúlio Vargas. To obtain values in 1953 NCr$, the implicit GNP deflator
was used.

parent from columns 10 through 14 of Table 1. Table 3 shows that total tax revenue in real terms remained approximately constant between 1961 and 1963 and that federal tax revenue continued until 1965 below its 1960 level. The federal consumption tax advanced satisfactorily, but the income tax hovered around its 1960 level, with a drop in 1962. After an 8.4 percent jump in 1961, the real value of state taxes also stagnated until 1964. As a result of these changes, the ratio of indirect to total taxes in the public sector as a whole increased by one percentage point with respect to that prevailing under Kubitschek (Table 1, col. 17), reaching a level of 69.9 percent.

These divergent trends in expenditures and receipts caused the public sector deficit-GDP ratio to rise to its maximum recorded average level of 3.8 percent. Public savings on current account were practically wiped out, which meant that nearly the whole of government investment had to be financed through the printing press, the fraction financed by compulsory and voluntary loans being negligible. As a consequence of the government's financial mismanagement, the wholesale price index increased at a rate of 83 percent in 1963. A vicious circle resulted from the fact that an increasing rate of inflation spelled a decline in real tax collection, and the latter combined with increasing real government expenditure implied a widening deficit, a faster increase in the issue of currency, and a faster rate of inflation.

Castello Branco

After Goulart's ouster, the revolutionary government of Castello Branco attempted to reorganize the chaotic state of public finances by curbing certain types of expenditure and raising the country's tax burden. The results achieved during the next three years are shown in Tables 1 and 3. The ratio of public consumption to GDP was reduced by slashing expenditures other than the wages of civilian and military employees, which continued rising in relation to GDP. On the other hand, transfers rose substantially and subsidies reached an all-time high with respect to GDP. As a consequence of these diverging trends in the different components of government spending, the average ratio of current expenditure to GDP remained practically unchanged with respect to the Quadros-Goulart years. The same was true of public capital formation, and the average proportion of total expenditure to GDP dropped only very slightly.

If the net result of the government's anti-inflationary efforts was almost negligible with respect to public-sector expenditure, the same cannot be said regarding its receipts.[15] Tax revenue increased its average ratio to GDP by no less than 3.6 percent. With the exception of import duties, all the most important types of tax contributed to this rise, the star performers being the fuel tax and social security contributions, followed by the state sales tax *(impôsto de vendas e consignações)* and the federal income tax. The average ratio of indirect to total taxes, however, remained practically unaltered. In spite of the favorable trend in taxes, the ratio of current revenue to GDP rose very little on account of the sharp fall in "other current receipts"—so sharp, in fact, that this item turned negative.[16] Because of this, the average ratio of the public sector deficit to GDP decreased more slowly than was to be expected in view of the government's firm anti-inflationary stance.

Costa e Silva

During the first two years of the Costa e Silva government, which are the only ones for which data for the entire public sector were available at the time of writing, the pattern of public consumption varied little with respect to its predecessor's. Slight declines took place in the ratios to GDP of consumption as a whole and of its two components. On the other hand, the ratio of transfers to GDP underwent a sizable increase, reaching in 1968 its all-time high of 8.0 percent. The slight drop in the subsidies-GDP ratio, which had peaked in 1965 at a level of 1.9 percent and fell to 1.1 percent in 1968, was partly ascribable to the policy of "corrective inflation" which had been initiated under Castello Branco. One of its aims was to induce unprofitable public utilities and transport enterprises to increase the relative prices of their services and become gradually less dependent on subsidies. The ratio of public investment to GDP maintained the same average level of the previous ten years. The net effect of these changes was an appreciable rise in the average ratios of current and total expenditure to GDP, both of which reached their maximum recorded levels.

Tax revenue increased to an average level of 25.0 percent of GDP. For the first time in postwar Brazilian history, this was achieved by increasing direct taxes at a perceptibly faster rate than indirect ones. This was largely a result of the increase in social secur-

15. While the ratio of public-sector expenditure to GDP remained practically constant, there was a significant drop in the real expenditure of the federal government.
16. See footnote 13.

ity contributions, however, since the real value of income taxes remained below its 1965 level (Table 3).[17] Since other current receipts, which were negative, continued decreasing, current revenue increased less than tax revenue. The ratios of public savings and of the deficit to GDP oscillated considerably between 1967 and 1968.

What are the main features which stand out from this examination of budget policy in the sixties? Consumption expenditure rose to its all-time high in the early sixties and is the only category of expenditure to have been reduced in relation to GDP by the revolutionary governments, thanks to a sharp fall in its "other purchases" component. The ratios of the government wage bill and of public investment to GDP revealed themselves to be more rigid than any other expenditure ratio. The oft-expressed official hopes of effecting a reduction in the public sector's proportional absorption of the economy's output were achieved to only a limited extent (Table 1, col. 8). Both current and total expenditure reached their highest ratios to GDP toward the end of the decade, chiefly because of the impressive rise in transfer payments.

On the revenue side, the revolutionary governments succeeded not only in making up for the drop in the economy's tax ratio during the Quadros-Goulart years but in raising this ratio well above that experienced at any previous time.[18] This was probably the greatest single achievement of their fiscal policy and was brought about by a radical reform of the tax structure.

As a consequence of the increase in tax receipts, and in spite of the offsetting fall in other current receipts, the deficit-GDP ratio was gradually reduced in the second half of the sixties (but with a re-

17. This level was exceeded in 1969, when income taxes rose faster than any other type of federal tax (65.5 percent in nominal terms). Cf. *Conjuntura Econômica*, vol. 24, No. 3, 1970.

18. It should be noted that even in the first half of the sixties Brazil's tax ratio, though low in relation to the country's revenue needs as determined by the government's expenditure ratio, was very high by international standards for a country with its per capita income and participation in international trade. Defining a country's "tax effort" as the proportion between its actual tax ratio and that predicted by a 72-country regression equation using the above two indices as independent variables, Lotz and Morss have found that Brazil in 1963-65 ranked first in tax effort among these 72 countries. Cf. Jorgen R. Lotz and Elliott R. Morss, "Measuring 'Tax Effort' in Developing Countries," *International Monetary Fund Staff Papers*, November 1967. Their calculated value of Brazil's tax ratio was, however, based on a set of national income accounts which has since been superseded by that used in the present study.

lapse in 1967), during which the deficit, whether of the public sector as a whole or of the federal government, was no longer the most important cause of inflation. As we shall see, other factors accounted for the diminished, but far from eliminated, inflationary pressure to which the economy remained subject.

Resource Allocation in the Private Sector and Tax-Structure Change

A government's influence on resource allocation is hardly limited to the pattern of its expenditures. Just as important are the effects of its expenditure, tax, monetary, credit, price, and wage policies on allocation in the private sector of the economy. Since an adequate analysis of all these facets of public policy falls outside the scope of this chapter, attention will here be focused on the effects of the changing tax structure on private allocational decisions during the sixties.

The tax structure had undergone piecemeal reform before a new tax code was approved in October 1966 and incorporated in the Constitution of 1967. For example, in 1957 the import tax was changed from a specific base to an ad valorem one. The stabilization program introduced by Lucas Lopes in 1958 effected substantial improvements in the federal consumption and income taxes. The consumption tax was altered from a turnover basis to a value-added one, and its specific nature changed to an ad valorem one in line with the similar reform of the import tax. The income brackets used in computing income-tax liability were defined in terms of multiples of the minimum wage, thus avoiding unwarranted changes in the incidence of this tax arising from inflation.

In spite of these and other reforms, there is little doubt that Brazil's revenue structure produced considerable resource misallocation during the early sixties and that its inadequacies were exacerbated by the accelerating rate of inflation. The erosion of certain tax bases through inflation, coupled with the increasing need of revenue in the face of the rise (both monetary and real) in public expenditure, led the pre-revolutionary governments to raise the level of taxation on the most administratively convenient tax bases, regardless of any considerations of either fiscal equity or optimum resource allocation. A multiplicity of taxes was imposed on certain activities, increasing taxpayer resentment and resulting in considerable tax evasion, especially in view of the tax exemption enjoyed by other activities. Certain minor taxes resulted in smaller revenue than the cost involved in administering them. The lack of administrative continuity, exemplified by the fact that finance ministers between 1961 and 1964 enjoyed an average tenure of six months, contributed to the haphazard growth of the tax structure and prevented any effective attempt at tax reform.

The chief aspects of the tax structure leading to resource misallocation during this period were the following:[19]

The vertical integration of production and distribution was encouraged by the turnover tax at the state level *(impôsto de vendas e consignações)*, which accounted for a high and increasing fraction of state revenue (82 percent in 1961-63 and 87 percent in 1964-66) and was the most productive tax at any level of government (Table 3). The stimulus given to vertical integration was considerable since the I.V.C. was levied at an average rate of 6 to 7 percent (in 1965-66) on an average of three intermediate transactions per commodity. In addition to promoting the concentration of industry, it engendered a regional distortion in the pattern of production since it was levied at different rates in different states.

The production of luxury goods was encouraged by the protection afforded by the high import duties levied on these commodities, coupled with considerably lower rates of indirect taxation on equivalent domestic goods.

Misallocation of human and physical resources was engendered by the partial or total exemption from taxation of certain sectors of the economy and of certain professions, not warranted by economic considerations. For example, agricultural income was imputed on the basis of totally unrealistic land values estimated by the taxpayers themselves so that, in 1964, only 2 percent of taxable income originated in the agricultural sector. Some professions (writers, professors, journalists, judges) were totally and unjustifiably tax-exempt.

As part of the reform brought to the federal consumption tax in 1958, it was specified that its rate should vary inversely to the degree of "essentiality" of the commodity. Although some of the basic commodities which enter the budget of the lower-income groups were in fact exempted from this tax, in other cases little or no relation existed between the tax rate and the "essentiality" of commodities, given any of the necessarily arbitrary definitions of this term. The consumption tax thus resulted in the creation of excess burden and in a distorted

19. Cf. Ministério do Planejamento e Coordenação Econômica, *Plano Decenal de Desenvolvimento Econômico e Social*, Tomo II, Aspectos Macroeconômicos, vol. 1, *Política Tributária*, 1967.

structure of production, insufficiently offset by any socially desirable distributional side-effects.

An example of economically irrational use of the government's tax powers was the taxation of the "illusory profits" associated with inflation. These "profits" resulted from the calculation of the allowances for the replacement of both fixed and working capital on the basis of original cost rather than replacement cost. This tax therefore fell upon a cost item of the firms. Moreover, a special tax on "extraordinary profits" was based on the firm's "rate of return," calculated by dividing current "profits," including their illusory component, by the firm's capital valued at original cost. If, to escape part of this tax, the firm wrote up the value of its capital stock, it incurred a special tax on the monetary appreciation of the latter! Given the imperfection of the country's capital markets and the consequent importance of retained profits as a source of investment funds, these tax laws were prejudicial to sensible resource allocation, both within and among firms, and to economic growth.

The above was only one of the many untoward effects of inflation on resource allocation in Brazil. In so far as the tax structure in the early sixties was insufficiently elastic to finance rising public expenditure, the government resorted increasingly to the printing press, with typical effects on resource allocation in the private sector which have been amply discussed in the economic literature, both in the case of Brazil and in a wider context.[20]

Conflicts of tax interest between different levels of government had unintended and undesirable allocational effects. For example, the federal government's fiscal incentives to exporters were frequently canceled by export taxes levied by the states.

Upon coming into power, the Castello Branco regime carried out some immediate improvements in the tax structure, and a more pervasive reform was embodied in the new tax code of October 1966 (Law 5172). As a result of these measures, some of the distortions in resource allocation discussed above were either eliminated or reduced. The state sales tax was converted from a turnover tax to one on

20. See, for example, Arnold C. Harberger, "Some Notes on Inflation," in Werner Baer and Isaac Kerstenetzky (editors), *Inflation and Growth in Latin America,* (Homewood, Illinois: Irwin, 1964) and other articles in this volume; and Mario Henrique Simonsen, *A Experiência Inflacionária no Brasil,* Instituto de Pesquisas Econômicas e Sociais, Rio de Janeiro, 1964.

value added, with the name *impôsto de circulação de mercadorias.* Limits were set to the extent to which the rate of this tax could vary among states. The incidence of income taxation was made more equitable by abolishing the exemptions enjoyed by certain professions, combatting tax evasion by various means, such as increasing the proportion of income tax withheld at source and laying the foundations for a more just taxation of the agricultural sector by carrying out a cadastral survey.

With regard to corporate taxation, the revolutionary government made compulsory every year rather than optional the monetary correction of firms' capital stock. The government first lowered, then abolished altogether, the tax on this correction. Firms were permitted to calculate depreciation allowances on the basis of either the monetarily corrected purchase price of capital equipment or its current replacement cost, instead of its original cost. Similar criteria of monetary correction permitted firms to maintain the real value of their working capital.

The tax reform of 1966 embodied in the Constitution of 1967 has undoubtedly removed many of the distortions in resource allocation engendered by the previous tax structure. Improvements were also made in the efficiency of tax collection and administration: several uneconomic taxes were abolished, tax powers were distributed more rationally among the different levels of government, and monetary correction was applied to tax debts, thus eliminating the previously existing incentive to postpone tax payment. In addition to introducing greater economic rationale into the tax structure, the resulting sizable increase in tax revenue is one of the most important successes of the revolutionary governments' economic policy.

At the same time, much remains to be done to simplify a tax system which presents numerous complications even to tax experts, as witness the hundred or so laws governing income taxation. The federal consumption tax, now denoted as *impôsto sôbre produtos industrializados,* has not yet been the subject of satisfactory reform, in spite of its vast and increasing importance in Brazil's tax structure (Table 3). The deficiencies in its administration have been compounded by the government's using it for anticyclical purposes by reducing the rates levied on commodities produced by industries suffering from excess capacity. This anticyclical device seems of dubious value, if not actually harmful, because of the allocational distortions resulting from continuous changes in relative after-tax prices. Moreover, it defeats the original intention of securing a better distribution of income by a differentiated taxation of commodities according to their supposed degree of essentiality.[21]

The governments of many developing countries plan their tax structures not only with the aim of minimizing interference with resource allocation as determined by the market. In view of the multitude of existing market imperfections, they use instead a variety of fiscal and nonfiscal incentives to promote certain economically and socially desirable ends. Since 1966 the Brazilian government has granted tax advantages in order to fulfill certain national objectives such as reforestation, the expansion of the fishing and tourist industries, and the growth and diversification of exports. It has stimulated private savings, not only by generalizing the use of monetary correction on debt instruments and improving the state of the capital markets, but also by allowing taxpayers to deduct from their taxable income certain percentages of the investment made in indexed treasury bonds, the shares of incorporated enterprises, and other specific uses. Interest and dividends have also enjoyed privileged tax treatment, and capital-gains taxation has been nonexistent.

The most striking example of the use of the government's fiscal powers to attain desired allocational effects has been the impressive array of fiscal incentives in favor of Brazil's backward regions in the Northeast and the Amazon basin. Although fiscal incentives for the development of the Northeast have existed since 1956, it is only since the creation of the *Superintendência do Desenvolvimento do Nordeste* (SUDENE) that they have assumed crucial importance for the

---

21. Among the many allocational effects of the present tax and expenditure structure about which little is known, two in particular deserve detailed study. The first concerns the desirability of the present distribution of taxing and spending powers between different levels of government and the efficiency of the scheme of intergovernmental grants adopted in 1966 *(Fundo de Participação dos Estados e Municípios)* whereby states and municipalities are granted stated (but not constant) percentages of the federal income tax and of the I.P.I. A second question worth investigating is the allocational impact of the fuel tax, which almost doubled in real terms between 1964 and 1968 (Table 3). The proceeds of this tax are earmarked for expenditure mainly on highway construction and maintenance; smaller amounts are assigned to help finance the railroad deficit, petroleum prospecting by Petrobrás and the construction of airports. The continuity over time in highway construction projects which the fuel tax has permitted since its creation in 1940, independently of the vicissitudes of the federal budget, has probably offset the potential allocational disadvantages caused by the presence of earmarked revenue in the over-all tax structure. Similar remarks also apply to the tax on the use of electric power.

Northeast's development.[22] SUDENE's first Guiding Plan in 1961 permitted domestic firms to reduce their income tax liability by 50 percent by investing the corresponding amount in a northeastern industry approved by SUDENE. The second Guiding Plan of 1963 exempted SUDENE-approved firms from income tax for a period of 10 to 15 years and allowed both domestic and foreign-owned firms to invest up to 50 percent of their income tax liability in approved projects in the Northeast. In 1964, individuals were allowed tax exemption in relation to (at most) 50 percent of their taxable income if they invested it in registered shares of incorporated enterprises installed in the Northeast. Other fiscal incentives included the exemption from import duties and other taxes of imported capital equipment. Similar tax advantages have been available to the Amazon region since the creation of SUDAM in 1966.

Since 1962 these fiscal incentives have resulted in a dramatic flow of investment into the Northeast.[23] Although a detailed analysis of SUDENE's policies is obviously outside the scope of this chapter,[24] a few general remarks should be made regarding the effectiveness of fiscal incentives in promoting the Northeast's development. SUDENE's data show that the type of industrial structure whose growth has been stimulated by these incentives has been considerably more capital-intensive than that previously existing, in spite of the crying need to absorb large numbers of unemployed and disguisedly unemployed in the industrial sector.[25]

While the nature of modern technology is in part responsible for this, a good share of the blame must be laid on the government's fiscal

22. The events and personalities leading to the creation of SUDENE are described in Albert O. Hirschman, *Journeys toward Progress*, (New York: Twentieth Century Fund, 1963), Chapter 1.

23. Data up to 1967 can be found in Albert O. Hirschman, "Industrial Development in the Brazilian Northeast and the Tax Credit Scheme of Article 34/18," *The Journal of Development Studies*, October 1968. Hirschman is optimistic about both the efficacy of the fiscal incentives for developing the Northeast and the pattern of industrial growth induced by them.

24. Cf. David E. Goodman, "Industrial Development in the Brazilian Northeast: An Interim Assessment of the Tax Credit Scheme of Article 34/18," Chapter Seven of this volume.

25. Indeed, it has been estimated that between 1959 and 1965 total industrial employment in the Northeast *fell* by 14 percent. Cf. Otto G. Wadsted, "A Industrialização do Nordeste—Alguns Aspectos de Longo Prazo," in *A Economia Brasileira e suas Perspectivas*, VII, APEC Editôra, Rio de Janeiro, 1968.

incentives. By artificially lowering the relative price of capital with respect to that of labor, they have induced entrepreneurs to adopt the most capital-intensive techniques of production in the most capital-intensive lines of industry. Greater labor absorption, though possibly at the expense of a smaller increase in output, would have occurred had the government chosen a type of fiscal incentive specifically biased in this direction, such as an annual subsidy, for a limited period of time, applicable to a firm's operating costs rather than, as at present, to its initial (mostly capital) costs.

By concentrating its energies on attracting funds which would have otherwise gone to the treasury and supervising their allocation among industrial enterprises, SUDENE has neglected the more comprehensive approach to northeastern economic problems, which had motivated its creation in 1959. It has so far avoided a fundamental attack on the problems of irrigation in the *sertão* and crop diversification in the *zona da mata*, whose solution still awaits the implementation of an effective agrarian reform. The results of this neglect were visible during the drought which struck the Northeast in 1970. Without the increase in agricultural productivity resulting from a well-planned and executed agrarian reform, it will be difficult to create an adequate market for the rapidly expanding flow of industrial goods coming out of northeastern factories.

This points to the conclusion that while fiscal incentives can be a powerful tool to redress regional imbalances, they should be so designed as to permit the utilization of the backward region's relatively abundant factors. Moreover, they can be expected to be fully successful only as part of a package program which includes reform of the traditional power and property structure, which is, needless to say, politically much more difficult to accomplish.

Stabilization Policies since 1964

While cyclical fluctuations of economic activity affect developed and underdeveloped countries alike, their effect on the latter can be more damaging since either mounting inflationary pressure or the cyclical underutilization of industrial capacity can seriously jeopardize the achievement of a satisfactory growth rate. Recessions are nearly always associated with a sharp decline in the rate of investment and consequently in the economy's growth potential. The prospect of a runaway inflation may also have this effect and will in any case tend to distort the pattern of investment and lower its social marginal productivity.

Since the Second World War, the governments of both advanced and underdeveloped capitalist countries have assumed the responsibility of reducing as much as possible the cyclical fluctuations of output, price level, and employment to which their economies have been subject; and Brazil has been no exception. In this section we shall focus attention on the stabilization policies pursued by successive Brazilian governments since the Revolution of 1964, both because of the widespread interest with which these policies have been followed inside and outside Brazil and because of lack of space in which to discuss the half-hearted stabilization attempts undertaken up to that time.[26]

Upon taking power, the Castello Branco regime was well aware that the resumption of a satisfactory growth rate depended on the nature of its anti-inflationary policies. The necessity of introducing a stabilization program to bring the inflation rate down from the peak level reached in the first quarter of 1964 carried with it the danger of a prolonged recession, leading to social unrest or to the recrudescence of inflation following the abandonment of the program. For this and other reasons, the government opted for a gradual attack on inflation rather than a shock treatment of the type recommended by foreign lending institutions such as the International Monetary Fund.[27] It expressly linked the control of inflation to the resumption of economic growth. These two objectives were not deemed incompatible: just as the high rate of inflation experienced in 1963 (76 percent, as against 50 percent in 1962) was assumed to be one of the main causes of the low growth rate of 1.5 percent in that year, so was a decreasing rate of inflation thought to be consistent with an increasing growth rate. The Costa e Silva government placed an even greater emphasis on a higher rate of economic growth while conditioning it to further progress in the fight against inflation.

At first sight, the revolutionary government's program appears

26. For a description of the pre-1964 stabilization attempts, with an emphasis on the political factors and personalities involved, cf. Thomas E. Skidmore, *Politics in Brazil, 1930-1964*, Oxford University Press, New York, 1967.

27. Cf. Ministério do Planejamento e Coordenação Econômica, *Programa de Ação Econômica do Govêrno 1964-1966*, Rio de Janeiro, 1964, pp. 33-34. The stabilization policies of the Castello Branco regime are described and analyzed in Howard S. Ellis, "Corrective Inflation in Brazil, 1964-1966," in *The Economy of Brazil*, ed. by Howard S. Ellis, (Berkeley and Los Angeles: University of California Press, 1969), and Alexandre Kafka, "The Brazilian Stabilization Program, 1964-1966," *The Journal of Political Economy*, August 1967, *Supplement* (Issues in Monetary Research). Both authors defend the gradual nature of the disinflationary strategy adopted by the government.

to have been fairly successful. As shown in the Appendix Table, column 10, the annual rate of inflation as measured by the index of wholesale prices has declined continuously from its peak of 81 percent in 1964 to only 19 percent in 1969. Moreover, this decline has been associated with a gradual increase in the growth rate of GDP from 2.9 percent in 1964 to 9.0 percent in 1969, with only two minor regressions in 1965 and 1967 (cols. 1 and 2).[28] This apparent "success story," however, is subject to the following qualifications:

The average annual growth rate of GDP in the revolutionary years 1964-69 was practically identical to that in the prerevolutionary years of the sixties, 1959-64 (6.0 percent versus 5.9 percent).[29] It was lower than that experienced under the Kubitschek administration (6.8 percent for the period 1955-60) or in the decade of the fifties as a whole (6.5 percent). The revolutionary governments thus succeeded only in steering the economy back to the trend growth path of the first half of the sixties, which had been adversely affected by the political turmoil and runaway inflation of that period. It still remains to be seen whether their policies can produce, during the seventies, an average economic growth rate equaling or surpassing that attained during the period of import substitutive industrialization.

The growth rates of the agricultural and industrial sectors (cols. 3 and 4) are more revealing than that of GDP. The agricultural growth rate, being affected by climatic factors, was largely beyond the government's control. The industrial growth rate during the stabilization program, instead, depended critically on the government's compensatory policies. The sudden reversals in the latter's direction from expansionist to deflationary and vice versa during the Castello Branco government, depending on its changing appraisal as to whether recession or inflation constituted the worse danger, were chiefly responsible for the violent year-to-year changes in the industrial growth rate from 1964 to 1967. The fact that the rate of growth of GDP followed a fairly steady upward trend between 1964 and 1969 in spite of the abrupt changes in the industrial growth rate can be attributed to a fortuitous circumstance: in each year since 1965, any decline in the industrial growth rate with respect to the previous year was off-

28. All column references in this section relate to the Appendix Table. Several variables in this table are given on an index basis with 1964=100 (or 1963=100 if they are end-of-year values) so as to facilitate the comparison of their behavior before and after the Revolution of March 1964.

29. Note, moreover, that the high growth rates for 1968 and 1969 are preliminary estimates.

set by an increase in the agricultural growth rate, and vice versa. This caused the variance of the growth rate of GDP to be smaller than that of either its agricultural or industrial component.

If the revolutionary governments' growth record leaves something to be desired, this may be set against their success in gradually reducing the rate of inflation by 1969 to less than one quarter of that experienced in 1964. On taking a closer look at the price record, however, one notes substantial intra-year variations in the rate of price increase. Indeed, if instead of taking price indices as annual averages we were to consider indices relating to the end of December of each year, the rate of inflation since 1964 appears to have obeyed a damped oscillatory path rather than a damped steady one. As shown by column 11, the rates of increase of the wholesale price index in 1966 and 1968 were higher than those in 1965 and 1967 respectively. The apparent contradiction between the smooth decline in the rate of inflation of column 10 and the oscillatory one of column 11 springs from the fact that prices frequently increased faster in the second half of the year than in the first. The considerable variations in the inflation rate during the stabilization program were caused partly by the government's own fiscal, monetary, credit, wage, and exchange-rate policies and were accompanied by fluctuations in the pace of business activity.

In retrospect, the revolutionary governments' disinflationary policies appear to have been too gradual. The *Programa de Ação Econômica do Govêrno* of Castello Branco prescribed rates of inflation of approximately 25 percent in 1965 and 10 percent in 1966. While the first of these targets was reasonably well attained, the rate of inflation in 1966 actually exceeded that in 1965 (col. 11). Moreover, the economic growth rates achieved during the Castello Branco years were well below the planned target of 6 percent annually. The economy's recovery was thus much slower than had been anticipated in spite of the fact that the control of inflation proved to be considerably more gradual than specified in the government's "gradual" program. In the last three years of the decade, the annual rate of inflation remained practically constant, raising some doubts as to the government's willingness or ability to lower it much below 20 percent (cols. 11 and 13).

In spite of these qualifications, the revolutionary governments did succeed in lowering the rate of inflation to about one quarter of its value in 1964 and, in the last two years of the decade, in achieving high rates of economic growth. We now proceed to a summary appraisal of the most important tools which they used to attain their anti-inflationary and anti-cyclical objectives: fiscal, monetary, credit, and wage policies.

Fiscal Policy

The revolutionary governments' foremost preoccupation was to reduce drastically the union budgetary deficit *(déficit de caixa)*, whose association with the rate of inflation had been well established.[30] Until 1967 a considerable success was scored in this endeavor. After rising from 2.8 percent in 1960 to 4.2 percent in 1963, the deficit to GDP ratio was reduced steadily to 1.1 percent in 1966. It is noteworthy that the deficits, measured in real terms and even in nominal terms, decreased between 1964 and 1966 (cols. 5, 6, and 7). In 1967 the deficit/GDP ratio rose to 1.7 percent but fell again in the next two years to just 0.6 percent in 1969. The decrease in the real budgetary deficit was accomplished at first by a reduction in real union expenditures coupled with a substantial increase in real revenue, then, in 1968 and 1969, by a rise in expenditure accompanied by a much faster rise in revenue (cols. 8 and 9). In spite of the reiterated lip service which the revolutionary governments paid to the need to reduce the economy's tax burden, the ratio of taxes (both federal and total) to GDP was higher at the end of the sixties than at any previous time.

The success in reducing the size of the deficit in both nominal and real terms during the Castello Branco years was compounded, in the eyes of the government, by the fact that an increasing proportion of it was financed in a noninflationary way through the sale of indexed treasury bonds. The fact that the latter financed almost the entire deficit in 1966, and more than covered it in 1969, attests to the popularity of this new financial instrument. Private corporations, however, were adversely affected to the extent that they found a sizable part of the capital market pre-empted by the government bond issues, forcing some of them to borrow from financial intermediaries at higher interest rates. In 1967 and 1968 the proportion of the deficit financed by public borrowing fell off considerably with respect to 1966, allegedly because of the Costa e Silva government's unwillingness to burden the capital market in view of its own professed aim of lowering the rate of interest.

30. Cf. Antonio Delfim Netto, et al. *Alguns Aspectos da Inflação Brasileira,* Estudos ANPES No. 1, (São Paulo: Editôra Gráfica Piratininga, 1965), chapter 4. The term "union" includes the federal government and the federal *autarquias.*

The government's one-sided concern with reducing its deficit, while understandable in terms of its anti-inflationary stance, appears to have prevented it from using its spending and taxing powers for the purpose of deliberate compensatory policy. Indeed, the sharp rise in real taxes during the Castello Branco years, combined with a fall in real government spending at both the union and federal levels, contributed in no small measure to the depressed level of industrial output. And while the reduction in the budget deficit was instrumental in attacking inflation from the demand side, the higher level of taxation added considerably to firms' costs, contributing to the cost-push inflation which characterized a good part of that period, as evidenced by the coexistence of continued price rises with a sizable underutilization of industrial capacity. The need to expand aggregate demand was recognized in 1967 by the incoming Costa e Silva government. While budgetary policy doubtless stimulated the economic recovery of 1967, however, it made no contribution to the economy's upsurge in 1968 and 1969: in those two years the union government's real revenue increased at a much faster rate than its real expenditure (cols. 8 and 9).

Administrative procedures and various contingent factors were responsible for the monthly pattern of accrual of the union deficit in any given year (as well as for large deviations from its planned level in certain years). Noticeably absent was any conscious attempt to influence this pattern so as to smooth out the economy's fluctuations. By the government's own admission, it was sheer coincidence that the deficit in 1967 was concentrated in the first half of the year, contributing to the economy's recuperation from the recession caused by the tight money policy of 1966.

While the government did not carry out compensatory fiscal policy in the traditional sense of the word, it did implement various tax measures with anticyclical aims. In the middle of 1964 it increased the scope of withholding at source of the income tax and made income tax debts subject to monetary correction, thus eliminating the previously existing incentive to postpone tax payment. These measures, together with the increase in tax collection arising from better administration, enhanced the built-in flexibility of the tax structure.

Certain discretionary tax measures were undertaken to control prices, offset slumps in demand in various sectors of the economy, and provide firms with working capital. In 1965 the Castello Branco government reduced the rate of the federal consumption tax, postponed its collection or granted outright exemption from it to industries suffering from nonseasonal decreases in sales. These tax advantages, which were maintained for limited periods of time, were made conditional on the "stabilization" of prices in order to make the consumer the ultimate beneficiary. Thus in 1965 and 1966 the rate of the corporation income tax was varied in accordance with the percentage by which firms had increased their prices since a base date, penalizing those firms whose price increases had exceeded specified limits. Other forms of tax and nontax incentives were also introduced with the same objective, such as a variable tax rate on the monetary correction of firms' capital assets.

In 1967, incoming Minister of Finance Antonio Delfim Netto diagnosed the main bottleneck preventing aggregate output from responding to increasing demand as the scarcity of working capital in the industrial sector. Instead of creating appropriate debt instruments he decided to postpone the collection of the I.P.I. (the federal tax on industrialized products which had substituted the consumption tax) by 30 to 45 days, thus pumping, or rather failing to withdraw, an estimated NCR $300 million of liquidity into the business sector. In addition, the government raised the exemption level of the income tax in an attempt to offset somewhat the squeeze on wages resulting from the misapplication of the wage policy adopted in 1964. For similar reasons, the deadlines for payment of the I.P.I., the income tax, and the state sales tax were extended in 1969.

In certain respects, these discretionary countercyclical tax measures were of doubtful value. The changes in the commodity rates of the I.P.I. in accordance with the degree of distress of the industry in question distort resource allocation and are inferior to a general reduction in income taxes or an increase in transfers in conformity with the prevailing norms of distributional justice. The attempt to control prices through the granting of tax advantages may be effective if the economy has entered a period of continuous disinflation leading entrepreneurs to believe in its irreversibility. If, however, the behavior of monetary aggregates is inconsistent with this belief (as was the case, for example, in 1965 and 1967), this type of price control proves worse than useless. Finally, the creation of suitable debt instruments, accompanied by a liberalization of monetary policy, is a more efficient way to provide firms with working capital than the postponement of their tax payments, unless a tax reduction were needed for anti-cyclical reasons and the government wished the business sector to be its sole beneficiary.

Monetary Policy

Monetary policy has been the Achilles' heel of the revolutionary governments' stabilization program. The Castello Branco regime planned to bring the rate of inflation under control by reducing the budget deficit, introducing an austere wage policy and letting bank credit expand in proportion to the money supply. The latter was to expand in accordance with the government's monetary budget, which specified growth rates of 70 percent in 1964, 30 percent in 1965 and 15 percent in 1966. In line with the government's gradual policy of disinflation, it was not its intention to curtail credit drastically, but rather to adapt its growth to the rise in firms' costs without allowing it to contribute to demand inflation.

As was pointed out above, the revolutionary governments achieved considerable success in gradually reducing the union deficit, both in real terms and as a proportion of GDP, and in financing part of it through the sale of indexed treasury bonds. It thus greatly diminished what was considered the chief source of inflationary pressure. In spite of this, both the money supply and the rate of inflation grew at rates well above those initially intended. Although these growth rates were considerably lower at the end of the decade than they had been in 1964, they were still very high compared with those prevailing in advanced economies and behaved in a markedly unstable manner during the intervening years, as shown by columns 11 and 16. From the latter we note that the money supply targets were exceeded by a sizable margin in 1964 and even more so in 1965. Although the monetary growth rate in 1966 coincided with that planned for that year (15 percent), it jumped to 43 percent in each of the following two years, dropping to a still excessive level of 33 percent in 1969.

The government's lack of success in its monetary policy in the second half of the sixties can be traced to its relatively small control over some of the factors responsible for variations in the supply of money.[31] I shall examine the causes both of primary and secondary monetary growth. The chief factors affecting the primary expansion of the money supply—the increase of currency in circulation—were the fraction of the treasury deficit financed by the monetary authorities; the net resources (loans less deposits) granted by the monetary

31. The deficiencies in the execution of monetary policy during the Castello Branco years are discussed by Alexandre Kafka, *op. cit.*, and Howard S. Ellis, *op. cit.*

TABLE 4
CAUSES OF CURRENCY ISSUE DURING THE SIXTIES
(annual changes in millions of NCr$)

	1960	1961	1962	1963	1964	1965	1966	1967	1968	1969
Treasury net requirements	+75.4	+128.9	+215.6	+432.6	+748.4	+264.6	+ 42.8	+699.9	+ 889.8	-1018.2
Net loans[a] to autarquias and other government agencies	-14.3	- 35.7	- 13.6	- 38.0	-219.9	-131.6	-314.7	+ 79.9	- 540.0	- 744.4
Net loans[a] to private sector	+35.3	+ 45.6	+118.8	+175.3	+252.0	+ 60.4	+774.1	+438.3	+1482.9	+2104.2
Net loans[a] to commercial banks	- 9.8	- 31.2	- 92.6	-180.4	-233.9	-758.4	-146.2	-421.9	- 336.2	- 326.6
Foreign exchange operations	-24.2	- 3.4	- 81.8	- 42.8	- 9.1	+1135.0	+724.8	-241.2	- 357.4	+ 268.1
Import-export transactions and other accounts	-13.3	- 6.1	+ 35.8	- 3.0	+ 21.5	+123.1	-413.0	+161.3	+ 373.1	+ 960.3
Currency in circulation	+49.1	+ 98.1	+182.2	+343.7	+559.0	+693.1	+667.8	+716.3	+1512.2	+1243.4

a. "Net loans" means loans granted by the monetary authorities less deposits with them

Source: APEC, A Economia Brasileira e suas Perspectivas and Relatório do Banco Central, various issues.

authorities to the *autarquias* and other government agencies, the non-bank private sector, and the commercial banks; and the financing of foreign exchange operations.

As shown in Table 4, the relative importance of these factors has varied from year to year. One feature, however, distinguishes the years up to and including 1964 from those following that year. Between 1960 and 1964, the fraction of the budget deficit financed by the monetary authorities always exceeded the increase in currency; the reverse has been true since 1964. In the first half of the sixties, the deficit was the single most important factor accounting for the increase in currency. In the second half this was no longer the case: in 1966 only a very small percentage of the deficit was financed by the monetary authorities, and in 1969 the treasury actually became a net creditor vis-à-vis the authorities by selling a much greater number of indexed bonds than needed to finance the deficit.

Some of the other factors responsible for the issue of currency remained outside the control of the government and were not adequately counteracted by it. For example, contrary to forecast, Brazil ran large balance-of-payments surpluses in 1965 and 1966 ($331 and $153 million respectively) thanks to a good export performance coupled, in 1965, with a recession-induced drop in imports. The government's purchase of the foreign currency flowing into the country was the most important factor accounting for the large currency expansion in 1965 and an important subsidiary factor in that of 1966, both of which were well in excess of their planned levels.[32] Minimum price-support schemes for various agricultural products, the most important of which was coffee (whose financing is included with "foreign exchange operations" in Table 4), also produced unpredictable annual variations in currency expansion, depending on the climate's influence on the size of the crops.

The financing of foreign-exchange operations and of price-support schemes was not, however, the most important cause of primary money expansion during the second half of the sixties. In 1966, 1968, and 1969 the growth in currency was mainly attributable to the excess of the nonbank private sector's demand for loans from the monetary authorities over its increase in deposits with them. The union deficit was the most important cause of monetary expansion only in 1967 and was then closely followed in importance by the non-bank private sector's net requirements. It is interesting to note that the commercial banks exerted throughout the sixties a net negative effect on currency expansion in spite of the sizable increase in rediscounts during certain years.

The government could do little to counteract the impact of foreign-exchange transactions on the stock of currency in 1965 and 1966 since it lacked weapons of monetary control such as open-market operations which were not feasible in view of the embryonic state of the market for government securities. Various institutional inadequacies also hamstrung the effectiveness of monetary control, such as the ill-defined and at times overlapping division of powers between the Central Bank of Brazil and the Conselho Monetário Nacional, both of which began functioning in 1965.[33] On the other hand, the inordinate increase in loans granted by the monetary authorities to the private sector, particularly in 1968 and 1969, raises some doubt as to the government's willingness (as opposed to its ability) to reduce substantially the rate of monetary growth and with it the rate of inflation.

The main determinants of the secondary expansion of the money supply were the compulsory and voluntary reserve ratios of commer-

32. As shown by cols. 14 and 16, in 1965 the currency expansion of 49.4 percent was exacerbated by the even faster growth in demand deposits, leading to a money supply expansion of 75.4 percent instead of 30 percent as planned. In 1966 the planned target of a 15 percent money supply growth was achieved only because of a sharp drop in the deposit/currency ratio: the expansion of currency in that year was 32.2 percent.

33. Cf. Howard S. Ellis, pp. 187-197.

cial banks and the public's preference for currency versus demand deposits. The last two of these factors fluctuated considerably throughout the sixties and lay practically outside the government's control (cols. 18 and 19). The banks' voluntary reserve ratios behaved in accordance with their willingness to lend to the private sector. The public's preferred ratio between currency and demand deposits was also fairly variable, in some years exacerbating, in others attenuating, the growth of primary liquidity (cf. cols. 14-18).[34] The one cause of secondary money expansion over which the government could exercise full control was the variation in the compulsory reserves of commercial banks (col. 20). Far from using this tool of monetary control to stabilize the level of economic activity and offset undesired changes in primary monetary growth, however, the Castello Branco regime actually used it in a destabilizing fashion, magnifying the economy's cyclical fluctuations.[35]

Considering the various causes of Brazil's primary and secondary money expansion and the small degree of government control to which some of them were subject, it is not surprising that the rate of total monetary growth fluctuated, at times violently, during the stabilization program, jeopardizing its success in inducing a permanent reversal of the public's inflationary expectations. Column 21 reveals an interesting trend in the money supply deflated by the wholesale price index. After remaining roughly constant during the first half of the sixties and behaving erratically during the Castello Branco years, the real money supply increased substantially in the last three years of the decade, reaching at the end of 1969 a value 64 percent higher than that at the end of 1963. The counterpart of this phenomenon was a gradual decline in the income velocity of circulation (col. 23), cal-

34. Cf. Jan Peter Wogart, "Secondary Expansion of Money Supply and its Underlying Variables in Post-war Brazil," in *A Economia Brasileira e suas Perspectivas*, VIII (Rio de Janeiro: APEC Editôra, 1969). Wogart emphasizes the precedence of behavioral over policy variables in explaining the secondary expansion of the Brazilian money supply over the period 1947-66. He finds that the currency-money ratio was related negatively to the rate of inflation and positively to per capita income, and that, during the Castello Branco stabilization program, the commercial banks' excess reserve-deposit ratio varied inversely with the level of economic activity. See also Antonio Delfim Netto, "Tentativa de Explicação das Causas que Determinaram a Expansão dos Meios de Pagamento em 1964-1965," in *A Economia Brasileira e suas Perspectivas*, V (Rio de Janeiro: APEC Editôra, 1966).

35. The same feature characterized the alterations made in the quantity of rediscounting during that period. Cf. Howard S. Ellis, *loc. cit.*

culated as the ratio between gross domestic product and the average annual money stock.

In general, a fall in velocity is a natural consequence of a continued decline in the rate of inflation, which leads to the expectation that it will continue: when the public realizes that the monetary unit is depreciating more slowly than before, it is less reluctant to hold a part of its assets in the form of money. Indeed, precisely this argument has been used by Finance Minister Delfim Netto to defend the continued high rates of monetary growth. The argument certainly has some validity. At the same time, the rate of inflation as measured by the wholesale price index (col. 11) or the Guanabara cost of living index (col. 13), remained practically constant over the years 1967-69, during each of which the monetary stock grew at a faster rate. This situation does not appear to be tenable over a longer period of time, for if the public has grown accustomed to a steady rather than a declining rate of inflation, it will no longer be content, other things being equal, to continue increasing its stock of real cash balances at a faster rate than is warranted by the increase in real income.[36]

If any recrudescence in inflationary expectations were to occur as a consequence of the inordinate growth in the real money supply, the resulting increase in the income velocity of circulation coupled with the present abnormally high monetary stock would lead to a return to higher rates of inflation with disastrous consequences for the stabilization program. Hence the government should exercise greater control over the basic causes of monetary expansion, particularly the loans granted by the monetary authorities to the private sector, and should hasten to improve such tools of monetary policy as open-market operations.

Even had better techniques of monetary control been available, in an initially stagnating and inflationary economy where the level of industrial activity is closely correlated with the amount of real credit granted to industry, the government is faced with a dilemma. A tight rein on the supply of credit will in all likelihood nip in the bud any incipient tendency toward economic recovery. On the other hand, any loosening of credit, while allowing the industrial sector to recover, may do so only at the cost of continued inflationary pressure.

36. The "other things being equal" clause in this sentence is intended to suggest that the demand for money is affected by other variables than income and the public's inflationary expectations. For example, if the rates of return to other financial and non-financial assets were to decline, the public's preference for cash balances would to that extent increase and the stated conclusion need no longer hold.

Columns 24 through 29 show that the Castello Branco and Costa e Silva regimes differed in their responses to this dilemma. Under the former regime the value of real loans to the private sector was kept within strict bounds, particularly those granted by the monetary authorities, which were maintained, in real terms, below the level prevailing at the end of 1963. The consequent lack of working capital in the private sector condemned many firms to operate at low levels of capacity and was rendered even more serious by the tight fiscal policy of that time. The alternate tightening and loosening of liquidity introduced great uncertainty in the business community and caused both the level of industrial output and the rate of inflation to fluctuate. A much more liberal credit policy characterized both the monetary authorities and the commercial banks during the Costa e Silva government, as a result of its desire to restore dynamism to the economy. Indeed, the amount of total real credit available to the private sector at the end of 1969 was virtually double that at the end of 1966. In its laudable desire to stimulate the level of economic activity, the government has probably expanded the supply of credit—and consequently the money supply—to an excessive degree, thus not only preventing substantial further progress in its fight against inflation but adversely affecting (if not actually rekindling) the public's inflationary expectations.

Wage Policy

The one aspect of the revolutionary governments' stabilization program in which they can claim to have been largely successful has been their wage policy. It is true that in 1964, soon after the inauguration of the Castello Branco regime, excessive wage increases were granted for political reasons to government employees at the federal level, both military and civilian, and in the *autarquias*, encouraging similar wage liberality in the private sector. Beginning in February 1965, however, the government applied a much tougher wage policy by raising the minimum wage at a smaller rate than the increase in the cost of living since the previous wage adjustment. In July of that year it extended the scope of application of its wage policy also to the private sector.

The criterion underlying this wage policy was the so-called *reajustamento pela média*, by which was meant that when the time came for a wage readjustment the government would not restore the previous peak purchasing power of workers. Instead, it would raise nominal wages only by the amount necessary to guarantee that the workers' average purchasing power during the following year would equal its average during the previous two years, adjusted for any productivity increase. Since the government expected the rate of inflation to decline as a result of its disinflationary program, the purchasing power of wages immediately following any wage readjustment would be lower than that prevailing at the time of the previous adjustment. This apparent inequity would be compensated for by the smaller subsequent rate of decline in real wages resulting from the deceleration in the rate of inflation.

In theory, the government's wage policy was reasonable in its intention of depriving wage readjustments of any inflationary impact. If, at the time of its introduction, the distribution of income between labor and capital had been socially desirable, this policy would also be equitable, since it would tend to preserve this initial distribution. Unfortunately, its execution fell far short of the government's expressed intentions. This is illustrated by columns 30 through 32, which give the real value of the minimum wage in Guanabara (using the cost-of-living index as deflator) on an index basis with 1964=100, its annual growth rate, and the ratio between the nominal values of the minimum wage in Guanabara and of per capita GDP. The first of these columns shows that the real minimum annual wage in Guanabara, calculated as the average of twelve monthly real values, has decreased continuously since 1964, its over-all decline by 1969 being 16.4 percent. Moreover, this decline has been taking place since at least 1959.

Workers earning the minimum wage have therefore suffered during both the pre-1964 acceleration and the post-1964 deceleration in the rate of inflation, in contradiction to the oft-repeated claim that the reduction of the rate of inflation would be beneficial to the working class.[37] The steady decline in the real minimum wage since 1964 is all the more surprising when one realizes that productivity in the economy as a whole was slowly increasing during that period. The ratio between the minimum wage and average productivity, using GDP per capita as a proxy for the latter, has decreased more drastically than the real minimum wage since both 1959 and 1964, its decline

37. If a section of the community has benefited unduly by an accelerating inflationary process, distributional equity may require its being correspondingly penalized in the course of a subsequent stabilization program. This argument, however, cannot be used to justify the regressiveness of the Brazilian government's wage policy in the latter half of the sixties since the labor share in national income seems to have begun declining well before 1964.

over the decade as a whole being almost 50 percent (col. 32).[38]

The explanation of these results is that the government, though rigorously adhering to its wage formula, consistently underestimated the rate of inflation expected to prevail during the year following each wage readjustment. For example, the "residual inflation" forecast for 1966 was only 10 percent, consistent with the monetary expansion target of 15 percent. As it turned out, the cost of living in Guanabara increased that year by 41 percent. As a result of the criticisms leveled at its predecessor's underestimation of residual inflation, the newly inaugurated Costa e Silva regime raised the latter's forecast for 1967 to 15 percent. In spite of this, a large discrepancy arose once more between expected and realized rates of inflation, since in that year the cost of living increased by 24 percent. The downward trend in the real value of the minimum wage continued, though at a somewhat lesser rate, in 1968 and 1969. These results are an ironic commentary on the government's slogan of "promising less and giving more."

The question arises, Why did the government not make up for its underestimation of the rate of inflation in any given year at the time of the following wage adjustment? One reason may be that until 1968 its chosen wage formula did not allow for any compensation to workers when its previous forecast of residual inflation had been too low. Another is that, from 1967 on, the arrôcho salarial was consistent with the official policy of attacking inflation from the cost side, although why this should result in an actual decrease in the real wages of laborers earning the minimum wage was never explained.[39]

In general, a decline in the real minimum wage need not imply that the real average wage declines as well. The available evidence, however, shows that the average real wage of industrial workers also

38. Although the figures in columns 30 and 32 relate to the state of Guanabara, similar results are obtained for the trend in the minimum wage in other states.

39. In a discussion, Affonso Celso Pastore has advanced the interesting hypothesis that the revolutionary governments' wage policy sprang not so much from a concern with the cost of labor as from the fact that many prices (the foremost example being rents) were tied to the level of the minimum wage. From this point of view,, wage policy was just one facet of public policies aimed at the repression of prices, minimum wage earners being the unintended victims of the fight against inflation. Of course, to avoid this untoward distributional effect the government could have based monetary correction on some price index rather than on the minimum wage.

tended to decrease in Brazil between 1964 and 1968.[40] Although certain categories of skilled personnel in the industrial and service sectors undoubtedly experienced some increase in real wages, it is safe to conclude that unskilled workers suffered an appreciable drop in their standard of living.[41] In spite of the lack of published statistics on the functional distribution of income between wages, profits, interest, and rent, one can also infer that the labor share in national income has fallen since 1964. This would be implied by a decline, or even a constancy, in average wages in a period during which productivity is rising and employment in the industrial sector increases insignificantly. Whether intentionally or not, the working class of Brazil has been made to bear the brunt of the stabilization program, being adversely affected both by the government's wage policies and by the changes in relative prices arising from its policy of corrective inflation. This decline in the purchasing power of wages is not only inequitable towards the working class but, by acting as a damper on the

40. It is unfortunately impossible to find a strictly consistent series of average wages in manufacturing industry covering this time span and relating to Brazil as a whole. Using the annual data of GETEI *(Indústrias de Transformação, Aspectos Gerais, Grupo Especial de Trabalho para as Estatísticas Industriais* of IBGE) for 1963, 1964, and 1965 and the *Pesquisa Anual* data of DEICOM *(Departamento de Estatísticas Industriais, Comerciais e de Serviços* of IBGE) for 1966 and 1967; deflating these two series by the São Paulo cost of living index *(Conjuntura Econômica,* Vol. 24, No. 3, 1970) and linking them together, one finds that the average real wage of all industrial workers (white-collar and blue-collar) declined by 4.1 percent between 1963 and 1967, while that of blue-collar workers *(pessoal ligado à produção)* declined by 7.9 percent.

Using the monthly GETEI data published in *Inquéritos Econômicos* for 1965 and 1966 and linking them with the *Pesquisa Trimestral* data of IBGE-IBE-DEICOM for 1967 and 1968 by means of the same deflating procedure yields a 2.1 percent drop in the average wage of all industrial workers between 1965 and 1968. The same data for the first six months of 1969, however, indicate a sharp rise with respect to 1968.

I am indebted to David E. Goodman for pointing out the difficulties associated with the comparability of these various data sources. See also IBGE-IBE-DEICOM, *Produção Industrial,* 1966, Volume I.

An interesting reference on wage behavior, in spite of its geographical limitation, is "Salários na Guanabara," in *Conjuntura Econômica,* Vol. 24, No. 2, 1970, which shows, on the basis of a sample survey, that the real average wage of workers in Guanabara employed in industry, commerce, and certain service categories declined slightly between 1964 and 1968.

41. To the extent that the welfare of workers depends not only (positively) on the average level of their wages but also (negatively) on the variability of the latter over time, the fall in average wages has been partly offset by the fact that, with the reduction in the rate of inflation, the variance of real wages between wage readjustments has also been reduced.

expansion of total effective demand, raises some doubts as to the viability of the country's growth process in the years ahead.[42]

The various stabilization measures implemented since 1964 have so far been considered more or less in isolation. When we analyze them simultaneously and in the context of the diagnoses of the state of the economy made by the first two revolutionary governments, distinctive patterns of economic policy emerge. The Castello Branco regime diagnosed that the inflationary process which had gathered momentum during the first years of the sixties was mainly attributable to excess demand pressures engendered by both the government and private sectors. Its tools of economic policy were accordingly oriented toward a reduction of aggregate demand. Central government expenditure was cut in real terms and the economy's tax burden substantially increased, thus decreasing both private and public demand as well as the budget deficit. While after-tax income was being reduced by the government's tax policy, before-tax income of workers was adversely affected by its wage policy. The real values of both the minimum wage and the average industrial wage declined because of the government's consistent underestimation of the economy's "residual inflation."

The government intermittently starved the industrial sector of the working capital it needed to operate at normal levels of capacity utilization and maintained the average real value of private-sector loans below that of the first half of the sixties. The periodic loosening and tightening of monetary and credit policies, combined with the lack of governmental control over some of the basic causes of monetary expansion, introduced great uncertainty in the business community. The availability to firms of internal financing for both fixed and working capital was reduced both by higher taxes and by the lower corporate profits resulting from the recession into which the economy had slid, while external financing was rendered both difficult and costly by massive borrowing by the government to finance part of its deficit. This policy of "overkill" of excess demand pressures by a combination of policy instruments precipitated the result which the government had intended to avoid—an industrial recession accompanied by a sharp drop in real private investment. Despite this recession,

42. Cf. Werner Baer and Andrea Maneschi, "Import-Substitution, Stagnation and Structural Change: An Interpretation of the Brazilian Case," *The Journal of Developing Areas*, January 1971.

the rate of the inflation, while halved with respect to its 1964 peak, still exceeded 40 percent in 1966; and the coexistence of considerable underutilization of industrial capacity with a high rate of price increase showed that the government's diagnosis of the inflationary process as arising from excess demand, if it had been valid for the previous years of the sixties, was now no longer so.[43]

The newly inaugurated Costa e Silva regime took note of these various factors and tailored its economic policies to a different analysis of the inflationary process. It found firms' cost structures to have been adversely affected by their increased tax liabilities, by the more realistic exchange-rate policy implemented since 1964, by the higher prices of certain important inputs (some produced by public enterprises) permitted by the policy of corrective inflation, and by the increased cost of borrowing resulting from the credit squeeze and the heavy government demands on the bond market. With unit costs rising because of the lower level of demand, firms raised the prices of their products, generating cost-push pressures and causing the new administration to alter the previous diagnosis of the inflationary process.

The new government adopted an economic strategy which was in many respects the reverse of its predecessor's. It allowed demand to expand, using budgetary policy to this end in 1967, and liberalized drastically the supply of credit to the private sector. Underlying this policy may have been the conviction that the price level would not rise any faster through an increase in demand than through the continuance of cost-push pressures resulting, among other things, from a depressed volume of sales in the industrial sector; or that even if the rate of inflation did not drop as fast as it would otherwise have done this would be amply compensated for by a higher rate of economic growth. The government attempted a stricter control of industrial costs and pressured commercial banks to lower their interest rates. The budget deficit was permitted to rise considerably in 1967, and in both 1967 and 1968 the government decreased the percentage of its deficit financed by borrowing.

Thanks to the government's efforts, the economy's growth rate rose appreciably in 1968 and 1969 while the inflation rate showed, at

43. For a similar appraisal of the Castello Branco government's economic policies, cf. Celso L. Martone, "Análise do Plano de Ação Econômica do Govêrno (PAEG), 1964-1966," in Betty Mindlin Lafer (editor), *Planejamento no Brasil* (São Paulo: Editôra Perspectiva, 1970).

least, no tendency to increase. At the same time, the austerity of the previous wage policy was alleviated only to the extent of freezing real wages rather than allowing them to decline as before. The liberalization of credit and the consequent expansion of the money supply were so great that they may prejudice any substantial further progress in the near future in reducing the rate of inflation. The second revolutionary government was certainly more skillful than the first in reconciling economic growth with the control of inflation through its mix of fiscal, monetary, and other economic policies. Nevertheless, in addition to the reservations expressed in our previous analysis of the latter, certain doubts—discussed below—remain as to the government's over-all economic policy.

Conclusions

This chapter has emphasized the results of government action during the sixties, which often differed considerably from the intentions expressed in the government plans. A different kind of analysis, of interest to both economists and political scientists, could usefully investigate the causes of the numerous deviations observed between plan targets and public actions during the sixties, and the effectiveness of planning under successive governments given the available planning machinery and the reality of the Brazilian power structure both inside and outside the public sector.[44]

Various policy implications arising from our discussion of the Brazilian public sector have been noted in the previous sections and need only be briefly summarized:

In order to maintain constant the share of the wages of government employees in GDP, the successive governments of the sixties have reduced considerably that of all other consumption expenditures. Moreover, the share of government investment in GDP has shown no tendency to rise. Neither of these allocational choices seems to have been wise from the point of view of the development of the Brazilian economy.

The 1966 tax reform has not been as beneficial as was originally intended. The welter of existing tax laws creates considerable confusion for taxpayers, and the tax legislation has been continually altered in response to changing economic conditions and governmental

44. Two useful studies of economic planning in Brazil during the postwar period are Robert T. Daland, *Brazilian Planning: Development Politics and Administration* (Chapel Hill: The University of North Carolina Press, 1967), and Betty Mindlin Lafer (editor), *Planejamento no Brasil, op. cit.*

attitudes. The frequent changes in the commodity rates of the federal tax on industrial products have been of dubious countercyclical effect and detrimental to good resource allocation in the private sector. No significant steps have yet been taken to turn the tax structure into a vehicle of income redistribution by increasing either the ratio of income taxes to total taxes or the effective progressivity of income taxes.

The fiscal incentives in favor of the Northeast have resulted in much tax erosion and have not made an effective contribution to solving the economic needs of that region, especially in terms of creating employment. In addition, they have turned attention away from the far more pressing problems of land tenure and irrigation, which still await a satisfactory solution.

The revolutionary governments are frequently praised for their effort in reducing drastically the ratio of the Treasury deficit to GDP between 1964 and 1969. It is true that by so doing they have brought under control what up to 1964 was the most important source of inflationary pressure. Their single-minded concern with reducing the size of the deficit, however, has prevented them from using fiscal policy to stabilize the level of economic activity around its long-run upward trend. At the same time, they deliberately encouraged the chief cause of currency expansion and of continuing inflation in the second half of the sixties—the granting of loans by the monetary authorities to the nonbank private sector. The present government's powers of monetary control still appear deficient compared with those of fiscal control, raising some doubts as to its progress in reducing the rate of inflation in the near future.

To conclude this chapter, I propose now to take a broad look at the main aims of the economic policies implemented by the revolutionary governments since 1964 and compare them with the four objectives of public policy: resource allocation, income redistribution, stabilization of output and price fluctuations, and economic growth. It becomes apparent that the first revolutionary government stressed the stabilization of the price level above all else, while its successor emphasized the resumption of economic growth, conditioning it to a further decrease in the rate of inflation. These objectives were invested with such importance as to relegate the others to relative obscurity.

Certain measures were doubtless taken to improve the efficiency of resource allocation in the public sector. The budgetary structure was rationalized considerably in the last decade, and the first steps taken toward the formulation of multi-annual capital budgets. Nevertheless, much remains to be done before the performance or program approach can be adopted for budget organization. The fact that no functional breakdown is yet available of past public sector (or even federal government) expenditure makes it impossible to analyze adequately the past or future efficiency of this expenditure. The *Programa Estratégico de Desenvolvimento* of Costa e Silva specifies a planned breakdown of both federal government and private-sector investment for the years 1968-70 according to "strategic areas," such as agriculture, basic industries, electric power, transportation, housing, education, and health.[45] No justification is given for this sectoral distribution even on an intuitive basis, let alone by calculated rates of return or benefit-cost ratios. Even if this plan were technically irreproachable, it is far from clear that the present Brazilian government disposes of the organizational machinery or the policy tools needed to execute it.

It is interesting to note that in their economic plans neither of the first two revolutionary governments adopted even in principle the objective of promoting a more equitable distribution of income. Instead, they both pledged themselves to maintain the current share of labor in national income by allowing real wages to rise in proportion to real per capita output. As was argued in the preceding section, even this objective has not been attained. Since the wage policies which were implemented militated against it, it is doubtful whether it was ever meant to be attained. In practice, income distribution has been treated as a residual category, that is, as the consequence of the distributional implications of policies aimed at the achievement of other objectives and particularly of price-level stabilization.[46] The *Programa Estratégico*, while deploring the regressive impact of wage policy since 1964 and stressing the desirability of raising the purchasing power of the working class, does not formulate any policy designed to compensate workers by restoring the former values of either the share of labor in national income or of real income per worker. This is rather paradoxical in view of the emphasis which this plan places on the need to raise over-all demand so as to bring the economy to higher levels of capacity utilization and to expand the markets for traditional industries. In sum, the first two revolutionary governments have failed to advocate a more equitable distribution of income either

45. Ministério do Planejamento e Coordenação Geral, *Programa Estratégico de Desenvolvimento 1968-1970*, 1968, Vol. I, Part II, Chapter I.

46. In addition, the numerous tax advantages granted to savers, who of necessity belong to the higher-income groups, have eroded the nominal progressivity of the tax structure and weakened its redistributional function.

on the ground of justice or as a vehicle for increasing aggregate demand and have not attempted to reverse the worsening of this distribution which has taken place since at least 1964. On both these grounds, the redistributional functions of public policy ought to be carefully considered and implemented by Brazilian policy-makers during the current decade.

Much has been said and written in Brazil during the sixties about the need to reduce or, at worst, prevent any further increases in the share of public expenditure in total output so as to alleviate the tax burden on the private sector. The economic plans of both revolutionary governments included this among their policy aims. There is much to be said in favor of thinning the swollen government bureaucracy, and steps were in fact recently taken in this direction. At the same time, the very size of the public sector in relation to national income and the preponderance of public enterprises in several key sectors of the economy place in the hands of Brazilian policy-makers a powerful base for effective economic planning. The patterns of public expenditure and taxation could be so altered as to serve the interests of genuine economic development, which implies both an expansion of total output and a participation in this expansion by all sections of the community. The fact that the Brazilian public sector had reached by the end of the sixties the largest size ever recorded in relation to national income can therefore be viewed as a positive by-product of fiscal policy, with favorable potential consequences for the seventies.

APPENDIX TABLE
OUTPUT, BUDGETARY PRICE MONETARY CREDIT, AND WAGE DATA FOR BRAZIL DURING THE SIXTIES

Year	(1) Real Gross Domestic Product index 1964 = 100	(2) %	(3) Industrial Production %	(4) Agricultural Production %	(5) Union Deficit (déficit de caixa) millions of NCr$ current prices	(6) Union Deficit constant prices of 1965-67	(7) Union Deficit/GDP	(8) Union Government Expenditure (index 1964 = 100)	(9) Union Government Revenue (index 1964 = 100)	(10) Wholesale Price Index %	(11) Wholesale Price Index %[a]	(12) Guanabara Cost of Living Index %	(13) Guanabara Cost of Living Index %[a]	(14) Currency in Circulation %[a]	(15) Currency held by the Public %[a]	(16) Money Supply %[a]	(17) Money Supply[a] / Currency in Circulation[a]	(18) Money Supply[a] / Currency held by Public[a]
1959	75.1				40.7													
1960	82.4	9.7	9.6	4.9	77.6	1120	2.8	76.5	78.4	31	35	29	24	40.6	33.4	38.2	3.50	4.09
1961	90.9	10.3	10.6	7.6	137.5	1420	3.4	83.4	80.6	40	53	33	43	49.7	51.0	50.5	3.55	4.10
1962	95.7	5.3	7.8	5.5	280.9	1920	4.3	95.0	84.1	50	46	52	56	61.6	55.1	63.4	3.56	4.29
1963	97.1	1.5	0.2	1.0	504.7	1960	4.2	99.4	89.3	76	83	71	80	71.9	72.2	64.0	3.40	4.09
1964	100.0	2.9	5.2	1.3	728.2	1560	3.2	100.0	100.0	81	84	91	87	69.0	69.2	85.9	3.74	4.49
1965	102.7	2.7	-4.7	13.8	592.9	828	1.6	95.1	111.4	54	31	66	46	49.4	49.7	75.4	4.39	5.26
1966	108.0	5.1	11.7	-3.2	586.6	581	1.1	98.7	122.5	41	42	41	41	32.2	35.5	15.0	3.84	4.49
1967	113.1	4.8	3.0	5.7	1224.7	957	1.7	97.0	110.7	27	21	31	24	26.1	25.6	42.6	4.32	5.07
1968	122.6b	8.4b	13.2b	1.7b	1226.7	781	1.2b	112.6	136.7	23	25	22	24	43.7	38.6	43.0	4.30	5.23
1969	133.7b	9.0b	10.8b	6.0b	755.8	404	0.6b	118.6	154.4	19	19	22	24	25.0	31.9b	32.5b	4.55b	5.26b

a. End-of-year values
b. Preliminary estimates
% = Percentage change

228

APPENDIX TABLE-(CONTINUED)

Year	(19) Voluntary Reserve/Deposit Ratio of Commercial Banks (annual averages)	(20) Compulsory Reserve/Deposit Ratio of Commercial Banks (annual averages)	(21) Real Money Supply[a] 1963=100 index	(22) %	(23) Income Velocity of Circulation (=GDP/Money Supply)	(24) Total Real Loans to Private Sector[a] 1963=100 index	(25) %	(26) Total Real Loans by Monetary Authorities to Private Sector[a] 1963=100 index	(27) %	(28) Total Real Loans by Comm. Banks to Private Sector[a] 1963=100 index	(29) %	(30) Real Minimum Wage in Guanabara 1964=100 index	(31) %	(32) Minimum Wage in Guanabara / GDP per capita
1959			98.5			113.2		100.4		120.9		135		2.45
1960	0.180[a]	0.116[a]	101.3	2.8	4.83	118.7	4.9	101.3	0.9	129.0	6.7	115	-14.8	2.05
1961	0.184[a]	0.115[a]	99.5	-1.7	4.92	107.1	-9.8	101.3	0.0	110.6	-14.3	134	16.3	2.22
1962	0.162	0.133	111.7	12.3	5.19	118.2	10.4	119.6	18.1	117.3	6.1	119	-10.7	1.90
1963	0.165	0.179	100.0	-10.5	5.94	100.0	-15.4	100.0	-16.4	100.0	-14.8	108	-9.5	1.62
1964	0.167	0.166	100.8	0.8	6.16	97.8	-2.2	94.2	-5.8	99.7	-0.3	100	-7.3	1.58
1965	0.165	0.165	134.5	33.4	5.37	117.2	19.8	88.8	-5.7	134.1	34.5	96.9	-5.1	1.65
1966	0.157	0.162	108.9	-19.1	5.68	110.1	-6.0	98.2	10.6	117.3	-12.5	90.0	-7.2	1.52
1967	0.150	0.152	128.1	17.6	5.63	141.5	28.5	112.1	14.1	159.3	35.8	87.0	-3.3	1.51
1968	0.106	0.183	146.8	14.6	5.50[b]	183.8	29.9	154.5	37.8	203.0	27.4	85.9	-1.3	1.35[b]
1969	n.a.	n.a.	163.6[b]	11.5[b]	5.51[b]	219.2	19.3	198.2	28.3	232.8	14.7	83.6	-2.7	1.26[b]

a. End-of-year values
b. Preliminary estimates
% = Percentage change
n.a. = not available
Note: Money supply and loans are deflated by the wholesale price index; the minimum wage in Guanabara is deflated by the Guanabara cost of living index.

Sources: cols. 1-4 from Fundação Getúlio Vargas, Centro de Contas Nacionais; cols. 5, 8, 9, 14-16, 19, 20, 24, 26, 28 from Relatório da SUMOC, Relatório do Banco Central and Conjuntura Econômica, Vol. 24, No 5, 1970; cols. 10-13 from Conjuntura Econômica, Vol. 23, No 12, 1969 and Vol. 24, No 2, 1970; col. (30) from Anuário Estatístico do Brasil, 1969.

229

7 DAVID E. GOODMAN

Industrial Development in the Brazilian Northeast: An Interim Assessment of the Tax Credit Scheme of Article 34/18

WHEN SUDENE, the federal development agency for the Brazilian Northeast, was established in December 1959, it represented a radical departure in federal policy towards the region.[1] Its proponents
adhered to the view that only sustained economic growth would
provide a definitive solution of the Northeast's economic and social
problems and that an autonomous regional planning agency was required for this purpose. Nevertheless, although this view had gained
ground steadily by the mid-1950s, it is more appropriate to regard
the creation of SUDENE as a direct response to the crisis engendered
by the 1958 drought rather than as the logical outcome of intellectual
argument and debate. In this respect, it may be seen against the background of the Brazilian preference for institutional innovation when
tackling intractable policy issues as opposed to entrusting new tasks
and policy instruments to existing institutions. Previous droughts also elicited institutional modifications and there is little reason to
anticipate a change in this pattern as events surrounding the 1970
drought unfold. However, these considerations are beyond the scope

1. The Northeast has an area of 600 thousand square miles, approximately 19
percent of Brazil, and includes nine states ranging from Maranhão in the north to Bahia
in the south. The estimated population is 30 million, slightly less than one third of
Brazil's total population, and the region in 1967 generated 15 percent of national income at factor cost.

231

of the present chapter and only a brief description of the circumstances which led to the establishment of SUDENE is attempted here.[2]

Beginning with the First National Commission of Inquiry into the severe drought of 1877-79 until the late 1940s, the central concern of federal policy in the Northeast was to mitigate the effects of the periodic droughts which assail the region's vast semiarid interior zone, known as the *sertão*. The construction of reservoirs and dams (*açudes*) and the improvement of communications between the heavily populated humid coastal strip and the interior constituted the common element of federal programs in this period. In drought years, these public works programs were accelerated to absorb the rural unemployed and supplemented by the distribution of emergency relief funds and food supplies to state and municipal authorities. Several factors in the early and mid-1950s combined to shift the focus of federal policy away from what Hirschman has called "the hydraulic or engineering solution" towards a more comprehensive strategy for the region. A partial change towards broader developmental objectives had occurred previously with the establishment of the São Francisco Valley Commission (CVSF) and the São Francisco Hydroelectric Company (CHESF) in 1948. The CVSF was to formulate and implement a multiple-purpose river basin development program while CHESF was created to exploit the hydroelectric power potential of the Paulo Afonso Falls. Doubts concerning the efficacy of public works programs in combating the effects of the drought were dramatically confirmed in 1951-53 and 1958 when temporary work fronts and food distribution centers had to be opened hastily to cope with the *flagelados* or refugees. The National Department for Works against the Droughts (DNOCS), which was responsible for these programs and the co-ordination of emergency relief measures was further discredited by the frequent allegations of administrative irregularities and outright corruption.

Dissatisfaction with the performance of DNOCS in 1951-53 prompted the creation of a new regional agency, the Bank of the Northeast of Brazil (BNB), in 1952. The BNB was intended primarily to finance medium- and long-term investment projects, particularly those involving cultivation of drought-resistant agricultural crops. In practice, the BNB largely neglected its investment and development

2. For a more detailed analysis see Albert O. Hirschman, *Journeys Towards Progress*, (New York: The Twentieth Century Fund, 1963), pp. 18-86. Also, Riordan Roett, *The Politics of Foreign Aid in the Brazilian Northeast*, (Nashville: Vanderbilt University Press, 1972), especially chs. 5 and 6.

banking functions in the 1950s in favor of short-term commercial financing. This change was followed in 1954 by the formation of an Investments Commission to co-ordinate federal expenditures in the region and undertake detailed studies to serve as the basis for public policy. Although the commission failed to fulfil this mandate, it represented an initial step toward acceptance of the need for regional planning and policy co-ordination. The new Kubitschek administration encouraged further initiatives in this direction,[3] and in 1956 the Working Group for the Development of the Northeast (GTDN) was established. The GTDN lacked autonomy and executive status, but in 1958, under the intellectual leadership of Celso Furtado, it produced an incisive and timely report on the Northeast situation.[4]

The drought of 1958 again demonstrated the ineffectiveness of the DNOCS approach while public indignation against the misappropriation of federal funds and food shipments reached a new pitch. These practices, characterized by the term *industriais da sêca* or "drought industries," were widely publicised in the Center-South press.[5] In seeking to resolve these difficulties, President Kubitschek requested Furtado to examine the region's problems and to suggest a program of action. The new report,[6] which drew on the analysis and results of the earlier GTDN document, was submitted to Kubitschek in early 1959, and in February 1959 the bill to establish SUDENE was before Congress. A prolonged legislative struggle ensued, however, before SUDENE obtained the necessary budgetary appropriations and the authority to coordinate and control the activities of other federal agencies in the Northeast.[7]

The application of economic analysis to a problem which previously had been discussed almost solely in social and political terms was a novel feature of the Furtado document. Thus, the toll exacted by the drought in terms of human suffering and the disruption of

3. For example, a series of measures recommended by the First and Second Meetings of the Northeastern Bishops held in 1956 and 1958 were approved by President Kubitschek. See Roett.

4. *O Diagnóstico Preliminar da Economia do Nordeste* (Rio: Grupo de Trabalho para o Desenvolvimento do Nordeste, 1958).

5. The term is attributed to the journalist Antonio Callado. See *Os Industriais da Sêca e os "Galileus" do Pernambuco*, (Rio: Editôra Civilização Brasileira, 1960).

6. *Uma Politica de Desenvolvimento Econômico Para o Nordeste* (Rio de Janeiro: Conselho do Desenvolvimento, GTDN, 1959).

7. Although the bill to establish SUDENE was passed in December 1959, approval of the first Master Plan detailing the proposed allocation of federal resources for the years 1961-63 was delayed until December 1961.

economic activity was shown to be a consequence of the region's economic backwardness. Moreover, Furtado argued that previous policies against the drought had aggravated such characteristics of underdevelopment in the *sertão* as overpopulation and widespread reliance on subsistence agriculture for food supplies. Briefly, Furtado proposed a radical transformation in the economic structure of the region through industrialization, crop diversification, and new land-use patterns in the humid coastal zone, the encouragement of migration from the *sertão* and the colonization of the moist soils of Maranhão. These measures would provide alternative sources of income, growth, and employment and permit agricultural specialization in the semiarid interior along lines more suited to the ecological environment: cattle-raising based on drought-resistant forage crops and the cultivation of xerophilous commercial crops, particularly *mocó* cotton.

The Furtado document is noteworthy not only for the economic analysis of Northeastern development problems and the comprehensiveness of its policy recommendations. It also presented an extremely skillful case in favor of intensified federal development efforts in the region by marshalling "technical" arguments and quantitative evidence to support new political initiatives. The crux of this case was the demonstration of marked inter-regional disparities in income per head and divergent rates of growth between the Northeast and the Center-South in the period 1949-56. Such trends, it was suggested, were "cumulative and hardly reversible at all."[8] Furthermore, it was argued that rapid economic development in the Center-South partly had been achieved at the expense of the Northeast through such mechanisms as exchange rate overvaluation and import controls which had transferred resources from the region.[9] While these arguments may be questioned, it must be noted that this analytical approach established a completely different framework of discussion for the Northeast problem. It traced the catastrophic effects of the drought to the more general phenomenon of regional underdevelopment which in turn was attributed to differential rates of regional economic growth. The policy implication was that eradication of the drought

8. *GTDN*, page 9. All page references are to the second edition of this report. See *Uma Política de Desenvolvimento Econômico Para o Nordeste* (SUDENE, Recife, 1967).

9. Furtado's analysis in this respect was not original. See, for example, *The Economy of Brazil*, Report of the Joint Brazil-United States Economic Development Commission. Institute of Inter-American Affairs, Foreign Operations Administration (Washington, D.C., 1953) pp. 123-126.

problem required an ambitious development program in the North-east to reduce inter-regional disparities.

In fact, the attenuation of such inequalities generally has been accepted as the major aim of regional policy in the 1960s. This commitment and concern with global objectives, however, has tended to inhibit the use of alternative criteria in evaluating the SUDENE program and its sectoral components. This chapter seeks to offset this bias by undertaking an interim assessment of the tax-credit scheme used to stimulate private industrial capital formation in the region. The scheme, known as Article 34/18, was introduced in 1961-62 and constitutes the central core of SUDENE's industrialization policy.[10] It may be observed here that the agency, despite its broad initial aims, has been active primarily in the promotion of industrial investment and the provision of social overhead capital. In recent years, fiscal incentives similar to those embodied in the 34/18 legislation also have been extended to the Amazon region and several neglected sectors.[11] It seems appropriate, therefore, to examine the effects of this novel instrument in the Northeast, where it has been applied most intensively.

The Tax-Credit Mechanism

The fundamental element of the 34/18 tax-credit mechanism is that registered Brazilian corporations *(pessoas jurídicas)* may reduce their annual federal income tax liability by 50 percent by opting to invest the corresponding tax savings in projects approved by SUDENE. Such funds are deposited initially in a blocked account with the Bank of the Northeast of Brazil (BNB), the regional financing agency. Subject to certain conditions, legal title to such deposits not committed to approved projects within a period of two years reverts to the federal government. The 34/18 deposits invested in approved projects must be combined with additional resources *(recursos próprios)* provided by firms undertaking the projects. At present, projects are classified into five categories, and 34/18 funds may constitute from 30 percent to 75 percent of the total equity, depending

10. The name derives from legislation regulating the activities of SUDENE. That is, Article 34 of Decree No. 3995 (December 1961) and the amendments introduced by Article 18 of Decree No. 4239 (June 1963).

11. These programs, with the date of their eligibility to receive tax savings in parentheses, are the Amazon region (SUDAM: October 1966); tourism (EMBRATUR: November 1966); reforestation (November 1966), and the fishing industry (SUDEPE: February 1967).

on their ranking by SUDENE.[12] An intrinsic feature of the scheme is that the 34/18 depositor is not required to contribute any further funds to the project receiving his deposited tax savings. As Hirschman has observed, agreements between depositors and entrepreneurial groups supplying the fresh funds component are reached at the project level.[13] A system of investment brokers and consultants performing intermediary functions has emerged to facilitate the operation of this capital market.

Investments of 34/18 deposits usually take the form of preferential, nonvoting stock, negotiable only five years after the conclusion of the project.[14] Recently, however, SUDENE has sought to accelerate the absorption of 34/18 funds in approved projects and several other forms of participation have evolved. Since 1966, beneficiary firms have been able to receive 34/18 funds as loan capital, repayable five years after the project becomes operational.[15] A recent regulation permits the beneficiary firm to redeem such loans either in cash or by conversion into equity in the enterprise. Under certain conditions, 34/18 funds also may be used to provide working capital and to amortize long-term domestic and foreign currency loans. It is important to observe that access to 34/18 funds is not restricted to firms with deposited tax savings. Any new or established firm with a project approved by SUDENE may negotiate the investment of 34/18 funds with depositors. In effect, these firms have a captive source of equity financing within the limits determined by SUDENE. Moreover, with freedom to restrict the amount of 34/18 investment by any individual depositor and to opt for different forms of 34/18 participation, the beneficiary firm may achieve an equity structure in which it retains effective control.

A second powerful investment incentive, and an integral part of regional development policy is provided by the BNB in the form of long-term loans. This agency may finance, in foreign or domestic

12. The proportions are 30, 40, 50, 60, and 75 percent of total investment, which is defined to include working capital but not loan financing. See Article 31 of Decree No. 64.214 (March 18, 1969).

13. Albert O. Hirschman, "Industrial Development in the Brazilian North-East and the Tax Credit Scheme of Article 34/18," *The Journal of Development Studies*, Vol. 5 (October 1968), p. 6.

14. The period is ten years for projects which received 34/18 funds before July 11, 1963.

15. Annual interest rates may not exceed 12 percent and monetary correction is not paid on either interest payments or the principal. See paragraph 3, Article 15 of Decree No 64.214 (March 18, 1969).

currency, up to a maximum of 50 percent of the additional "own resources" contribution to total equity, which beneficiary firms are required to invest in their projects. The reduction in the initial outlay of own equity or risk capital needed to establish an industrial enterprise in the Northeast, achieved by combining 34/18 funds and BNB financing, is the principal inducement to invest offered by the tax credit scheme. SUDENE also may confer a more conventional range of investment incentives on firms locating in the Northeast, including exemption from federal income tax for ten years.[16] In combination with the Customs Policy Council (CPA), SUDENE may grant tariff exemptions and reductions on imported equipment and components. Finally, individual state and municipal governments offer a variety of incentives in an attempt to influence location decisions within the region. However, for present purposes, it is unnecessary to review the many industrial incentive policies in elaborate detail.

Flows of 34/18 Resources

Table 1 summarizes the flow of resources under the 34/18 scheme. Although the rate of growth of deposits in real terms varies considerably, there is some indication that this rate has declined in recent

TABLE 1
INFLOW, COMMITMENT AND DISBURSEMENT OF 34/18 RESOURCES
(NCr$ million)

Year	34/18 Deposits		Commitments to Approved Projects		Disbursements	
	(a)	(b)	(a)	(b)	(a)	(b)
1962	5.7	61.4	-	-	-	-
1963	7.7	47.0	7.0	42.7	0.1	0.6
1964	37.3	125.6	26.0	87.5	3.4	11.4
1965	149.4	328.0	35.0	76.7	8.0	17.5
1966	226.6	353.1	152.0	236.9	39.0	60.8
1967	351.1	432.3	496.0	610.7	157.0	193.3
1968	456.7	456.7	511.0	511.0	315.7	315.7
1969	626.6	520.0	581.3	482.4	432.0	358.5
TOTAL	1,861.1	2,324.1	1,808.3	2,047.9	955.2	957.8

Note: Columns (a) and (b) are in current and 1968 prices, respectively. The wholesale price index, excluding coffee, of the Getulio Vargas Foundation is used as the inflator.

Sources: BNB; SUDENE; Ministério da Fazenda.

16. The reader may refer to Decree No. 64.214 (March 18, 1969).

years. Any firm conclusion is complicated by the annual fluctuations in the level of economic activity, which is a major determinant of the influx of new funds. Thus, the general economic recovery initiated in 1968 is generating higher real flows of tax savings not only into the 34/18 scheme but also to the other programs eligible for such investment. However, as shown below, this apparently favorable situation masks a growing tendency for investors to place their tax-credit funds outside the SUDENE program. In short, as in 1969 for example, SUDENE may enjoy a higher real inflow of resources despite a declining participation in total tax-credit funds.

A second point from Table I is that the margin of uncommitted resources, given by the difference between the accumulated inflow of 34/18 funds and allocations to approved projects, is disappearing rapidly. In real terms, such allocations represented 88.1 percent of accumulated deposits in the years 1962-69. A significant acceleration in the absorption rate of accumulated deposits is evident after 1966 and commitments of 34/18 funds exceeded deposited tax savings in the period 1967-69. This improvement may be attributed mainly to the wider project choice available to depositors and measures taken to broaden the possible forms of 34/18 participation in beneficiary firms. A further stimulus to rapid absorption is SUDENE's recent decision to reduce the period in which depositors may choose freely between approved projects from three to two years.[17] In addition, the depositor is required to do more than merely nominate the beneficiary firm which is to receive his 34/18 funds. Such funds now are considered to be "invested" only when this participation has been legally incorporated in the firm's capital and recorded with the appropriate authorities.

Given present trends in the inflow of new 34/18 funds and their absorption in projects, the stage is approaching in which the annual volume of investment approved by SUDENE will be constrained by the *current* inflow of new deposit resources. Concomitantly, with no backlog of uncommitted deposits, the future scope of the program will depend more closely on depositors' evaluation of investment opportunities in the Northeast vis-à-vis those arising under the other schemes eligible to receive tax savings. In fact, recent statements by SUDENE officials suggest that a deficitary situation may arise in the very near future. Current estimates of the eligibility for 34/18 funds of new projects now being reviewed by SUDENE evidently exceed

17. Article 13 of Decree No. 64.214 (March 18, 1969).

the anticipated inflow of new tax savings by a substantial margin. Although further information is needed for a more accurate assessment, the keener competition already observed between beneficiary firms seeking to obtain their approved share of 34/18 funds may be cited in support of this view. Several significant changes in the operation of the market in 34/18 deposits, which have occurred in the past year or so, are discussed below.

A marked lag in the disbursement of 34/18 funds allocated to approved projects also is shown in Table 1. The slow rate of project implementation is suggested by the fact that, at 1968 prices, only 46.8 percent of the 34/18 funds committed in the period 1962-69 actually were spent. Despite significant improvements in this ratio in 1968 and 1969, there has been a serious lag between the commitment and expenditure of 34/18 funds and, correspondingly, a pronounced accumulation of deposits. This may be seen from a different angle using information on total approved industrial development and estimates of *realized* investment in this sector. (Table 2). The accumulated totals for the years 1962-69 indicate that realized expenditures represent only 37.3 percent of anticipated total investment.[18] It is evident, therefore, that this disbursement lag has reduced the short-term impact of the 34/18 program significantly. Of course, this impact will rise as increasing numbers of projects enter the implementation phase and absorb the past accumulation of resources. This assumes that projects currently at this stage already have secured their full entitlement to 34/18 deposits or at least will encounter no difficulty in this respect. As noted previously, however, there is now a real possibility that the 34/18 deposit requirements of newly formulated projects presently under review *(en análise)* by SUDENE may exceed such flows. In the short term, however, a far more serious and immediate constraint on project execution will arise if the BNB continues to have difficulty in financing the foreign-currency requirements of approved projects. This question is known to be a matter of acute concern in official circles, although its gravity is difficult to assess because of the paucity of quantitative information. It appears that loans recently concluded between the BNB and international credit institutions have temporarily averted a critical situation in this respect, at least for those

---

18. The position is modified if projects approved in 1969 are excluded and realized investment for 1969 is re-estimated by applying the participation of 34/18 funds in 1968 projects to actual 1969 disbursements. On this basis, realized investment in the period 1962-69 represents 45.4 percent of projected total investment.

TABLE 2

APPROVED 34/18 INVESTMENT AND ESTIMATED REALIZED INVESTMENT
IN INDUSTRY

(NCr$ million; 1968 prices)

Year	Total Approved Investment	Disburse-ments[a]	34/18 Participation in Approved Investment (%)	Estimated Realized Investment
1962	165.9	-	-	-
1963	222.2	0.6	20.1	3.0
1964	449.2	11.4	19.8	57.6
1965	304.6	17.5	23.8	73.5
1966	522.6	57.0	45.4	125.6
1967	1,354.1	152.7	44.8	340.8
1968	953.8	283.5	53.4	530.9
1969	946.0	358.5	51.0	702.9
TOTAL	4,918.4	881.2		1,834.3

a. Disbursements relating exclusively to working capital participation are excluded.

Source: SUDENE.

projects presently in execution. Firms with projects now entering this stage, however, are by no means assured of access to foreign financing and may be compelled to postpone or scale down their expenditures unless the required funds are forthcoming. Clearly the sustained momentum of the 34/18 program depends on a successful solution of this problem.

Changes in the allocation of tax-credit funds between the various incentive programs can be considered only briefly as the information available is rather limited. As shown in Table 3, SUDENE has been losing ground steadily to the SUDAM scheme in relative terms. Since 1967, however, both schemes have suffered from the extension of tax incentives to tourism, the fishing industry, and reforestation as investors have diversified their tax savings-financed portfolios. This is more pronounced in the case of SUDENE, and particularly with reference to allocations in the state of São Paulo, its major source of funds (Table 4). Investors in that state have reduced their allocations to SUDENE from 60 percent in 1968 to 52 percent during the first half of 1969, whereas SUDAM has maintained its share in options (Table 5). The most notable change in allocation involves SUDEPE, whose participation has risen sharply from 5 percent to 14 percent in the same period. This switch largely confirms impressions gathered in interviews undertaken in São Paulo and Guanabara in mid-

TABLE 3
FLOWS OF TAX-CREDIT RESOURCES TO SUDENE AND THE
AMAZON REGION (SUDAM)

| YEAR | (NCr$ million; 1968 prices) | | $\frac{(B)}{(A)} \times 100$ |
	SUDENE (A)	SUDAM (B)	
1963	47.0	-	-
1964	125.6	-	-
1965	328.0	-	-
1966	353.1	74.7	21.1
1967	432.3	128.3	29.7
1968	456.7	163.1	35.6
1969	520.0	215.9	41.5

Sources: BNB; Bank of the Amazon.

TABLE 4
PARTICIPATION OF SEVERAL STATES IN 34/18 DEPOSITS

| State | YEAR | (%) | | January-June, |
	1966	1967	1968	1969
São Paulo	57.1	51.6	46.1	48.4
Guanabara	17.2	22.2	27.3	19.0
Minas Gerais	5.2	6.2	7.2	8.4
Rio Grande do Sul	5.6	5.6	5.7	4.6
All Others	14.9	14.4	13.7	19.6

Source: Ministério da Fazenda.

1969. Potential investors of tax-credit funds, without their own projects in the SUDENE/SUDAM areas, expressed a strong preference for programs which would benefit locally based entrepreneurial groups and the Center-South region generally. In short, regionalism is an important factor in this type of investment decision. Despite their surprisingly parochial character, such attitudes indicate a tendency for tax-credit flows to become regionalised to the detriment of the SUDENE/SUDAM areas with their limited tax base.

The patterns of industrial investment, employment and location associated with the 34/18 scheme are examined below. Some relevant aspects of the pre-34/18 situation are described briefly to introduce the discussion of the probable effects of the tax-credit system.

TABLE 5
DISTRIBUTION OF TAX-CREDIT FUNDS BETWEEN ELIGIBLE
PROGRAMS BY MAJOR STATES, 1968 AND 1969

(%)

Program	1968					1969[a]				
	Total	SP	GB	MG	RGS	Total	SP	GB	MG	RGS
SUDENE	64.5	59.9	80.3	76.4	45.5	56.1	51.7	67.2	81.6	39.6
SUDAM	22.8	26.7	12.1	19.6	21.6	23.4	26.4	16.8	8.8	21.7
SUDEPE	6.1	4.8	2.6	0.5	26.5	12.8	14.2	9.3	2.3	27.9
EMBRATUR	5.0	6.2	4.7	2.1	6.0	4.1	3.8	5.9	1.9	8.5
Reforestation	1.6	2.4	0.3	1.4	0.4	3.6	3.9	0.8	5.4	2.3

a. First six months of 1969. The figures refer to options stated in corporate income tax declarations.

Source: Ministério da Fazenda.

Industrial Structure

The sectoral composition of industrial gross value-added in 1959 and 1966 and 34/18 investment is given in Table 6 for purposes of comparison. The dominance of the consumer nondurable goods industries in the pre-34/18 structure is readily apparent, despite some reduction in their relative weight between 1959 and 1966. More significant for present purposes is the fact that these industries have articulated strong linkages with the region's raw material and agricultural base. The importance of nonferrous metals, mainly cement, and the chemical industry also reflects the influence of similar locational factors. The chemical industry comprises two distinct branches: oilseed processing and a modern, dynamic sector based on the exploitation of petroleum resources in Bahia by the federal autarquia, PETROBRÁS. This sector has made a vital contribution to recent industrial growth and the petrochemical complex in the Recôncavo region of Bahia is emerging as a significant "growth pole."

Conversely, the past weakness of the metallurgical and metalworking sectors is evident and they have assumed a secondary, passive role in previous industrial expansion. Their raw materials and semimanufactured inputs originate primarily in the Center-South, while assembly-type operations are common in the electrical and transport-goods sectors. Small firms and workshops predominate, particularly in the metallurgical industry, specializing in general maintenance and "one-off" replacement services rather than the pro-

TABLE 6
SECTORAL DISTRIBUTION OF GROSS VALUE ADDED
AND 34/18 INVESTMENT[a]
(%)

Sector	Gross Value Added		Approved 34/18 Investment			
	1959	1966	(a) Total	(b) New.	(c) Moderni- zation	(b) as % of (a)
Nonmetallic Minerals	8.1	7.5	11.5	9.2	21.2	64.2
Metallurgy[b]	2.1	4.3	14.7	17.6	2.7	96.4
Machinery	0.1	0.8	2.4	2.8	1.0	92.1
Electrical Equipment	0.2	1.0	4.1	4.7	1.5	92.7
Transport Equipment	0.8	0.6	2.8	3.4	0.1	99.1
Wood Products	1.7	1.1	1.9	2.3	-	100.0
Furniture	1.6	1.3	0.4	0.4	0.3	83.0
Paper, cardboard	1.7	0.7	4.8	5.8	0.6	98.2
Rubber	0.3	0.4	0.4	0.4	0.4	81.4
Leather	2.3	1.1	0.8	0.5	1.8	54.5
Chemicals	14.9	16.8	25.6	30.4	5.7	95.6
Pharmaceuticals	0.3	0.3	0.2	0.2	0.1	95.7
Perfume, Soap, etc.	1.4	1.3	0.1	0.1	0.1	79.8
Plastics	0.1	0.4	0.7	0.8	0.3	91.2
Textiles	24.1	20.9	16.8	7.6	55.0	36.5
Clothing, Footwear	2.2	2.3	1.8	2.1	0.6	93.4
Food Products	29.7	28.0	6.4	6.3	6.9	79.1
Beverages	3.0	4.5	3.6	4.4	0.5	97.3
Tobacco	3.1	3.8	0.1	0.1	0.3	34.5
Printing, Publishing	1.9	2.5	0.2	0.2	0.2	76.1
Miscellaneous	0.4	0.4	0.7	0.7	0.7	81.5
TOTAL	100.0	100.0	100.0	100.0	100.0	80.6

a. 34/18 investment approved before December 31, 1968.

b. If the USIBA project is excluded, the share of metallurgy in total investment is 8.1 percent and 9.7 percent in new project investment.

Sources: (i) *Gross Value Added:* 1959 Industrial Census and *"Pesquisa Industrial de 1966"* (DEICOM-IBGE)
(ii) *34/18 Investment:* SUDENE

duction of standardized components. These characteristics are revealed clearly in a recent unpublished study by SUDENE which merits wider circulation.[19] This study also gives emphasis to the limited interdependence between the various subsectors of these industries. Without extensive modernization and rationalization of their traditionally

19. This study was undertaken in 1966-67 and analyzed 194 firms in these sectors.

diverse product-mix, it is doubtful that pre-34/18 firms in the engineering sectors[20] can meet the input requirements of the modern firms now entering the region. On this point, the small proportion of total investment in these sectors devoted to modernization projects suggests the possible emergence of a sharply dualistic structure. The following discussion of the input-output relationships of newly established firms in these sectors confirms that this interpretation has considerable validity.

As shown in Table 6, the relatively high proportion of 34/18 investment absorbed by the metallurgical, engineering, and chemical industries represents the most obvious deviation from the inherited industrial structure. Of course, the eventual sectoral composition of output will not correspond exactly to the distribution of 34/18 investment because of intersectoral differences in capital-output ratios. Nevertheless, it is evident that the pattern of industrial output will be modified significantly, more closely approximating that of the Center-South. The fact remains, however, that the truly revolutionary elements of the 34/18 scheme are not fully revealed by reference to shifts in sectoral investment allocation. These elements compose the changes in market orientation, input flows, and production techniques being introduced principally by firms from the Center-South.

Hirschman preferred to emphasize the allocative aspect, stating that the 34/18 scheme is achieving "a more diversified and sophisticated industrial structure . . . with sharply increased representation of industries that are both dynamic and rich in linkage effects."[21] This result must not be taken for granted on the basis of a priori considerations however. The important point is whether the linkage effects actually being articulated will stimulate a significant degree of input-output complementarity within the Northeast. As Hirschman remarked, "it would be unfortunate if the 34/18 funds were to lead to the establishment of wholly uneconomic activities, such as the hauling of raw materials over long distances to the Northeast and then the return of the finished product to the South, merely for the purpose of taking advantage of the available 34/18 funds."[22] Sadly, an interim assessment suggests that this is quite an accurate description of many 34/18 projects in the capital and durable consumer-goods sectors.

20. In Brazilian nomenclature these sectors are known as *estamparia, funilaria,* and *serralharia.*

21. Hirschman, pp. 15-18.

22. Hirschman, p. 24.

A partial view of the input-output relationships in the new industrial sector may be constructed from the project analyses *(pareceres)* submitted to SUDENE and interviews of beneficiary firms. The project information must be used cautiously since firms are known to misrepresent details of their projects to gain more points under the SUDENE ranking system and hence obtain a higher proportion of 34/18 funds in their equity. This bias primarily affects estimates of labor force, regional sales distribution, and market demand projections rather than input purchases. Moreover, the geographical origin of inputs may be verified easily and the project information corrected, although this proved to be necessary in very few cases. Since the project analyses for all sectors were unobtainable, attention was given to new projects in the following industries: metallurgy, machinery, electrical and transportation equipment, nonferrous metals, paper, and two subsectors—industrial chemicals and artificial fibers. The information on the regional origin of inputs is summarized in Table 7. This demonstrates the remarkably limited degree of interdependence, through input purchases, between the machinery, electrical and trans-

TABLE 7

REGIONAL ORIGIN OF INPUTS OF NEW PROJECTS IN CERTAIN SECTORS[a]

(%)

Sector	Coverage of Projects Analyzed[b]	Origin		
		Northeast	Center-South	External
Nonmetallic Minerals	52.0	65.0	30.0	5.0
Metallurgy	50.0[c]	23.0	67.0	10.0
Machinery	82.0	7.0	92.0	1.0
Electrical Equipment	91.0	5.0	71.0	24.0
Transport Equipment	41.0[d]	2.0	96.0	2.0
Paper Cardboard	88.0	76.0	17.0	6.0
B - *SUBSECTORS*				
Industrial Chemicals	11.6	31.0	26.0	43.0
Artificial Textile Fibers	85.0	4.0	1.0	95.0

a. All project information was expressed in March 1968 prices. Purchases of fuel oil, electricity, water, etc. are excluded.

b. Percentage participation of the projects analyzed in total investment approved in the respective sector or sub-sector up to December 31, 1968.

c. Excluding the USIBA projects.

d. The Willys Overland project, which represents 31 percent of investment in the sector, is not included due to lack of input data. This project is essentially an assembly operation using components from the Center-South.

Source: Project analyses *(pareceres)*, SUDENE.

portation equipment industries and Northeastern sources of supply. Repercussions from the high backward linkage typically attributed to these sectors will be felt primarily outside the region, at least in the medium term. This also is true of the metallurgical sector, but to a lesser extent. In sharp contrast, the input structures of the nonferrous metals and paper industries are much more closely integrated with the resource base of the Northeast. The seven industrial chemical projects analyzed here do not really provide an adequate basis for generalization, although the considerable leakage into imports may be noted. Finally, firms producing polyester and acrylic fibres are almost entirely independent of domestic input sources at present.[23]

The origin of domestic inputs is presented in greater detail in Table 8, which again demonstrates the limited reliance on Northeastern sources.[24] It reveals also that input structures in the metallurgical and engineering industries are dominated by *intrasectoral* purchases and here the Northeast has a very insignificant role indeed. In other words, this type of interdependence is not emerging between 34/18 projects and established firms nor is it found in relationships between new firms, at least as revealed by the project data. This finding obviously casts doubt on the efficiency of SUDENE's methods of sectoral programming. It implies also that as a rule firms incur the additional costs associated with the long transport hauls from the Center-South and the higher inventory investment caused by irregular input supplies. Moreover, the strength of the intrasectoral linkages with the Center-South in these sectors suggests that many projects involve essentially assembly operations. Interviews of beneficiary firms and careful study of project analyses confirm that this frequently is the case, particularly in branches producing durable consumer goods, machinery, machine tools, and vehicles. Products in this category include refrigerators, air conditioners, radios, television sets, jeeps, buses, lathes, elevators, and excavation equipment. Such projects typically rely on the parent firm and its traditional network of suppliers in the Center-South for their manufactured components. In some instances, although this is less common, the Northeast plant receives components from the parent company to manufacture and assemble intermediate parts, which are returned to the main Center-South plant for the final stages of the production process.

23. The import coefficient in this subsector will be reduced considerably once several recently approved projects enter production.

24. A large steel project, USIBA, was approved initially in 1964 but it has since undergone several design changes, and implementation has barely begun.

TABLE 8
REGIONAL AND SECTORAL ORIGIN OF DOMESTIC INPUTS [a]

Sector	Metallurgy		Machinery		Electrical Equipment		Transport Equipment		Paper Cardboard	
	A[b]	B[c]	A	B	A	B	A	B	A	B
Agriculture	-	-	-	-	-	-	0.1	100.0	32.3	100.0
Mining	7.4	100.0	-	-	2.0	100.0	-	-	1.0	100.0
Manufacturing: Total	92.6	19.0	100.0	8.0	98.0	6.0	99.9	1.6	66.7	72.0
Nonmetallic Minerals	1.8	-	1.8	30.0	1.2	19.0	0.01	57.0		
Metallurgy	77.3	14.0	71.8	6.0	29.4	2.0	10.4	-	0.4	-
Machinery	-	-	16.1	1.0	14.9	3.0	5.8	4.0		
Electrical Equipment	0.9	90.0	5.1	10.0	37.1	3.0	4.3	-		
Transport Equipment							72.0	-		
Wood Products							1.3	95.0		
Furniture										
Paper, Cardboard	0.01	100.0			1.4	31.0			17.3	81.0
Rubber	0.03	-	3.3	38.0	0.2	-	5.1	-		
Leather	-	-			-	-				
Chemicals	8.6	69.0	1.9	47.0	9.7	18.0	0.09	6.0	32.9	58.0
Pharmaceuticals										
Perfume, Soap										
Plastics	3.2	-			3.7	-				
Textiles	0.03	12.0			0.2	6.0			6.4	90.0
Clothing, Footwear					-	-				
Food Products	0.01	-			0.2	19.0			9.7	99.0
Beverages										
Tobacco										
Printing, Publishing										
Miscellaneous										

a. See note a of Table 7. The coverage is that given in the first column of the table.

b. Percentage share of each sector in the value of total domestically-produced inputs at March 1968 prices.

c. Percentage share of North-East inputs in the value of total inputs originating from each sector.

Source: See Table 7.

This discussion certainly gives reason to doubt that investment under the 34/18 scheme represents an efficient resource allocation along lines of dynamic regional comparative advantage. A more definitive judgment on this issue, however, must be founded on a detailed analysis of transportation and inventory charges and interregional cost differentials.

In his analysis of the SUDENE scheme, Hirschman confidently dismisses the possiblity that the 34/18 incentives may induce an inefficient pattern of industrial location on the grounds that "the way in which individual firms view these funds makes it unlikely that many uneconomic decisions . . . will be taken."[25] Yet precisely the type of resource flows Hirschman associated with "wholly uneconomic activities" characterizes numerous projects in the four sectors under consideration. That is, the Center-South is not only the principal source of raw materials and manufactured inputs but also of vital importance as a market. Indeed, this position is typical of firms producing durable consumer goods. Interviews of beneficiary firms in production and industry specialists leave little doubt on this point.[26] Of course, the dependence on the Center-South market varies, but firms selling 50 percent or more of their output outside the SUDENE area are encountered frequently. Several reasons can be given for this. Plant size obviously exerts a major influence on marketing policy, and the investment decisions of beneficiary firms fall into three broad categories in this respect. First, the size of branch plants designed specifically for the Northeastern market often is based on recent sales by the Center-South parent firm in the region. In this case, the Center-South market essentially provides a safety valve to avoid temporary under-utilization of the Northeastern plant. Firms in a second category, however, possibly because of the influence of scale economies, design their plants to exceed the size of the regional market substantially, and here the Center-South market assumes great importance in determining capacity utilization and profitability. While these firms tend to sell the major proportion of this output locally, nevertheless its regional distribution often is flexible, depending on the firms' over-all national marketing policy. Such firms thus benefit from the tax incentives, protect their Northeastern market position and retain considerable room for maneuver.

A third, closely related category includes firms with limited Northeastern sales which, attracted by the tax incentives, establish branches primarily as an alternative to new plant investment in the Center-South. That is, such plants are designed explicity to meet the anticipated increase in demand in the national market and this rather than the narrow regional market determines their scale. A variant of

25. Hirschman, p. 24.

26. The project analyses submitted to SUDENE are a notoriously precarious source of data on marketing intentions. Thus, firms may indicate sales in both the national and regional markets but the distribution between them usually is not specified. Secondly, the regional market may be included merely to raise the possible participation of 34/18 funds in the project.

this occurs where the products of the Northeastern plant are intended to complement or extend the firm's existing line of products, all of which are marketed nationally. Casual empiricism indicates that the 34/18 investment decisions of Center-South firms more frequently reflect the circumstances described in the final two categories. All three explanations of plant size and the corresponding marketing policy, however, were encountered in interviews, and the question of which is the most decisive must remain open at the moment, casual empiricism notwithstanding.

The comments above raise serious qualifications concerning the efficiency of resource allocation in these four sectors and, by implication, in other industries. Above all, numerous firms have a significantly greater degree of input-output complementarity with the Center-South and few locational ties with the Northeast, apart from the 34/18 incentives. Radical modification of the situation would involve regional production of the wide and complex range of metallurgical and engineering components required by firms in the equipment and durable consumer-goods sectors. Obviously, output expansion in these sectors will gradually create viable opportunities for local production of such components and intermediate goods. Conversely, the tendency to pursue this objective indiscriminately through the 34/18 mechanism must be resisted in order to avoid a wasteful repetition of the import substitution process, only recently completed in the Center-South, in a region presenting immeasurably greater problems of market size, industrial infra-structure, etc. There is an urgent need to define the aims of SUDENE's industrialization policy more precisely; at present, these seem to comprise duplication of the diversified industrial structure found in the Center-South. Indeed, the agency's investment criteria give specific inducement to projects which substitute imports from outside the region. Although greater regional autonomy eventually may be achieved by a policy of "forced regionalization" of input structures, it would exact a high price in terms of slower national economic growth and impair the competitiveness of Brazilian industry by the increased fragmentation of its capacity. In other words, a solution other than a comprehensive policy of regional "import" substitution must be sought to overcome the limited articulation of intraregional linkages by 34/18 projects. One suggestion is that SUDENE devote greater attention to the identification of investment opportunities which exploit regional comparative advantage. Within this framework, the possibility of creating integrated industrial complexes deserves careful consideration. This orientation would provide a rational basis for the consolidation of the present industrial structure and enhance the competitive ability of 34/18 firms in regional and national markets.

It is recognized, of course, that these conclusions are derived primarily from projects in the four metal-working industries and a limited series of interviews. The information used here also refers to a static situation which may be modified substantially by new projects, although their effects will be felt only in the medium term. It is believed, however, that the circumstances described above prevail in several other important industries, with only slight differences in the degree of input-output dependence on the Center-South. One major point to emerge from this discussion is that the relationships associated with 34/18 investment projects certainly merit closer study than they have hitherto received.

Employment

The industrial employment situation in the Northeast was extremely bleak at the time SUDENE was established. Thus, in the decade 1949-59, the monthly average employment of industrial workers (operários) declined at an average annual rate of 1.4 percent, representing a net loss of 26.3 thousand jobs in the region.[27] This depressing situation was accentuated by the fact that the labor force engaged in textiles and food processing, the major sources of industrial employment, contracted by 42 thousand. In contrast, urban population growth in the 1950s was rapid, averaging 5 percent per year, with even higher rates in the larger centers.[28] This expansion represented a continuing process of rural-urban migration; the outflow reached dramatic proportions in drought years, however, with the flight of thousands of destitute rural families from the semiarid interior.

The severe open unemployment and underemployment found in the urban centers clearly made a strong impression on the authors of the GTDN report. "The mass of underemployment accumulating day by day in Northeastern cities constitutes, in itself alone, an enormous obstacle to be overcome by any regional development policy."[29] Industrialization was given a prominent role in the GTDN program because it promised to provide both an autonomous source

27. Industrial Census data for 1949 and 1959.
28. The population in centres of 100,000 inhabitants, which grew from 1.1 to 2.8 million in this decade, represented 36 percent of the regions' urban population in 1960.
29. *GTDN*, p. 53.

of economic growth and substantial employment opportunities. "The absorption of large masses of labour, at a high level of productivity. . . . *only* is possible with the installation of manufacturing industry."[30] In the first economic plans elaborated by SUDENE in the early 1960s, labor absorption continued to form part of the rationale to justify the policy goal of accelerated industrial growth. Unfortunately, the results so far achieved by the 34/18 scheme in terms of direct employment creation do not instil confidence that this strategy will resolve the region's grave employment problems. This may not be so surprising after all, given that the subsidy to industry is applied through the capital input.

The sectoral distribution of total industrial employment in 1959 and that associated with the 34/18 projects approved in the years 1960-68 is shown in Table 9.[31] Estimated total employment in the latter amounts to 112,000, with modernization projects accounting for 52,000 or 46 percent. On the assumption that all projects are implemented and working at full capacity by 1971, projected employment represents an increase of 53 percent over the 1959 level, or an average annual rate of growth of 3.6 percent for the period 1959-71. If the employment attributed to modernization projects is excluded, this proportion falls to 29 percent and the growth rate to 2.1 percent. With the significant exception of textiles, which retains its relative position, the 34/18 scheme is achieving a more balanced employment structure. This is particularly evident if only new projects are considered. In contrast, the dominance of textiles in the modernization category is quite remarkable, such projects contributing approximately 36,000 jobs or 27 percent of total projected employment under the 34/18 scheme.

There is, however, a more fundamental analytical reason for drawing a clear distinction between the employment effects of new and modernization projects. That is, employment attributed to the latter does not necessarily represent a positive net contribution to the supply of employment opportunities. The official employment estimates for these projects represent the labor force required after modernization and not the difference between pre- and post-modernization employment, which can be either positive or negative. SUDENE chooses to ignore this distinction and presents these estimates as if

30. *Ibid*, p. 83. Emphasis added.
31. The published SUDENE figures for total employment usually do not distinguish between production and administrative personnel.

TABLE 9
SECTORAL DISTRIBUTION OF EMPLOYMENT[a]

| | 1959 % | 34/18 Employment[b] | | | | | |
| | | Total | | New Projects | | Modernization Projects | |
Sector		Absolute	%	Absolute	%	Absolute	%
Nonmetallic Minerals	12.5	9,431	8.4	6,460	10.8	2,971	5.7
Metallurgy	1.9	8,773	7.8	6,058	10.1	2,715	5.2
Machinery	0.2	2,224	2.0	2,014	3.4	210	0.4
Electrical Equipment	0.2	5,901	5.3	4,996	8.4	905	1.7
Transport Equipment	0.8	2,717	2.4	2,699	4.5	18	-
Wood Products	2.2	2,482	2.2	2,482	4.2	-	-
Furniture	2.9	1,261	1.1	1,072	1.8	189	0.4
Paper, cardboard	0.8	3,970	3.6	3,781	6.3	189	0.4
Rubber	0.2	1,033	0.9	864	1.4	169	0.3
Leather	2.2	1,125	1.0	298	0.5	827	1.6
Chemicals	4.5	9,957	8.9	7,006	11.7	2,951	5.7
Pharmaceuticals	0.3	226	0.2	190	0.3	36	0.1
Perfume, soap	1.0	243	0.2	158	0.3	85	0.2
Plastics	-	1,217	1.1	1,121	1.9	96	0.2
Textiles	28.2	35,217	31.5	4,557	7.6	30,660	58.8
Clothing, footwear	4.1	6,922	6.2	6,299	10.5	623	1.2
Food Products	30.2	13,848	12.4	6,276	10.5	7,572	14.5
Beverages	2.6	3,089	2.8	2,443	4.1	646	1.2
Tobacco	2.2	910	0.8	-	-	910	1.7
Printing, publishing	2.6	218	0.2	127	0.2	91	0.2
Miscellaneous	0.5	1,148	1.0	883	1.5	265	0.5
TOTAL	100.0	111,912	100.0	59,784	100.0	52,128	100.0

a. Employment comprises production and administrative workers.
b. As given in projects approved up to December 31, 1968.

Sources: 1959 Industrial Census; SUDENE.

they represent newly created jobs.[32] Clearly, on the most favorable of
assumptions, modernization initially will imply no more than
maintenance of the previous labor force and is more likely to release
labor in the vast majority of cases. In other words, it is supremely
optimistic to expect that the net direct employment effect of modernization projects will be zero; this effect undoubtedly is negative,

32. To justify this treatment SUDENE argues that failure to modernize will result
in the eventual closure of the firm due to inefficiency. See SUDENE, "IV Plano
Diretor, 1969-73" (Recife: Ministério do Interior, 1968) p. 93.

although estimation of its magnitude provides fertile ground for argument. With regard to textiles, however, which represents more than half the investment and employment in this category, engineers and economists in the Northeast entertain no illusions about the highly negative direct employment effects of modernization. Informed observers estimate that such projects dispense with between 30 percent and 50 percent of the pre-modernization labor force. In short, the SUDENE employment figures for these projects are extremely ambiguous and are unacceptable in their present form.

What is still more disquieting is that even the official "employment" figures given for textile modernization projects may be substantially overestimated. This possibility emerges from a SUDENE survey, so far unpublished, of firms financed under the 34/18 scheme and the textile re-equipment program, which were in production in December 1966. The survey includes seven textile firms whose modernization projects, initiated in the early 1960s, have been completed. The official SUDENE employment figures attribute 9,337 jobs to these seven projects or 27 percent of total modernization employment in textiles for the period 1960-68. In contrast, the survey gives combined employment in these firms as 7,887, 6,359 and 6,065 for the three years 1964-66, respectively, a range of 16 percent to 35 percent below the official total. In one extreme case the published official estimate exceeds actual employment in 1966 by 70 percent. Of course, these seven modernization projects in the survey may be wholly unrepresentative of the sector and, given due allowance for various shortrun difficulties, actual and estimated employment may correspond reasonably well. Perhaps so, but this further doubt concerning the validity of official estimates can be removed only by a steady flow of information on current employment trends in completed modernization projects.

These considerations sharply diminish confidence in the efficiency of the 34/18 scheme as an instrument to accelerate labor absorption. Investment in new projects approved in the period 1960-68 will generate directly some sixty thousand new jobs as firms reach full-capacity levels of output. This increase, which will not be achieved before the early 1970s, is hardly going to transform employment patterns in the region. Thus, it is estimated that 274 thousand jobs are needed in the 1970s merely to maintain the manufacturing sector's present 8 percent share in total employment. To raise this participation to 12 percent by 1980 implies the creation of 838 thousand new jobs, equivalent to an average annual growth rate of 7 percent in manufacturing employment in this decade.[33] It may be noted that acceptance of the official SUDENE figures on the over-all net direct employment creation associated with the 34/18 scheme does not alter this conclusion significantly. As argued previously, however, actual employment creation probably is reduced well below this figure by the negative employment effect of modernization investment. The magnitude of the adjustment required to correct for this factor remains a matter of speculation at present but the position of the textile industry may be taken for purposes of illustration. Thus, a contraction of 30 percent in the labor force it employed in 1959, the year immediately preceding the initiation of the textile re-equipment and 34/18 programs, would involve a loss of 17.3 thousand jobs. In more general terms, the limited contribution of the 34/18 scheme assumes an even more discouraging aspect when set against the absolute decline in blue-collar employment in the 1950s. One final observation here is that estimates of *indirect* employment induced by 34/18 investment which are based on official direct employment figures are quite precarious in the absence of more accurate information on the latter.

These comments lead to the rather ironic conclusion that the industrialization strategy is failing to eradicate precisely those critical problems which led to its adoption. That is, high rates of urban unemployment and an occupational structure in which the mass of the labor force is concentrated in low-productivity employment. Of course, perhaps the high hopes of the first generation of SUDENE planners in this strategy were misplaced. Indeed, some observers now contend that the absorptive capacity of modern industry is limited and that the indirect employment effects of industrial investment are much more significant in quantitative terms.[34] Apparently this view is now shared by SUDENE, and its present five-year plan demonstrates an abrupt loss of faith in industry's absorptive capacity. "The experience of recent years emphasizes the impossibility of basing a vigorous policy of labor absorption on the industrial sector." This conclusion is based on "the level and nature of technological development, (and) the need for competitiveness in Northeastern industry, implying a high density of capital."[35]

33. These calculations are based on IPEA projections of the economically active population in the 1970's.

34. W. Galenson, "Economic Development and the Sectoral Expansion of Employment," *International Labor Review* (June 1963), pp. 505-519.

35. SUDENE, *IV Plano Diretor, 1969-1973*, p. 93.

Although it is not clear whether this statement is an ex post characterization of 34/18 investment, SUDENE typically has neglected to exercise its formal powers of control over the technological choice of beneficiary firms. No well-defined policy has been pursued to recommend or disseminate information on alternative, efficient techniques, where these exist, with a view to more rapid labor absorption. In this respect, firms have encountered few constraints on their freedom to maximize private rather than social benefit. This omission has various causes, not the least being the outside pressure on SUDENE to reduce the accumulation of 34/18 deposits. Similarly, the agency must attract firms to the Northeast against the competition of the alternative industrial incentive schemes. SUDENE, therefore, is constantly aware that projects may be lost to the region if its project evaluation procedures are markedly more rigorous and time-consuming than those employed by its rivals. In these circumstances, it is obviously difficult for SUDENE to remain impervious to local economic and political pressures. These factors have led to an open-door policy to facilitate the inflow of investment and a corresponding reluctance to restrict the scope for private decision-making. In addition, SUDENE generally has lacked sufficient qualified personnel to subject projects to a detailed screening process and make specific recommendations concerning their technical specifications. The high rate of turnover in its corps of *técnicos*, largely a result of the more attractive salaries offered by private enterprise, has further aggravated this situation. At the same time, it must be emphasized that the SUDENE ranking system favors investment in the capital and basic intermediate goods sectors on the grounds that such projects are "essential" to regional development.[36] Techniques in these sectors tend to be capital-intensive with relatively limited possibilities for factor substitution in the actual production process. While this moderates the previous criticism, the rationale for this discrimination against traditionally more labor-intensive sectors is dubious.

Personal observation and interviews give the overwhelming impression that firms actively seek to implant the most modern capital-intensive techniques available, frequently importing both the equipment and production layout from abroad. A general indication of the high capital-labor ratios found in new firms, particularly those in the capital and intermediate goods sectors, is given in Table 10. Several

36. See SUDENE, *Incentivos Fiscais e Financeiros para o Nordeste*, (Recife: Ministério do Interior, 1969).

TABLE 10
CAPITAL-LABOR RATIOS OF 34/18 PROJECTS[a]

Sector	New Projects		All Projects	
	NCr$	US$	NCr$	US$
Non-Metallic Minerals	37.7	11.7	40.2	12.5
Metallurgy	77.5	24.1	55.5	17.3
Machinery	36.5	11.4	35.9	11.2
Electrical Equipment	25.2	7.9	23.0	7.2
Transport Equipment	34.1	10.6	34.1	10.6
Wood Products	25.1	7.8	25.1	7.8
Furniture	9.5	3.0	9.7	3.0
Paper, Cardboard	41.0	12.8	39.7	12.4
Rubber	13.6	4.2	14.0	4.4
Leather	47.4	14.8	23.1	7.2
Chemicals	115.4	36.0	84.9	26.4
Pharmaceuticals	29.4	9.2	25.8	8.0
Perfume, Soap	20.8	6.5	16.9	5.3
Plastics	18.0	5.6	18.1	5.6
Textiles	44.6	13.9	15.8	4.9
Clothing, Footwear	8.8	2.7	8.6	2.7
Food Products	26.6	8.3	15.2	4.7
Beverages	48.1	15.0	39.1	12.2
Tobacco	-	-	3.6	1.1
Printing, Publishing	31.4	9.8	24.1	7.5
Miscellaneous	22.0	6.9	20.8	6.5
TOTAL	44.5	13.9	29.5	9.2

a. Ratios expressed in terms of March, 1968 prices and in thousands of new cruzeiros (NCr$) and US$ dollars.

Source: SUDENE.

factors may be cited to explain the tendency to adopt the latest imported technology. The most obvious is that the tax credit mechanism distorts relative factor prices, giving a strong subsidy to the cost of capital, which induces firms to use more capital-intensive techniques than would otherwise be the case. In short, the incentive scheme has caused a rightward shift in the supply of capital schedule in the Northeast which, it may be hypothesized, has lowered the marginal cost of capital vis-à-vis the Center-South and hence influenced technological choice. The magnitude of this differential, of course, will depend on the slope and position of the demand for capital schedule in the Northeast. In institutional terms, the tax-credit scheme furnishes capital to firms with no 34/18 deposits of their own at a lower price than is available from alternative domestic sources.[37] Indeed, if official credit agencies are excluded, domestic firms would experience great difficulty in raising any long-term venture capital whatsoever from external sources as the public capital market presently is restricted to a few, well-established companies. The SUDENE scheme therefore confers advantages of "availability," as well as price, on firms in this position. Similarly, firms able to finance the 34/18 requirements of their projects themselves obtain risk capital cheaply in relation to prevailing long-term market rates. Certainly, as Hirschman has emphasized, there is a real opportunity cost involved in this use of such funds, namely, the return on investment in third-party projects.[38] This does not, however, alter the fact that all beneficiary firms enjoy access to an institutionalized capital market on terms not generally available elsewhere in Brazil.

While these circumstances alone may explain the choice of capital-intensive techniques, interviews of beneficiary firms suggest some additional reasons. With regard the unskilled labor, firms are convinced that wage costs per unit of output are not significantly lower in the Northeast. This view is debatable, however, as may be seen from the rather crude estimates of regional wage and labor productivity differentials given in Table 11. Lower standards of health and nutrition are most frequently advanced as causes of the lower labor productivity in the Northeast. In this respect, several firms are impressed by the improvement in productivity following the provision of free or subsidized canteen meals. Further reasons given for low labor productivity include the higher rates of labor turnover and poor work discipline.[39]

All firms expressed concern about the limited supply of skilled labor and some regard it as the most critical obstacle to the establishment of a successful enterprise in the Northeast. As a general rule, firms recruit such workers and supervisory personnel in the Center-South. In several cases, firms had advertised for skilled Northeastern migrants to return to their native region. For example, one producer of bus chassis recruited a large proportion of its skilled manpower needs by hiring Northeastern workers away from the São Paulo auto-

37. Moreover, before 1969, long-term BNB financing for approved 34/18 projects was available at a *nominal* annual interest rate of approximately 12 percent, plus 2 percent commission. That is, a sharply negative rate in real terms.

38. Hirschman, pp. 21-22.

39. The comments on high turnover rates made in interviews lend themselves to an interpretation in terms of a backward-sloping supply curve of labor.

TABLE 11
WAGES AND GROSS VALUE ADDED PER WORKER (OPERARIO) IN THE
NORTHEAST IN RELATION TO THE STATE OF SÃO PAULO AND BRAZIL
(%)

Sector	Wages per Worker		Gross Value Added per Worker	
	São Paulo	Brazil	São Paulo	Brazil
Nonmetallic Minerals	45.0	55.0	67.0	74.0
Metallurgy	50.0	54.0	75.0	77.0
Machinery	56.0	60.0	72.0	73.0
Electrical Equipment	63.0	67.0	70.0	72.0
Transport Equipment	40.0	43.0	37.0	40.0
Wood Products	45.0	64.0	42.0	58.0
Furniture	49.0	61.0	52.0	64.0
Paper, cardboard	51.0	60.0	39.0	42.0
Rubber	38.0	42.0	36.0	40.0
Leather	56.0	62.0	61.0	70.0
Chemicals	107.0	105.0	57.4	55.9
Pharmaceuticals	47.0	48.0	24.0	28.0
Perfume, soap	43.0	55.0	31.0	46.0
Plastics	33.0	36.0	54.0	54.0
Textiles	48.0	59.0	58.0	70.0
Clothing, footwear	50.0	55.0	68.0	80.0
Food Products	47.0	63.0	30.0	45.0
Beverages	43.0	50.0	38.0	51.0
Tobacco	19.0	37.0	19.0	36.0
Printing, publishing	56.0	60.0	58.0	64.0
Miscellaneous	44.0	50.0	45.0	52.0
TOTAL	45.0	54.0	52.0	62.0

Source: *"Pesquisa Industrial de 1966"* (DEICOM-IBGE)

mobile firms. It is often necessary, however, particularly for engineering firms, to bring workers from the Northeast for periods of intensive training in their Center-South factories. The firms interviewed are virtually unanimous that the labor costs incurred for skilled and supervisory personnel are higher in the Northeast. Wages and salaries evidently exceed those paid in equivalent grades in the Center-South by a substantial margin and usually more nonwage benefits are provided. In general, firms state that they are compelled to pay more attention to welfare and personnel management problems. This concern reflects the high turnover rates arising from the intense competition for this type of labor, which all firms have experienced. Firms have encountered similar difficulties in contracting management and administrative staff locally and the Center-South is the major source. Such personnel apparently have a high transfer price as all firms report paying salaries and fringe benefits significantly above those prevailing for similar functions in their Center-South management structure. It is abundantly clear that management executives enjoy a sellers' market in the Northeast and this is confirmed by firms' complaints of high turnover and lack of company loyalty.

While these interviews give some insight into certain problems faced by beneficiary firms, it is difficult to decide on their importance in the choice of relatively capital-intensive techniques. Given the substantial subsidy to capital under the 34/18 scheme, labor recruitment difficulties and "distortions" in regional wage and productivity differentials probably are secondary rather than decisive factors. Moreover, there is always the danger that reference to labor problems is an *ex post* rationalization for a certain decision whereas, in fact, the variability of technical coefficients of production may be very limited. In sectors where this is the case and labor costs also represent only a small proportion of unit costs, the choice of the most modern technology available may be a reasonable rule of thumb.[40] This point was never put forward explicitly in the interviews; it nevertheless, deserves serious consideration. It may also explain the impression given by several firms that technological choice was basically a question of visiting the North American and European suppliers and trade fairs. Nor should one forget that modern technology seems to exercise a fascination of its own for some entrepreneurs. In one admittedly extreme case, the owner of a petrochemical plant was moved to state that "The project may never earn a profit, but what a beauty it is technologically!"

Industrial Location

The 34/18 beneficiary firms from the Center-South, following established lines of industrial location in the Northeast, are concentrated in the coastal zones of the states of Pernambuco, Bahia, and Ceará (Table 12). In each of these states, the capital city and its immediate suburbs has 75 percent or so total approved investment in new projects. These cities are better endowed with the necessary infrastructure and transportation links and more closely approximate the

40. On the assumption, of course, that market size permits operation at efficient output levels. There are cases where even this aspect seems to have been neglected as, for example, in the synthetic rubber project, COPERBO, located in Recife.

TABLE 12
DISTRIBUTION OF INVESTMENT AND EMPLOYMENT
IN NEW PROJECTS BY STATES[a]

State	Investment (%)	Employment (Absolute Numbers)
Bahia	38.4	15,528
Pernambuco	35.7	20,563
Ceará	8.6	9,779
Alagoas	6.7	2,616
Paraíba	4.1	5,576
Rio Grande do Norte	2.1	2,631
Maranhão	2.1	969
Minas Gerais[b]	1.2	1,576
Sergipe	0.7	541
Piauí	0.4	275

a. Investment approved before December 31, 1968, excluding modernization projects.

b. Several municipalities (municípios) of the northern part of Minas Gerais are included in the area eligible to receive 34/18 resources.

Source: SUDENE

urban culture of the Center-South, an important consideration in the recruitment of administrative staff and skilled technicians. SUDENE has recently taken steps to discourage further concentration in the vicinity of Recife and Salvador. New projects locating in these areas may receive no higher than a "B" ranking, which limits the possible participation of 34/18 resources in total equity to 60 percent.[41] This is a precipitate move at this juncture in view of the excellent facilities offered by state government industrial parks in these centers and the possible exploitation of external economies. Moreover, the most probable outcome is that firms will choose locations on the periphery of the area now eligible for "A" ranking and as close as possible to these established centers, implying a wasteful duplication of infrastructure. SUDENE's locational criterion in this respect is the "drought polygon," whose definition owes far more to geographical or territorial considerations than to economic factors which influence industrial location decisions.[42] A detailed discussion of the intraregional location of 34/18 projects, however, is beyond the scope of this chapter.

41. Articles 32 and 33, Decree No. 64.214 (March 18, 1969). Projects with "A" ranking can receive a 75 percent participation of 34/18 funds.

42. The drought polygon originally defined the area of action of federal government drought relief agencies in the Northeast.

At the interregional level, there is little question that the 34/18 incentives are the decisive factor in location decisions. Most beneficiary firms from the Center-South indicate that, by comparison, the presence of local markets, raw materials, and low-wage labor, in the Northeast are very much secondary considerations. In the present case at least, these determine location within the region but rarely are fundamental elements in choice at the inter-regional level. Indeed, in the absence of the 34/18 scheme, the vast majority of firms undoubtedly would have extended their existing Center-South facilities and continued to supply the national market from this base. The beneficiary firms interviewed confirm this point but consider the 34/18 inducements as being simply too attractive and powerful to disregard. Several firms rationalize their locational decisions more explicitly, stating that these inducements outweigh the loss of scale economies owing to the duplication of capacity and the administrative and other advantages of concentration around the Center-South plant. If this is generally the case, it raises the obvious question of whether policy-makers recognize and accept the social opportunity cost incurred in promoting the regional dispersion of industrial capacity.

Apart from the basic motivation given by the 34/18 incentives, other subsidiary factors have influenced the investment decision of Center-South beneficiary firms. Several have been mentioned in the previous discussion of plant size and it is unnecessary to repeat them here. In some instances, firms are motivated by the knowledge that their competitors in the national market intend to establish a Northeastern plant. The incentive to secure their position in the regional market is strengthened by the fear that SUDENE will approve only a limited number of projects. The desire to retain traditional Center-South clients provides a further motive for investment in the Northeast in the case of firms producing intermediate goods. Other firms state that their location decision reflected an urgent need for additional capacity combined with the substantial accumulation of 34/18 deposits of their own. A related situation occurs where firms become dissatisfied with the results of investment in third-party projects and a Northeastern plant offers a more profitable outlet for their 34/18 funds. While these factors are of interest, however, the attractiveness of the 34/18 incentives per se adequately explains why beneficiary firms have preferred branch plants to further expansion of their Center-South facilities as a means of acquiring additional productive capacity.

Industrial Investment

Estimates of changes in the region's industrial capital stock associated with the 34/18 scheme coincide with those made by Hirschman;[43] that is, taking 1964 as the base, the implementation of total
industrial investment approved before 1969 will double the industrial capital stock in the Northeast. The application of an average capital-output ratio of 2.5 to industrial production in 1964 gives the
capital stock as NCR$ 3,348 million at 1968 prices.[44] This may be
compared with approved 34/18 investment of NCR$ 3,325 million.

I now turn to the supply side of the market in 34/18 deposits.
Some factors which determine depositors' investment decisions are
presented, as well as a brief survey of past variations in the terms received from beneficiary firms. The sources of information for this discussion include interviews of depositors and beneficiary firms and the
brokers and commercial banks which perform intermediary functions
in this market. The interviews reveal that depositors differ substantially in their approach to investment decisions involving 34/18 funds.
Three broad classes can be distinguished according to the criteria used
in project evaluation. As will become apparent, however, this taxonomy is not rigidly defined and certain characteristics are common to
each group.

The few large firms which make up the first category give relatively more weight to objective criteria in selecting between available
investment projects. Inter alia, these firms examine the feasibility of
cost and revenue estimates, market demand projections, and the
project implementation schedule. The preliminary screening and
analysis frequently is undertaken by the international accounting
firms which serve these companies. The depositor's evaluation of the
quality of management of the beneficiary firm, however, is consistently
presented as the principal investment criterion. This has some objective basis in the present case since the recent profit and dividend performance of the company controlling the 34/18 project is taken into
account. Nevertheless, a subjective appraisal of the "character" and
"trustworthiness" of the administrative team in question, based
on the depositor's personal knowledge and dealings with the men

---

43. Hirschman, p. 15.
44. The estimate rises to NCR$ 4,017 million using a capital-output ratio of 3.0.
The Getúlio Vargas Foundation figure for industrial production in 1964 has been revised upwards.

concerned, carries great weight. Once such firms are satisfied on this point, their investment decision depends on estimates of future profitability. In this respect, they tend to be risk-averters, preferring projects which promise low but secure returns to those with a low probability of high rates of return. Thus, *ceteris paribus,* such firms favor investment in new projects already in operation and undergoing expansion, despite the lower dividend rates on preferential shares commonly offered in these cases. All firms diversify their 34/18 investments but this is dictated by circumstances rather than efficient portfolio selection policies. That is, beneficiary firms generally prefer a widely-based 34/18 participation to reduce the possibility of a few large contributors exerting pressure on management in the future. Moreover, depositors also believe that a wide distribution of their funds throughout the various Northeastern states has a valuable public relations effect. Participation in the 34/18 projects of their Center-South customers reflects a similar motivation.

Depositors in this category generally require that the terms offered by beneficiary firms on preferential nonvoting stock meet certain criteria. The most common prerequisite is that preferential shareholders be granted rights of "full participation" *(participação integral)* in the enterprise. This means that preferential and ordinary shares receive equal rates of return in the form of dividend payments. That is, once ordinary shares have been paid the agreed preferential rate, any earnings remaining for distribution are to be allocated without distinction between them. In addition, these rights insure that new share issues arising from the revaluation of fixed assets or the capitalization of undistributed profits are distributed between all shareholders in accordance with their participation in the firm's initial capital. Depositors emphasize that "full participation" is now particularly important since few beneficiary firms have yet paid dividends, preferring to capitalize whatever profits they earn. As regards loan participation in 34/18 projects, large depositors require some provision for monetary correction and accept informal agreements to this effect to circumvent legal restrictions. Such practices clearly demonstrate why personal contacts and mutual trust are important elements in depositors' investment decisions. Other conditions to be satisfied by beneficiary firms vary widely between individual depositors. For example, one depositor rejects projects where the controlling group has an equity interest in firms which supply inputs or purchase the output on the grounds that profits may be made "at either end of the operation rather than in the middle." Finally, large depositors typically refuse to deal with brokers and intermediaries or to pay beneficiary firms for permission to participate.

Depositors in this first category are exceptional in that they assign high-level executive staff to supervise project evaluation, make recommendations, and report periodically on their 34/18 investment portfolios to the board of directors. It is this decision to allocate scarce administrative resources to the task of managing their 34/18 funds efficiently which distinguishes them most clearly from the vast majority of depositors.[45] It shows an awareness of the opportunity costs involved and a corresponding determination to invest these funds profitably, as if they were "free resources" with no restrictions on their use.

A second category of depositors may be distinguished, however, with attitudes toward 34/18 investment which are far more representative. These depositors differ from the preceding group largely in terms of the administrative effort expended on project evaluation. Management performance again is the leading criterion but usually is assessed only on the basis of personal knowledge of the group engaged in the 34/18 project and the general reputation it enjoys in business circles. Estimates of future rates of return at times are naively equated with such casual assessments of management quality. Thus, the fact that a leading Center-South firm is undertaking a 34/18 project may be regarded as an adequate assurance of future profitability. In short, although profitability is pertinent to investment choice, it is not based on a systematic analysis of the alternative projects available. Consequently, the range of 34/18 projects effectively considered by these companies is generally limited to those controlled by entrepreneurial groups from the same city or region and within their circle of personal and commercial contacts. Moreover, as investment decisions depend on informal, personalized factors, a "bandwagon effect" frequently may be observed with the few large firms, known to analyse 34/18 projects more objectively, acting as "investment leaders." Once the business community learns that the latter have selected certain projects, other firms rush to follow suit. This phenomenon is clearly recognized by brokers, who are quick to exploit such participation as a selling point to attract depositors.

Companies in this second group are less restrictive concerning the terms received from beneficiary firms, although demands for "full

45. This category probably accounts for 5 to 10 percent of total 34/18 deposits, although this estimate is only an informed guess.

participation" generally are the rule here too. As in the previous case, portfolio diversification is also undertaken for its public-relations effect. In this respect, numerous depositors impose quite arbitrary ceilings on their 34/18 investments, usually as a convenient decision rule to achieve some diversification. This again illustrates the unwillingness, stressed repeatedly in interviews, to divert skilled personnel from general managerial functions. In similar vein, some firms reduce the task of evaluation further by informal agreements committing their present and future 34/18 deposits to projects undergoing expansion or well-known groups contemplating investment in the Northeast. These practices partly explain why small projects and Northeastern companies which lack a national reputation often experience difficulty in raising 34/18 funds. The informal, subjective approach to investment decisions has fragmented and localized the market in 34/18 deposits and, to this extent, is an inefficient allocative device.

The third category of depositors has similar characteristics but exhibits much greater indifference in the application of 34/18 deposits. Indeed, it is at times difficult to decide why some firms even trouble to take the 34/18 option. One reason was advanced rather succinctly by a large depositor who commented that "The worst present from SUDENE is better than paying the tax." The attitude here is that investment in a 34/18 project is a gamble but not one worth taking very seriously, particularly if this would absorb managerial resources. Such pessimism also may stem from the fact that few depositors have received dividends from their investments with any regularity. The interviews reveal that this class is by no means confined to small depositors, although it would be hazardous to estimate the proportion of total 34/18 deposits involved. It may be noted here that the latter encounter special difficulties in finding an outlet for their deposits. Both beneficiary and brokerage firms are reluctant to accept small 34/18 contributions because of economies of scale in the administration of large deposits. Evidently, some brokerage firms continue to charge small depositors a fee for placing their funds.

These comments raise further doubts concerning the allocative efficiency of the market in 34/18 deposits. In the present case, these stem mainly from an explicit decision by many depositors to expend as few managerial resources in project evaluation as possible. It may of course be argued that the onus is on the beneficiary firms, under SUDENE supervision, to select projects efficiently. Nevertheless, as long as the scheme calls for private participation and decision-making on the supply side of the market, there is a case for measures which induce depositors to treat their tax savings as "own resources," whose misallocation imposes higher, more easily discernible opportunity costs. This point is strengthened by the fact that firms taking the tax-credit option also determine the distribution of these resources between the several tax-incentive programs. One suggestion here is that depositors be required to invest certain of their own funds in the project selected. This contribution could be made in two installments, the first coinciding in time with the deposit of tax savings to encourage careful consideration of the decision to take this option. The second payment would be made at the time depositors allocate their 34/18 funds to beneficiary firms. Although such changes would introduce greater administrative complexity in the SUDENE scheme, they would stimulate a wider use of rational methods of investment choice than is now the case.

Following is a brief review of the terms negotiated between depositors and beneficiary firms since the inception of the SUDENE scheme. The scarcity of projects in relation to 34/18 funds between 1961 and 1965 limited depositors' bargaining power with beneficiary firms. These commonly offered a fixed preferential dividend rate of 6 percent and many refer to the waiting list of depositors ready to invest on these terms. In this period, brokers' commissions from depositors ranged as high as 10 or 15 percent of the sum invested, although these often were shared with the beneficiary firm concerned. Such firms continued to receive free brokerage services until 1966 when some brokers evidently charged both parties. This situation has been transformed since 1967 by the more rapid rate of project approval and the more intense competition between beneficiary firms. Their weaker negotiating position has given rise to various inducements which supplement the legal contractual terms offered to depositors. These terms now customarily include a preferential dividend rate of 10 percent and rights of full participation, as defined previously. Moreover, beneficiary firms absorb brokerage fees which at present vary from 6 to 12 percent of the sum invested. These charges have stimulated direct negotiations with larger depositors, who frequently receive a "commission" on the investment of their 34/18 funds. A second device to attract depositors involves beneficiary firms in gentlemen's agreements to pay an annual "dividend" to preferential shareholders, whether this is warranted by their earning position or not. In fact, firms typically regard such payments as interest charges with the twofold advantage that the "loans" are not amortized and the "interest rate" is below current commercial bank rates and therefore negative in real terms at present rates of inflation.

Such practices emphasize the variable, individual nature of terms negotiated in this market. It is doubtful also that the outcome of this process is independent of the size and reputation of the firms involved, although an examination of this relationship is beyond the scope of this chapter. For present purposes it is sufficient to note this additional evidence of market imperfections. It indicates that measures are needed to avoid more widespread resort to illegal financial inducements and thus insure that beneficiary firms have access to 34/18 financing under more nearly equal conditions. If the present situation continues, the viability of many projects will be threatened either by long delays in implementation or by onerous financial costs assumed in the struggle to obtain such financing.[46] Some observers believe that these costs already have weakened the competitive position of many small and medium-sized firms and that their survival is doubtful.[47] Of course, these devices may be regulated by stricter administrative and accounting controls over beneficiary firms. Alternatively, and more simply, the demand for 34/18 funds arising from new project approvals must be related more closely to their availability and the requirements of existing projects. In recent years, SUDENE has tended to present the volume of investment approved in a given period as a meaningful index of administrative competence, at least in its public pronouncements. This emphasis obviously is misplaced if financing difficulties inhibit the implementation and operational efficiency of projects approved previously, as now seems to be the case.

Conclusion

In seeking to modify Hirschman's highly optimistic assessment of the 34/18 scheme perhaps the negative aspects have in turn been overemphasized in this chapter.[48] To redress the balance, it is readily admitted that all sectors have attracted viable, well-designed projects

46. Sixty-eight firms, mainly in the small-to-medium-size range, have withdrawn their projects in the period 1961 to April 1969. They represent 12 percent of the total number of approved projects.

47. See "BC Semanal," No. 399 (December 1, 1969), p. 8.

48. A recent round-table discussion held to mark the tenth anniversary of SUDENE also emphasized several of the shortcomings noted here. See "SUDENE: dez anos desenvolvendo o Nordeste," Caderno Especial, Jornal do Brasil, December 14, 1969 (Rio de Janeiro), pp. 4-5. See also the criticisms by the governor of Maranhão, Sr. José Sarnei, reported in the Jornal do Brasil, December 17, 1969 (Rio de Janeiro).

which exploit locational advantages in the Northeast. In many cases also, the tax-credit mechanism merely served to accelerate the timing of decisions by Center-South firms to establish branch plants. The action of SUDENE and the BNB also has transformed the competitive position of local firms in the traditional northeastern sectors, which are closely linked to local raw materials and agricultural products. These agencies have performed a vital promotional function, arousing entrepreneurial awareness of industrial investment opportunities and infusing a growing sense of confidence in the region's future. In sum, SUDENE's industrialization policy and its activities in other sectors have given a powerful impetus to regional development.

While this positive contribution is acknowledged, the possibility of serious resource misallocation arising from 34/18 investment decisions clearly must be recognized. This stems, in great part, from the absence of carefully formulated priorities in development and industrial policy. Lack of definition and direction at this level, in turn, has led to failure to impose rigorous methods of project evaluation and a correspondingly excessive reliance on private investment decisions.[49] Thus, the general GTDN aim "to create an autonomous centre of manufacturing expansion in the Northeast" has yet to be formulated as a consistent program of sectoral growth, output, and employment targets. At present, this objective is interpreted as the achievement of a diversified industrial structure modeled on the Center-South pattern. Neither regional nor national interests are well-served, however, by a scheme in which "every project is more or less automatically given a rating and all, or almost all, are approved."[50] As argued previously, this approach neglects considerations of compartive advantage and threatens to compromise the viability of the emergent industrial sector. These considerations suggest that greater weight be given to macro-economic criteria which focus attention on possible conflict between 34/18 investment decisions and other national policy objectives and clarify the trade-off involved. Closer co-ordination at this level also would avoid any tendency to pursue an autarkic import-substitution process on a regional basis. This places responsibility squarely on the federal planning authorities to formulate the priorities of *national* industrial policy as concisely as possible. In this respect, it is vital to review the function of all incen-

49. In terms of private opportunity costs, it is quite possible that these decisions represent a rational response to policy distorted relative factor prices.

50. Hirschman, p. 8. The term "rating" here refers to the percentage participation of 34/18 funds in total capital.

tive programs and determine the appropriate degree of autonomy for the administrative agencies concerned.[51]

It is conceded that various points pertinent to a fuller assessment of the 34/18 scheme have been neglected here. These include, inter alia, investigation of secondary employment effects, the input-output structure of all approved projects, and the results achieved by beneficiary firms already in production. A more general evaluation also should attempt to estimate the contribution of industrialization to the reduction of regional income inequalities and the social cost involved in this approach. Similarly, alternative regional development strategies which may achieve the desired results at lower social opportunity cost should be examined. For example, the relative merits of applying the subsidy to Northeastern industry either wholly or in part through the labor input may be evaluated. These wider themes certainly require exploration before a definitive conclusion as to the effectiveness of the 34/18 scheme can be reached. This analysis, however, has drawn attention to certain omissions and allocative distortions in the implementation of SUDENE's industrial program and emphasized the need for further empirical investigation of this process. Finally, these critical comments are offered in a constructive spirit and are not directed against the fundamental decision to reduce inter-regional income disparities through accelerated economic development of the Northeast.

Epilogue

The drought of 1970 marked yet another turning point in regional economic policy, and it is necessary to refer briefly to the changes it has set in motion. Unjustly or otherwise, the calamitous situation created by that drought was widely taken to indicate the failure of SUDENE's policies and, as in 1958, new solutions to this perennial problem are being proposed. Indeed, close parallels may be drawn between the current situation and that of 1958, when the DNOCS strategy was rejected in favor of industrialization and regional economic planning. Whatever the final outcome, it is already clear that SUDENE has lost considerable ground politically and will play a more secondary role in regional economic policy in the 1970s.

51. For example, the Commission for Industrial Development (CDI) grants a variety of incentives in nine industrial sectors to firms locating outside the SUDENE/ SUDAM regions. In the period 1964 to August 1969, the CDI approved 1,610 projects accounting for US$ 2.3 billion in fixed investment. In addition, a network of intermediate credit agencies has been created to supply various types of industrial financing.

It is interesting to ask why the drought again proved to be the agent of change in federal policy in the Northeast. A partial answer seems to lie in the misguided tactics of SUDENE in responding to the political pressures generated by this crisis. As in previous drought years, irregular rainfall during the planting season for subsistence crops in the *sertão* and the exhaustion of seed supplies provoked the retreat of agricultural workers and small holders to nearby urban centres in search of food and employment. Municipal authorities in the interior, unable to cope with the influx of migrants and facing the threat of food riots, requested financial aid from the state governments. These, in turn, brought pressure on SUDENE to release special drought-relief funds and implement a long-standing emergency public works program prepared for such a contingency. Despite the rising tide of criticism by state governors, however, few work fronts were established before May 1970, and SUDENE steadfastly refused to decree a state of "public calamity" and held its emergency plan in abeyance. This stand possibly reflected apprehension that such a declaration would create adverse publicity and operate against SUDENE's interests at a time when firms were filing corporate tax returns and opting between the various incentive schemes. If so, it represented a very short-term view as subsequent events were soon to demonstrate. By this time, news of widespread suffering and the sacking of stores, warehouses, and trains by destitute *flagelados* were provoking concern in the Center-South and receiving detailed coverage from the mass media. In the process, SUDENE's image became badly tarnished and its administrative competence was held in question. The marked contrast between SUDENE's muted response to the crisis and these reports, together with the state governors' appeals for more drastic action, promoted President Médici to visit the region in early June 1970 and undertake a personal evaluation of the situation.

The policy measures announced only ten days after this visit combine the traditional short-run palliatives and sweeping new initiatives. Thus, the flow of federal funds into the construction and improvement of roads and *acudes* has been increased sharply. In August 1970, approximately 140 work fronts employed an estimated 400,000 men and this number rose above 500,000 by the end of the cotton harvest in October. The longer-term measures comprise construction of the Trans-Amazonian highway, the creation of colonization settlements along its route, and the acceleration of irrigation programs in the Northeast. These projects are incorporated in the Program of National

Integration, *(Programa de Integração Nacional:* PIN), which is being financed by appropriating 30 percent of all corporate tax incentive funds in the fiscal years 1971-1975.[52] Although still in process of elaboration, the principal innovation of the PIN clearly is the joint solution it offers for the development problems of the North and Northeastern regions. Within this wider policy context, it proposes to stimulate the migration of surplus labor from low-productivity agriculture in the *sertão* to populate the empty lands of the Amazon region and the Central West. In essence, the PIN seeks to exploit the complementarity between the factor endowments of the two regions and, in the process, reduce the population base in the drought-afflicted areas.

It is worth observing that two components of the PIN solution were recommended in the original GTDN report, although admittedly on a less ambitious scale. That is, exploitation of irrigable lands in the proximity of public dams and reservoirs and the colonization of Maranhão. SUDENE, however, never enjoyed the political and financial support required to implement these then controversial proposals. Force of circumstance and political realities compelled SUDENE to focus on the industrial sector, the one area where it had effective decision-making power and an adequate flow of resources. It is ironic, therefore, that SUDENE has been criticized in the present crisis for neglecting agriculture and failing to effect a spatial redistribution of the population from the areas subject to the ravages of the drought.

Although SUDENE apparently will continue to administer the 34/18 program, the nature of its future role in regional economic policy is difficult to define. While flows of 34/18 funds will be substantial, it is clear that this source is no longer inviolate and further depredations may occur. Furthermore, SUDENE's authority to "supervise, co-ordinate and control" investment projects of other federal agencies in the region has been eroded sharply in recent years. Few central government bodies now even bother to submit their regional investment plans to SUDENE, let alone seek its approval. Federal budget allocations to the agency also have been reduced, and in 1967 SUDENE's investment expenditure represented only 10 percent of public sector investment in the region. The emergence and rising importance of state government planning units and development banks presents a further challenge to SUDENE's supervisory

52. See Article 5 of Decree Law No. 1.106 (June 16, 1970).

function. These entities are heavily dependent on central government finance for capital investment projects and hence more responsive to overtures concerning co-ordination from this source. To a considerable extent, therefore, the situation has reverted to that of the 1950s, with numerous loosely co-ordinated agents participating in the regional development process. It remains to be seen whether the PIN will bring institutional changes in its train which represent a second attempt to centralize decision-making in this field of public policy.

Social Change in Brazil:
The Priorities of a Decade

8 DOUGLAS HUME GRAHAM

The Growth, Change, and Reform of Higher Education in Brazil: A Review and Commentary on Selected Problems and Issues

DURING THE sixties, Brazil encountered a new set of development problems. Discussions began in Brazilian political and intellectual circles on a range of topics that had been neglected in the past. The decade became an era of painful re-evaluation. The economy suffered its first prolonged recession in recent history, and the fragile political structure proved incapable of dealing with the accumulated social and economic problems that came to a head during the early part of the decade. At that time Brazilian intellectuals and policy-makers grew increasingly concerned with questions of structural reform rather than merely achieving certain quantitative targets of growth and development. The élan of the fifties was replaced by the pessimism of the early and middle sixties. The problems of growth were then considered more complex than had hitherto been recognized and the path of future progress was by no means as certain as it had seemed in the previous decade.

Among the issues raised during this period of re-evaluation and

I would like to thank Stanley Nicholson, Andrea Maneschi, Martin Katzman, Keith Rosenn, and Emilio Willems for their helpful critical comments on an earlier version of this chapter. In addition, Miguel Colassuonno, Werner Baer, Jose Francisco Camargo, Paulo Haddad, Samuel Levy, and Isaac Kerstenetzky have been a constant source of counsel and information on developments in the Brazilian educational system. All remaining shortcomings and errors are the responsibility of the author.

reinterpretation of Brazilian economic growth was the prospective role of human capital, more particularly, the importance of the educational sector in this process of growth and transformation and the consequences of relying upon external sources for technological change and development. This chapter will treat some of the more important issues associated with the evolution of the higher educational sector during this period. In so doing, attention will be directed toward the results of several recent attempts to analyze the quantitative and qualitative features of the Brazilian higher educational system. The question of equity and the financing of higher education will also be discussed along with the issue of foreign aid in this area and the problems associated with the recent creation of graduate centers in the country. The analysis will close with a brief discussion of educational planning in Brazil and some of the more recent attempts of university reform in the Brazilian setting.

A common question that occurs to those who have witnessed the development process in Brazil and elsewhere is the following: To what extent can a country continue to industrialize on a broad front without being forced to reform radically, modernize, and expand its educational system and significantly increase its commitment of national resources to this end? While I do not pretend to have any specific answer to this question in the context of contemporary Brazil, some general thoughts and speculations are in order before moving on to a more selective discussion of some of the issues and problems that arose in higher education in Brazil during the sixties.

First, it is apparent that the pace of economic growth and related structural change of the economy far surpassed the capacity of the educational system to service that growth with quality output. As will be seen, the structure and content of the Brazilian educational system has lagged far behind developments in other sectors of society, especially the industrial sector.[1]

One feature of this is that few fruitful links were developed between the university community and industry in terms of scientific

1. For a more generalized view and interpretation of this differential growth and performance between the educational system and the economy in recent Latin American history see Luis Ratinoff, "Problems in the Formation and Use of Human Capital in Recent Latin American Development," *Studies in Comparative International Development*, Vol. IV, No. 9. For comments on the consequences of this differential in the Brazilian context, see Werner Baer, *Industrialization and Economic Development in Brazil*, (Homewood, Ill.: Irwin Press, 1965), pp. 187-190; and Joel Bergsman, *Brazil: Industrialization and Trade Policies* (New York and London: Oxford University Press, 1970) pp. 68-69.

and technological research and development activity or wide industrial support for improved professional expertise and training within the universities. In part, this is because of having an important modern component of industrial growth growing out of foreign investment, and in part because industry more generally reserves its effort for the not unimportant role of engaging in extensive on-the-job professional training of the imperfectly trained graduates.

Nevertheless, it is clear that while improved educational inputs could have added impetus to the growth process of lowering costs and increasing productivity, the lack of this basic structural reform did not constitute an insuperable obstacle to economic growth in the post-war era. In this sense, development of the educational sector and the associated capacity for local autonomous technological development were most certainly not prerequisites for successful economic growth. A pattern of substitution existed for these missing prerequisites in the form of readily available imported inputs of technology made available through direct foreign investment and extensive capital goods imports, technical assistance contracts and licensing agreements for domestic producers.[2] Similarly, in the early stages of growth immigrant groups supplied essential ingredients of entrepreneurial and technical skills. Finally, widespread on-the-job training largely substituted for the lack of an adequately developed formal educational system in meeting the demand for skilled manpower.[3]

A pattern of economic growth somewhat different from that which characterized the industrial growth of the late-comers (Germany, Russia, and Japan) at the end of the nineteenth and early part of the twentieth century emerges from this experience.[4] Whereas these

2. For analysis of the important role of patterns of substitution for missing prerequisites in the process of European economic growth, see Alexander Gershenkron, *Economic Backwardness in Historical Perspective*. (Cambridge: Harvard University Press, 1966) ch. 1.

3. For a review of the important role of on-the-job training in Brazilian industrialization, see Werner Baer, *The Development of the Brazilian Steel Industry* (Nashville: Vanderbilt University Press, 1969) ch. 5; and Nathaniel Leff, *The Brazilian Capital Goods Industry, 1929-1964* (Cambridge: Harvard University Press, 1968) ch. III. For an illuminating historical analysis of the role of immigrants in the earlier phases of industrialization in Brazil see Warren Dean, *The Industrialization of São Paulo* (Austin and London: University of Texas Press, 1969) ch. IV.

4. An interesting insight into the contrasting patterns of nineteenth-century industrialization and the current twentieth-century experience in Latin America can be found in Albert O. Hirschman, "The Political Economy of Import-Substitution Industrialization in Latin America," *Quarterly Journal of Economics (QJE)*, Vol. LXXXII, No. 1, (February 1968), especially pp. 4-12.

late industrializers did not have and therefore had to find substitutes for certain basic prerequisites common to the earlier English, American, and French patterns of growth, they at least were not as educationally backward and so completely technologically dependent upon their predecessors as the currently industrializing countries. Even in the face of unbalanced growth that created what we refer to today as dualistic societies, these countries were never far behind their predecessors and, in the case of Germany, an equal in many of the important fields of scientific and technological investigation. Germany and later Russia and Japan were able to develop enclaves of scientific and educational excellence in the midst of their economically underdeveloped societies. Some original research and imaginative technological innovation and adaptation were possible and, indeed, eventually played a crucial role in supplying essential qualitative inputs to their growth process. It is true that all three of these countries (especially Russia and Japan) "borrowed" heavily from technologically more advanced societies in their earlier phases of growth; however, this importation of skills built upon a growing base of local technological capacity and innovation. Their technological dependency would appear to have been less comprehensive than is typical of the late-late industrializers of the post World War II era and, in contrast to Latin American countries, much less dependent on foreign investment.

Brazilian experience thus shows that the rapid change and modernization of the educational sector has not been necessary as a prerequisite for past economic growth. The lack of significant investment in this area, however, did create costly bottlenecks forcing many firms to import technology and technical assistance and invest in expensive on-the-job training programs for skilled workers and middle-level managerial and technical personnel. The failure to make up for this deficiency in "social overhead capital" in the future through increased investment in education could prove even more costly for future growth.

Many Brazilians would now argue that their country currently needs a much greater self-sufficient technological and educational base. In this view, the educational sector would not merely evolve in a passive fashion, reacting to the growing needs for certain professional and occupational skills of the growth process, but also actively promote significant local research and innovation that would be instrumental in altering the local processes of production. Important to this view is the fact that Brazil is passing beyond the earlier and easier import-substitution phase and must now direct its policies toward creating more competitive, lower-cost industries that can reach a larger local market and begin exports as well. Local research and development more linked to local factor conditions could presumably play an important role in this drive, perhaps counteracting the technological "bias" toward large-scale, capital-intensive techniques imported from abroad. This would appear a reasonable and promising local initiative in those sectors such as agriculture and light industry where the range of efficient technology is not so rigidly fixed in scale and technique.

Nevertheless, there is no reason to believe that Brazil necessarily has to imitate the expensive strategy to attain a high level of technological self-sufficiency followed by the aforementioned latecomers to industrial growth. To begin with, the climate for the international transfer of technology in the form of direct foreign investment, on one hand, and capital goods imports, licensing, and technical assistance agreements on the other is much more developed commercially today than it ever had been during the nineteenth century when the late industrializers engaged in their self-sufficient strategies of growth. Despite the inherent bias toward the production technology of developed countries in the transfer of skills and techniques through international trade and investment, it still makes sense for Brazil to exploit these opportunities for "borrowing" technology in a "selective" fashion and thus avoid a costly strategy of duplication in this field.[5] Also it is important to bear in mind that in the foreseeable future most sectors of Brazilian industry (and the relevant policy-makers in government) are very likely unprepared to accept and support the degree of austerity and costly independence that would be implicit in any large-scale change to eliminate Brazil's current technological dependence from the developed countries.

5. For a discussion of this point in the Brazilian context see Leff, *op. cit.*, ch. IV. An important qualification to the foregoing should be added here. Too heavy a dependence on imported technology, especially in the form of extensive foreign investment, could be undesirable if technology is transferred and disseminated more widely through the medium of domestic enterprises (especially public sector or mixed firms) than through foreign firms. Similarly, local public and private producers may be more forceful lobbyists for the expansion and modernization of technical and higher education and the associated local capacity for research and development than foreign firms, since the latter tend to rely more on foreign sources for many of these inputs, especially the research input. For a perceptive analysis of the possible inhibiting features of extensive direct foreign investment on the development of local entrepreneurial and technological capacity in the lesser developed countries, see Hirschman, *How to Divest in Latin America and Why,* Essays in International Finance, No. 76, November 1969, International Finance Section, Department of Economics, Princeton University, pp. 4-9.

The Brazilian higher educational system needs to be modernized, if only to meet the current needs of national development. Quality considerations and a more discriminatory allocation of national resources for this end will have to be made. Any attempt to achieve near autarchic technological autonomy is clearly ill-advised, however, given Brazil's still-limited resources and the present context of technological transfer in the world economy which can still be exploited selectively for Brazil's needs. Clearly, at issue here is the degree and level of technological autonomy and related technical and scientific development advisable for Brazil in the next decade and the nature and direction any national effort to this end should take. This will undoubtedly be one of the continuing questions asked by Brazilian policy-makers in the future with many possible repercussions on the changing nature of the Brazilian educational sector, its structure, content, and purpose. In this chapter, however, I address myself to the more modest task of merely reviewing some of the more important issues and problems of the higher educational sector as it evolved through the decade of the sixties and the various efforts of the several governments to deal with these problems. I shall emphasize the formidable task confronting the country's leaders if they are serious in their determination to reform this sector to service an economic policy that stresses more technological and educational development growing out of greater research and improved professional training within the system of higher education.

Higher Education in the 1960s: Its Expansion and Related Problems

Enrollment data are useful benchmarks to indicate the evolution of the educational sector in Brazil. Table 1 highlights the rapid growth of enrollments during the decade of the sixties, especially in higher education. Indeed, it is apparent that from 1960 to 1968 enrollment at this level increased much more rapidly than enrollment for other levels of education. From 1964 to 1968, remarkably high rates of enrollment can be seen in Table 3 with a 30 percent increase recorded in 1967-68. Preliminary but still unpublished data indicate that the rapid rate of increase of enrollment in higher education is continuing up to the present. Comparing the decade of the sixties to that of the fifties (Table 2) the data suggest that by 1970 primary school enrollment will have increased at roughly the same percentage rate in the sixties as it did in the fifties, while secondary school enrollment will have increased at a rate two times the corresponding rate in the fifties and enrollment in higher education by 1970 will very likely have increased

TABLE 1

ENROLLMENT IN ELEMENTARY, SECONDARY AND HIGHER EDUCATION IN
BRAZIL FOR SELECTED YEARS

Years	Elementary	Secondary	Higher Under-graduate	Graduate	Total
1950	4.352.043	538.346	44.097	N.A.	4.934.486
1960	7.458.002	1.177.427	93.202	2.489	8.731.120
1965	9.923.183	2.154.430	155.781	1.649	12.235.043
1966	10.695.391	2.483.212	180.109	1.790	13.360.502
1967	11.182.746	2.816.440	212.882	2.440	14.214.508
1968	12.353.000	3.205.851	278.295	4.358	15.841.554

Source: *Anuário Estatístico do Brasil*, IBGE, (Various years); *Atualidade Estatística do Brasil 1969*, IBGE, pp. 320-329

TABLE 2

PERCENTAGE INCREASE OF ENROLLMENTS IN BRAZIL FOR
SELECTED YEARS

	Level of Education Elementary	Secondary	Higher Education
1950/60	71.4	118.7	117.0
1960/68	65.6	172.3	195.4

Source: Table 1

TABLE 3

PERCENTAGE INCREASE OF ENROLLMENT FOR HIGHER EDUCATION IN
BRAZIL FOR SELECTED PERIODS

1965/1966	15.5
1966/1967	18.3
1967/1968	31.3
1960/1965	64.5
1965/1968	79.5

at a rate 3 to 4 times as high as the rate in the fifties.

The over-all and sectoral growth and change of the Brazilian economy during this period acted as a partial stimulant to the growth of certain disciplines as employers began to look for more university-trained graduates in such areas as engineering and business administration. The rapid increase in the supply of secondary school graduates, however, was an equally important factor in generating a demand for expanding university education. Given the lack of a well-developed technical and vocational orientation in Brazilian secondary schools, most graduates at this level have been trained to do little other than continue their formal education at the university level. Table 1 certainly highlights the rapid increase in secondary-school enrollment. While it took ten years to double secondary school enrollment in the previous decade (1950 to 1960), it took only five years to accomplish the same feat in the decade of the sixties (1960 to 1965).

Similarly, candidates for the college entrance exams increased only 20 percent from 1957 to 1961. In the four-year period from 1962 to 1966, however, the number of candidates almost doubled in size.[6] This pressure point on the supply side was instrumental in creating the *política dos excedentes* in the sixties: demonstrations and political agitation to expand university enrollment for the *excedentes* (those who passed the entrance exams but could find no openings in the faculties of their choice). Finally, this growing demand was facilitated by the fact that about half the institutions of higher education are public and tuition free.

Increased pressure for expansion at this level also grew out of the past geographical imbalance in the opportunities for higher education in Brazil. Many politicians promoted the creation of numerous isolated professional schools to service the growing number of secondary-school graduates in their states and counties, since the part-time work and study regimen and lack of dormitory facilities in the big urban universities work against student mobility to secure higher education far from home.[7]

The rising expectations and desire for social status of the growing number of middle-class secondary school graduates (and their families) constituted a political pressure or social demand for expansion of higher education that the governments of the sixties felt they could not ignore. Unfortunately, this expansion appears to have been largely unco-ordinated and unplanned. The public and private

6. Data on candidates for the college-entrance exams come from the statistical service of the Ministry of Education and Culture (MEC). See J. D. Ryder, "Study of Enrollments" in *Relatório da equipe de assessoria ao planejamento do ensino superior,* (MEC) (Rio de Janeiro, 1969), p. 265.

7. This lack of mobility is even more marked among professors. It is very common for members of the teaching body in institutions of higher education to be associated with the same school from which they received their degree. This lack of any significant professorial or student mobility among regions and schools leads to an inbred provincial view of national problems and an equally uninformed view of professional competence.

professional schools generally responded to these pressures by merely increasing their input of students without also undertaking measures to increase sufficiently the number of well-trained professors and to introduce the administrative and academic reorganization necessary to service this growing number of students with a satisfactory level of quality education.[8]

The quality of many of these faculties that proliferated in the interior and in some of the major urban centers is in great doubt, leading one to wonder whether the rapid increase in the enrollment and the graduates in many of these schools does not hide "quality equivalents" little if any above the level of the good high schools in the urban centers. The students generally come from weak secondary schools, and the professors recruited from the area to service these new faculties are from equally weak backgrounds, usually being high-school professors or professional men of questionable credentials teaching only part-time, usually at night, with no serious intellectual or academic vocation. The facilities are usually in old buildings, frequently shared with high schools, and hardly conducive to creating a promising and productive higher-educational environment. There are rarely any library or laboratory facilities. The absenteeism of professors and students is quite high, and the drop-out rate is considerable. The teaching methods and content are suspect, given the lack of any research capabilities or library resources. There are few independent projects or term papers. Instruction is based on the professors out-dated notes *(apostilas)* with examinations emphasizing simple rote memorization instead of developing problem-solving techniques testing alternative hypotheses with relevant empirical data.

It is difficult to see how the expansion of enrollment in higher education of this nature plays any positive role in fulfilling the development needs of Brazil. Indeed, one can conceive of this questionable pattern of expansion emphasizing the wrong kind of education, fostering the wrong kinds of values and attitudes, and producing improperly trained professionals as constituting a net burden rather than a contribution to the country's current development needs with negative implications for future socioeconomic change.

8. It could be argued further that there was a hidden or unexpected social cost in this rapid expansion, since the decline in quality associated with large, unmanageable classes was clearly apparent to most students and played no small role in their growing disillusion with the unsatisfactory state of their higher education. This widespread dissatisfaction was no doubt of some importance in the growing student unrest and agitation throughout the decade with all its attendant social disorder.

A recent study analyzing the evolution of establishments in higher education within the state of São Paulo highlights these features under discussion.[9] The entering classes in higher education in São Paulo numbered only 1,000 in 1940, rose to 8,656 by 1960, then increased to 34,577 by 1968. In 1940, practically all the enrollment was in the city of São Paulo. By 1968, almost 50 percent of the total enrollment was outside the capital. Obviously some expansion in the growing urban centers of Campinas, Santos, and Ribeirão Preto was justified; however, the rate of expansion raises a question about the standards of quality achieved. Of the total of 8,400 professors in 1968, only 26 percent could be considered full time, and within private institutions this precentage drops to 5 percent.[10] Some of the law schools operate only on weekends, and about 80 percent of the schools of economics function only at night. Libraries and laboratories are minimal or nonexistent. This is hardly indicative of a teaching body engaged in research or even competent professional instruction. It is important to remember that this refers to the most developed state in the nation. It would appear reasonable to assume that this helter-skelter pattern of expansion with all its characteristic features of dubious quality is even more pronounced in other states.[11]

Manpower surveys of a carefully selected sample of these graduates would be most helpful in establishing educational policy. For

9. José Pastore, *O ensino superior em São Paulo: Aspectos quantitativos e qualitativos de sua expansão*, relatorio elaborado por solicitação das Secretarias de Educação e Planejamento do Estado de São Paulo, Instituto de Pesquisas Econômicas, Universidade de São Paulo, 1969. For reference to cited data, see ch. 1.

10. *Ibid.* ch. 1. Well-trained and well-motivated part-time teachers can play an important role in bringing valuable experience from their professions into the classroom. When the teaching body is almost wholly dependent upon part-time professors, however, it is difficult to inculcate a serious academic commitment on the part of the students or the professors.

11. For perceptive insights into the law schools in Brazil outlining their obsolete curriculum, archaic organization, and negative impact in developing the legal profession to deal with the development problems of Brazil, see Keith S. Rosenn, "The Reform of Legal Education in Brazil," *Journal of Legal Education*, Vol. 21, No. 3, (1969).

For an equivalent critical analysis of the low quality of economics training in Brazil and the problems and issues of attempting to reform and modernize this profession to meet the development needs of the country, see the special issue devoted to a discussion and analysis of this field in *Revista Brasileira de Economia*, Ano 20, Numero 4, (December 1966). See also John M. Hunter "Sobre o ensino de economia do Brasil," *RBE*, Ano XXII, No. 2, (September 1968) and ERGO, *Análise do ensino de economia no Brasil*, estudo elaborado para o Escritório de Pesquisa Econômica Aplicada, Ministério do Planejamento e Coordenação Econômica, Rio de Janeiro, 1966.

example, it would be useful to have some relevant empirical data on the job profile and remuneration of these students after their higher education. Such data could help one arrive at some firm conclusions concerning their absorption into professional labor markets. With this information, one could evaluate the efficiency of allocating resources into these scattered, isolated faculties. If many of the current graduates are moving largely into subprofessional or nonprofessional occupations, then it doesn't make sense to continue developing those professional schools that obviously are not performing their function of training professionals. It makes more sense to redesign these programs for shorter periods of training, geared to less pretentious and more market-oriented subprofessional occupations to fill the demand that exists for intermediate-level technicians and administrative personnel in a more forthright and efficient manner. Advanced professional training could then be more appropriately redirected to the larger metropolitan university centers which have a comparative academic advantage in competent professors, libraries, and laboratory facilities.

Changing the focus from over-all enrollment to that of particular disciplines, Table 4 indicates that economics (which includes the much lesser developed business administration field), philosophy, letters and science (largely preparing secondary-school teachers), and engineering grew the most rapidly, while the traditional fields of law and medicine declined in the relative growth of enrollment over the past decade. The rapid growth of philosophy and letters was in part owing to the need to service the growing demand for secondary-school teachers. The slow growth of enrollment in medicine is more a result of the deliberate policy to restrict entry into the profession and the high cost of expansion rather than any lack of demand, popularity, or suitable candidates. The relative decline in law enrollment, however, would appear to reflect a changing social preference for other disciplines such as engineering and economics, fields whose popularity have understandably grown in the milieu of recent economic development.

It is clear that it was much less costly to permit an expansion of enrollment in fields such as economics, philosophy, and letters where laboratory and other expenses are unnecessary. Thus it would appear that the role of satisfying the growing social demand for higher education fell to these two fields. It is also of interest to note that economics, the field that grew most rapidly in the sixties, is the discipline that has come under the severest attack for having failed

TABLE 4
DISTRIBUTION OF UNIVERSITY UNDERGRADUATE ENROLLMENT IN
BRAZIL BY COURSE 1958-1968

Course	1958 Enrollment—%		1968 Enrollment—%		% Increase 1958-1968
Philosophy, letters and science	17,372	20.6	76,799	27.6	342.1
Law	22,302	26.4	52,856	19.0	137.0
Engineering	9,672	11.4	37,552	13.5	288.3
Business administration and economics	6,812	8.1	36,796	13.2	440.2
Medicine	10,535	12.5	25,226	9.0	139.4
Odontology	5,145	6.1	7,791	2.8	51.4
Agriculture	1,627	1.9	5,597	2.0	244.0
Social Work	1,265	1.5	4,248	1.5	235.8
Pharmacy	1,583	1.9	3,736	1.4	136.0
Architecture and urbanism	1,720	2.0	3,635	1.3	111.3
Veterinary medicine	763	.9	2,512	.9	229.2
Others	5,685	6.7	15,211	7.8	167.6
TOTAL	84,481	100.0	278,295	100.0	229.4

Source: *Sinopse Estatística do Ensino Superior,* March 1969 p. 13; *Anuário Estatístico do Brasil,* IBGE, 1958, p. 383.

lamentably to give adequate training to its students.[12] While the growth and change of the economy created a need for economists and managers, the faculties were clearly unaware of how to rearrange their curricula and teaching skills to service this demand. A large number of students chose this field through the misunderstanding that the microeconomics of the firm would train them for a business career.[13] This of course is decidedly not the case, as any well-trained economist knows. What is needed are fewer economics faculties and more business administration faculties, since most of the graduates of economics faculties find themselves working in the business area and not exercising the profession of economists.

Even for those whose interest was economics, the curriculum and the instruction in most of these schools are seriously inadequate to train students to be effective economists. The lack of any rigorous

12. See references cited in footnote 11.
13. On this point, see Hunter, *op. cit.;* and Claudio de Moura Castro "O que Faz um Economista," in the *Revista Brasileira de Economia,* Ano 24, No. 4, (October-December 1970).

training in mathematics, statistics, and econometrics is characteristic
of all but a few faculties in this field. Without these essential tools of
the trade it is impossible to teach students applied or theoretical economics at an acceptable level of sophistication. Equally important here
is that the part-time professors have practically no experience in research, so that their students receive very little if any training in
learning how to collect, organize, and critically analyze empirical data,
test hypotheses with various statistical techniques, and learn the all-
important perspective of acquiring a problem-solving mentality. As a
result, most graduates fall into subprofessional or nonprofessional
occupations with much of the public and private demand for well-
trained economists being filled, in part, by engineering graduates who
by virtue of their more quantitative backgrounds are able to adapt
themselves more readily to such tasks as planning and project analysis. It was precisely this state of affairs in the economics profession
that led to the creation of a limited number of "quality-oriented"
graduate programs of economics in the mid-sixties.

Turning our attention now to engineering, Table 4 shows that
this discipline also experienced significant growth. There is a current
general feeling in many circles that an oversupply of engineers exists
in certain specialties, especially in civil, mechanical, and metallurgical
engineering, with low salaries established in the market for these
areas. This has caused a diversion of graduates into business management, economics, and less technical careers. Several points can be
made here. Evidence indicates that the rapid expansion of enrollments in this field very likely affected the quality of training. Taking
São Paulo again as a frame of reference, of the 23 faculties of engineering in the state in 1968 more than 15 had been created within
the previous eight years. Incoming first-year classes numbered only
925 students for all engineering faculties in São Paulo in 1960. By
1965 this number had risen to 2,568 and by 1968 to 5,598.[14] Thus in
three years, first-year enrollment grew more than 100 percent, an
alarming rate by any standard and obviously the result of unco-ordinated growth by both public and private faculties.

Evidence of the lack of quality in this expansion can be seen by
the fact that much of this growth occurred in many isolated faculties
unconnected to existing universities. Of these schools, thirteen have
still not received any accreditation by the Federal Council of Education. The libraries associated with these schools number at most no

14. Cf. José Pastore, op. cit., pp. 58-60.

more than a few thousand volumes, and most of these are outdated works. Only one third of the existing faculties have any systematic circulating library. Mimeographed apostilas appear to be most characteristic form of teaching, and no more than four or five of these faculties have any semblance of a loosely defined full-time staff of any importance.[15] Practical laboratory experience is greatly underdeveloped except in the most prestigious schools such as the University of São Paulo and ITA (in São José dos Campos). It should thus not be surprising that some engineering graduates are currently finding jobs in their professions scarce, with salaries less than they expected. Given the low quality of training associated with some of this expansion, many of these graduates are very likely far from being engineering graduates in any professional sense of the word, but rather intermediate technicians whose marginal productivity is accurately reflected in the lower salaries they are currently earning in the market.

Beyond this important fact, however, it is still conceivable that there is a current temporary oversupply relative to demand for even well-trained engineers in certain specific fields as mentioned above. In the rapidly changing industrial environment of Brazil where new technologies are quickly imported and established, the composition of the market demand for certain specific engineering skills is bound to change more rapidly than the composite supply available from the existing network of professional schools. Because of this lagged adjustment typical of slowly adjusting educational systems, past scarcity frequently leads to an overreaction which in turn results in a later oversupply in certain specialties.

In short, premature specialization tends to lock an educational infrastructure into past, obsolete patterns of demand, while current demands are left unmet. In view of this, a more flexible curriculum postponing specialization in the early years of engineering schools would appear advisable so as to adjust more readily to the changing shortages and surpluses of specific high-level manpower. Along the same lines, more emphasis should probably be given to the development of the broader field of industrial administration, since many young engineering graduates are discovering that technically informed business managers are probably in even greater demand than mere engineers.

Turning now to the available aggregate expenditure data, Table

15. *Ibid.*, pp. 58-75.

5 shows that as a percent of GNP there has been a gradual increase in expenditures devoted to all educational levels throughout the sixties. The current government has frequently emphasized this point as a counterargument to the charge that they have neglected education. The meaningfulness of this increased expenditure, however, is unclear until more detailed cost data become available showing which levels of schooling, which disciplines, programs, and regions have benefited from this increased expenditure. Also of some importance here is the expenditure per student. With reference to higher education, it is possible that, because of the remarkable rise in enrollments during the decade, the expenditure per student has been declining significantly, while the expenditure GNP ratio for higher education may have been rising. New methods of instruction and academic reorganization could conceivably create higher quality training at less cost per student; however, with the possible exception of the University of Brasília, there is no evidence to indicate that this has occurred in Brazil in any marked fashion in the traditional or isolated faculties. The proliferation of faculties and enrollments undoubtedly accounts for much of the increased expenditure in higher education and, as discussed earlier, there is no strong evidence to indicate that this particular pattern of expenditure was efficient or carried any high return for the development needs of the country.

TABLE 5

TOTAL EXPENDITURES ON EDUCATION IN BRAZIL IN CONSTANT CRUZEIROS 1960 to 1970[a]

Year	Public	Private	Foreign[c]	Total	Foreign/ Total (%)	Gross Domestic Product	Total/ GDP (%)
1960	1,921,891	415,100	4,000	2,340,991	0.2	95,604,800	2.4
1961	2,148,480	429,700	14,900	2,593,080	0.6	102,587,000	2.5
1962	2,471,055	454,700	4,600	2,930,355	0.2	110,203,800	2.6
1963	1,951,293	461,000	247,200	2,659,493	9.3	113,560,300	2.3
1964	2,606,728	468,000	20,800	2,549,528	0.8	115,205,800	2.2
1965	3,290,260	477,100	19,800	3,787,160	0.5	117,337,700	3.2
1966	3,589,556	481,000	104,200	4,174,756	2.5	124,156,400	3.4
1967	4,095,025	507,800	114,300	4,717,125	2.4	128,673,500	3.7
1968	4,356,419	501,000	121,000	4,978,419	2.4	143,842,100	3.5
1969[b]	5,238,327	560,500	180,000	5,978,827	3.0	158,017,800	3.8
1970	5,780,200	578,000	181,000	6,539,200	2.8	172,239,400	3.8

a. Cr$1,000 of 1970; all figures corrected for inflation through applying index no. 2 of the *Conjuntura Econômica.*

b. Data for 1969 and 1970 are preliminary estimates.

c. From 1960 to 1967 data on foreign resources applied to education represented signed agreements for the years in question thus implying that some of these funds could actually be spent in later years. Data for foreign resources from 1968 through 1970 however represent actual expenditures for the years in question.

Source: Instituto de Pesquisa Economia Aplicada do Ministério do Planejamento e Coordenação Geral.

However, other areas of great importance to the development potential of the country have been supported, such as the creation and financing of the growing "development oriented" graduate-level training programs throughout the country in such disciplines as engineering, economics, the agricultural sciences, and some of the basic and applied sciences. In these fields, budgetary sources outside the Ministry of Education and traditional university budgets have been employed along with foreign financing. It is not altogether clear whether all these nontraditional domestic and foreign sources of financing have been included in the data on educational expenditures in Table 5. Of interest here, however, is that much of the initiative to develop and finance "quality-oriented" programs in higher education during the decade came from outside the usual sources of educational finance in Brazil. These developments will be discussed in more detail in Part V.

Higher Education in the 1960s: The Changing Issues

Many events of importance affected the evolution of the higher education sector in 1960s and, even more importantly, affected the attitude of Brazilian policy-makers with respect to the role of education in national development. Only a succint résumé is attempted here. In the early sixties, questions of reform and change in higher education were still discussed in more traditional humanistic terms. The latter sixties saw a change in attitude among many Brazilian policy-makers and intellectual circles. Education was more frequently interpreted and analyzed as a scarce resource to be allocated efficiently to promote national economic growth and independence. This sector thus received growing critical attention through the decade as policy-makers and technocratic circles in the Ministries of Finance and Planning, among others, became more aware of the importance of education for economic development.

In 1961, the passage of a federal law governing the principles and guidelines to use in administering various spheres and levels of education concentrated on the traditional issues of administrative jurisdiction and allied questions of centralization and descentralization of the administrative control of the various levels of education. To a large extent, these questions were the debated issues of the day along with the issue of privately versus publicly supported education. Within certain educational circles of administrators and professors there was also extensive debate on the role and nature of the university. These discussions were frequently broad philosophical discourses drawing on the past work of European and American educators and dealing with the issues of what should constitute the Brazilian university.[16] There were rarely any empirical data, however, on the Brazilian educational system presented in these papers and conferences and never any explicit discussion of education as an economic good which could conceivably be analyzed in quantitative terms. Indeed, this very thought would have been considered crass and materialistic in the eyes of most traditional educators, student groups, and intellectuals who dominated the scene at that time.

Even within this more traditional framework, however, useful insights and promising new approaches to university development did emerge as evidenced in the debate and discussion which led to the creation of the University of Brasília.[17] Instead of following the current dysfunctional model of isolated faculties or professional schools with little interdisciplinary contact and lifetime chair professors dominating most fields, the concept of a university made up of a departmental organization of disciplines was developed with no chair professors. New fields were developed at Brasília and an emphasis was placed on interdisciplinary programs and research. Central institutes in the physical and social sciences were developed to handle the basic courses for all students regardless of degree program. Thus the costly duplication of having a large number of professors teaching the same basic courses in many different isolated faculties was largely eliminated. This centralization of the elementary courses in many fields into a central institute serving all departments and students meant that fewer and better professors could now handle many more students with obvious savings (less cost per student) through the economies of scale gained. Finally, establishing the administrative and

16. A representative sample of these debates and essays in the early sixties can be found in *Simpósio sôbre problemática universitária*, Universidade de Recife, Imprensa Universitaria, 1965. For lucid and informative critical reviews of the state of the Brazilian Universities in the early sixties, see Newton Sucupira, "A universidade Brasileira: Sua idéia e sua realização," in *Simpósio . . . op. cit.*, and Darcy Ribeiro "A universidade e a nação," in *Educação e Ciências Sociais*, 10 (19), January/April 1962. For a highly personal but interesting point of view, see Rudolph P. Acton, *Rumo à reformulação estrutural da universidade Brasileira*, Ministério da Educação e Cultura, Diretoria do Ensino Superior, Rio de Janeiro, 1966.

17. See references in footnote 16 and, in addition, the wide collection of articles and commentary by many Brazilian educators and social scientists especially dealing with the issues of creating the University of Brasília, in *Universidade de Brasília*, (Projeto e Organização, Pronunciamento de Educadores e Cientistas, e Lei No. 31998 de 15 de Dezembro de 1961). Ministério da Educação e Cultura, Rio de Janeiro, Brazil, 1962.

financial affairs of the university in a foundation rather than as a part of the public administration bureaucracy of the Ministry of Education gave the university authorities more flexibility with regard to the recruitment and promotion of professors and the introduction of new programs.

The impact of this new university on the rest of the system of higher education was unfortunately much more limited than its founders and supporters had hoped for, with very few lateral spillover effects on the existing network of traditional faculties and universities which were generally mere conglomerations of isolated disciplines making up a university more in name than in fact. It was still an isolated experiment with apparently little thought having been given to designing a concrete strategy and establishing the machinery to introduce these new features into the rest of the system of higher education at that time. Following the political changes of March 1964, the University of Brasília experienced many dismissals and resignations among the faculty and administration at the insistence of the new government. Thus the spirit of innovation was at least temporarily checked, nevertheless it is clear that the plans for university reform developed later in the decade were, in part, influenced by the experience at the University of Brasília.

From 1964 onwards, the political climate changed abruptly in Brazil, and government attitudes and programs towards education were an ambiguous mixture of heavy-handed intervention and cautious reform. On the one hand, government authorities were determined to purge society of what they considered subversive elements and, in these sweeping measures, certain university professors and programs suffered dismissals and forced retirements. These measures unfortunately compromised the fragile concept of academic freedom in the Brazilian University setting and, in some cases, affected quality training and research through the dismissal of professors of professional stature. On the other hand, the new technocratic regime established after 1964 in the Applied Economic Research Office of the Ministry of Planning began a detailed and constructive review of the educational system with the purpose of providing a more solid quantitative base for effective reform than had ever been undertaken in the past. For the first time a wide range of revealing quantitative data on enrollments, attrition, graduates by level, discipline, and region were assembled and analyzed as a source of supply for current and future manpower demand. The studies on the supply and demand for high-level manpower forcefully underlined the way in which the present educational system was lamentably failing to guarantee any semblance of a growing educational opportunity for lower-income groups, equity in educational financing and efficiency in fulfulling the current and prospective manpower demands for economic growth.[18]

It is useful and instructive to summarize the major results of these studies since they did much to condition the attitude of the "modernizers" in the government toward higher education. First, as was demonstrated earlier, the unco-ordinated increase in the number of establishments of higher education, many of them isolated faculties with no possibilities of engaging in competent professional training, raised the question of the efficiency and the practical value of this aimless policy. Certainly many fields were allowed to expand beyond any reasonable measure of the effective market demand for their poorly trained graduates while others were held back despite a demonstrated need for their graduates.

Another indicator of the inefficient allocation of resources centered around the comparatively low student-professor ratio for higher education in Brazil which in the early 1960s was about 4 or 5 to 1. This contrasts sharply to ratios two to three times higher in many developed countries and thus, at first glance, would indicate a remarkably favorable balance for quality education in Brazil. The fact that higher education in Brazil is not noted for its quality indicates that this ratio is misleading. The data on professors does not correct for the fact that many teach in more than one institution. Beyond this, however, the overwhelming part-time component in the teaching body undoubtedly accounts for this figure along with the fact that many professors were paid but did no teaching (among whom were many *catedráticos* who hired *assistentes* to do their teaching). More to the point here would be the number of man hours taught rather than the number of professors. Finally, there are remarkably peculiar ratios in some schools in certain esoteric or semivocational fields where there are more professors than students.[19]

By far the greatest example of the misallocation of teaching resources (and an important factor behind the above mentioned low student-professor ratio) is the absurd duplication or multiplication

18. Escritório de Pesquisa Econômica Applicada (EPEA), *Educação diagnóstico preliminar*, Volume I e II, Ministério do Planejamento e Coordenação Econômica, June 1966, Rio de Janeiro.

19. For some examples here, see Mário Henrique Simonsen, *Brasil 2001*, APEC Editôra, Rio de Janeiro, 1966, p. 234.

of courses and teachers within the same area. This can be frequently seen within the same university as a result of the rapid expansion of numerous separate faculties. Notorious examples of this duplication are in basic courses of mathematics and the natural and physical sciences but also appear in the social sciences. An example of this multiplication of similar *cadeiras* or specialties spread throughout numerous neighboring professional schools was documented in the Federal University of Rio Grande do Sul, where in 1960, more than seventy-five professors of basic and specialized courses in chemistry were teaching in seven separate faculties or professional schools of the same university (medicine, veterinary science, nursing, engineering, geology, agronomy, and basic sciences).[20] No doubt some of these professors were of questionable professional stature. The situation (repeated in many other settings) obviously called for the creation of centralized departments or institutes for these fields within which a much smaller number of the better trained full-time professors could service all the faculties in question with a higher quality of instruction. In short, higher quality could result from the economies of scale gained at lower cost per student. Unfortunately, at least before the current university reform, most universities have resisted this solution with the various faculties frequently engaging in political maneuvers to prevent each other from controlling the appropriations and posts within the proposed centralized institutes.

The classic example of the inefficient allocation of resources in this area was the phenomenon of idle capacity. This reached extreme proportions in the half-built, unused and partially abandoned monumental structures lying idle in many poorly planned University Cities on the outskirts of Rio, Recife, and other urban centers while poorly paid, part-time professors taught poorly prepared, part-time students in outmoded buildings downtown. The immense waste involved in such grandiose schemes only added to the argument that the relevant question with respect to higher education was not whether the government was allocating a fair share of its budget to the growth and development of this sector, but whether the existing structure deserved any greater share of development funds until it

20. See ERGO. *Análise Econômica das Universidades Brasileiras*, Estudo Elaborado para o Escritório de Pesquisa Econômica Aplicada, Ministério do Planejamento e Coordenação Econômica, (Rio de Janeiro, 1966), ch. IV, p. 18. This little disseminated study under the co-ordination of David Carneiro was the first breakthrough in analysing Brazilian universities in economic terms and as such was the precursor to the succeeding volumes by EPEA, cited earlier.

could overcome its apparent inability to allocate and administer these resources in an efficient manner.

Finally, these analyses brought forth the question of costs and equity in higher education. Estimates of the unit cost of higher education in 1960 in Brazil ranged as high as $1,500 per student.[21] While this estimated unit cost is lower than those typical of developed countries, it nevertheless represents a much higher relative financial burden if we bear in mind that this unit cost in Brazil is about six times the level of Brazilian per capita income while the unit cost of higher education in developed countries would at most be no more than twice the level of per capita income. Thus it is expensive to offer even imperfectly developed professional training in Brazil, and the need to introduce a note of efficiency and rational planning was made even more apparent.

The cost burden also raised the question of whether the students should not be expected to share in some of these expenses and thereby contribute a fair share to their own education. This question takes on greater significance when it is recognized that the high unit costs of higher education mentioned above result primarily from the expenses incurred in the publicly supported federal and state universities rather than in the private faculties in this sector where the students bear a greater proportion of the direct costs of their education. The question of equity and the financing of higher education in Brazil is a delicate and complex one which will be treated below. Of interest here is that the arguments for efficiency in the planning and allocation of resources in higher education led to the inference (unpopular in most student and many intellectual circles in Brazil) that university students should contribute more toward the cost of their education than was characteristic in the past when the European concept of free higher education prevailed.

---

21. Data on unit costs are still sparse and subject to errors. The above average estimate for higher education grows out of a limited survey conducted by the statistical service of the Ministry of Education (SEEC) in 1966. For a review of this data, see J. D. Ryder, "Unit Cost in Higher Education" in *Relatório da equipe de assessoria . . . op cit.*, Apendice C./3. Important factors contributing to this high unit cost are the low student-teacher ratio, idle capacity in public universities, and the widespread duplication of facilities and professors mentioned earlier. A more recent estimate of the total direct costs per student at the University of São Paulo for all disciplines combined in 1968 comes to approximately the same figure of $1,500. See *Análise econômica do sistema educacional de São Paulo*, Vol. 1, by Samuel Levy, Egas Moniz Nunes, and Antonio C. Campino, Instituto de Pesquisas Econômicas (São Paulo, 1970), p. 191.

The Equity Question in the Financing of Higher Education in Brazil

Who should pay for the costs of education is a question with many ramifications. It is strongly held that since the external economies or benefits to society at large are clear and present in extensive primary and secondary education, the government should strongly subsidize education at these levels by offering free, even compulsory public education. Without this support, fewer resources would be devoted to primary and secondary education than is considered ideal from a social welfare point of view since, with the existence of significant external economies (spillover benefits to others), the social rate of return is higher than the individual or private rate of return. This argument has not been commonly used in reference to higher education, although external economies clearly exist here as well. Society obviously benefits from having trained professional people. But there are significant private monetary returns from advanced professional training at the university level. College graduates are presumably in a position to capture through the market a large part of the total economic benefit associated with their training than are primary or secondary school graduates since, for the latter, external economies make up a greater part of the total economic benefit of their education and, as such, are unable to be appropriated by them in the market. Thus the question arises whether the private beneficiary of advanced training should not be expected to make some contribution to the costs associated with his education if he is in a position to gain much of the total monetary benefit associated with his training.

In the Brazilian context, an important question that has been rarely asked until very recently is, Who really pays for higher education in Brazil? First we should recognize that about half of the establishments in higher education are private and thus these students pay an important part of their total costs (though by no means all since these private faculties also frequently receive subsidies from public sources). In the federal and state universities however, the student pays at most only a token fee. For all practical purposes, his education is free in terms of direct costs.

We should also remember that students incur an additional indirect cost through their foregone income while they follow a four- or five-year university course of study. This represents the amount they could have earned if they had been free to work full time instead of attending school. In the American context, this represents an important component of the total cost of higher education as has been pointed out in numerous studies.[22] In Brazil, however, many students work part time, hence the income they sacrifice by attending school part time is much less than for American students. To the extent that a Brazilian student is primarily working and only attending school on the side, his foregone income is minimal indeed. This would probably be characteristic of those students who attend the less prestigious and weaker faculties which demand little of his time. Nevertheless, in the more difficult disciplines and stronger faculties such as medicine and engineering full-time students are much more common and thus foregone income much more important.[23]

To return to the question of direct costs and focus attention on the public or federal universities, however, the students contribute little and the government an overwhelming proportion of the resources in the form of direct subsidies from the Federal Ministry of Education. Hence the relevant question to ask to determine the equity or fairness in this arrangement is, Who are the students and who are the taxpayers in terms of socioeconomic level?

University students do not come from very low income families or they would not have reached the university level of education.[24]

22. See for example Gary Becker, *Human Capital: A Theoretical and Empirical Analysis with Special Reference to Education*, (New York: Columbia University Press, 1964), pp. 169-174; and Theodore Schultz "Capital Formation in Education," *Journal of Political Economy*, LXVIII, No. 6, (December 1966), 571-583.

23. In financing higher education, the lower foregone income (and hence lower initial costs) associated with part-time work and part-time study should not necessarily be construed as being cheaper and more efficient in the long run than full-time study and higher foregone income. If there is a negative correlation between hours of outside work and academic performance, the longer the gestation period to gain a degree the less completely and meaningfully trained is the graduate in the end, thereby compromising his ability to progress in his profession. In short, he pays a price in future income foregone through being less well trained in drawn out part-time courses of study. In formal terms, as Merrett has pointed out, one would have to compare the excess of present value over present costs for both part-time and full-time study. There is no reason to believe this comes out in favor of part-time training. See Stephen Merrett, "Student Finance in Higher Education," *Economic Journal* (June 1967) p. 292.

In the present situation of low-quality professional training in Brazilian universities, however, it should be pointed out that in some fields, such as law, simultaneous part-time work in the relevant professional milieu, such as being an apprentice in a law firm, may be almost the only effective way to become well trained in the profession and to gain contacts for future employment.

24. A study in 1960 emphasized the predominance of children from higher-income families in the universities, see Bertram Hutchinson and C. Castaldi, *Mobilidade de Trabalho*, Centro Brasileiro de Pesquisas Educacionais (Rio de Janeiro, 1960). A more recent study in 1969 by the Instituto de Pesquisas Econômicas of the University of São

The barriers to the progress of poorer children through the tortuous pyramid of Brazilian education is widely known. Attrition or drop-out rates are still very high in primary and secondary school, though this is less pronounced in the progressive South than elsewhere. Furthermore, more than half the secondary schools in the country are private and at least in major urban centers not inexpensive to attend. Finally, to master successfully the college entrance examination, private costly cram courses or *cursinhos* of one to two years are frequently required after high school. Thus by any measure of income distribution it would appear that most students in higher education in Brazil are clearly in the middle- or upper-income classes, though the rapid enrollments in higher education in recent years may very likely have reached down into less high income groups than was typical ten years ago.

In contrast to this, the incidence of taxation in Brazil is decidedly regressive, at least from the middle-income level upwards with the lower- and middle-income groups paying a greater proportion of their income in taxes than the higher-income groups. This is largely because of the still predominant role of indirect taxes in the tax structure of Brazil combined with the absence of any tax on capital gains and the well-known difficulties of effectively implementing and collecting direct personal income taxes in an underdeveloped country, especially in the liberal professions and the self employed.[25]

This evidence strongly indicates that many beneficiaries of subsidized public higher education in Brazil come from higher-income groups than many taxpayers who contribute most to the general

Paulo indicates a slight increase in the enrollment of the lower-income classes in higher education but still far more than half of the students in the higher educational establishments in the state of São Paulo come from the middle- and upper-income classes. See *O ensino superior em São Paulo, op. cit.* Part II.

25. Recent research pointing out the regressive features of the Brazilian tax system from the middle-income level upwards can be found in Henry Aaron, "Estimates of the Distributional Impact of Brazilian Taxes and Expenditures," written for the Council for International Progress in Management (USA) Inc. under contract with AID, mimeo, 1968. See also Gian Sahota, *Tax Evasion in Brazil,* and *The Distribution of Tax Burden in Brazil,* mimeographed, Instituto de Pesquisas Econômicas, Universidade de São Paulo, 1968. For an interesting analysis of how the inequitable features of financing higher education appear to prevail even in a developed country such as the United States, see Lee Hansen and Burton Wesbrod *Benefits, Costs and Finance of Public Higher Education* (Chicago: Markham Press, 1969).

revenues of the government (as measured in terms of relative incidence). This inequity is reinforced when those students who have
been able to pay handsomely for their private primary, secondary,
and tutoring education (and thus come from the higher socioeconomic
groups) successfully gain admission to the smaller number of prestigious, publicly subsidized faculties (the federal and state university
faculties), while those who are forced to follow the less costly public
primary and secondary education route and come from lower socio-
income groups are less prepared and end up in the weaker but more
costly (to them) private faculties that have been set up in recent
years. Thus among the university students themselves it is quite
probable that students from relatively better-off families receive more
of a subsidy for their higher education than those from families less
well off to the extent that they gain admission to the limited openings
in the better public universities while the latter are detoured into the
less prestigious private faculties where the yearly tuition can be
significant.[26]

Finally, many graduates (and some dropouts) of at least the
stronger publicly supported universities are in a position to earn
relatively high incomes compared with many who bear the tax burden
through their privileged membership in professional or semi-
professional groups thus perpetuating the vicious circle of an ever-
widening unequal distribution of income in the country. On balance,
the current method of financing public higher education (and education in general in Brazil) would seem to exacerbate rather than reduce the unequal income distribution in the country.

In recognition of this basic inequity in the financing of higher
education, the government through a special work group appointed
to study and make recommendations on university reform proposed
a scheme of financing by which students would be expected to contribute a growing proportion of the total direct cost of their education

26. This "within group" inequity would appear to be characteristic of São Paulo
and Belo Horizonte, where the free public universities offer much better professional
training in most fields, such as medicine, engineering, economics, and the applied sciences, than private schools in those areas. The only exception to this in São Paulo
would be in the area of business administration, where the highly reputable private and
costly program at the Getúlio Vargas Foundation stands out. In Rio de Janeiro, however, this quality distinction between public and private faculties appears less marked
in that the private Catholic University (PUC) in certain disciplines offers training equal
to and perhaps superior to that offered by the former National University.

as their family income rose as a multiple of the current minimum wage.[27] The proposal in effect included three different concepts of dealing with the role of the student's participation in financing higher education. Students whose family income was 35 times the prevailing minimum wage, the report argued, should be expected to pay a realistic tuition covering the administrative and maintenance costs associated with their training. Those whose income fell between 15 and 35 times the minimum wage would cover the administrative and maintenance costs associated with their training through long-term loans with up to 15 years for repayment and with the first payment due only some two to three years following graduation. For those whose income was less than 15 times the minimum wage, all costs would be waived and, in addition, a maintenance stipend would be offered to guarantee their full-time attendance. Finally, the proposal strongly recommended that the above measures represent an addition to, rather than a substitution for, the current subsidization of higher education through normal channels. This last recommendation was no doubt made in order to facilitate the political acceptance of this proposal. It should be recognized, however, that on grounds of both equity and efficiency any public expenditures saved through having greater student contribution to the costs of higher education should probably be applied to expanding public investment in primary and secondary schools where the barriers to a more democratic access to education are most pronounced and the social rate of return to public investment in education very likely much higher.

Returning now to the substance of the proposal, it would appear incongruous to pay students to attend the university while professors are still underpaid and teaching part-time. Thus the practice of paying out a significant stipend to a large number of lower-income students to guarantee their full-time devotion to study could create opposition among the teaching body itself unless the issue of decently remunerated full-time teaching is resolved first. Second, the possibility of determining the income levels of students in order to determine who deserved to pay and who deserved a loan would necessitate that the student or his family produce evidence of their income, such as income-tax returns, for the relevant university authorities. While this is not inconceivable and in principle ideal, there is a

27. *Reforma Universitaria*, Relatorio do Grupo de Trabalho Criado pelo Decreto No. 62.937/68, Ministério da Educação e Cultura, Ministério do Planejamento e Coordenação Geral e Ministério da Fazenda, Rio de Janeiro, 1968. See pp. 58-60.

real question whether the university authorities will be able in practice to enforce a policy of this unprecedented nature on unco-
operative parents without strong governmental support.

The foregoing suggests that a loan scheme might be easier to implement than a complicated scholarship formula, though there is
clearly an appropriate place for both in the present system. In discussing loans, two alternatives come to mind: deferred payment
through a fixed-income obligation and deferred payment through an
income-tax mechanism with one's income level determining one's repayment schedule.

The income-tax scheme is frequently referred to as the most
equitable way to repay an educational loan. In repaying according to
some fixed or variable percentage of one's income, the future earning
capacity of the student is taken into account in establishing his repayment, with conceivably no repayment required below a certain
minimum income level. A fixed income obligation on the other hand
would unnecessarily discriminate against those who chose or fell into
a poorly remunerated career since they would be required to repay a
fixed sum despite having a low income.

While the argument in favor of an income-tax scheme to repay
educational loans appears convincing in the context of a developed
country such as the United States, the inherent regressive features of
the Brazilian tax system raise important questions concerning the use
of this mechanism to help finance higher education in underdeveloped
countries. There is an obvious discrimination in the collection of personal income taxes in underdeveloped countries. In practice, only
those who appear on a public or private sector payroll pay their fair
share of income taxes in Brazil (in large part because their taxes are
withheld at the source). Those who earn income outside the organizational framework of a public- or private-sector payroll (all independent professionals, self-employed businessmen, wealthy farmers,
tradesmen and merchants) can escape a good part of their income-tax
obligations. Even more importantly, higher-income groups enjoy an
added advantage in that capital gains are not taxed in Brazil. Thus
any proposal designed to have graduates repay part of the costs of
their higher education through a fixed percentage of the gross income
as reported in their future income tax returns would very likely
penalize the less affluent graduates (those subject to payroll deductions) and favor the more affluent (those in the upper-income groups
not subject to payroll deductions and able to enjoy untaxed capital
gains). It would be unfortunate indeed if the original objective of in-

troducing equity into the financing of higher education in Brazil through using a deferred payment linked to the income tax would, in the end, result in another inequity with those most able to pay the cost of their education escaping much of their repayment through the route of a defective and imperfectly administered income-tax system.

The above-mentioned structural defect in the tax system points toward a loan program with deferred payment as the most appropriate means to complement the existing public subsidization of higher education in Brazil. Furthermore, the burden of a fixed-income obligation would be much less than the critics of this scheme imply if there is a positive correlation between the cost of education and the level of one's future income made possible through this education. As a first approximation, this would appear to be true. On the average, the income-earning potential of those whose education is costly, such as doctors or engineers, is considerably above the average income level of all university graduates. Thus the burden of their repayment would be correspondingly much less. At the other end of the spectrum, those whose future income would be far below the average of all university graduates, such as high-school teachers, would very likely not have incurred a heavy repayment burden since it is not expensive to train people in these disciplines.

Finally, it should be made clear that any complementary source of financing should not require the student to pay the full direct cost of his education since, as mentioned earlier, there are external economies associated with an increased number of university graduates. The government through its traditional channels of finance should obviously continue to finance a substantial portion of the total cost of higher education. Also, given the important break with past practice here for the federal and state universities, any policy of student participation in the financing of higher education should be introduced gradually not only to facilitate the change for the students but also to permit a periodic evaluation of the operation of the various means of financing adopted.

Although loan schemes have been implemented in various private medical and engineering faculties and at the Getúlio Vargas Foundation Business School in São Paulo, to date no practical measures have been taken by the government to implement any of the loan measures for public universities proposed in the Report of the Work Group on University Reform. In time, however, it would appear likely that some form of student participation in sharing the costs of higher education will emerge, though the precise form of this arrangement is still unclear and the appropriate pace and degree of implementation still open for discussion.

The Experiment with Graduate Centers (Pós-Graduação)

For Brazil to develop a local capacity for highly trained specialists and to engage in research that satisfies the development needs of the country, policy-makers 'and educators will find they are in effect engaging in import-substitution in the educational sector. Instead of importing expensive expertise in the form of foreign technicians and advisors and instead of sending local talent abroad for advanced training, it is possible to consider reorganizing higher education to create graduate research and training centers *(pós-graduação)* to produce this product domestically.[28]

Thus the embryonic graduate centers in Brazil in such fields as the applied sciences, engineering, agricultural sciences, and general economics can be looked upon as the capital goods subsector of the educational sector. As in any import-substitution process, the long-run goal of achieving greater self-sufficiency in certain selected areas of specialized training and research implies that during the short- to medium-run period a rather heavy reliance upon foreign technical assistance is helpful and in some areas almost indispensable. During the decade of the sixties there was a marked increase in the amount of foreign aid to Brazil and, more particularly, in the amount of technical assistance for educational activities, especially on the graduate level. Even though there was a marked growth in Brazilian resources devoted to education after 1964, Table 5 shows clearly that foreign resources grew even more rapidly to reach a level representing about 3 percent of the total resources applied to education in Brazil by 1970. A large part of these foreign resources were directed toward the development of these young graduate centers.

As an illustration of the foreign effort in one field alone, six economics graduate centers have been established in the past ten years in Brazil. These centers, taken together, are currently training approximately 100 masters-level economists annually with reasonably paid

---

28. A distinction should be made between graduate training in general and graduate centers. There are many loosely defined one-year courses of graduate training all over Brazil in many disciplines. In practice, most of these are little if any above the level of the undergraduate programs in their areas. The graduate training centers under discussion here, however, are institutes and not merely courses. They are far fewer in number, more serious in intent and, as will be made clear subsequently, far more important in their impact upon their respective professions and higher education in general.

full-time staffs ranging from 8 to 15 professors engaging in research and instruction in each center. At the same time, from this pool of students, approximately 150 Brazilians have been sent to the United States and elsewhere over the past ten years for advanced training leading to the masters or doctoral degrees in economics. A significant number of these students have returned and have been effectively reabsorbed into the local professional job market as full-time professors and research specialists in the regional economics graduate centers, some undergraduate faculties, and strategic agencies in the public sector. Their impact on teaching, research and policy-making is becoming more and more significant.[29]

Foreign grants from such sources as USAID and the Ford Foundation have been instrumental in supporting these graduate programs through financing visiting foreign professors, library development, extensive local and foreign scholarships, and supplemental salaries for full-time teaching and research for the local Brazilian staffs. The crucial role of foreign technical and financial assistance in many of these centers merely underlined the difficulty of initially developing these experiments in graduate education through domestic sources of finance and expertise alone.

The discussion of these graduate centers will focus on such questions as their autonomy, financial survival, organizational requirements, and, finally, the issue of the appropriate number of such centers to support and the possibility for national co-ordination among centers. The discussion will be heavily influenced by the author's experience with several economics graduates centers; however, the problems and issues raised should be pertinent to other disciplines.

Within the traditional university undergraduate environment a

29. Advanced professional instruction on a graduate level in economics is occurring in the following six centers: the Instituto de Pesquisas Economicas (IPE) of the University of São Paulo; the Centro de Desenvolvimento e Planejamento Regional (CEDEPLAR) of the Federal University of Minas Gerais; Escola de Pós Graduação em Economia (EPGE) of the Getúlio Vargas Foundation in Rio de Janeiro; Centro de Aperfeiçoamento da Economistas do Nordeste (CAEN) at the Federal University of Ceará; the Programa de Mestrado em Economia of the Federal University of Pernambuco, and the Centro de Treinamento de Economistas (CENDEC), of the Ministry of Planning in Brasília. The first two centers mentioned above are already making substantial professional contributions in applied economic research in such areas as regional economics, the economics of education, and tax policy in Brazil. Furthermore, the staffs and graduates of all these centers are playing an instrumental role (as advisors or full-time staff members) in upgrading the technical competence of such policy entities as the Central Bank, the Ministries of Finance and Planning, and important regional development agencies.

certain suspicion and jealousy toward these experiments was not un-usual in the beginning. Among the more politically active student groups, questions were raised concerning the implication of having such an important foreign influence in their educational system, and, among the traditional part-time professorial groups, a certain jealousy occasionally appeared since these centers had not grown up from within the traditional faculty structure that administered the extensive undergraduate programs. Invariably they were established as separate institutes beyond the direct control of the traditional undergraduate faculty with the bulk of their financing coming from sources external to the university and frequently foreign in nature.

The initial financial and professional exclusiveness of these cen-ters could perhaps be defended as having been a necessary short-run policy in the early and mid-sixties in order to guarantee that these cen-ters (largely staffed by a small handpicked group of the better trained professors in the undergraduate faculties) would not be overwhelmed by the professional mediocrity that prevailed in the traditionally ori-ented undergraduate faculties of the universities. Indeed, the special treatment accorded to these centers was considered essential to in-troduce successfully research into the university milieu of Brazil and develop professional training and expertise more in line with interna-tional standards of excellence. Nevertheless, an open dialogue and close co-operation and exchange with their parent undergraduate de-partments or faculties is necessary to introduce better teaching meth-ods, stimulate curriculum reform, and develop a greater awareness of research on national problems within the undergraduate faculties. The closer integration of these young graduate centers into their heretofore traditional undergraduate faculties is one of the successful organiza-tional changes occurring in the current university reform.[30]

By far the most serious challenge confronting these young gradu-ate programs is their source of future financial support. The important foreign financing will eventually come to an end and the question arises as to what local sources of funds will be available to replace these external sources. Fortunately, in many of these programs the burdensome foreign-exchange costs of training a large number of Bra-zilian scholars and technicians abroad will have been largely under-

30. Of importance here is that the staffs of these graduate centers are not forced into a heavy undergraduate teaching load, thereby compromising their research and graduate-school teaching. The integration of several economics graduate institutes with their parent undergraduate faculties has already occurred successfully at the University of São Paulo and the Federal University of Minas Gerais.

taken before the major sources of foreign financing begin to cut back on their aid. In short, a promising stock of human capital will have been effectively established in these graduate centers, but how are they to be maintained?

The highly trained teaching and research staff in these centers will demand a much more market-competitive salary for their full-time devotion to academic and research pursuits than has been typical in the part-time undergraduate faculties of the past. Moreover, research projects will have to become a permanent feature of these centers if they are to remain truly "graduate" in character. It is unlikely that the traditional university budgets can absorb the increased costs of a full-time, high-quality staff associated with these expensive graduate centers in the face of the rapid growth of the undergraduate faculties which will require much more financing. Tradition and practical politics will force the usual sources of university finance to opt for supporting these growing undergraduate programs with less financial support for graduate work.

In view of this, nonuniversity public-sector sources of finance will have to play more of a role in supporting these graduate centers. Other ministries, public agencies, and *autarchias* can benefit by giving institutional grants to promote advanced professional training and by farming out a good amount of applied research to the staffs of these graduate centers rather than engaging in exclusive in-house research. In so doing, they would be playing an instrumental role in developing professional and technical competence within the university milieu in those fields of major importance for public policy.[31] Fortunately, recent policy in the Ministries of Planning and Finance and in such *autarchias* as the National Development Bank, SUDENE, the Bank of Northeast, the Bacia Paraná Commission and others indicates that policy-makers in many important circles of government are beginning to think and act precisely along these lines with several economics graduate centers benefiting significantly from outside research agreements and general institutional support. It is to be hoped that such

31. It is important that these public entities promote genuine research activities within these institutes and not merely use them as data-gathering branches and that the agencies control their natural proclivity to steal men from the institute's staff. This form of an intersectoral brain drain will disappear the moment these institutes can pay adequate salaries above those possible in the public sector. Fortunately, salary differentials favorable to the institutes are already emerging in several economics graduate centers known to the author.

arrangements can continue to grow in importance in the coming decade.[32]

While admitting the importance, indeed the necessity, of such extra-university financing, one should be aware of the implicit bias such support could introduce into the nature and direction of research. Till now this has not been a serious issue in the field of economics; however, there is always the possibility of a divergence between the specific research questions of interest to the financing agency and the important areas of research in the eyes of the professional staff in the graduate centers. To the extent that the technical staffs in these centers acquire prestige it is quite likely that their expertise could influence the demand from the public-sector agencies through direct professional lobbying for certain lines of research and, at the same time, influencing policy-makers on more appropriate lines of research and policy action.

It is important to recognize the dangers of contract research as the primary base for financial support in a graduate institution. The more that client-oriented research comes to dominate a university environment, the less open and flexible are the intellectual interests and activities of the staff and the more the institution comes to be dominated by its service function to outside interests, public or private. In short, it becomes more difficult to develop a broad intellectually stimulating academic environment when more specific, pragmatic, and specialized research concerns overwhelm the equally important broader educational purpose of graduate training. In view of this, it is to be hoped that the sources of financial support from the university budgets themselves will grow larger over time so as to insure that some degree of less client-oriented research can always form an important part of the research activities in these centers and more general "academic" values will influence the intellectual milieu.

Subject to the caveat mentioned above, an important function of these centers should lie in the application of knowledge for social uses, such as, engaging in relevant research to aid public policy in improving industrial and agricultural productivity, launching agrar-

32. It is clear that such arrangements naturally tend to favor the more technical fields of interest to public policy, such as general and agricultural economics and applied science and engineering. What is needed to balance this bias is an entity such as the National Research Council (CNPq) designed to dispense funds to promising scholars and programs in the humanities and the social sciences similar to the activity of the Social Science Research Council in the United States.

ian reforms and urban renewal, investigating the structure and incidence of monetary or fiscal policy, and introducing more rigorous
analysis in broader areas of economic and social planning. In this regard, nonuniversity financing is clearly in order, indeed essential,
given the development needs of Brazil. To the extent that this research
effort can be allocated to the graduate centers of the universities, the
greater are the probable "spillovers" or external economies in improving the traditional undergraduate schools through more relevant
teaching and more respectable professional training geared to national problems.

The foregoing suggests that graduate training in Brazil will
evolve in a fashion different from that characteristic of the universities
in the United States. American universities initially developed graduate research and training from within the university milieu itself and
with a strong emphasis on basic research. The applied and later the
troublesome client-oriented features emerged only much later in the
process of change toward the "multiversity." Brazilian graduate centers will necessarily have to emphasize the service function earlier in
its evolution. As mentioned before, the scarcity of resources in general, and of traditional educational resources in particular, have forced
the young Brazilian graduate centers to lobby for funding from more
client-oriented public sponsors. Given the pressing development
needs of Brazil, this arrangement should not appear surprising nor illogical. Furthermore there is growing public pressure emphasizing the
social obligation that these graduate centers have to service the short-
and medium-run goals of public policy in broad areas of social and
economic development. It would thus appear that in the present development context of contemporary Brazil, Brazilian graduate centers
will not enjoy the luxury of a large, basic non-client-oriented source
of funds for some time. The service function toward society will
necessarily stand out more than the traditional role of general education and research to advance the fund of knowledge typical of earlier
United States graduate institutions.

It should be apparent from the above that this new role for the
Brazilian university, that is, the pragmatic role of engaging in contract research and creating graduate institutions to service this function, will require a new style of administration which will have to
be more professionally and technically oriented than has heretofore
been typical in university circles. The administration and the staff
will have to be more closely integrated, given the technical nature of
much of its teaching and research. Furthermore, the multifaceted ties

with the outside world—to the government, to industry and international organizations—will require a sophisticated entrepreneurial talent to lobby and successfully negotiate for a wide range of institutional support and contract research activities. These managerial tasks will have to include the challenge of knowing how to co-ordinate professional staffs to meet certain deadlines as well as supervising the academic responsibilities associated with graduate training. Finally, all of this should be done in such a way as to emphasize the joint responsibilities of the staff and the teamwork needed for both teaching and research. In short, given the degree of professional expertise that would have been built into the largely foreign-trained local staff, a sense of joint direction and decision-making through frequent staff meetings would be necessary to maintain morale and a spirit of institutional loyalty to these graduate centers.

The above-mentioned organizational challenge would be impossible to undertake within the old fragmented university structure of part-time teachers, inbred lifetime-chair professors with no research experience, and infrequent staff meetings. Furthermore, the nature of administering a graduate center represents a marked change from the task of running an undergraduate school. In view of this, the current university reform should recognize that in supporting these centers within the appropriate undergraduate faculty, great care should be taken to guarantee a large degree of administrative autonomy for these centers to operate within their new university status.

Two further points should be made: It makes no sense to proliferate the number of graduate centers as was done with the undergraduate schools in the sixties. This tendency to permit an unlimited number of institutions to develop will only guarantee a decline in quality in all. The federal and relevant state government educational and planning authorities should realize that the costs are high and the human resources needed for these undertakings scarce and difficult to mobilize and thus not permit a wholesale creation of insufficiently funded graduate schools. No more than six to seven comprehensive graduate centers should be developed throughout the country, obviously within the major federal and state (for São Paulo) metropolitan universities.[33] Some exceptions could be made for certain separate

33. Many more programs offering quick one-year graduate training courses will no doubt be established if only to serve as a vehicle for manufacturing quickly the postgraduate credits considered necessary for university teaching staffs under the university reform. As in the past, these courses can be set up at very low cost and the training that

centers of established quality such as ITA (the Aeronautical Technological Institute in São José dos Campos) and the Vargas Foundation (both in Rio and São Paulo). Expanding much beyond this number, however, will only mean less for all with the loss of a chance to maintain a critical minimum effort and scale of activities necessary to guarantee professional and technical excellence. It is time that Brazilian educational authorities paid attention to creating quality instead of merely increasing the quantity of schools and students. In graduate research centers this is of paramount importance.

Finally in recognition of their privileged status it is incumbent upon the professional staffs of these centers to establish and maintain contact with their colleagues in the same discipline at other centers and help develop a national network of graduate centers. An exchange of professors and students would be useful here as well as periodic professional meetings reviewing current research and training activities. Joint research efforts should be worked out between centers and an extension program could be developed through which the more prestigious and better financed of these centers would lend professors and research specialists to the lesser developed centers in other parts of the country for varying periods of time to upgrade their instruction and research activities. Finally, joint funding arrangements could be worked out with the nonuniversity sources, thereby emphasizing the complementary and co-operative effort needed to create a national profession of scholars in the discipline in question.[34] This would be a welcome change from the inbred parochialism that characterizes all undergraduate faculties.

---

results is little if any above the undergraduate level. The comprehensive regional graduate centers, however, should be expensive centers of excellence where quality research, training, and consulting are expected to prevail and where the first integrated doctoral (Ph.D.) programs should be established. This need to concentrate resources in only a limited number of centers was recently recognized by MEC through Decree Law 67350 of 6 October 1970 in which recognized graduate-level training centers are to be limited to five universities strategically located throughout the country, (São Paulo, Rio de Janeiro, Belo Horizonte, Porto Alegre, and Recife).

34. To a large estent, the above-mentioned features of a well developed extension program emphasizing the exchange of professors and research specialists, joint research and funding agreements, and finally the formal creation of a national association of scholars exclusively associated with the graduate centers have been worked out in recent years in the field of economics among regional economics graduate centers in the universities in São Paulo, Rio de Janeiro, Belo Horizonte, Fortaleza, Recife, and Porto Alegre, and the Vargas Foundation in Rio de Janeiro.

A Note on Educational Planning in Brazil

The increasing emphasis on analyzing the educational system in Brazil in terms of providing valuable human resources for the development of the country has naturally led to a growing discussion of planning within this sector. Other factors reinforce this emphasis. First, as many observers have noted, there are particular features inherent to education that argue for some degree of planning. The long-run gestation period in carrying students through all levels of schooling, the "feed-back" feature by which the educational sector necessarily supplies its own inputs in the form of teachers, and finally the possibilities of creating many structural imbalances within the educational system through bottlenecks and waste by level and discipline point out the need to engage in at least some limited degree of planning.

Second, the limited resources in a country such as Brazil dictate that more rational investment criteria be used in all areas, education being no exception. Finally, the succession of economic plans from the early sixties to the present in Brazil has created a technocratic planning environment in which education was bound to be included within the over-all planning exercises owing to its role of supplying critical manpower for economic growth.

Following the initial comprehensive diagnosis of the educational sector discussed in an earlier section of this chapter, the Human Resource Division of IPEA produced a volume of the over-all Ten Year Plan (1967-76) in which an elaborate exercise in manpower planning was presented with its implications for educational enrollments and the necessary teaching personnel outlined for the succeeding decade.[35] Later in the Strategic Three-Year Development Program (1968-70), the earlier manpower enrollment and, more particularly, the current and prospective programs and reforms at various levels of education were reviewed in detail, frequently including planned budgetary costs.[36]

The growing need to promote a more efficient allocation of resources in the educational sector has highlighted the need for more relevant and up-to-date data upon which these plans depend. Of im-

35. Ministério do Planejamento e Coordenação Econômica, *Plano Decenal de Desenvolvimento Econômico e Social*, Tomo VI Volume I, *Educação e Mao de Obra*, Rio de Janeiro, March 1967.

36. Ministério do Planejamento e Coordenação Geral, *Programa Estratégico de Desenvolvimento 1968-1970*, Área Estratégica IX, Infra-Estrutura Social, Volume I, Educaçao e Recursos Humanos, Rio de Janeiro, February 1969.

portance here is the obvious need to have detailed cost data on a continuing basis covering not only the various levels of education but also a breakdown by discipline and program within higher education so that various educational strategies and reforms can be properly evaluated at this level. Also, a continuing review of the current stock and flow of students and teachers in an equally disaggregated fashion is necessary for successful educational planning. Further, this disaggregation should be of such a degree that the growth and future performance of specific centers of quality training in both graduate and undergraduate education can be separated out for individual projections and analysis. Fortunately, as mentioned above, the emphasis on planning in recent years has begun to make data more available.

Of equal importance here are periodic data reviewing the current and prospective stock and flow of high-level manpower in the economy and the market wages and salaries of this specialized manpower including graduates from the various professional schools in higher education as well as from vocational and secondary schools. Given the high unit costs of most vocational and university training, it is important to know how much cost (and possible waste) might be involved through expanding enrollments in these areas. Hence past and current wage and salary data are useful indicators to establish the changing market demand for and the possible degree of underemployment in given occupations. PNAD (the National Household Survey of the IBGE) has made a start in this direction by periodically publishing regional wage and salary data for various occupations. It is to be hoped that this salary survey can be expanded to include occupations associated with higher education. An additional survey strategy in this area of professional remuneration would be to focus surveys on the major public and private sector enterprises employing professional manpower and use this information to complement the household survey data covering self-employed professionals.[37] In summary, with these periodic cost and wage data made available the authorities responsible for educational planning will have more suitable information to undertake more sophisticated cost-benefit studies of the various current and proposed strategies of educational innovations than they have been able to do up to now.

The growing need for planning in this area and the recognition of the data needs to undertake useful analysis and evaluation lead

---

37. Conceivably the occupational surveys conducted under the law of two thirds by the Ministry of Labor could be used for this purpose.

to the final stage of implementation and it is here that a note of uncertainty arises. All the initiative in the past to support or engage in
a more sophisticated quantitative analysis of the educational structure highlighting its interrelation with the process of economic
growth has come from the technocratic ministries, more particularly
from the Human Resources section of the Applied Economic Institute
of the Ministry of Planning. Unfortunately, until very recently there
has been very little awareness or understanding of these developments
within the more traditional bureaucracy of the Ministry of Education
and Culture (MEC), the major implementing organ for any new
direction in higher education. No effective machinery had been established within MEC to study and deal with the wide range of planning and modernization needed to reform higher education. Thus the
possibility exists that despite the recent growth of more useful and revealing research on the issues and problems of higher education,
very few new policy directions will result owing to either the active
resistance or general indifference of the bureaucratic leaders responsible for policy within MEC.[38]

Several factors probably account for the lack of rapport between
these two ministries in the past. First, it should not be surprising that
the educators and bureaucrats within the Ministry of Education
with a more humanistic and nontechnical background would find the
new economic analysis of education confusing and disturbing. Treat-
ing education as an economic good whether in manpower or rate-
of-return analysis no doubt strikes many of these educators as highly
irregular and unnecessary if not misleading.

Second, it is also quite apparent that in the pecking order of
political importance the Minister of Planning in the past has been a
far more important and influential cabinet head than the Minister of
Education in the policy-making councils of the government and,
hence, in a position to lobby for his department's view and policy
prescription in such areas as education. To some extent the civil ser-
vants and policy-makers within MEC could not help feeling that
another ministry had encroached upon their presumed area of competence and responsibility.

While this divergent view existed between the planners and
educational bureaucrats in the past, there are indications that this is
changing in the present. The current Minister of Education, Jarbas

38. On this point, see Mario Henrique Simonsen, *Brasil 2001*, (Rio de Janeiro:
APEC Editôra, 1969), p. 243.

Passarinho, is a much more dynamic and effective administrator than were his predecessors. Furthermore, being a former labor minister, he has an awareness of the manpower implications in education and has earned the respect of the technocrats in other ministries for his administrative competence and leadership. His initial appointments and directives appear to be creating a more propitious milieu for the effective implementation of innovations in the educational sector in general and in higher education in particular, where the ministry exercises its greatest influence.

Finally, it is instructive to note that the recent Work Group on University Reform was made up of an interministerial commission (from finance and planning as well as education). This clearly grew out of a growing recognition in government circles that any major plan to reform higher education would necessarily have to draw upon the technical and professional staffs of other ministries as well as professional educators. It is apparent that any program to alter or redesign the current flow of human capital being produced by the higher educational system obviously would affect future social and economic growth and, as a result, technocrats responsible for such economic planning should also have a role in designing any major reform of the current university reform.

University Reform

Ideas for university reform have been germinating throughout the decade in Brazil. Furthermore, as mentioned earlier, the growing discussion in recent years highlighting the inefficiency and waste in the university system gave further impetus to this movement. At the risk of overgeneralization, the major intent of the recommendations set forth by the recent Interministerial Work Group was to transform the older European-type professional school milieu with its separate isolated faculties, nontechnical bias and lifetime-chair professors into a more American-type system with a departmental structure, more interdisciplinary programs, and a stronger emphasis on research and training in technological fields serving the development needs of the country. In brief, the attempt is to transform the older classical university into a more up-to-date "multiversity" serving society through emphasizing a closer connection with government and industry in both research and professional training.

It is premature at this point to judge the results, since the reform has only barely begun. University statutes are still being changed, and many important features of the reform have yet to be implemented in certain areas, schools, and disciplines. In view of this, the author feels that it is only possible to outline the major recommendations of the aforementioned work group, and then close out with an admittedly impressionistic conclusion concerning the degree to which these recommendations are apparently being implemented, ignored, or altered, as seen from the author's limited vantage point.

The first area of concern for the work group was preuniversity training. Recommendations were made to reconstruct many current academic secondary schools to include more subprofessional, market-oriented training, thereby preparing the high-school graduate to be more easily absorbed into a productive job and not fall into the pattern of pushing on for university training merely because he had not been trained to do anything else. Also a common "vestibular" or university entrance exam for all disciplines and schools within a given region was proposed as a strategy with the aim of reducing the number of "excedentes" that appeared to grow out of the earlier uncoordinated system of decentralized testing by individual faculties. In addition, a centralized testing service would be in an excellent position to collect a wide range of valuable socioeconomic data as well as information on past academic history from the candidates for university admission. These data could then be correlated with their scores and future academic performance. Such information on a continuing basis could prove invaluable for future educational policy as well as sociological and economic research. Evidence indicates that measures are being undertaken to implement both these features. The reconstruction of the secondary school curriculum, however, will take much longer and only proceed in stages in selected areas.[39] The consolidated entrance exam is already becoming a reality in various regions.

Within the university environment itself, the major focus of the reform recommendations centered around the following: eliminating the lifetime-chair-professor tradition and creating a departmental structure in which all members of the department would presumably have an equal voice and no individual member would "own" or be the exclusive professor of a given specialty and in turn paternalistically controlling the future of his assistants; creating basic institutes to handle the early years of instruction in general science, mathematics, social sciences, and the humanities among others (this would elimi-

39. As of this writing, the pilot projects implementing this structured curriculum are currently programmed for only four states (Minas Gerais, Espírito Santo, Bahia, and Rio Grande do Sul).

nate the inefficient and wasteful duplication of having each individual faculty or professional school hire its own professors to handle these courses for their own students and afford students an opportunity to experience various fields before choosing their professional specialization in the later years of their university experience); instituting a more extensive adequately paid full-time teaching body; utilizing existing facilities more efficiently and moving separate faculties and schools to a central campus to facilitate interdisciplinary programs and to consolidate many of the professors from scattered faculties into the relevant basic institutes for general instruction; establishing short (2 to 3 year) operational courses for middle-level technicians to better serve the labor market for subprofessional skills in such areas as medicine and engineering; developing closer links to the community through an extensive apprenticeship program through which students in their final years would contribute their services in their area of training to the community at large; gradually introducing the practice of having the student participate in the financing of his university education through a system of long term loans; and, finally, developing graduate centers, *(pós-graduação)* to train future professors for the university system and institute research on national problems.

It is premature to judge the degree to which these measures have been effectively implemented, since the reform has only recently begun and private faculties and state universities will undoubtedly incorporate these features in a style and pace somewhat different from that of the federal universities. In addition, despite the savings and greater efficiency of some of these measures (such as creating the basic institutes), much of the success of these reforms will depend upon growing financial support on a larger scale than in the past (especially to support full-time teaching and graduate training). The degree to which these funds will be forthcoming is still unpredictable. In view of the fact that the author has already discussed at length the issues of partial student financing in higher education and the development of graduate centers, the following will limit itself to the areas of full-time teaching, interdisciplinary studies, the departmental organization, and outside influence on the university.

Full-Time Professors

As already demonstrated, full-time professional work in both teaching and research is clearly needed in the new Graduate Centers. University budgets will apparently not be able to absorb the full cost of supporting these graduate-center staffs on a full-time basis; however, other public-sector and some private-sector institutional and contract research support appears to be a possible source of continuing support at adequate levels of financing for many of these centers. Full-time professors in the undergraduate schools pose a different problem. First, it should be recognized that excluding part-time teachers may not be in the best interest of certain specialized disciplines. Engineering, medicine, business administration, and law come to mind as areas in which outstanding practitioners are also needed on a part-time basis to complement the students' formal education with practical experience. In Brazil, it is difficult if not impossible to be well informed or well trained in these specialized professions today unless one is actually practicing the profession itself. This explains why some of the most popular and stimulating professors in Brazilian universities are precisely these part-time experts who have distinguished themselves in their professions and thus have much to give to the students from the experience of their demanding and highly relevant professional careers. These part-time men should always form a part of any professional faculty, and the current division of professors into full-time, half-time and part-time categories by the reform measures appears to recognize this.

Nevertheless, there is an obvious need to have more full-time professors handling other courses within the professional faculties and in the basic fields of the arts and sciences. It is impossible to offer significant university education that has any lasting educational quality without a substantial full-time component of both students and professors. Anything less transforms the university into a part-time vocational school for subprofessional graduates. Unfortunately, financial constraints within the higher educational sector will undoubtedly restrict the range and extent of implementing full-time teaching for some time to come. It is financially impossible to create an adequately paid full-time teaching body in a short time within all the fields in all Brazilian federal universities.

To illustrate this point, the newly promulgated higher salary scales will pay a full-time full professor as much as $1,000 a month (at the current cruzeiro rate of exchange). This relatively high pay is necessary (and in some cases not enough) to attract top talent into full-time teaching in most priority disciplines in the major urban universities. Unfortunately, this salary level, not too different from American academic salary levels, represents a relatively heavy financial burden for a country at Brazil's level of income. For example, this yearly salary of about 12,000 dollars is about 40 times the level of Brazil's current per capita income, while a full professor's salary in the United States (say between 25 and 30 thousand dollars as a high estimate) would be no more than 5 to 6 times the per capita income level of the United States. This extreme relative salary differential (with respect to per capita income) merely reflects the equally extreme relative scarcity of high-level manpower in lesser-developed countries. This fact makes it difficult indeed to apply this highly remunerative salary scale indiscriminately throughout the country. There is the additional issue that many of the current professors are hardly deserving of such largesse. This has been recognized in the university reform, and currently the higher pay scales recently promulgated by the Ministry of Education to stimulate more full-time teaching in federal universities are being applied gradually to only a limited number of disciplines considered high-priority areas for Brazil's development needs (science, technology, and teacher-training among others).

It is interesting to note that this recent ad hoc strategy of applying the new higher pay scales for full-time teaching to certain limited priority areas is the first time the Ministry of Education has ever in effect allowed the market principle to enter into the salary structure for university professors. The civil-service-like salary rules for federal university professors have never allowed any salary differentiation according to region, discipline or merit. Paying professors in less important fields at the same rate as professors in crucial priority areas only compromises the development of these priority areas. While the current strategy of permitting only certain priority disciplines to enjoy immediately the benefits of the higher full-time pay scales is, in effect, a welcome differentiation, this has been an indirect and inadvertent result that may be only temporary. It is important that this principle of salary differentials becomes a more explicit and permanent feature in the current university reform and not an inadvertent, temporary effect brought about by the exigencies of the moment.

Finally, it should be pointed out that while differentiation by discipline may be an improvement over no differentiation at all, it is nevertheless an incomplete and wasteful criterion by itself. More to the point are specific programs within disciplines. It is important to focus on the existing strong programs and schools within a discipline, given the obvious fact that there will never be sufficient educational resources in the near future to pay these higher scales across the board to all disciplines. Furthermore, it is quite conceivable that some specific programs in some lesser-priority disciplines would be of such high caliber that they would deserve special treatment before all the schools or faculties in the priority areas receive these benefits. As an example, the current work in certain select programs in the social sciences or the humanities may be of such outstanding merit by national or even international standards that it would make sense to give them more concentrated support before the fund of higher pay scales is exhausted in paying high salaries to third- or fourth-rate faculties in the usual high-priority technical or scientific areas. This dual criterion of program as well as discipline would assign the highest weight to the most promising programs within the top-priority field. Once this group was served, however, it is possible that the high weight assigned to a particularly impressive program in a lesser-priority area would more than counterbalance the lower weight assigned to its field and place it ahead of the less promising programs or schools in the priority areas.

Interdisciplinary and General Studies

With respect to the prospects for an interdisciplinary milieu in the current reform, several features are apparent. First, in the short run the prospects are slim for major changes from past specialization in most places. A central campus is almost a necessity in order to create the physical setting permitting students access to a variety of departments. Many "university cities" are still in construction and will be for some time in the future. Furthermore, the development of centralized institutes handling the basic subjects for all departments is only now under way and, in some cases, the reassignment of professors and courses to these institutes is encountering resistance and modification. Thus at best the prospects of creating viable institutes cutting across departmental and faculty lines will be a long, arduous process.[40]

Second, the faculty or department still remains the seat of power in the university. The student in his first year enters and later receives

40. In addition to the natural reluctance of the older faculties and current departments to surrender an important part of the students' education to non-specialized institutes, there are two problems appearing in this area. First, in organizing the teaching body for these basic institutes, there is some difficulty in overcoming the friction and, at times, animosity among professors of allied disciplines who have been previously trained and conditioned in different intellectual and methodological traditions by their former specialized and separate faculties. Second, in having the student admitted and accepted first by the institutes in the university (instead of by the faculty as in the current practice), a programming problem could appear later, since there would be no easy way to guarantee that the specialized faculties can count on a set number of majors coming out of the earlier pool of nonspecialized students within the Institutes.

his diploma from a specific faculty. In the meantime, he may be in a position to take an occasional course from other faculties. Such initiative is likely to be discouraged, however. His intellectual experience and training will still essentially be determined for some time by all the rigid rules and required curriculum of the faculty in question. This is unfortunate, since high schools do not engage in any career counseling or orientation, and a broader-based academic training in the early university years could prove invaluable in steering the student into a career more appropriate to his aptitude or latent interest. Similarly, it could help alleviate the personal loss and social cost associated with many students discovering late in their university career that they have an interest or vocation in another specialty. Frequently the only present recourse for students in this untenable situation is to begin all over again by taking the entrance exam in the new faculty or department with little credit being awarded for past work in another field.[41]

In summary, a more broadly constructed education during the early years of university training could represent a much more flexible and efficient allocation of human resources in Brazilian universities. Premature specialization, in addition to compromising the chance for a richer educational background for the student, also incurs a high social cost through making it more costly and difficult for the schooling system to adjust to the shortages and surpluses for various types of specialized manpower that invariably occur in the process of rapid and uneven economic growth.[42]

The Departmental Concept

The tradition of the *catedrático* chair professor has been formally abolished in all the emerging university statutes, and departments have been created in which academic and educational policy can now become a collective concern for all grades of professors in the teaching body. As a result, a more centralized and coherent departmental policy could presumably emerge than was characteristic in the former more decentralized *catedrático* tradition where the chair professor ruled as an absolute monarch in his own specialty.

This change represents an improvement over the former system,

41. For a personal commentary underscoring this drawback, see Mario Henrique Simonsen, *Brasil 2001, op, cit.,* p. 232.

42. An informative discussion of the social costs of premature specialization can be found in Marc Blaug, "Approaches to Educational Planning," The Economic Journal, Vol. LXXVII, No. 306 (June 1967) esp. p. 277.

and, in those faculties with an aggressive group of young junior professors, departmental policy is more open to their views and concerns than was possible in the earlier tradition. Nevertheless, certain questions remain. It would appear that the influence of the former *catedráticos* (as a class or group) has been carefully preserved in many new departmental arrangements through giving each of them a full vote in departmental affairs, while the lower professorial ranks have only one voting representative for each rank. This unnecessarily limits the influence of younger faculty members in departmental affairs, a particularly unwelcome prospect in view of the fact that within the university community the spirit and drive to reform the current out-dated university structure has invariably come from the younger and not the older members of the teaching body.

Another undersirable feature that has been associated with the creation of departments within some former faculties is that of using the organizational concept of a department so loosely that too many departments are created. This in effect preserves some of the older *cadeiras* or chair-professor specialties under the guise of a department. When this is combined with the aforementioned restrictive voting arrangements, former chair professors or small groups of them are in a position to preserve their former status and influence.[43]

Finally, the principle of rewarding excellence and guaranteeing quality instruction in the university would be better served if arbitrary procedures forcing outstanding young men to remain in each professorial rank for specified time periods regardless of their accomplishments and publications were relaxed. This becomes important as many foreign-trained Brazilian scholars return to Brazil with outstanding credentials far superior to the elders in their department. Arbitrarily holding them in the lower echelons of the department unnecessarily compromises the contribution they could be making to departmental affairs.

Outside Community Influence

Among groups interested in university reform, some feel that the new statutes give insufficient attention to developing a strong role for the outside community in the affairs of the university. Brazilian universities have traditionally been quite inbred. Geographical mobility and turnover among professors has always been low. Professors, ad-

43. This practice appears to be characteristic of the law schools' adaptation to the emerging reform statutes.

ministrators, and rectors are frequently graduates of the same university in which they work. Thus all past practices and tradition have tended to reinforce an academic inbreeding which unfortunately has had a tendency to segregate the university from significant outside influence.

Since much of the support for university reform has come from outside the university proper, and, further, since much of the spirit of the current measures has centered around putting the university in a better position to contribute to the community at large, recommendations have been made to permit a wider participation within the governing councils of the university for representatives from interested outside entities actively engaged in promoting social and economic development. It is argued that the nonacademic vision of these prospective representatives derived from valuable executive responsibility in public or private enterprises dealing with the problems of change would presumably prove invaluable in helping the university adjust to the changing needs of society. At first glance, there is much to be said for this view. Certainly the entrepreneurial drive and imagination of many of these men would be a welcome change, offering a more innovative managerial perspective to the problems of change within the university environment than what has been characteristic in the past. There is no sure formula, however, that would guarantee that the particular representatives from these outside entities and associations would be men of this caliber and vision. It is equally possible that these posts could be used for political interference and anti-intellectual attacks upon the proper role and function of the university. In view of this, the universities are acting cautiously by admitting only a limited number of outside representatives on the *conselhos universitários*.

To the extent that there will be significant curriculum reform and improved teaching methods affecting the substance as well as the form of general and professional education, this will more likely be brought about, not so much through direct outside representation within the university councils, as through the combined influence of the growing number of effective full-time undergraduate professors in selected priority areas and programs, and the long-run impact of the regional graduate centers with their more up-to-date and internationally trained full-time staffs. Moreover, it is already evident that through the close co-operation and special arrangements between these graduate centers and a growing number of development-oriented public agencies, these centers are already performing a valuable role in acting as a bridge between the university and the outside community. This outside influence properly filtered through the more acceptable professional medium of the graduate centers can possibly play an increasingly important role in inducing the undergraduate faculties to adapt to the changing times by engaging in a more pragmatic and productive reorientation of their outmoded administrative procedures, imperfect departmental organization, and weak curricula.

Finally, as pointed out in an earlier section, the political events from 1964 to the present have introduced a more authoritarian rule for the country. This has inevitably had its effect on the university community, as various programs have been discontinued and professors have been dismissed or forcibly retired on the grounds that they were political risks. Academic freedom has thus been brushed aside. Two points can be made here. First, it is lamentable and, very likely, counterproductive that the state has felt it necessary to interfere in this arbitrary fashion in the university setting. Teaching and research would be much better served in an environment more securely anchored to the principle of free and open academic inquiry and criticism. Unfortunately, this principle is difficult to nurture in a society that does not also encourage a more open and democratic political system. Secondly, however, it is important to recognize that outside political interference has always been present to some degree within the imperfectly developed Brazilian university milieu. Abrupt changes in national leaders and political institutions are frequently reflected in the university community in most developing countries such as Brazil. In the present context, however, with the prospects for meaningful change in the universities present, government officials should be forcefully reminded that effective university reform will be difficult to promote unless the more arbitrary acts of interference with academic freedom are held to a minimum if not eliminated altogether.

Conclusions

It is clear that education in Brazil has become an area that is too important to be left to educators alone. Educated manpower is now a major concern of the technocrats responsible for economic planning in the country and, consequently, their counsel will very likely grow in importance in future policy measures affecting higher education.

The growing tendency to analyze education as an economic good has been helpful in forcefully underlining the widespread inefficiency and inequity in the past practice of financing and administering higher education in Brazil and underscoring the need to focus on quality as well as quantity. In line with this trend, it is hopeful to note that not only in the Ministry of Planning, but also and more importantly, within the Ministry of Education itself, measures are being taken for the first time to investigate the questions of allocation and efficiency within higher education and the effective use of the output of this sector within the professional labor markets of the country.

The creation of graduate centers in several universities in the late sixties has for the first time introduced meaningful research and quality instruction in various disciplines important for the development needs of Brazil. Further, these centers are, at the moment, the most appropriate vehicle permitting constructive outside influence to enter the university milieu. The degree to which these centers can exercise a decisive influence on the undergraduate faculties, however, depends upon the degree to which the new university statutes will permit the faculties to take advantage of these new approaches to professional training.

Finally, it is clear that the Brazilian universities, which were incapable of making any major contribution toward promoting and supporting social and economic growth in the sixties, had to change. Recognition of this fact led to university reform. As outlined above, there is reason to believe that, at least in the short run, the reform will not eliminate some of the negative features of the earlier tradition. Nevertheless, the current reform measures should not be looked upon as a single event never subject to change but as an ongoing process. Furthermore, in the medium and long run the growth of the regional graduate centers and meaningful full-time teaching in selected priority undergraduate disciplines and programs will exercise a crucial role in attracting a much more professionally competent and talented group of individuals into the university community than ever before. These people will undoubtedly play an important, perhaps a decisive, role in pressuring the more reluctant university administrators and department heads to eliminate the remaining negative features of the earlier tradition and accept the challenge of effectively reforming Brazilian universities in the seventies.

9 EMILIO WILLEMS

The Rise of a Rural Middle Class
in a Frontier Society

CONCENTRATION OF land ownership among the members of a small privileged class has long been recognized as one of the most serious problems hampering the development of rural Latin America. The dominance of the *latifundio* or large agricultural estate is believed to be causally related to the widespread occurrence of the *minifundio*, an agricultural holding too small to provide an adequate level of living for a single family. Holders of *minifundios* are believed to share much of the poverty of the rural proletariat, and most agragrian structures of Latin America are depicted as two-class societies "with a small elite at the upper extreme and a huge mass of impoverished, largely dependent people at the other, the two being separated by a vast void in all parts of the range that would correspond to middle-class status."[1]

In a recent Unesco-sponsored publication, Jacques Lambert accused the large rural estate, the *latifundio*, of monopolizing all avail-

Field work leading to this chapter was conducted in 1967 and financed by the National Science Foundation (Grant No. G-1444). The author is indebted to Professor Leo C. Rigsby for advice on statistical procedures and to Kenneth Westhues for an earlier version of that part of the chapter dealing with census data on size distribution of landholdings.

1. T. Lynn Smith, *Brazil, Peoples and Institutions*, p. 301.

able land and of thus depriving Latin America of the social advantages of the frontier. According to Lambert, frontier situations are "exceptional" in Latin America, but where they occur, as in northern Paraná (Brazil), they have had "the same economic and social value as in the United States."[2]

The alleged monopolization of land resources by the agricultural estate appears to be a recurrent theme in the literature on Latin America. Writing on Middle America and the Antilles, Wolf and Mintz, drawing on earlier statements by Sergio Bagú and E. Gruening, noted that "by monopolizing the supply of land in its immediate vicinity," the *hacienda* prevented the agricultural labor force from "seeking economic independence . . . by cultivating land not owned or controlled by the hacienda."[3]

Referring to Brazil, T. Lynn Smith, in unison with Brazilian reformers, remarked that large landholders withheld lands from production "so that they might have enough to distribute among their numerous heirs."[4]

Whatever the frequency, geographic distribution, intended functions, and social significance of these trends, they should not prevent the researcher from perceiving and evaluating divergent developments. Those who accept the unqualified view that all agricultural resources of Latin America remain in the grip of a few powerful and wealthy feudal barons will perhaps experience surprise in learning that, under certain circumstances, land ownership may not be an undivided blessing and that it may be economically more advantageous to divide the land and sell it piecemeal in the open market. Furthermore, the acquisition of large tracts of land, developed or undeveloped, for the sole purpose of parceling and offering it for sale may become a more profitable enterprise than its retention and cultivation. This is exactly what has happened, at least in Brazil. In some regions this kind of enterprise has been extensive enough to make it appear a major factor in redistribution of land.

The history of coffee agriculture in Brazil, particularly in the state of São Paulo, clearly shows at least two main factors determining the spontaneous fragmentation of many *latifundia* and their conversion into numerous smaller holdings. First, the diminishing yields of the

2. Jacques Lambert, "Requirements for Rapid Economic and Social Development: The View of the Historian and Sociologist," p. 59.
3. Eric R. Wolf and Sidney W. Mintz, "Haciendas and Plantations in Middle America and the Antilles," p. 389.
4. Smith, *Brazil, Peoples and Institutions*, p. 353.

older plantations and the availability of huge tracts of cheap virgin land elsewhere gradually, but ineluctably, led to the abandonment of the exhausted estates and their division into smaller holdings. In a classic study, Sergio Milliet retraced this development and its impact on land ownership.[5]

Entering São Paulo from the north, coffee agriculture invaded the central region of the state and gradually moved toward the west during the last hundred and fifty years. The settlement of northern and western Paraná appears to be part and parcel of this process.

Second, in the late twenties and thirties, unceasing expansion of coffee production in Brazil and elsewhere led to a highly critical situation of the world market. Coffee prices dropped to a level that spelled disaster to many plantation owners and determined the fragmentation and piecemeal sale of many of the less productive *fazendas*. Far from monopolizing the land, many big owners thus had to relinquish their holdings, and since these could usually not be sold in one piece—either because the soil was too impoverished to allow the traditional one-crop system or because coffee agriculture had ceased to offer profitable investment opportunities—they had to be divided and sold in small or medium-sized lots.

Third, urban development, particularly since 1930, has been successfully competing with commercial agriculture for scarce capital resources. Urban real estate, especially high-rise office and apartment buildings, have been offering investment opportunities far more attractive than agricultural estates. Even in northern Paraná, a partial shift from rural to urban investments is clearly visible in such cities as Londrina and Maringá.

The emergence of a veritable retail market for agricultural land tends to produce a mobilizing impact on the society, both in the geographical and social sense of the term, *if* the land is totally undeveloped and *if* enough of it has been amassed to generate its primary occupation on a large scale. Wherever these conditions prevail they will be referred to in terms of frontier, meaning a society starting from scratch and taking advantage of economic opportunities not to be found in "older" areas. In this sense, Northern Paraná has been a frontier but not a "hollow" or a "big man's" frontier. By this, Benjamin Higgins means the sort of frontier condition which leads to the formation of large estates offering no chances whatever to smaller operators. According to Higgins, the Latin American frontier was

5. Sergio Milliet, *Roteiro do Café e outros ensaios*, p. 31 ff.

exactly the opposite of the North American frontier which was a "small man's frontier."[6] The assumption that Northern Paraná does not conform to Higgins's classification constitutes one of several hypotheses to be tested in the present chapter.

It was noted initially that Lambert recognized Northern Paraná as the only Brazilian frontier offering opportunities similar to those of the North American frontier. Although it is beyond the scope of this chapter to disprove Lambert's implication that frontier conditions in the American sense did not prevail elsewhere in Brazil, it ought to be pointed out briefly that genuine frontier conditions existed in those regions of western São Paulo that were named after the railway companies which performed a crucial role in the "opening" of the west. (Alta Sorocabana, Alta Paulista, Noroeste, Alta Araraquarense). The frontier conditions of this huge area adjacent to Northern Paraná were studied in *Pionniers et Planteurs de São Paulo* by the French geographer Pierre Monbeig whose findings demonstrate that considerable upward social mobility accompanied the occupation of that area.[7] Genuine frontier conditions are by no means confined to Paraná and São Paulo. They existed or still exist in Minas Gerais, in Western Santa Catarina, in the northern state of Maranhão, and along the new highway linking Brasília to Belém. In fact, as Charles Wagley pointed out, the vast fringe area of sparsely populated Central Brazil bears frontier character.[8] Any one of these areas could have been chosen for the kind of study proposed here. Our final choice of Northern Paraná was largely determined by two facts: recurrent contact with the area since 1936 and the recency of its occupation in comparison with most frontier areas of western São Paulo.

It is assumed here that the availability of land resources combined with frontier opportunities may lead to the emergence of a rural middle class largely through the mechanisms of upward social mobility. Although this chapter is concerned with facts referring to the existence and relative size of such a class rather than with mobility processes, it ought to be noted that in Northern Paraná upward mobility has been common enough to be taken for granted by the local society. As a matter of fact, among 900 high school students whose

6. Benjamin Higgins, "Requirements for Rapid Economic Development in Latin America: The View of an Economist," p. 171

7. Pierre Monbeig, *Pionniers e Planteurs de São Paulo*, pp. 145-146 and passim.

8. Charles Wagley, *Introduction to Brazil*, p. 88 ff.

fathers owned or operated farms, more than 75 percent were found to belong to upwardly mobile families.[9]

Frontier opportunities mean little in a society that feels strongly attached to the land and therefore disinclined to face the uncertainties and risks of long-distance migration. Far from clinging to the land, Brazilians, particularly rural Brazilians, migrate often and easily. Higgins pointed out that "the internal migrants constituted 8.5 percent of the total population in 1940 and 10.3 percent in 1950."[10] These figures, suggesting "that the Brazilian population is one of the most mobile in the world,"[11] do not indicate a new trend but merely a new version of a cultural tradition that is as old as Brazilian history.[12] The many facets and historical manifestations of this migratory pattern cannot be explained merely in terms of rural poverty. Monbeig and others before him noted that the flow of migrants who opened the west of São Paulo and the north of Paraná was not exclusively composed of poor, landless proletarians but that all social classes participated, to some extent, in the westward movement.[13] So far as Paraná is concerned, the census of 1940 registered among its 1,236,276 inhabitants 214,256 who had been born in other states. In 1950, this figure had risen to 661,456 or 31.2 percent of a total population of 2,115,547.[14] At least 90 percent of these migrants settled in Northern Paraná.

The extraordinary spatial mobility of the rural working class suggests the existence of an excessively large labor force in search of scarce employment opportunities. Actually, it is a well-known fact that rural labor has been chronically and often critically scarce in most regions of Brazil, particularly in the rapidly developing south. Frontier areas cannot rely on surplus labor, but they have to compete with "older" regions by paying substantially higher wages and by offering other contractual advantages which, from the standpoint of the laborer, often constitute the difference between stagnation and betterment.[15] In predominantly coffee-growing Northern Paraná, the main contractual advantage is the right of the worker to raise other crops

---

9. Processes and mechanisms of social mobility in Northern Paraná will be analyzed in another work I am preparing with Jack C. Dailey.

10. Higgins, p. 202.

11. *Ibid.*, p. 203.

12. Roberto C. Simonson, "Recursos econômicos e movimentos das populações."

13. Monbeig, p. 107 ff.

14. Higgins, pp. 201-203.

15. Monbeig, pp. 139-140.

in the open spaces among the rows of coffee trees. Many rural workers entered the area as *empreiteiros* or contractors who assume the
responsibility of starting a coffee *fazenda* from scratch by clearing the
ground, planting the young trees, and tending them during the first
years while no yield is to be expected. Thus, most of the virgin soil
can be used for raising such crops as corn, beans, and manioc. Assisted by wife and children, a frugal worker may be able to amass, within
a few years, the amount of cash necessary to make a down payment
on a small piece of land. Often enough, the land owner seeks to attract scarce labor by providing a piece of land for the exclusive cultivation by each worker, or he may offer sharecropping arrangements
to some of his workers. All these different mechanisms constitute steps
on the ladder leading to land ownership. But one should never lose
sight of the fact that they are effective only within the context of an
agricultural frontier.

Before 1920, the entire northern and western regions of the state
of Paraná were virtually uninhabited and completely undeveloped.
Beginning in 1919, the state government issued a series of decrees selling large tracts of land to individuals or private companies with the
understanding that the land be divided and sold to agricultural set-
tlers. Between 1919 and 1940, eleven major land concessions were
made, the largest by far being the Companhia de Terras Norte do
Paraná (henceforward called the "Company"). Established with predominantly British capital, this company purchased, between 1925
and 1927, approximately 3,000,000 acres or almost 4,700 square miles
of virgin land, either directly from the state of Paraná or from private
concessionaries most of whom held titles of dubious value. The quality of the soil in most of Northern Paraná is exceptionally high, probably higher than in any other region of Brazil, yet to attract large
numbers of buyers, the Company had to invest heavily in the development of an infrastructure designed to link the region to the existing
markets, mostly São Paulo and, to a lesser extent, the southern region
of Paraná. As a matter of fact, from the very beginning the Company
engaged in long-range planning the dimensions and thoroughness of
which seem to have no precedent in Latin America. The Brazilian and
British directors of the project visualized a densely populated area
developing along the axis of a railway and internally articulated by a
network of roads facilitating the outflow of agricultural products.
Several urban centers were projected dividing the area into local ecological systems. Among these centers, four cities (Londrina, Maringá,

Cianorte, and Umuarama) were planned for a population of 100,000 or more.

The settlement policy pursued by the Company was designed to attract large numbers of buyers, few of whom could afford to purchase more than a relatively small tract. In fact, it was the stated purpose of the Company to encourage small and medium-sized holdings by extending credit to purchasers who could afford no more than the required down payment. Thus, the average size of the lots sold by the Company over a period of thirty years was 14.6 alqueires, or approximately 87 acres.

In 1928, the Company purchased the stock of a railway which a few major landholders had constructed between Ourinhos and Cambará. Located just across the state line separating Paraná from São Paulo, Ourinhos was already served by the Sorocabana railway which links São Paulo city (and Santos) to a prosperous agricultural region named after the railway it serves. In 1929, the Companhia de Terras Norte do Paraná began to extend the existing twenty nine kilometers of track toward the Tibagi River which was reached in 1932. In 1935, the first train arrived in Londrina, the administrative seat of the Company and the first of the projected cities. Construction continued without interruption, and in 1943 the line reached Apucarana, 269 kilometers west of Ourinhos. Apucarana has remained the terminal point of the line, which in recent years has lost much of its former importance owing to the construction of modern highways articulating North Paraná with the São Paulo highway systems, with Curitiba, the state capital, and with Paranaguá, the seaport of the state.

Before selling the first land, the Company began to build local roads following the ridges of the rolling countryside. These roads constituted the axes along which the individual tracts were surveyed and lined up in such a way that each property had access to a road and to one of the numerous small streams following the valley bottom. From the very beginning, the Company adhered strictly to the policy of selling holdings which had already been provided with these facilities. Each local road system articulated all agricultural holdings with the next town and its railway facilities. Road construction proceeded at the average rate of 300 kilometers per year until it reached, in 1967, the total of 5,000 kilometers.

The third major component of the infrastructure provided by the Company was the hydroelectric power plant of Apucarana, part of which became operational shortly after 1950.

The Companhia de Terras Norte do Paraná was not an immediate success. The worldwide depression of 1930 seriously affected the Brazilian economy. Prices of agricultural products were extremely low, and large quantities of coffee—unsalable in the world market—were burned. Under these conditions it seemed most unlikely that large-scale enterpreneurs should risk scarce capital resources to invest in unpromising agricultural ventures. This was perhaps one of the reasons why the Company concentrated on the almost untapped market of people willing to risk their modest savings or proceeds from the sale of impoverished land owned elsewhere in Brazil in a frontier venture which, to judge from rumors and posters, seemed promising enough. It is perhaps significant that the first four land sales in 1930 were made to Japanese immigrants who, over the years, entered the area in increasing numbers to constitute, at the present time, the only sizable ethnic minority of the region.

Table 1 shows the percentage of plots of four size divisions sold in each of six time-intervals and the whole 35-year period between 1930 and 1965. The results of the table are perhaps more meaningful if expressed in acres: 54 percent of all plots sold by the Company have been fewer than fifty acres in size, 81 percent fewer than one hundred acres, 88 percent fewer than 125 acres, and only 12 percent more than 125 acres.

TABLE 1
PERCENT DISTRIBUTION OF LAND SALES IN SIZE CATEGORIES,
NORTH PARANA LAND COMPANY

| | Hectares | | | | | |
	1-20	20-40	40-50	50+	total	holdings
1930-35	45.8	34.7	8.1	11.4	100.0	N= 2,744
1936-40	53.0	31.5	7.2	8.4	100.0	N= 3,828
1941-45	45.8	34.2	7.7	12.1	100.0	N= 9,436
1946-50	34.1	28.9	11.0	26.0	100.0	N= 8,646
1951-55	67.5	25.1	3.9	3.4	100.0	N= 6,798
1956-65	82.5	13.5	1.6	2.3	100.0	N= 5,908
TOTAL	53.6	27.8	6.8	11.8	100.0	N=37,360

Source: Company records.

The question may be raised, however, whether the initial prevalence of medium-sized and small holdings was not followed by a phase of concentration of rural property in the hands of relatively few land owners. There is also a possibility that while most of the plots remain of small size, their total area may be small compared with that of the smaller percentage of large holdings. Furthermore, what is the legal status of the holder with regard to the land he occupies? If absentee ownership prevails, a few proprietors may own a number of farms entrusted to administrators or leased to tenant farmers.

To find out about the present situation, the most recent census data (1960) were used. Since the divisions used in the census are not coterminous with the boundaries of the area developed by the Company, precise measurement is impossible. The major tract of land initially purchased by the Company includes all or portions of thirty one *municipios* in 1960 (Alto Paraná, Araruna, Cianorte, Cruzeiro do Oeste, Cruzeiro do Sul, Engenheiro Beltrão, Floraí, Jussara, Marialva, Mandaguarí Maringá, Nova Esperança, Paraná City, Rondon, São Jorge, São João do Caioá, Terra Boa, Apucarana, Arapongas, Astorga, Bom Sucesso, Cambé, Ibiporã, Iguaraçú, Jandaia do Sul, Lobato, Rolândia, Sabaudia, Santa Fé, and Londrina).

To get as precise figures as possible on the Company area, thirteen of these municipios which also include land not developed by the Company were omitted in the collection of data (Rondon, Cruzeiro do Oeste, Araruna, Engenheiro Beltrão, Paraná City, Lobato, Cruzeiro do Sul, Astorga, Iguaraçú, Apucarana, Santa Fé and Ibiporã). Hereafter, "Company Municipios, 1960" refers to all those except the thirteen just named.

Table 2 shows the percentages of holdings and area, first in eleven size categories, as reported by the census, and then collapsed into three size categories. The census categories were maintained on all tables to show the degree of differentiation in the size distribution of the holdings which obviously stands in sharp contrast to the facile dichotomization, *minifundio* versus *latifundio*, that is supposed to charac-

TABLE 2

PERCENT OF HOLDINGS AND OF AREA IN SIZE CATEGORIES
LAND COMPANY MUNICIPIOS, 1960

Number of Holdings: 32,193
Area in Hectares: 863,584

| | Hectares | | | | | | | | | | |
	0-1	1-2	2-5	5-10	10-20	20-50	50-100	100-200	200-500	500-1000	1000+	Total
Holdings	.2	.7	13.0	22.7	32.6	23.2	4.5	1.8	1.0	.2	.1	100.0
Area	.0	.0	2.1	6.6	16.7	26.2	12.0	9.3	10.7	6.2	10.2	100.0

	0-20	20-200	200+	Total
Holdings	69.2	29.5	1.3	100.0
Area	25.4	47.5	27.1	100.0

Source: *Recenseamento do Brasil de 1960*

terize the agrarian situation of Brazil. Holdings under five hectares which could conceivably be classified as *minifundios* represent no more than 13.9 percent of all holdings and 2.1 percent of the total area. Yet these holdings do not generate the social problems usually associated with the concept of the *minifundio,* mainly because virtually all of them are truck farms located in the vicinity of local urban markets. Furthermore, most of their owners are part-time farmers who live in town and have other sources of income.

Holdings between 10 and 20 hectares constitute the largest percentage of all farms, and the area they occupy is the second largest of all size categories. Together with all holdings under ten hectares they represent 69.2 percent of all farms covering 25.4 percent of the area under scrutiny. All these holdings may be safely classified as small by local standards.

Before approaching the concept of the medium-sized holding, it may be preferable to consider briefly the less controversial concept of the large holding. The *fazenda* Boa Vista in the municipio of Londrina may serve as an example of what locally is considered a large holding. It covers 368 hectares and employs forty workers under a full-time administrator. One hundred fifty thousand coffee trees produce about 25,000 sacks of coffee in "good" years. As do most large *fazendas,* Boa Vista has its own plant to process and classify coffee. Of course, Boa Vista is not a *latifundio,* and its owners are certainly not members of the landholding "aristocracy."

By local standards, it is probably correct to classify any holding measuring more than 200 hectares as "large," although there are transitional zones from one size category to the next which may be expected to raise some doubt regarding classification. It seems quite conceivable that some local people should be inclined to consider a holding of 200 hectares as medium-sized, and one of 20 hectares as small, but on the whole holdings of more than 20 and fewer than 200 hectares are locally defined as medium-sized. It appears that 29.5 percent of the farms and 47.5 percent of the land are in the medium-sized category, and no more than 1.3 percent of all holdings occupying 27.1 percent of the land may be classified as large.

The meaning of the findings reported on Table 2 is also clear in comparison to those of Table 3 showing the size distribution of land in Latin America. Here not 73 percent but 69 percent of the holdings are of fewer than twenty hectares in size, and these holdings (of fewer than twenty acres) account for 25.4 percent, rather than 3.7 percent, of the land. In northern Paraná, holdings measuring between

TABLE 3
DISTRIBUTION OF LAND IN LATIN AMERICA

| Size-groupings | Holdings | | | | Acre | |
	No. (000)	% of total	Cumula-tive %	Hectares (mill.)	% of total	Cumula-tive %
Below 20 hectares	5,445	72.6	72.6	27.0	3.7	3.7
20-100	1,350	18.0	90.6	60.6	8.4	12.1
100-1,000	600	8.0	98.6	166.0	22.9	35.0
Above 1,000	105	1.4	100.0	470.0	65.0	100.0
TOTALS	7,500	100.0	—	723.6	100.0	—

Source: Jacques Chonchol, "Land Tenure and Development in Latin America," In Claudio Veliz, ed., Obstacles to Change in Latin America, (New York: Oxford University Press, 1965) p. 82.

20 and 100 hectares account for 27.7 percent of the holdings and 38.2 percent of the land, while in Latin America 18 percent of the holdings and only 8.4 of the land ranked in this category. In Northern Paraná holdings of more than 100 hectares account not for 8 percent of the holdings and 88 percent of the land but for 3.2 percent of the holdings and 36.4 percent of the land. The very large estates of more than 1,000 hectares (latifundia proper), which account for 1.4 percent of the holdings and 65 percent of the land in Latin America as a whole, account for only .1 percent of the holdings and 10.2 percent of the area in the Company municipios. It is obvious then that the over-all statistics regarding distribution of land ownership in Latin America, and the stereotype in which such summary statistics result, do not fit the case of this portion of Paraná. Not only is the population of small landholders numerically large as a proportion of the rural landholders, but they also control most of the land.

Since the Company pursued the policy of favoring small landholdings, it seems worth while to examine the actual effects of such a policy and to determine the distribution of land ownership outside the Company area. For this purpose, 69 municipios were scrutinized. All are located in northern and western Paraná, and together they constitute almost the entire regional frontier not controlled by the Company (Table 4). Here 58.7 percent of the holdings making up 15.4 percent of the land measure fewer than twenty hectares. These figures are considerably lower than the corresponding ones on Table 2. The opposite is true of the medium-sized farms measuring from 20 to 200 hectares, for here 39.1 percent of the holdings account for 56.2 percent of the land. So far as holdings of more than 200 hectares are

TABLE 4
PERCENT OF HOLDINGS AND OF AREA IN SIZE CATEGORIES
69 MUNICIPIOS OUTSIDE COMPANY AREA, 1960

Number of Holdings: 125,262
Area in Hectares: 4,195,244

Size categories	0-1	1-2	2-5	5-10	10-20	20-50	50-100	100-200	200-500	500-1000	1000+	Total
Holdings	.2	1.1	17.4	16.4	23.6	28.5	7.6	3.0	1.6	.4	.2	100.0
Area	.0	.0	2.0	3.8	9.6	26.6	17.0	12.6	15.4	8.0	5.0	100.0

Size categories	0-20	20-200	200+	
Holdings	58.7	39.1	2.2	100.0
Area	15.4	56.2	28.4	100.0

Source: *Recenseamento do Brasil de 1960*

concerned, there is little difference between the figures of Table 2 and those of Table 4.

The differences found between the two areas with regard to the relative position of the small holding suggest that the policy of the Company has indeed been effective, but the point will be taken up again in connection with the *development* of size distribution of farms in both areas.

The census also offers information concerning the legal status of the occupant with regard to the land: whether he is owner, administrator, renter, or squatter who pays no rent. Since this question refers directly to the hypothesis that the area is dominated by small and medium-sized independent holdings, the status of the occupant, even though the plot be small, appears to be important. The most secure would presumably be owners, the least secure the squatters, with administrators and renters forming an intermediate group the characteristics of which could only be determined by more extensive research. Table 5 shows the size and area distribution of land holdings by status of occupant. Fifty-two percent of the holdings and 46 percent of the land is owner-occupied. The mean size of such holdings is about sixty acres. This category, which forms a majority in the area, seems comparable to what has been the dominant pattern of land ownership in the United States: the family farm. The larger farms tend to be controlled by administrators, but these account for less than one tenth of the holdings and less than a third of the land. The remainder of the land and holdings is in the hands of renters, except for a small and insignificant number of squatters who control less than one percent of the land.

Outside the Company area, the proportion of owners is 49.9 per-

TABLE 5

DISTRIBUTION IN PERCENT OF LANDHOLDINGS AND
AREA BY STATUS OF OCCUPANT LAND COMPANY
MUNICIPIOS, 1960

Total Number of Holdings: 32,193
Area in Hectares: 863,584

	Owner	Adminis-trator	Renter	Squatter	Total
Holdings	51.8	8.6	37.7	1.9	100.0
Area	46.3	31.3	21.4	1.0	100.0
Mean Size (ha)	24.0	97.4	15.2	13.4	

Source: *Recenseamento do Brasil de 1960*

cent and the land they control amounts to almost 51 percent (Table
6) of the total. These proportions are only slightly different from
those prevailing in the Company area. The role of the administrator,
however, is essentially less important than on Company land. Here
only 5.7 percent of the holdings comprising 22.1 percent of the land
are controlled by administrators. Even more significant is the difference regarding the role of renters. Here only 21.0 percent in contrast
to 37.7 percent of the holdings are occupied by renters, and the area
controlled by these accounts for only 6.6 percent of the land, in contrast to 21.4 percent reported for the Company area. The very high
percentage of occupants classified as squatters and the large area controlled by these—more than one fifth of the total acreage—can only
mean that these squatters have not been able to obtain titles to the
land they occupy. This is not surprising in view of the fact that much
land in northern and western Paraná has been under litigation. The

TABLE 6

DISTRIBUTION IN PERCENT OF LANDHOLDINGS AND AREA
BY STATUS OF OCCUPANT IN 69 MUNICIPIOS OUTSIDE
COMPANY AREA, 1960

Number of Holdings: 126,504
Total Area in Hectares: 4,636,435

	Owner	Adminis-trator	Renter	Squatter	Total
Holdings	49.9	5.7	21.0	23.4	100.0
Area	50.8	22.1	6.6	20.5	100.0

Source: *Recenseamento do Brasil de 1960*

Company, however, was very careful in securing clear titles to all land purchased before transacting any sale.

Even granting that independent landowners are relatively dominant in this area of Paraná, the question may be raised as to whether the pattern of land tenure has changed during the last thirty years or so. It seems conceivable, for example, that recent decades have seen a process of smaller holdings being gradually swallowed up by large holdings so that, although the 1960 distribution seems widely spread in comparison with that of Latin America as a whole, it may in fact be much more concentrated than it was in 1950 and 1940. The answer to this question may be provided by a comparative analysis of patterns of land ownership in 1940, 1950, and 1960. There is of course the problem of finding census divisions approximating the boundaries of the Company area, but it seems fairly certain that the entire developed area was in the *municipio* of Londrina in 1940, so that the 1940 census data for this single *municipio* have been used. With reference to the 1950 census, six *municipios* were used; Londrina, Cambé, Rolândia, Arapongas, Apucarana, and Mandaguarí. Since the Company had sold by 1950 several thousand more than the total of 10,635 holdings included in those six *municipios*, the estimate probably underrepresents the area we would wish to include. Since the use of these data, however, is comparative with respect to land ownership patterns, underrepresentation may not distort the results to be obtained.

Table 7 shows the number of holdings and the area they encompass for 1940, 1950, and 1960. The results are clear: land ownerships shifted from concentration in the upper categories to those in the lower. In 1940, holdings of more than 200 hectares accounted for 55.2 percent of the farmland; by 1950 their proportion had dropped to 48.3 percent; by 1960 to 27.1 percent. On the other hand, medium-sized holdings which accounted for only 39.3 percent of the land in 1940, and for 42.4 in 1950 included 47.5 percent of the farmland in 1960. And the area represented by small holdings grew from 5.5 percent in 1940 to 9.3 percent in 1950, and to 25.4 percent in 1960. One can only conclude that during the last thirty years the distribution of land in this area has gradually come to favor the small- and middle-range landholder, the man who owns a *sitio* rather than a *fazenda*. The trend existing in the former Company territory found an even stronger expression in the sixty-nine *municipios* outside that area. Table 8 shows that that the land made up of holdings of more than 200 hectares decreased from 63.1 percent in 1940 to 28.4 percent in

TABLE 7
PERCENT OF HOLDINGS AND AREA IN SIZE CATEGORIES
COMPANY MINICIPIOS, 1940, 1950, and 1960

Categories	Hectares											
	0-1	1-2	2-5	5-10	10-20	20-50	50-100	100-200	200-500	500-1000	1000+	Total
1960												
Holdings	.2	.7	13.0	22.7	32.6	23.2	4.5	1.8	1.0	.2	.1	100.0
Area	.0	.0	2.1	6.6	16.7	26.2	12.0	9.3	10.7	6.2	10.2	100.0
Categories	0-20						20-200			200+		
Holdings	69.2						29.5			1.3		100.0
Area	25.4						47.5			27.1		100.0
1950												
Holdings	1.0	4.4	26.3	27.7	24.2	13.3	2.3	.6	.2	.0	.0	100.0
Area	.0	.0	.4	1.5	7.4	19.5	12.0	10.9	14.7	6.9	26.7	100.0
Categories	0-20						20-200			200+		
Holdings	83.6						16.2			.2		100.0
Area	9.3						42.4			48.3		100.0
1940												
Holdings	.0	.1	3.7	5.7	27.2	38.7	11.8	6.3	4.2	1.3	1.0	100.0
Area	.0	.0	.1	.5	4.9	16.1	11.5	11.5	17.1	11.9	26.2	100.0
Categories	0-20						20-200			200+		
Holdings	36.7						56.8			6.5		100.0
Area	5.5						39.3			55.2		100.0

Source: *Recenseamentos do Brasil de 1940, 1950, 1960*

TABLE 8
PERCENT OF HOLDINGS AND AREA IN SIZE CATEGORIES
MUNICIPIOS OUTSIDE COMPANY AREA, 1940, 1950, and 1960

Categories	Hectares											
	0-1	1-2	2-5	5-10	10-20	20-50	50-100	100-200	200-500	500-1000	1000+	Total
1960												
Holdings	.2	1.1	17.4	16.4	23.6	28.5	7.6	3.0	1.6	.4	.2	100.0
Area	.0	.0	2.0	3.8	9.6	26.6	17.0	12.6	15.4	8.0	5.0	100.0
Categories	0-20						20-200			200+		
Holdings	58.7						39.1			2.2		100.0
Area	15.4						56.2			28.4		100.0
1950												
Holdings	.1	.3	5.4	9.4	22.6	37.6	11.1	7.7	3.9	1.0	.9	100.0
Area	.0	.0	.2	.9	4.2	15.4	10.9	13.8	15.9	9.2	29.5	100.0
Categories	0-20						20-200			200+		
Holdings	37.8						56.4			5.8		100.0
Area	5.3						40.1			54.6		100.0
1940												
Holdings	.0	.3	5.6	8.5	19.6	34.4	12.3	9.9	5.7	2.0	1.7	100.0
Area	.0	.0	.2	.6	2.8	11.0	8.8	13.5	17.7	13.1	32.3	100.0
Categories	0-20						20-200			200+		
Holdings	34.0						56.6			9.4		100.0
Area	3.6						33.3			63.1		100.0

Source: *Recenseamentos do Brasil de 1940, 1950, 1960*

1960. In the medium-sized range, the total area grew from 33.3 percent in 1940 to 56.2 percent in 1960. As in the former Company

territory, the number of middle-range holdings declined during that
period. The land controlled by small holders outside the Company
area increased from 3.6 percent in 1940 to 15.4 percent in 1960, a
growth rate almost identical with that of the Company territory.
There is no doubt, however, that by 1960 the relative importance of
small holdings in terms of both total area *and* number of farms was
more pronounced in the former Company territory than in the outside *municipios*. The opposite is true of medium-sized holdings.

Considering the comparative position of the two areas in 1940
and 1950, particularly in the latter year, it seems probable that the
differences revealed by the census data have some relationship with
the Company policy favoring the development of small holdings and
that the figures referring to 1960 continue to express the effectiveness of that policy.

Table 9 presents the distribution of land by the tenure status
of the occupant. Here several distinct trends are apparent. The relative importance of the independent landowner has declined in the
last twenty years as seen both in percent of holdings and percent of
the acreage for which owners are responsible. Nevertheless, the
owner-operated farm remains the dominant kind of tenure through
1960. Administrator-operated holdings rose in percent of the total
area between 1940 and 1950 but have declined somewhat since. Of
great interest is the increasing importance of renters, who accounted
for only 6.3 percent of the holdings in 1940 but for 37.7 percent in

TABLE 9

DISTRIBUTION IN PERCENT OF LAND HOLDINGS AND AREA BY
STATUS OF OCCUPANT, COMPANY MUNICIPIOS 1940, 1950, and 1960

	Owner	Adminis-trator	Renter	Squatter	Total	Total Number of Holdings and Total Area
1960						
Holdings	51.8	8.6	37.7	1.9	100.0	32,193
Area	46.3	31.3	21.4	1.0	100.0	863,584
1950						
Holdings	76.1	10.8	5.8	7.3	100.0	12,704
Area	55.1	38.2	3.1	3.6	100.0	714,835
1940						
Holdings	78.2	10.2	6.3	4.1	100.0	3,114
Area	64.6	25.8	4.5	5.1	100.0	231,897

Source: *Recenseamentos do Brasil de 1940, 1950, 1960*

1960, while the corresponding area increased from 4.5 percent in 1940 to 21.4 percent in 1960.

Outside Company territory, the percentage of owner-operated farms rose between 1940 and 1950 but has declined since. (Table 10) The area encompassed by these holdings declined after a sharp rise between 1940 and 1950 but was, in 1960, still slightly higher than in 1940. As in Company territory, owner-operated farms constitute by far the dominant form of tenure. Table 10 shows that administrator-operated holdings have declined rather drastically and consistently since 1940. Figures referring to the relative position of the renter reveal a sharply differing situation if we compare Tables 9 and 10. In 1940 the proportion of renters and of the land controlled by them was much higher than in Company territory. It decreased sharply in the following ten years. The figures of the 1960 census reveal a drastic rise, but the over-all position of the renter appears to be far less important than in Company territory. In fact, renters controlled only 6.6 percent of the land in contrast to the 21.4 percent they control in Company territory. Table 10 also shows that the squatter problem is a recent one, which means that it reached its present proportion as the frontier extended to the western part of Paraná.

TABLE 10

DISTRIBUTION IN PERCENT OF LAND HOLDINGS AND AREA BY STATUS OF OCCUPANT, MUNICIPIOS OUTSIDE COMPANY AREA, 1940, 1950, 1960

	Owner	Adminis-trator	Renter	Squatter	Total	Number of Holdings and Total Area
1960						
Holdings	49.9	5.7	21.0	23.4	100.0	126,504
Area	50.8	22.1	6.6	20.5	100.0	4,636,435
1950						
Holdings	76.0	10.3	5.6	8.1	100.0	17,387
Area	57.3	32.5	1.7	8.5	100.0	1,274,033
1940						
Holdings	71.2	11.5	14.9	2.4	100.0	7,134
Area	49.8	40.8	7.4	2.0	100.0	715,868

Source: *Recenseamentos do Brasil de 1940, 1950, 1960*

The results of our scrutiny of census data may be stated as follows:

In both areas small holdings of fewer than 20 hectares account for the largest proportion of land holdings, but there is a rather significant difference between Company area and outside *municipios*. In the Company territory, this size category accounts for one fourth of the land or 10 percent more than in the outside *municipios*.

In both areas, middle-range holdings measuring between 20 and 200 hectares account for the largest proportion of the land, but in the Company territory that proportion is significantly larger than in the outside *municipios*. The opposite is true regarding the number of medium-sized holdings.

The proportion of the land controlled by large holders is nearly the same in both areas, while the number of holdings is slightly higher outside Company territory.

In both areas the trend since 1940 has been away from large holdings and toward the small and medium-sized categories, at least so far as the proportion of the land is concerned. In both areas the number of medium-sized farms was significantly smaller in 1960 than in 1940. This means that the size of the holdings within the middle-range has become larger.

In both areas, the proportion of the land controlled by very small holdings (fewer than five hectares) has risen, but it is still negligible in the over-all picture.

In both areas, owner-operated holdings constitute the dominant form of land tenure.

In both areas since 1940, administrator-operated holdings have declined both in number and percentage of area.

In the Company territory, the number of renters has grown since 1950, and so has the area under their control. The same is true of outside *municipios*, but to a far lesser extent.

In both areas, the size of holdings is, on the average, largest for administrator-operated holdings, smaller for owner-operated holdings, and smallest for renter-operated holdings.

The facts presented here further indicate that there has been no attempt by any particular class or group to monopolize available land resources; the existing agrarian structure cannot be dichotomized in terms of the *latifundio-minifundio* stereotype; there is a relatively large rural middle class, something which is not widely believed to exist in Brazil, except perhaps in areas settled by migrants of recent European extraction. Now at least 70 percent of the local population is of Brazilian extraction, and the majority of these Brazilian migrants came from the neighboring state of São Paulo.

It would be arbitrary to draw rigid lines of demarcation identifying size categories of landholdings with social classes. It would be equally arbitrary, however, to disregard the size of holdings as unrelated to the existing class structure. True enough, a closer analysis not exclusively based on the size criterion may produce facts suggesting a higher degree of class differentiation. Economically, even small holdings represent an investment large enough to place most owners safely outside the range of the underprivileged strata of the local society. In 1967, the current market value of farmland, in the *municipio* of Londrina and neighboring areas, was $450 per acre. This was only one third of what the price of farmland had been in 1964. According to the deflated price of 1967, a farm of 20 hectares had a market value of $22,500. It would thus seem that the economic situation of the small holder in Northern Paraná does not fit the conventional image of the poverty-stricken *minifundista*.

Taking into account the facts that land values vary within the area under scrutiny and that many small holders are renters rather than owners, one may wish to exclude from middle-class status farmers with fewer than 20 hectares. If small holders and *fazendeiros* owning more than 200 hectares are excluded from the ranks of the middle class, a residual category is left which comprises 29.5 percent of all holdings and 47.5 percent of the Company area, as well as 39.1 percent of all holdings and 56.2 percent of the area outside Company territory. We propose to name this residual category the rural middle class of Northern Paraná.

This suggestion is based on the assumption that, in a broad sense, farm size and land tenure carry implications the sum total of which could be defined as rural middle-class culture. These implications presumably cover housing and consumption patterns, agricultural techniques, the interpretation and actual use of available institutional facilities, such as savings and commercial banks, cooperatives, agricultural extension services, schools and churches. Such a descriptive account would be the next logical step in a systematic study of the rural middle class of Northern Paraná.

REFERENCES

Chonchol, Jacques. "Land Tenure and Development in Latin America," in Claudio Veliz, ed., *Obstacles to Change in Latin America*. New York: Oxford University Press, 1965.

Higgins, Benjamin. "Requirements for Rapid Economic Development in Latin

America: The View of an Economist," in Egbert de Vries and José Medina Echavarria, ed., *Social Aspects of Economic Development in Latin America*, Vol. I, Paris: United Nations Educational, Scientific and Cultural Organization, 1963.

Instituto Brasileiro de Geografia e Estatística. Serviço Nacional de Recenseamento. *Recenseamento Geral do Brasil*, 1940, 1950, 1960.

Lambert, Jacques. "Requirements for Rapid Economic and Social Development: The View of the Historian and Sociologist," in Egbert de Vries and José Medina Echavarria, edgo, *Social Aspects of Economic Development in Latin America*. Vol. I. Paris: United Nations Educational, Scientific and Cultural Organization, 1963.

Milliet, Sergio. Roteiro do Café e outros ensaios, São Paulo: Coleção Departamento de Cultura, Vol. XXV, 1939.

Monbeig, Pierre. *Pionniers et Planteurs de São Paulo*. Paris: Librairie Armand Colin, 1952.

Simonson, Roberto C. "Recursos econômicos e movimentos das populações." *Revista Brasileira de Estatística*. Ano I, No. 2, 1940.

Smith, T. Lynn. *Brazil, People and Institutions*. Baton Rouge: Louisiana State University Press, 1963.

———. *Studies of Latin American Societies*. Garden City: Doubleday & Company, 1970.

Wagley, Charles. *Introduction to Brazil*. New York and London: Columbia University Press, 1963.

Wolf, Eric R., and Sidney W. Mintz. "Haciendas and Plantations in Middle America and the Antilles." *Social and Economic Studies*, Vol. VI: 380-412.

10 ROWAN IRELAND

The Catholic Church and Social Change in Brazil: An Evaluation

THIS CHAPTER does not represent a completed sociological investigation; it is a serious study in two senses. It was an attempt to summarize research up to the point that the major documentary sources easily available to the author had been consulted. It was meant, in this sense, to clarify questions for subsequent research: hence it is at once formal and opinionated. It was to be used as an instrument in further research. It was written as a sort of provocation and was presented to church leaders as a basis for subsequent interviewing.

In the early sixties the Catholic Church, as one of Brazil's great national institutions, was looked to by many observers, Catholic and non-Catholic, as a source of radical socioeconomic change. The hopes varied from an overoptimism that seems, in 1970, from an age past,[1] to the more cautious assessments of the kind that asked "how else but through the church can such-and-such a change be realized?"[2]

1. For an example from within the church, see the declarations by Padre Tiago G. Cloin, C.SS.R., written after he had seen the work being done in Natal from the mid-fifties on under the leadership of Bishop Dom Eugênio Sales, in *Revista da Conferência dos Religiosos do Brasil*, July 1962.

2. An example from a well-informed foreigner working in the Northeast before and for some time after the Revolution is Timothy L. Hogen, *A report on the Cooperative League in Northeast Brazil* (Chicago: The Cooperative League of the U.S.A., 1966).

As we shall see, even the cautious assessments of the early sixties seem, in many respects, overoptimistic in 1970. But this is not to deny the importance of an understanding of what was happening in the Catholic Church and of what it was doing as an active promotor of various types of socioeconomic change during the sixties. From the vantage point of the 1970s we can say that too many people hoped for too much not only from the church but also from other institutions and movements. But it may be that we can best attain perspective about the complexities of social change in Brazil in the sixties by pinpointing why the hopes were dashed and what sort of bases existed for entertaining any hopes at all.

The Catholic Church is involved in the complexities of social change in Brazil during the sixties in two ways. It is involved as an organization looming large in the shifting landscape of the old order. In this respect the church as an organization is worth study in itself, for in some of its features as a complex organization it reflects, even epitomizes, key features of the old order, while in others, it exemplifies organizational problems of adjustment to change. Analysis of the church as a changing organization should thus provide some of the data about change and resistance to change in Brazilian society at large. The church is involved in social change through the sixties as an active agent in the play of continuities and discontinuities in Brazilian society. Analysis of the church in this aspect, of its changing roles as a social institution, may help us clarify the sources and extent of some of the changes that were taking place in Brazilian society in the sixties.

The Catholic Church as Changing Organization

Change in the church, as in any other complex organization, may be analyzed through changes in key sets of relationships within the organization. In this case the following relationships will be identified:

—The relationships between the layers of the formal hierarchy—the degree of isolation of strata and the degree of centralization of authority.

—The relationships between groups on the same level of the formal hierarchy, performing the same or similar functions.

—The relationships between regional units of the organization.

—The orientation of elites in the organization vis-à-vis the environment.

Relationships between the layers of the formal hierarchy

During the sixties, elites in the church in Brazil, as elsewhere, became increasingly well aware of serious problems of communication between the several layers of the church's formal hierarchy. One of the structural correlates of lack of communication has been what Michel Crozier[3] in his analysis of problems of French bureaucracies, has called isolation of strata. Active pillars of the church remain aloof and incurious about the mass of practicing faithful. Active laity fail to share information with their priests, and priests make decisions without consulting laity. Priests conceal information from bishops and bishops deny participation by priests in diocesan decision-making.

The use of the present tense in the preceding paragraph may seem harsh to anyone acquainted with developments that have taken place in the Brazilian church during the last decade. Individual priests, such as Padre Geraldo Leite in the Recife-Olinda diocese, have even encouraged sharing of some clerical teaching functions with laymen from the lowest social strata. Especially since Vatican II, efforts have been made in many dioceses to provide at least the machinery for overcoming the isolation of the various strata. Priests within dioceses and regions can assemble regularly with their bishops. Some parishes have functioning lay councils which are supposed to advise and be consulted by priests on parish affairs. But studies completed by the church's Center of Religious Statistics and Social Research (CERIS)[4] reveal the limits of these organizational adjustments. Samples of priests in areas with some of the new machinery showed on the one hand a feeling of isolation from the hierarchy and on the other a strangely persistent clericalism in relation to lay-participation.[5] And, as we shall see, there are not nearly enough Padre Geraldos to go around.

Another structural correlate of the lack of communication has been centralization of decision-making. This centralization was exemplified in the sixties in relations between the bishops and Catholic

3. Michel Crozier, *The Bureaucratic Phenomenon* (Chicago: University of Chicago Press, 1964).
4. Pedro A. Ribeiro de Oliveira, *O papel do padre* (Rio de Janeiro: Centro de Estatística Religiosa e Investigações Sociais [CERIS], 1968) Vol. 1, chs. III and V.
Another study by Francisco Carta O.P., *A estrutura da igreja no Brazil* (Rio de Janeiro: CERIS, 1968) provides many examples of how the old isolation between the several layers continues to operate.
5. Pedro A. Ribeiro de Oliveira, Vol I, ch. V.

Action movements. As Catholic Action lay groups in the early sixties moved away from the militant evangelistic and apologetic emphases that they had had since the 1930s toward social and political involvement, there arose bitter squabbles between lay and clerical leaders. Most bishops insisted on maintaining the army-type centralized hierarchy that had been received from the militant Catholic Action movements of Europe in the thirties. This, among other things, insured decision-making on sociopolitical issues that was geared to papal directives that often distracted attention away from Brazilian sociopolitical realities. One outcome of the squabbles occurred in November 1966 when the student lay movements, Catholic University Youth (JUC) Young Catholic Students (JEC) and Independent Catholic Youth (JIC) cut themselves off from hierarchical control and the formal Brazilian Catholic Action organization (ACB). Dom Vincente Scherer, Cardinal-Archbishop of Porto Alegre, in a bitter radio broadcast, could not refrain from reminding the departing leaders that in cutting themselves adrift they were also forfeiting the use of church financial assistance.[6] This split in 1966 was no sudden break in previously good relationships. There was a major clash in 1962 between JUC and the hierarchy. After this conflict, many radicals left JUC and with other noncommunist radicals formed Ação Popular (AP). More conservative bishops were angered by the fact that many members of the Catholic youth organizations, against orders from the episcopal controllers of ACB, were active in AP, which seemed to become ever more Marxist.

In these examples, as in many others, centralization and isolation aid and abet one another. Those with central powers are unwilling or incapable of devolving them. Isolated groups lower down in the hierarchy see no incentive to share their resources of information and contacts. Similar patterns may be observed in certain Brazilian developmental agencies—always with the result of incapacity to cope with change.

But at least in the church, some bishops were conscious of the problem. The Plano de Emergência produced by the national conference of bishops (CNBB) in 1962 and the Plano de Pastoral de Conjunto published in 1966 consider the problem of formal discouragement of participation and responsibility at lower levels and call for organizational reforms to produce a more participatory church. More-

6. For a report see *Revista Ecclesiástica Brasileira* (REB henceforth) Vol. XXVII (March 1967), p. 187.

over, several movements within the church even before these plans were made departed radically from the old patterns of isolation and centralization. The outstanding example is the Movimento de Educação de Base (MEB) which grew out of experiments in Natal and Aracajú with radio literacy schools in the late fifties and was brought into being at the national level through an agreement between the CNBB and the Ministry of Education in 1961.[7]

From the start, MEB leaders were preoccupied with the need to escape organizational forms that plagued all Brazilian developmental agencies producing inflexibility and often re-introducing paternalism. And for once, not just in a few prize cases but on a wide scale, church leaders managed something more than statements of purpose. While possessing a sufficient national and state organization to tap and distribute resources from on high, MEB, until its demise after the revolution, functioned as a genuine grassroots organization. In 1963 it consisted of 60 systems (11 in 1961 and 31 in 1962). Most of these systems were organized around educational radio stations. Each system, through a local team, planned programs suited to the area and was responsible for training and selection of the "monitores" who actually ran the schools (there were 5,573 of these schools with 111,066 pupils in 1963). Reports of MEB activities reveal many defects and deficiencies. But the scheme seems always to have been consciously organized by church leaders to depend on voluntary grassroots initiative (from the monitors especially) to have done so actually, and to have reaped many of the intended benefits of this dependence. By 1963, monitors were coming from the ranks of graduates from the schools, and to the end, outside "animadores" who trained the monitors withdrew once present leaders were trained. By 1963 also, more conservative bishops were getting worried not only about decisions about reading materials, etc., being taken by some of the systems but about the very autonomy of the lower levels and the disturbing results of co-operation between elite lay groups and the schools. (In Pernambuco co-operation took place through MEB's relations with the Serviço de Extensão Cultural of the Federal Univer-

7. Details about collaboration between MEB units and other entities may be found in MEB Annual Reports. The 1963 report is especially inclusive. The most important link with professional educationalists was through Paulo Freire. Freire is by now quite well known in America for his theory and methods of literacy training. Texts by him and influenced by him were adopted by MEB. These texts reflect the theory that literacy training is most fruitfully combined with education towards understanding of the socioeconomic environment of the learner.

sity and through relations with Ação Popular). These reactions themselves are symptoms of the extent to which MEB challenged organizational customs. They also indicate that MEB was not the church.

Relationships between groups on the same hierarchical level

Even through the sixties, another type of structural isolation was
apparent in the Catholic Church. The church as organization may be
considered as divided within the several layers of the formal hierarchy into groups performing similar, even identical, functions, each
with its own hierarchy. Organizations may be considered to vary in
the degree to which such groups are isolated from one another—or the
degree to which they communicate and co-ordinate. In the national
society, lack of communication and co-ordination between agencies of
change and even between departments within large agencies is notorious as a source of inertia.[8] The church has been not just another
case manifesting this type of isolation; it has been an archetype.

The history of the Brazilian church's growth since the late 19th
century goes a long way toward explaining why the church remained
an exaggerated case through the mid-twentieth century. The patterns
of growth tended to produce a church that was a congeries of separate and often rival movements. The major feature of the church's
growth for more than seventy years was the arrival of waves of religious orders from Europe. From about 1889 on, the growth rate for
priests' religious orders may be taken as a rough indicator of the
influx of foreigners oriented to European conditions and ultimately
responsible to superiors in Europe. The growth rate for men's religious orders between 1889 and 1963 is nearly five times[9] the growth
rate for the secular clergy which remained always more Brazilian and

8. See for example comments on developmental agencies by Celso Furtado,
"Political Obstacles to the Economic Development of Brazil," in Claudio Veliz (ed.),
Obstacles to Change in Latin America (London: Oxford University Press, 1965) pp.
145-161.

9. This calculation is based on data presented by Father José Comblin in his essay
"Situação Histórica do Catolicismo no Brasil," *REB* Vol. XXVI (1966), p. 574ff. I am
relying heavily on Father Comblin's work in this section. Even in the sixties when the
clergy were beginning to become more demographically Brazilian, 55 percent of members of men's religious orders (N=7,515 in 1963) were foreigners as opposed to 16.5
percent of the secular clergy and more than 65 percent of all priests (12, 141 in 1963)
were members of religious orders. Several publications of CERIS contain these and related statistics. See especially Padre Zeno Osório Marques (ed.), *Algumas caracterís-
ticas estruturais da igreja no Brasil em gráficos e tabelas* (Rio de Janeiro: CERIS, 1969).

under the control of the local hierarchy. Considering priests' orders only, 165 European-controlled orders set up their own school systems, initiated their own favorite movements, always depending on directives from superiors overseas and employing models designed to cope with European needs. The result has been something like what we might expect in a factory with an extremely complicated and differentiated staff structure and an underdeveloped line organization: confusion about goals, duplication of effort, squabbles without end. Father Comblin has observed that ecumenism has been easier between the Catholic Church and other churches than between rival movements within the church.[10]

He is referring not just to relations between religious orders but to relations between movements that the orders themselves have often introduced. The CERIS church-structure study reveals that within parishes there is scarcely any communication and even less co-ordination between movements of the laity involved in similar activities. Whole parishes within a given area tend to relate to one another only indirectly through diocesan Curia. And, as Comblin has also noted, successive movements involving clergy and laity have come from Europe, made converts, lost momentum after a few years, and remained as isolated castes, each with a special language and arcane rites. The Italian Movement for a Better World, itself designed to provide renewal for flagging apostolates, seems to have become just the latest import to degenerate in this way.

During the fifties and sixties several efforts were made to remedy this form of isolation of groups within the church. The Plano de Conjunto produced in 1965 for 1966-70 is the most impressive statement of *purpose* regarding the problem. But the plan could not have been produced without two developments of the fifties. The first of these is the setting up in 1954 of a national organization of the religious orders, the Conferência dos Religiosos do Brasil (CRB). During the fifties the CRB concentrated on juridical administration and economic measures which resulted in, among other things, the setting up of CERIS (Centro de Estatística Religiosa e Investigações Sociais). And CERIS is not only a fruit of co-ordination but in studies produced under its auspices has documented the various forms of isolation mentioned in this article: it is a sign and producer of the

10. The comparison by no means implies the judgment that the church should function as an efficient factory. It does imply the judgment that there is much waste of human and financial resources.

church's growing self-consciousness of organizational problems. The
second development was the steady increase in co-operation between
the CRB and the national bishops' organization, from 1959 onward.
Since 1959 this co-operation has advanced in two ways: at the top
through the adoption by the CRB of the same regional divisions devised by the CNBB, and at lower levels in some dioceses through co-
operation by the orders in parish work, under the direction of bishops.[11]

During the sixties, several efforts were made to remedy the isolation of lay movements from one another. But moves in this direction revealed on the one hand the difficulty of the enterprise and on
the other hand the resistance of important bishops, apparently as
much for political as for pastoral reasons. The directives issued by the
Episcopal Commission for Lay Apostolates in 1960 to the Catholic
University Students' organization (JUC) consist of warnings and
condemnations against blurring of lines of authority and confusion
of spheres of action as between the "specialized" lay action movements. In its context, this document may be taken to be not only a
fearful reaction to the sometimes naïve effervescence of the students
but a sign of the bishops' incapacity to depart from models of organization received from Europe. Even where new post-Vatican II models
have been adopted, the CERIS studies of priests in Brazil and of the
structure of the church provide evidence of extremely limited effectiveness in encouraging more co-operation between groups on the
same level of the formal hierarchy.

Relations between Diocesan units.

Compounding the forms of isolation already mentioned was a
third form: isolation of diocesan units. Until 1952 the church lacked
national organization. All paths led to Rome: just as isolated parishes
communicated with one another only indirectly through diocesan
Curia, so isolated dioceses related directly to Rome and only secondar-
ily to each other. Fragmented into dioceses, the church reflected the
national polity, fragmented into states and fiefdoms, but was probably even slower to develop national or even regional coherence. The
same problems of sheer distance and physical isolation had the same
effect in the church as in the polity: the dominance of legalistic over
truly political relationships between isolated regional units. But

11. For more details on these and other changes see Padre Raimundo Caramuru
de Barros, *Brasil: Uma igreja em renovação* (Petropolis; Editôra Vozes, 1968).

whereas the federal system had a focal point for communications between its units, in Rio, the focal point in the case of the church was
outside of the country.

So even the first steps toward co-ordination of isolated dioceses
specifically in connection with plans for social change were under
Roman tutelage: the several meetings of the clergy of Amazônia, discussing agrarian reform from 1942 through the fifties, the joint pastoral on rural problems in Rio Grande do Norte in 1951, the 1952
meeting of clergy in the São Francisco Valley. All these were to a
great extent initiatives away from isolation of dioceses sponsored by
Vatican representatives. Even the setting up of the National Council
of Bishops in 1952 involved along with Monsignor Helder Câmara,
presently the famous Archbishop of Recife-Olinda, Monsignor
Montini, presently Pope Paul VI.[12]

Whatever the source of inspiration, from the late fifties through
the sixties there have been many developments in the direction of the
church's greater regional and national coherence. The church has been
divided into regions each with regional offices of the CNBB performing
several functions, such as organizing conferences and editing and dis-
tributing newsletters, designed to keep dioceses within the region in
communication and to encourage planning at the regional level. Indeed, there are signs that within less than twenty years the church has
developed organizational machinery for co-operation between dioceses
that is disproportionately complex given its grassroots weakness.[13]

12. Crucial meetings of bishops in the Northeast region in the later fifties seem to
have been more directly Brazilian in inspiration. These include (1) the Northeast
Meeting of 1956 in Campina Grande called by the National Conference of Brazilian
Bishops (CNBB) which in combination with Federal Government representatives, economists and technicians discussed the problems of the Northeast. The Superintendency
for the Development of the Northeast (SUDENE) may be considered, in part, an eventual product of this meeting. (2) The Second Meeting of the Bishops of the Northeast
in Natal in 1959 worked along similar lines. Dom Helder Câmara was secretary of the
CNBB through these years. He is well known now as the Archbishop of the Archdiocese of Olinda-Recife where he has been since 1964. Dom Helder is a Northeasterner
himself, born in Ceará, and his concern for the problems of the Northeast long precedes
his episcopate in the region. Since the military revolution of 1964, Dom Helder has
frequently criticized the government, inside and outside of Brazil. Most recently, he
has denounced torture of political prisoners to audiences in France. In Brazil, since the
Constitutional Act of December 1968 the heavily censored mass media have refused
him publicity.

13. The Northeast, for example, is divided into three subregions. These each have
their own conferences of bishops, clergy, and laity. But there are also regional conferences and, finally, national conferences.

And informal conversations with a few young priests and deacons attached to dioceses in the interior of the Northeast suggest, once again, that new machinery may mean very little in the day-to-day functioning of the church. But at least the sixties saw the church less plagued by inertia born of ignorance of regional needs and problems and less diffident about facing the difficulties of organizing to deal with the problems. A survey of the content of the religious news sections of the Revista Ecclesiástica Brasileira and diocesan news bulletins in Recife from the fifties through to the present is instructive in this regard. Brazil and regional problems and activities come to take up more space than Rome and canon law and the activities of purely diocesan organizations.[14]

The Orientation of Church Elites

The final feature of the church as an organization to be discussed here has already been hinted at: the orientation of clerical and lay elites within the church to their counterparts in Europe at the expense of an orientation toward the Brazilian grassroots. Church elites, isolated from lower strata and from one another, have faced outward from Brazil for inspiration and plans of action. This orientation outward and away, as we have seen, is partly a sort of demographic phenomenon: the indigenous Brazilian clergy from the late nineteenth century was swamped by foreign clergy in orders directed from Europe. It also reflects a cultural pattern which church elites have shared with other elites in Brazil. Levi-Strauss's reflections on the penchant of Latin American intellectuals in the thirties to consume the latest intellectual fashions imported from France held true of the church's[15] elite circles through the sixties. For example, analyses of what was going on in the university movements and proposals for action were often made in terms of what had been going on in the equivalent French movements.[16]

Not without pushes from Europe, paradoxically, there emerged

14. In the early sixties, when, for a while, Roman pronouncements and discussions of them again dominate the church journals, they are of a different kind from previously: the social encyclicals of John XXIII and Paul VI become the focus of discussion.

15. Claude Levi-Strauss: Tristes Tropiques (New York: Atheneum Paperback, 1967) ch. II.

16. For an example of such an analysis, within its frame of reference a very good one, see Monsignor Dr. Luciano Duarte, "Ação missionaria no JUC" in REB XXL, 1961, p. 883ff.

in the sixties what Padre Comblin has called a re-Brazilianization of the church. The Movement of Natal, though relying heavily on German financial support, led the way: Brazilian church elites in Natal asked serious and original questions about what was needed and devised new methods for dealing with problems of social change.[17] The Bishops' Emergency Plan and other declarations of the sixties show at least an awareness that the old foreign recipes are inadequate. Whereas the official devotions, the apparatus of rituals, of the church are still late-nineteenth-century European, a new generation of priests, in the Northeast at any rate, has been making serious efforts to investigate and develop popular religiosity. But a recent study of religious values of *camponêses* in the Zona da Mata areas of Pernambuco and Paraíba suggests that thus far such changes, though they might have gone very deep in a few areas, have not spread very far. To the *camponêses* interviewed, the church remains a custodian of laws from above (Heaven? Europe?),[18] a haven for the pious who belong to the proper movements.

In each of the four categories of organizational relationships examined, the church has undergone important and probably irreversible changes during the sixties. But these changes have to some extent been limited by political pressures on the church since 1964 and to an even greater extent by forms of inertia in the church itself. The isolation of vertical strata continues to limit the passage of information and inspiration from the grassroots, where the new church of the declarations and plans is supposed to be serving, to the top. The isolation of functionally similar groups continues to absorb the scarce energies of the church through duplication of effort and an over-elaboration of structure curiously reminiscent of Geertz's description of inertia-producing features of colonialist Javanese society. The isola-

17. The Movement of Natal refers to several developments initiated in the Archdiocese of Natal between 1954 and 1964 under the administration of the then auxiliary bishop Eugênio Sales. Dom Eugênio diverted Church funds to schemes for urban and rural workers. A Service of Rural Assistance (SAR) was set up. The co-operative sector of SAR was flourishing by the late fifties after earlier setbacks. The movement also included the prototypical developments of MEB and the rural unions. Natal was the source of ideas for change in the Northeast until 1964. In this sense, the word 'movement' refers to a sentiment of hope and a spirit of enthusiasm then emanating from Natal. Foreign organizations and groups such as Misericor (the German bishops social development fund), the Canadian bishops, the American Catholic Relief Service lent support to the movement.

18. Padre Eduardo Hoornaert, "A distinção entre lei e religião no Nordeste," in *REB*, September 1969, p. 580ff.

tion of basic administrative units, the dioceses, has been much modified, at least in terms of the degree of communication that is structurally possible. But various surveys of the opinions of priests indicate that such changes may amount to little given an unimaginative bishop. Some of the plans and activities of elites in the church during the sixties reveal an effort to think beyond the preoccupations nurtured by an excessive orientation to the church in Europe. But there are examples to the contrary in the early sixties—especially in intellectual apostolates and the masses being turned to remain remarkably ignorant of the change of heart. Despite the irreversible changes of the sixties, the church continues to provide interesting examples of organizational problems of social change in Brazil.

The Catholic Church as Agent of Change

Of course, in the sixties people interested in social change who placed hope in the Catholic Church were not thinking primarily of internal organizational change; interest was directed more to what the church was doing or proposed doing about outstanding problems of social change in Brazil. In the 1970s, it seems important to stress the interdependence of organizational factors and the institutional role of the church. But let us postpone discussion of this interdependence until a later section. Through the sixties the church was taking important initiatives in several problem areas.

One outstanding problem self-consciously attacked by various church-sponsored or church-initiated movements is that of inclusion of isolated marginal groups into Brazilian national society. As we have seen, the church in its various structural features not only manifested but even sustained the exclusion of rural illiterates from participation in the national society. Its reformed energies from the end of the nineteenth century on were concentrated on the urban middle classes or on the rural rich with urban connections. For the rural poor, the church was either merely absent or infrequently present as legitimizer, comforter to those lucky enough to reach the urban-located Casas Santas, forgiver of sins when the Santas Missões passed through town.

In the sixties, or a little earlier in the case of Natal, the church sponsored or directed a number of movements designed not only to shift the church itself from the traditional mould but to deal with the problem of exclusion of marginals in the national society.

The "Movement of Natal" from the mid-fifties through to the eve of the Revolution always placed a firm emphasis on inclusion of marginal groups into the national society as participating citizens. To Bishop Eugênio Sales, then auxiliary bishop of Natal, this meant three things: mass education of illiterates and low-level manpower training; the setting up of non-paternalistic co-operatives; and "concientiza-ção"—education of marginals into their rights as human beings and Brazilian citizens and education into the means of realizing those rights. Nor were these ends merely announced. By 1963 the Radio schools had more than 20,000 pupils; the co-operative schemes, after false starts which proved how difficult it was to avoid paternalism and financial ruin, were functioning well; and in 1962, a year after first efforts were made, membership in church-organized Rural Unions was more than 25,000.

Until the Revolution, Natal remained the star case of efforts to include marginal groups. But it did not remain a merely local phenomenon. The Natal Movement aims were adopted by MEB and the Rural Unions. And whatever criticisms may be justly leveled at these movements, there is no denying that in a very short time they mobilized large numbers of *camponêses*.

The participation figures for MEB have been presented in the previous section. In Pernambuco the numbers of *camponêses* involved by 1963 in the church-sponsored Rural Unions is truly impressive. By 1962, 62 unions in the state had been organized into a federation (60 of these Church-sponsored unions) with about 200,000 members.[19] In the Zona da Mata, within a couple of years, groups of canecutters formerly marooned in Sargassos of sugar were in contact with one another and achieving concessions through their co-ordination. It is important to note that the concessions were gained because sugar market conditions at the time allowed that they could be extracted without seriously threatening property owners. But the point remains that for the first time isolated groups, because they were in contact with one another *and* with the machinery for extracting concessions through a federation of unions, were able to take advantage of favorable conditions.

On a smaller scale, a few young priests labored in their parishes (and they or their successors continue to labor) to achieve the ends of

19. Mary E. Wilkie, *A Report on Rural Syndicates in Pernambuco* (Rio de Janeiro: Latin American Center for Research in the Social Sciences, 1964). A fuller and generally excellent history of the unions in Pernambuco is Cynthia N. Hewitt, *Brazil: The Peasant Movement of Pernambuco, 1961-64*, in Henry A. Landsberger (ed.) *Latin American Peasant Movements*, (Ithaca: Cornell University Press, 1969).

the mass movements. Those interested in radical social change in Brazil who are also acquainted with the post-Revolution political context in the Northeast, will realize that these individual initiatives, however well encouraged by such bishops as Dom Helder Câmara, are delicate experiments to be observed with restrained hope rather than welcomed as assured developments. And, as it turned out, the larger-scale movements were even more delicate.

These same movements had implications with regard to other problems of social change in Brazil which, though related to inclusion of marginals, deserve separate mention. Each movement stressed in its own way the need for collective struggle, the need for co-ordination of demands between groups on the same social level. This stress was especially explicit in some of the MEB readers and took organizational form in the relations between MEB and the Rural Unions in the Northeast: by 1962 MEB groups were founding unions, unions were setting up radio schools, and in Rio Grande do Norte, Pernambuco, Sergipe, Ceará and Maranhão specialized personnel in the MEB organization at state level devoted themselves to union affairs.[20] This emphasis on co-ordination appears especially important as a function of the church when contrasted to the lack of solidarity that has characterized Brazilian society at the grassroots.

A third important function of the church movements, related to the inclusion of marginals, lay in the intended and reasonably well practiced *mode* of inclusion. Tory and totalitarian modes involve inclusion at the cost of increases in paternalism: elites render services to masses which increase the dependence of the masses on their elite leaders. The church movements we have been examining were very conscious of this problem. And, until the Revolution, education of an *independent* grassroots leadership remained perhaps the most emphasized aim of elites in the Rural Unions and of MEB. The structure of MEB in 1963 reflects the realization of the anti-paternalistic ideology: of the 7,500-odd people rendering teaching or administrative services in MEB, only 530 were paid, often nonlocal experts and *animadores*.[21] As a matter of policy and necessity, the outsiders were withdrawn once local leaders had emerged. A proper degree of cynicism prompts speculation about the new forms of paternalism that might have developed had MEB and the Unions survived a few more

20. See the MEB Annual Reports for 1962 and 1963.
21. See MEB Annual Report of 1963.

years. But at the time these church-sponsored movements do seem to have been curiously more radical in their anti-paternalistic intent and practice than Julião's Leagues or the Communist unions. The former depended absolutely on Julião as *patrão* and the latter relied on a government handout method of attracting support; neither made any effort at training peasant self-leadership. But the church trained union leaders through the Serviço do Orientação Rural (SORPE), which was set up by Padres Antônio Melo and Paulo Crespo in 1961, and in 1963 *all* directors of the Federation of the church-sponsored Unions were peasants.

Another role of the church in the sixties that may be considered a contribution to social change is that of broker between the several layers of the national society. Certain "social bishops" and priests together with some lay groups performed this role simply—often too simply—through exhortation and propaganda. The church had captive elite audiences, means of propaganda and, as we have seen, increasing contacts with the rural and even urban poor. In a few cases, these resources were used to present interpreted information about lower-class conditions to upper-class audiences which were then exhorted, in the name of religious principles, to use their power and wealth to change things. If the exhortation sometimes merely echoed Julião and the plans of actions were often naïve, at least some sections of the church were attempting to hammer out and hammer home a Christian moral social ethic relevant to Brazil. Ivan Vallier has pointed to the lack of such a social ethic as one of the characteristics of the Catholic Church in Latin America that previously contributed to its inability to use its contacts with rich and poor to help produce change. In the Northeast during the sixties, some important groups and individuals within the church began to preach a social ethic that began to serve as a sort of rhetoric for communication about the exigencies of change across class lines.

It was only a beginning. Most of the exhortations were too bland (for example, the Emergency Plan and attendant declarations produced by the National Bishops Conference in 1962) or too oriented to the radical student milieux (the Ação Popular manifesto and supporting declarations by Catholic Action leaders) to serve as a rhetoric for across-class communication. But the 1966 declaration issued by the Commission of Bishops of the Northeast Region II[22] was explicit as

22. Pernambuco, Paraiba, Ceará, Alagoas make up this region.

to facts and ethics and was reacted to as such.[23] Father Crespo's
reports on conditions in the Zona da Mata in Pernambuco are of the
same mettle, though less publicized.[24] Dom Helder Câmara's radio
talks over Radio Olinda by no means live up to his reputation as a
demagogue. They are intended to serve as a basis for group discussions
and seem admirably designed to do so.[25]

A second way in which the church has served as a broker between social strata has been to use its prestige as an elite institution to
protect activists in lower-class causes. The action of Dom Valdir
Calheiros, bishop of Volta Redonda, who offered himself as a prisoner
in place of two workers, securing their release, is one dramatic example of a church dignitary laying his prestige on the line. The closing
of the churches in Fortaleza over Pentecost in 1969 as a protest against
the condemnation of Padre Geraldo Bonfim for his "agitation" among
the poor of his district is another dramatic example. (It is instructive

23. The bishops issued a statement commenting on reports of conditions affecting
rural and urban workers submitted by Catholic Actions groups. They condemned failure to pay minimum wages and transgressions by employers of the labor laws. Recife's
Jornal do Commercio failed to publish the statement but came out with a slashing attack accusing the church of interfering in things of the world. Despite conciliatory
gestures by the editor, this was followed up by another violent editorial blasting the
"demogogic solutions" of the bishops. A television debate between the editor and Dom
Helder was scheduled but canceled. The issue became a national one. It came out that
the paper had been under pressure from and supplied with editorial ammunition by
officers of the 10th military region (Fortaleza). Letters of support for Dom Helder came
in from all over the country. After a meeting with Dom Helder, President Castello
Branco apparently ordered that a conciliatory line be taken by the government. But at-
tacks and counterattacks went on for a long time. Recife's famous man of letters,
Gilberto Freyre, entered the lists against the bishops. For one side of the story, see
REB XXVI, 1966, p. 729. For another view, see *Jornal do Commercio*, 24 July 1966.
Visão 8/26/1966 has a comprehensive account.

24. For a relatively easily obtainable summary, see Alberto Tamer, *O Mesmo
Nordeste* (São Paulo: Editôra Herder, 1968) Ch. VIII. Padre Paulo Crespo, as noted
earlier, was with Padre Antônio Melo, one of the founders of the church-sponsored
rural union movement in Pernambuco. He is at present director of SORPE, the Serviço
de Orientação Rural de Pernambuco which he set up in 1961 as a scheme for training
rural leaders. He is also effective director of the Federation of Rural Workers of Pernambuco. The strength and scope of both of these organizations have been drastically reduced since the heady days before the Revolution, but Padre Crespo battles on gamely
from within the system. If a political label needs be attached, it would probably be most
appropriate to call Padre Crespo a Chilean-style Christian Democrat. But he is far too
immersed in Brazilian political and economic realities for even that label to apply
neatly.

25. Some 300-odd groups are still functioning in the poorer residential areas of
Recife and Olinda.

in considering the weaknesses of the church in its various roles to note that this dramatic action backfired: army chaplains celebrated Masses in most of the churches and the impact of the closing was almost entirely wasted.)

Let us allow the dust to settle on the most recent Dominican affair and alleged protection by priests of various terrorists before deciding what it may exemplify. A surer additional example is Dom Helder Câmara's unambiguous support of the impending Cabo strike in 1968, which, according to some accounts, resulted in swinging important grassroots support to the ultimately successful strike. Dom Helder's prestige was offered and at that stage could reasonably be accepted as a sort of security by camponese activists.[26]

Of course, this along with other sorts of brokerage is only a short-range contribution to change. Especially since Institutional Act No. 5, the sacrifices necessary to maintain the role have become very great. And far from being a protective haven, the church is becoming a tree in the electric storm—the last place for radical activists to seek protection. After the universities, it is *the* suspect institution. Moreover, its prestige has been much reduced. The affair of Recife's *Jornal do Commercio* versus the bishops of the second Northeast region of the CNBB in 1966 is only one fairly well documented case of a series of systematic officially sponsored attempts to discredit and silence the

26. Martha Duncan, "Consciousness versus Spontaneity: A Study of Peasant Movements in Northeast Brazil" (unpublished paper submitted to Professor Douglas A. Chalmers, Columbia University, March 6, 1969), pp. 46-58. Cabo is a town about 30 kilometers south of Recife. Since before the Revolution it has been the center of activities of Padre Antônio Melo. With Padre Paulo Crespo, he was among the first priests leading the rural unions before the Revolution. At present, he runs a large co-operative in the Cabo area. More than 500 camponese families, through the co-operative, own and cultivate land taken over from old, bankrupted fazendas. The rural union functioning in the area is *not* a part of the Federation of Rural Unions headed by Padre Crespo. Indeed, there are many differences between the two men: Padre Melo is more accommodating of the military government, more inclined to paternalism, more insistently apolitical. There are differences at Cabo too. In 1968, several issues came to a head in the area, such as nonpayment of back salaries, the failure to receive due social benefits, and further land redistribution. The president of the Cabo union, João Luis da Silva, urged a strike to resolve the issues. The land owners of the area and the Federal Government issued various threats against the strikers. Padre Melo urged the union not to strike. Dom Helder pledged support to the strikers, and João Luis called the strike. Most of the 3,000 peasant members joined the strike, and they were supported, as Dom Helder had promised, by food supplies organized by Catholic University students. The strike succeeded in its immediate aims. My sources on the strike included conversations and newspaper articles.

church, lower its prestige, and hence limit its mediating power.[27]

And silencing has been effected not only through tight government control of the mass media but through an increase in the risks of speaking out. The murder of Padre Henrique Pereira Neto in May 1969 among other events has set the stakes in the Northeast. Padre Henrique was a young priest sociologist, an assistant to Dom Helder, and a chaplain to many Recife students. His death has been attributed to the Communist-Hunters' Commando (CCC) which has also bombed Dom Helder's residence and disfigured the Episcopal Palace in Recife with "Dom Helder—Back to Moscow" and other signs.[28] In the South of Brazil, many nuns and priests have been imprisoned and in some cases tortured for alleged crimes that fit into the vague category of "the crime of psychological war and revolutionary war" for which the death penalty has recently been introduced.[29] Most recently, the imprisonment of JOC leaders in several Brazilian cities shows the laity the risks that they run. It is by now abundantly clear to all members of the church that to try to act as broker between classes or in any other of the roles promoting socioeconomic change involves risk of fierce retribution by rightist thugs within or outside of the government.

Even without such discouragement and active discrediting, processes of secularization, especially in the South, have taken the force out of the old church weapons of excommunication and interdict, though both have been tried as weapons to defend radical activists. The sixties may shortly be looked upon as a brief period in which the mediating role of the church blossomed and quickly withered.

Limits to the Possibilities of the Church as Agent of Change

The reader of Part I of this chapter and of the two preceding paragraphs will be alerted to the fact that however important were the contributions of the church to social change in the 1960s it remains important not to overrate them. The limits to change in the

27. Sources already referred to in Note 23.
28. I personally believe this attribution of guilt to be accurate but feel obliged to note that my evidence supporting this belief would not prove the case in a Brazilian or any other court of law.
29. The investigations and subsequent reports of Amnesty International, the International Association of Democratic Lawyers, the International Secretariat of Catholic Lawyers, and the International Federation for the Rights of Man can leave no further doubts on this score.

church as an organization placed limits to the role of the church as a change-inducing institution. And through the 1960s the church encountered new problems that limit its potential as a source of future social change. Let us discuss three of these problems in terms of a clash between needs created by the new plans (these will be simply asserted) and the possibilities for meeting these needs.

The church needs more clergy per head and a redeployment of clergy to fulfill its proclaimed new functions. But it is suffering from serious "demographic" problems which suggest that there is absolutely no chance of improving on the present state of affairs without changes in its structure far more radical than the changes of the sixties.

The ratio of clergy to population is already very low—for the whole of Brazil one priest per 6,800 and for the Northeast between one priest per 30,000 in Maranhão to one per 9,000 in Pernambuco.[30] This ratio will probably worsen in the near future under the operation of several factors. The birthrate is rising at a faster rate than the number of vocations.[31] At the same time as there is a leveling off in the number of vocations there is a huge increase in the number of priests and religious returning to lay life.[32] There are no signs that foreign clergy are going to answer in sufficient force to modify these trends; on the contrary, there has been, since 1964, a fall in the number of foreign priests arriving.[33]

Moreover, deployment of clergy is a serious problem. The clergy are not where the people are. Within Recife, for example, there are 5,000 people for one priest. But within many poor bairros the ratio is nearly 30,000 to one priest. At the same time, the church is demographically urban-based: one indicator of this is the ratio of priests per head of population in rural compared with urban areas. Whereas in Recife itself there are 5,000 people for one priest, in rural areas of

30. Padre Zeno Osório Marques. (The collection does not have page or table numbers.) There are 59 bishops in the Northeast, that is, 25 percent of the total number of Brazilian bishops for 30 percent of the population. There are 1,028 secular priests, 975 members of men's religious orders, and 5,384 members of women's orders. These statistics are mostly for 1964. They are presented in several places, including Godofredo J. Deelen, A sociologia a serviço da pastoral (Petrópolis R. J.: Editôra Vozes limitada, 1966) pp. 77-84.

31. Godofredo J. Deelen, "A ocupação do Clero," in Boletim Informativo CERIS (January-June 1967), p. 6.

32. For female religious orders, see Padre Zeno Osório Marques: For priests, see REB XXIX (December 1969), 924ff.

33. Boletim Informativo CERIS (January-June 1967), p. 7.

the archdiocese the ratio is one for more than 13,000, and Recife is probably a less dramatic case than others in the Northeast.[34]

To fulfill its new functions, the church needs a certain unity of purpose and stability among the active faithful. But just at the time that these things are needed, the active faithful are experiencing crises of faith and are split as never before on doctrinal and strategical grounds. Ivan Vallier has described four different and sometimes clashing stances of Latin American Catholics in the face of social change.[35] In Brazil his politicians, papists, pastors, and pluralists are all much in evidence and often at loggerheads. The Bishops' directives to JUC already cited present a classical statement of the papist position against the pluralists: the insistence of a clear line of hierarchical command as against lay autonomy; the call for application of a specifically Catholic social doctrine already defined as against eclecticism and flirtation with Marxist perspectives; an opposition to the principle of "humanize first, evangelize afterwards." Even fairly conservative papist bishops have felt and expressed the fear of open defiance from extreme papist laity of the Brazilian Society for the Defense of Tradition, Family and Property.[36] The latter group, based in São Paulo, sends bands of young men up to Recife regularly to distribute literature about the Red Archbishop Helder Câmara and subversive Dominicans. Even before the Revolution, conservative Catholic educationalists saw literacy-training literature of the kind the Catholic Paulo Freire was producing as Communist subversion.[37] At the same time, some of the fears of the papists and pastoralists seem to have been well founded: young people especially, entering in where angels had feared to tread, seem to have undergone crises of faith on a mass scale.[38] And, in general, the church is weakened as a short-

34. For statistics of this ratio for the various ecclesiastical divisions of Brazil, see *Boletim Informativo* CERIS (July-September 1966), p. 90. In the second Northeast region, about 1/8 of the population live in the capital cities. But more than one third of the priests and more than one half of female religious personnel work in these cities.

35. Ivan Vallier, "Religious Elites," in S.M. Lipset & Aldo Solari (eds.) *Elites in Latin America* (London: Oxford University Press, 1967).

36. *Paz e Terra* (Rio de Janeiro: Editôra Paz e Terra Limitada, 1968) No. 6, pp. 164-175.

37. *REB* XXIV (1964), p. 210ff. Other examples of publicized conflict include the vehement rejection by Bishop José Távora of the position taken by Archbishop Vincente Scherer in the case of imprisonment of priests in São Paulo in August 1967 and the letter of 30 priests to the bishops in *Paz e Terra* No. 6, p. 229ff.

38. See *REB* Vol. XX, 1960 p. 883ff. A French priest, expelled recently from Brazil, considers crises of faith to be one of two internal reasons for the collapse of Univer-

term force for social change because the very European influence that has provoked many of the changes in the church has introduced at the same time the uncertainties of modern Catholicism.

The realization of plans already made involves evoking a response at the grassroots, among people the new church is supposed to serve. But apart from the demographic problems mentioned earlier, there are several other reasons such a response might not be forthcoming:

—persisting clericalism
—the persisting foreignness of the church and the resulting inability to compete for allegiance with spiritists, pentecostalists, etc.[39]
—a system of financing that involves imprisonment of young priests in parishes in old functions that preserve the church as "the law" at the grassroots[40]
—the church's inability to protect grassroots activists from the political consequences of their actions.

Some of these phenomena have already been commented upon in other parts of this chapter. Here it is possible only to document the lack of response. One gross measure is Sunday Mass attendance. Surveys of Mass attendance have been done in the major cities of the Northeast. Using as a base the estimated Catholic population capable of attending Sunday Mass the proportion attending is at its lowest in Salvador—8.5 percent and never gets much above 16 percent. Perhaps even more important than these low over-all proportions are the relative proportions of literates and illiterates attending. In Aracajú, whereas 35 percent of the population is illiterate, only 8 percent of those attending Mass are illiterate. In Maceió, depending on the par-

---

sity Catholic Action movements. See *Informations Catoliques Internationales* No. 350 (December 1969).

39. Hoornaert contains some supporting data for this assertion. "Foreigners" is meant very broadly to refer to the late-nineteenth-century Italianization of the church and to the resistance against African religiosity.

Emmanuel de Kadt, "Religion, the Church and Social Change in Brazil," in Claudio Veliz (ed.), *The Politics of Conformity in Latin America* (London: Oxford University Press, 1967), pp. 192-220, provides valuable insights into this matter and indeed into many of the other issues raised in this chapter. This study, unfortunately, was not available to the author when this chapter was written.

40. For details that may, however, not be representative for the whole of Brazil, see Pedro A. Ribeiro de Oliveira, Vol. 1, ch. 3, and Carta, Vol. II, pp. 89-108.

ish, the proportion of illiterates among Mass-attenders is between 10 percent and 30 percent.[41]

These few statistics suggest that the church remains especially weak among the very class of people that it needs to respond to its new movements and reforms: the poor and underprivileged in areas where the church is, as it were, physically strongest. The growth rates of rival movements add some depth to the picture, suggesting that for all its development through the sixties the church is not able to satisfy popular religiosity under conditions of change. As poor migrants to the big cities cease Catholic practices, they take up spiritism. In Bahia during the decade 1950-1960 the number of professing spiritists increased 187.3 percent, but in the cities that are episcopal sees the increase was 224 percent.[42] In Pernambuco the percentage increase was slightly greater. As yet I do not have statistics for the episcopal sees, but some idea of the attraction of the spiritist groups in Recife may be given by a report from one of the priests who has worked there in a large, poor *bairro*. Tiny congregations turned up to the Masses celebrated in four churches by my informant and the four other priests with some responsibility for the area (population more than 180,000). In the same area more than 200 spiritist centers flourish.

Sources of Change

Having demonstrated the limits to change in and through the church, two summary assertions can be made. Given what Claudio Veliz has called "the resilient traditional structure of institutions in Latin America"[43] and the fact that the Catholic Church has seemed to epitomize this trait, the irreversible changes that have taken place in the church as an organization are important data that demand analysis from the student of social change in Brazil. In what the journalist Tamer has recently called simply "The Same Northeast," any initiatives in change demand analysis. It remains of more than academic interest to ask *how* the church could have changed in little more than a decade from being a pillar of order, and regarded as

41. For Sunday mass attendance statistics, see SUDEC (Superintendência do Desenvolvimento Econômico e Cultural), "Levantamento Socio-Religioso da Arquediocese de Fortaleza," 1968, and the following CERIS studies: "Aspetos da Prática Dominical de Maceió"; "A Cidade do Salvador"; "Analise do Recensaemento de Assistência a Missa em Aracajú."

42. *Boletims Informativos* CERIS (July-September 1966), p. 78.

43. Claudio Veliz (ed.), p. 1.

such, to being attacked publicly and clandestinely as a breeder of subversion.

A simple answer, often given, is that the church changed by reacting to challenges from the Left. This answer goes some way in explaining changes in the church's functions as a social institution. Father Crespo has outlined how the Catholic Rural Unions arose from a *reaction* by some priests and bishops to Julião's Leagues.[44] Statements from conservative clergymen supporting some of the changes in church organization and functions reflect a feeling of embattlement in the early sixties. For example, five conservative bishops in a letter welcoming the encyclical "Mater e Magistra" affirm support for the Rural Catholic Action movements only because of their potential as a counterbalance to atheistic Communism.[45]

Another form of the change-by-reaction hypothesis is that the church, considered as a clerical organization, found itself by the mid-fifties faced with new classes of clients. The church changed as it tried to regain a popular base which industrialization, urbanization, and the rise of new interest groups seemed to have withered away. In this view, the church reacted not so much against rival leftist ideologies but against the threat of marginalization. This hypothesis is supported by the many pronouncements by church leaders which drew attention to the fact the church would be left behind if it failed to participate in moves toward land reform and unionization. Dom Inocêncio Engelke in a pastoral letter provides an early (1950) and graphic example: "With us, without us, or against us, land reform will take place," he declared, urging of course, that the church respond so that reform should be "with us."[46]

But a reaction hypothesis focusing only on pressures for change within Brazilian society cannot be used to explain everything. In particular, the *form* of the reactions, their very originality at best, speak of something more than panicky reaction. Turning to other sources of change, the most obvious appears to be the church's own international structure. If the foreign links have had many disadvanta-

---

44. See A. Tamer, ch. VIII.
45. REB XXI (1961), p. 951ff. The tone of embattlement may be communicated through the following quotation, the final sentence of the bishops' letter: "The hour for prayers and sacrifices has arrived. Perhaps penetential processions and public prayers of petition are needed in order that our country, a home of Christianity, might remain faithful to Our Lord, Jesus Christ."
46. Padre Raimundo Caramuru de Barros, ch. 1.

geous aspects they have also been an antiparochial inspiration, a source of constant pressure, and a fount of financial resources.

Under the last three popes, Brazil, with the largest nominally Catholic population in the world, has been regarded as a sort of test-case of the church in the modern world. The Pontifical Commission for Latin America has continuously exhorted the Brazilian bishops to common action: the Emergency Plan in 1962 was solicited from them by Rome. The social encyclicals of Pope John XXIII and Pope Paul VI seem to have been written with Latin American problems especially in mind; they were certainly received as such in Brazil. The list of positive contributions from the European churches is a long one. European priests and European-educated Brazilian priests have contributed decisively to the growing self-consciousness of internal and national problems that has freed the church for change in the sixties. Fathers Comblin and Crespo come to mind in the case of the Northeast. German church aid was indispensable in the Movement of Natal. Technical and inspirational assistance from the European Churches seems to have been important in the development of the MEB radio schools. And, not least, the most important development in the postwar European church, the Vatican Council, seems to have finally corroded two pillars of the church's internal ossification and external conservatism in Brazil: the assumption that the church was an unchanging order depending ultimately on initiatives from Rome and the assumption that the church was bound to triumph in time.[47] Freedom from the illusions of the early sixties may be the decisive resource of the Brazilian church in the seventies.

Conclusions

Let us sum up this survey of the church in the sixties against the background of the first major church document of the seventies—the "Documento Pastoral de Brasília" issued during the Eleventh General Assembly of the Brazilian Episcopate.[48]

47. One gross indicator of the impact of the Vatican Council is the number of articles in church magazines on the council's deliberations and implications for Brazil. In 1963, more than 50 percent of all REB articles concerned the Vatican Council. In the years since the council, it is possible to document a shift in concern in published articles away from legalistic and apologetic preoccupations toward discussions of Brazilian pastoral problems, often with reference to the inspiration and authority of Vatican II.

48. The document is available in several places. My source was SEDOC (Serviço de Documentação) (R. J. Petropolis, Editôra Vozes Limitada) Vol. 3, (July 1970). This source has the advantage of including the bishops' votes on a number of important matters.

Unlike the great documents of the sixties, the Plano de Emergência and the Plano de Pastoral de Conjunto, the new document does not attempt to draw on the combined wisdom of the several layers of the church's hierarchy. It is of an older genre: a document speaking for those bishops whom Ivan Vallier would label "The Politicians." Its extensive footnotes interlacing references to the speeches of President Garrastazu Médici and papal encyclicals point an attempt to lean over backward in accommodation of the political status quo.

The great documents of the sixties analyzed the problems that lead to political polarization and social marginalization and called for radical solutions. But the Documento Pastoral de Brasília ignores those calls and belies the fact that such dangerous church-sponsored solutions as MEB ever existed. It sets up a sort of orthodoxy of the middle way, and anything either side is against the church and against Brazil. There is even advanced the promise that if Catholics hew to the middle line the church will emerge from present crisis to future triumph.

The church in the sixties, as we have seen, developed as an organization as it moved away from isolation of its several hierarchical layers and lack of communication between subgroups. In interdependence with internal developments were significant changes in the church's functions: decisive actions to deal with problems of marginalization in Brazilian society, new nonpaternalistic social services, developments in the church's role as broker between classes. The first important document of the seventies taken together with the votes of the assembled bishops on a series of important matters betokens a reassertion of hierarchical formalism. This and the new orthodoxy of the middle way seem to preclude the church's attempting on a large scale to build on the experiments in social change that distinguished it in the early sixties.

Of course, individual Catholics and groups within the church are not so precluded. And if MEB was not the church neither is a bishops' document. But the Documento Pastoral de Brasília confirms the fragility both of the internal changes in the church's organization and of its new functions in Brazilian society. It suggests that if disappointment and repression have freed some churchmen from illusions, it has led others, including some of the most important bishops, to crave security.

GLOSSARY
Of organizations and movements mentioned in the text

ACB   Ação Católica Brasileira. The official Catholic Action organization subsuming all lay apostolate movements such as JUC under the control of a committee of the CNBB.

AP   Ação Popular. A movement formed out of an alliance between political radicals of JUC who left after clashes in 1962 with the bishops running AC and secular radicals of the non-Communist left. To the bishops' dismay, many remaining members of JEC and JUC became active in AP. In the Northeast there were very close ties between AP and MEB. By the eve of the 1964 Revolution, AP was forming alliances with the far left, including Communist groups, rather than with the church-sponsored groups. In Pernambuco, for example, it backed Communist unions rather than Padre Crespo's Federation of Rural Workers. Emmanuel de Kadt in Claudio Veliz (op. cit.) pp. 210-218 has a succinct account of these relationships.

CERIS Centro de Estatística Religiosa e Investigações Sociais. The church's Center for Religious Statistics and Social Research. It is responsible to the CNBB and the CRB and is commissioned by these bodies to assemble available statistics or conduct sample surveys to gather data relevant to the church's problems and programs.

CNBB   Conferencia Nacional dos Bispos do Brasil. This body comprises all the bishops of Brazil and is the highest policy-making and administrative unit in the Brazilian church. Its various committees supervise Catholic Action, the conduct of the liturgy, and all other aspects of the church's official activities. Since the setting up of the CNBB in 1952 there have been 11 general assemblies of the bishops to discuss and vote upon key problems of the church. Dom Helder Câmara was secretary-general of CNBB during its first twelve years. Between assemblies, the CNBB is administered through a central commission.

CRB   Conferência dos Religiosos do Brasil. This body comprises representatives of all men's religious orders in Brazil. It was set up in 1954 and for the first year concentrated on smoothing out juridicial relationships between orders and investigating means of helping orders in financial difficulties. By the sixties, the CRB was more preoccupied with pastoral concerns and especially with co-operation with the CNBB in programs for the whole of Brazil. CERIS was established by the CRB.

JAC   Juventude Agrícola Católica (rural workers).
JEC   Juventude Estudantil Católica (secondary schools).
JIC   Juventude Independente Católica (mixed, white-collar, etc.).
JOC   Juventude Operária Católica (workers).

JUC   Juventude Universitaria Católica (university). These are the five youth movements within AC. Throughout the fifties and sixties these were the most vital organizations within AC. These organizations are not special to Brazil but are international organizations of the Catholic Church. JOC, for example, is known as the Y.C.W. in English-speaking countries

MEB   Movimento de Educação de Base. This movement has been fairly fully described in the text. It was set up through an agreement between the CNBB and the Federal Ministry of Education and Culture in 1961.

MMM   Movimento para um Mundo Melhor, the Movement for a Better World, originated in Italy and gained great momentum in Brazil from 1960 on. Its aim is education: it is designed to deepen Catholics' understanding of the religious dimensions of their various apostolates. In 1964, courses were provided for 46,907 people spread over 251 dioceses.

SAR   Serviço de Assistência Rural. The organization set up in the Archdiocese of Natal by the then auxiliary Bishop Dom Eugênio Sales. It It was designed to provide leadership and literacy training to rural workers and by the end of the fifties had developed a successful cooperatives section.

SORPE Serviço do Orientação Rural de Pernambuco, the Pernambuco equivalent of SAR. It adopted the same concerns. It still exists under its original leader, Padre Paulo Crespo. (See footnote 24.)

TFP   A Sociedade Brasileira de Defesa da Tradição Família e Propriedade. The Brazilian Society for the Defense of Traditon, Family, and Property originated in Chile. It is an organization of Catholic laymen who call on fellow Catholics to resist the erosion of traditional Catholic values by socialist-Marxist moral-relativist ideologies. It is especially strong in São Paulo but in numbers and influence has been growing nationally through the 1960s. Its ideology may be found pungently expressed in the magazine *Hora Presente*.

Literature
in the Sixties

11 ALEXANDRINO SEVERINO

The Brazilian Short Story:
Reflections of a Changing Society

WHATEVER ITS exotic indigenous qualities, the good literature of every nation expresses, at the same time, national and universal characteristics. Brazilian literature has been represented in the past by a composite of regional differences. At times, during periods of closer indentity with European values, the old capital of Rio de Janeiro became the center for cultural activity; on other occasions, however, when Brazil has sought to ascertain its national identity, regional traits have been emphasized.

Neither of these two currents has been instrumental in creating a really autonomous Brazilian literature. Till the end of the nineteenth century, the literature which sprang from cities along the Atlantic seaboard tended to express a hybrid European character, not surprisingly, for Brazilian writers were themselves a product of European influences. As a protest against European domination in Brazilian letters, the Modernist Movement, launched in the city of São Paulo in 1922, espoused purely Brazilian themes to be expressed in a language freed from academic control and hence more genuinely Brazilian. Culminating in a lesser but vital trend present in their literature from the beginning, the modernist writers broke away from their own cultural past as well as the European and adopted the regional literary traits as an over-all pattern for the expression of the Brazilian reality.

After the Second World War, a counter movement attuned the

375

Brazilian writer once more, not only to his own cultural heritage, but also to major European and American literary modes of expression. This counter trend was slow to develop, however, since the former emphasis on national realities had aroused Brazil's awareness of its national being while fostering its justifiable right toward political affirmation in the international scene. As the world became more aware of Brazil and its dormant potential for future development, Brazilian literature became known as the expression of appalling social inequalities, interracial conviviality, and of a quaint, exotic society—lush tropical climes, torrid passions, and voodoo religions. These are still the dominant traits for which Brazilian literature is known abroad.

It is difficult to tell, at the threshold of the seventies, whether the literary output of the last decade will herald the beginning of a truly autonomous Brazilian literature. It is possible, at least, to denote its major trends. These seem to be broadly defined by the assimilation of foreign esthetic and literary concepts into the indigenous experience. The result is a kind of literature both national and universal in character. The Brazilian writer of the sixties appears to be embarked on a literary experiment which will ultimately encompass the cumulative consciousness of a people projected into a universal context.

The gradual development of Brazilian literature toward maturity and its self-assertion during the sixties can be seen with special clarity in the short story. More than any other genre, the short story dominated the Brazilian literary scene in the past ten years; its study, therefore, can best reveal the literary renovation going on in Brazil at the present time.

In so far as literature portrays a fictional reality formed out of the human and social trends of a particular society, the study that follows, although primarily concerned with the special characteristics of the Brazilian short story in the sixties, may yield yet another perspective of Brazil's development during the sixties.

In spite of story-telling's being so much a part of Brazilian culture, the short story as an art form was slow to develop as an acceptable literary mode of expression. The Brazilian writer, until recently, regarded the short story as being more apt for children's ears than for the serious pursuit of imaginative literature. Machado de Assis (1839-1908), Brazil's first important short-story writer—to some the best the country has ever known—commented in 1873 on the short-story writer and the public's attitude toward the genre:

It's a difficult form, in spite of its apparent facility; I think this illusion of

ease is harmful to the short story, for it tends to turn the writer away; the
reading public, in turn, fails to give it all the attention it deserves.

Machado de Assis did give the short story the attention it deserved. In so doing, he not only brought the European-influenced
literary stream to an apex but transcended the genre to a degree of
artistic excellence unsurpassed even in our time. Nevertheless, there
is little reflection of the Brazilian social scene in Machado's stories.
The setting is the capital city of Rio de Janeiro—the seat of the im-
perial court at the end of the last century. The characters are for the
most part urbane and their conflicts domestic. The author's use of
language, although brilliant in its dexterity, may be ascribed to the
Portuguese literary tradition. Important in Machado de Assis's short
stories—beyond the mere considerations of technical and linguistic
accomplishment—is his constant use of irony—the slow unraveling of
a well-defined plot, laying bare the multifaced, paradoxical reality
with which he engulfs the reader.

Machado de Assis's contribution to the Brazilian literary tradition has not been fully acknowledged by the critics. In spite of the
extensive bibliography connected with his works—he is acclaimed by
university professors and by those who consider him a master of the
European-based nineteenth-century novel—Machado's legacy has
been repudiated by those who view Brazilian literature as a progressive recognition of the indigenous experience. For these, he fails to
reflect the Brazilian habitat as well as the particular kind of Portuguese
spoken in Brazil. As we consider the revival of the Brazilian short
story in the sixties, however, we must bear in mind that Brazil's
most important literary manifestation to date has been the short story
as engendered by Machado de Assis.

After Machado de Assis, the literary current which emphasized
the national character began to take hold within the Brazilian literary
tradition. Since the middle of the nineteenth century, when the country was seeking its independence from Portugal, Brazilian writers had
been calling for a new literature, set in the new land, with the Indian
as its "noble-savage" protagonist. They even advocated the adoption
of the Tupi language as a befitting vehicle for the new literary experiment. Being too closely identified with romantic ideals, however,
these elements were readily discarded once realism came into view.
Under this latter guise, the nationalistic strain manifested itself
through the portrayal of social conditions in Brazil's hinterland. The

inhabitants of the area, the backlandmen, were eulogized—their fortitude and moral stamina contrasted to the inhospitality of their environment. Brazilian literature became regional, that is, it drew away
from the cultural hegemony formerly held by the city of Rio de
Janeiro to accept the distinctive peculiarities of each of the four major
regions. In the process, it became a composite of several regional literary manifestations.

The regionalistic writers' contribution to the short story was
twofold. By choosing the short story as the preferred form for their
artistic effort, they helped to consolidate the genre within the
Brazilian literary tradition. By assimilating the backlanders' speech
in their work—a modified version of continental Portuguese containing many archaisms—they established an oral tradition which would
henceforth become the single most important factor in the attain-
ment of a really autonomous Brazilian literature. Technically, however, these stories were still crude, for the regionalistic short-story
writers were concerned more with subject matter than form. They
described the human conflicts sentimentally; they portrayed the
characters romantically.

When the modernist writers began calling for the adoption of
true Brazilian themes in their prose fiction, based on the folklore and
linguistic distinctiveness of the country, they were unwittingly drawing on the literary experiences of their regional predecessors. In São
Paulo, industrialization had given rise to a new society where social
injustices were as detrimental to the factory worker as the adverse
backland environment. These writers thought of the city as the "new
backland"—a befitting microcosm for the envisioned future Brazilian
society.

Two of the most important short-story writers connected with
the Modernist Movement launched in São Paulo in 1922 are Mário de
Andrade (São Paulo, 1899-1945), and Alcântara Machado (São Paulo
1901-1935). Both of these authors focus the problems brought on by
the new industrialized social order with a greater degree of realism
and objectivity than before. The Italian immigrant, as the greatest
component of the new labor force, is assimilated into the Brazilian
social milieu. Living in squalid slum conditions in the outskirts of São
Paulo—for example in Andrade's "Piá, Não Sofre? Sofre?" and Alcântara Machado's "Gaetaninho"—the Italian family begins to disintegrate; love degenerates into sex and further into prostitution.
Children are the pitiful victims, and both of these writers deal with
childhood tragedy with a great degree of pathos. These stories are

technically more accomplished: Andrade's by virtue of his objective realism; Alcântara Machado's through a cinematographic technique—the juxtaposing of several short sketches loosely tied together with no evident transition. They both assimilate the Italian peculiarities of speech into the narrative. Mário de Andrade goes back to the Tupi language of the Brazilian Indian as the source of some of his language innovations.

The early modernists failed in their attempt to unify Brazilian literature. The country was still too heterogeneous to withstand generalization. For the next quarter of a century, the section of Brazil known as the Northeast provided the background for the further entrenchment, within the realm of the Brazilian literary tradition, of the nationalistically inspired literary current. A group of writers born in this region purported to describe its afflicting social conditions. The novel, by virtue of its latitude, was best suited for their intentions; as a result, the short story gave way to the novel as the preferred art form. Since Brazilian literature in the sixties and the accompanying revival of the short story represented a reaction against the novel of the Northeast, however, let us take time to describe its major characteristics briefly before embarking on our subject.

Generally speaking, the novel of the Northeast is characterized by a deep concern with social problems in a particularly inhospitable and backward area of rural Brazil—the backland in the interior of the Northeastern states of Pernambuco, Ceará, Paraíba, Maranhão, and Bahía. Human conflicts are determined by the social realities. The long droughts which from time to time parch the area deepen the peasant's ever-present misery. The decadence of the old rural sugarcane aristocracy gives rise to a new social order based on capitalism, bringing with it the degeneration of time-honored human values, such as family cohesiveness, love, maidenhood, respect for the property of others, individual integrity, and honor. The governmental authorities, the rich, the bandits are the privileged classes under these social strata. The juxtaposition of human conflict and social determinism varies according to the author. In the most accomplished, the human predicament is more important, while in others the social conflict predominates. Circumstance, however, not character, dictates the action. In spite of the over-all objectivity that characterized these novels, the authors at times endeavor to influence the readers' conscience by bringing into their field of vision overt allusion to revolutionary ideologies. As would be expected, the northeastern novelists emphasized the regional peculiarities of speech in an attempt to show its singularity, rather unlike the early modernists who wanted to make their speech patterns common to the whole country.

As we have seen, the development of Brazilian literature up to the present time has been marked by a progressive assertion of the indigenous experience. This trend was first manifested through the acclaim, during the romantic period, of the new land and of the Indian as a superior moral being. Later, at the end of the last century, it called attention to the unfortunate, the derelict at odds with a constraining nature and victimized by social conditions in the country's hinterland. The backlander's basic human qualities were contrasted to the harshness of his environment. Since the middle and upper classes dwelling in cities along the Atlantic seaboard were hybrid products of the European tradition, this current in Brazilian literature consciously chose the backland reality as its major setting, for the destitute backlander was believed to represent genuine Brazilian qualities authentically. Always the social circumstances have been responsible for men's existential plight. Either the government would not take the necessary steps to ameliorate the peasant's lot or hard-set social inequalities hindered his betterment. Implied was the belief that once these restraining conditions were removed all would be well.

The Brazilian literature of the sixties, which continues a thematic and technical renovation begun after the Second World War, transcends social injustice and regional separateness to dwell on the general human condition of contemporary man compelled to subsist in an impersonal, incoherent, hostile world he has never made and is impotent to alter. The novel of the Northeast developed, after all, in a coherent society unified by common evils that once removed would improve man's condition. No such unity of purpose confronts today's writer. Global, organic, coherent visions are impossible. The short story, therefore, with its capacity for segmented analysis of reality— the illogical, unexplained apprehension of the fleeting present moment of truth—is the literary form most suited to the description of contemporary Brazilian society. A few authors persist in making the socio-political injustice affecting modern man the principal theme for their short stories, albeit with greater concern, proportionately, for the ensuing personal human tragedy. The most successful and representative, however, responding to the chaotic, diffuse, multifaceted world they inhabit as well as to the formalistic demands of the genre itself, endeavor to arrest the intensity of their private vision with the aid of innovating techniques and new forms of language expression:

Contemporary literature found its most representative form of expression in
the short story. . . . It is the genre most receptive to thematic and formalistic
change. Contemporary short-story writers approach a variety of subjects
ranging from the psychological to the regional in search for renewal or
formalistic revolution. If at times the pursuit leads to excessive
experimentation, it yields, nevertheless, new approaches to the literary
artifact.[1]

In the study that follows, we will endeavor to show the major
characteristics of the contemporary Brazilian short story manifested in
the most representative writers' work as they measure and transcend
the social realities of the sixties.

The short-story writers' first concern, as he grew weary of the
excessive social documentation in Brazilian literature, was to accen-
tuate the human universal qualities of the Brazilian man, no matter
what the conditions of his habitat. Fortunately, the task fell upon a
most accomplished craftsman, Guimarães Rosa (1908-1967), whose
short stories provide the necessary transition from the socially involved backland themes to those transcendentally universal. Guimarães Rosa, in his early and most influential work, continued to refer
to the backland as the setting for his stories. He was not concerned,
however, with social conditions merely. The backland provided an
appropriate setting for his work because personal relationships were
still meaningful in the rural community. Furthermore, the backlander's
simplicity heightened the effect of his ethical decisions—a frequent
theme in Guimarães Rosa's stories. While on one hand, the protagonists reveal their genuine Brazilian qualities as backlanders, their human conflicts cause them to transcend the rural milieu to become
universal representations of man's perennial metaphysical quest:

In Guimarães Rosa, Brazilian prose fiction found an exceptional moment of
literary vigor. Out of our most revolutionary literary trends—the regionalistic
themes—the author engenders a most original literary artifact, based on the
disclosure of our human problems and the incarnation of man's permanent
predicament.[2]

1. Antônio Cândido, "Movimento Geral de Literatura Contemporânea," *O Tempo
e O Modo no Brasil* (special issue), p. 87.
2. Maria Lúcia Lepeckni, "O Conto de Rubem Fonseca," *Minas Gerais: Suplemento Literário*, Ano III, No. 100 (July 27, 1968), p. 2.

Guimarães Rosa's most influential work, as far as the development of the short story in the sixties is concerned, was published in 1946—a volume of short stories entitled *Sagarana*. The stories in this volume include extensive, detailed descriptions of the backland milieu —adverse natural surroundings, disease, a poverty-stricken peasant class dominated by the old landed aristocracy who now exercise control through the electoral machine. Against these hard-set conditions, the only possible opposing force is banditry. The *cangaceiro*—(highwayman) and his band of followers raid the countryside, rival the rich in political power, and dispense their own special kind of social justice. The characters' actions are set against this background without necessarily being determined by it, since the climax arises out of human, not social, conflicts.

In "Sarapalha," for example, one of the volume's best-known short stories, the author depicts a backland community where malaria has taken its devastating toll. The region is desolate except for two men who have decided to remain, since they are bound to their inhospitable surroundings and to each other by the memory of a woman they had both loved. Slowly dying from malaria, they accept their physical desolation readily: "The malaria doesn't really matter. It even helped us to forget." Guimarães Rosa's characters do not react against their environment. Normally, they are complex human beings who control their adverse social conditions easily, only to rise or fall at the mercy of their human predicament or under the onslaught of deterministic forces. When their "time and day" approaches *(sua hora e vez)*, they reach an ethical decision which spirals them onto a metaphysical plane closer to God. The psychological and metaphysical impact of these stories derives from the magnitude of their choice.

Guimarães Rosa's growth as a short-story writer follows the development of the short story in the sixties. He becomes more and more concerned with the metaphysical decisions of his characters as well as with the aesthetic techniques required to achieve the compactness which characterizes his later work. His stories become more hermetic; local color disappears almost completely, the plot being practically nonexistent. For the purposes of the present study, however, Guimarães Rosa's greatest contribution to the development of the short story in the sixties lies in his ability to complement the backlander's genuine qualities with human, universal characteristics.

Contrasting to Guimarães Rosa's stories depicting the human and the metaphysical predicament amid rural, backward conditions, a new

breed of short-story writers began to look to the city and to the cos-
mopolitan milieu as their appropriate artistic setting. Rural conditions
exacted from men greater fortitude—their physical isolation and vicissitudes of nature warranted corresponding positive actions of an epical
magnitude. The city, on the other hand, brought together conglomerations of people living under the same impersonal, highly industrialized social conditions. What follows is a degeneration of human
values, a greater individual isolation based on the breakdown of human communication and, ultimately, a multiple sense of despair derived from the metaphysical insufficiency inherent to man.

Similarly, the destitute backlander has now been replaced as the
major protagonist. Urban problems do not arise solely out of socioeconomic inequality but engulf all classes and every ethnic group in
the same common human predicament. Thus, the rich, the apparently
well-adjusted to society, attain an increasingly more important role as
protagonists, as do foreigners, not necessarily immigrants, living in
Brazil. The universal human context that characterizes the short story
in the sixties precludes the artistic treatment of genuine Brazilian
types exclusively. Neither does the recent short story concern itself
with any specific ethnic group. The Negro—historically discriminated
against as a member of the poor classes and not as a symbol of an inferior race—is just one of many caught in the same human condition
with the poor, the middle class, and the rich.

Dalton Trevisan (born, Curitiba, Paraná, 1925) depicts the innate
human wickedness reigning in the city of Curitiba, Paraná. Since he is
most concerned with the absolute evil inherent in people—unlike the
Northeastern novelists who based their protest on the evil derived
from human institutions—Trevisan's city, Curitiba, maintains its provincial qualities in the midst of which the inhabitants are left to their
own wiles, unencumbered by the social ills of the modern city. The
gamut of men's perverted passions is endlessly and cyclically portrayed in short stories that do not normally exceed two or three pages.
The numerous gallery of characters, all caught in this malignant human society, include girls seduced by their boy friends and later abandoned to prostitution; maids raped by the master of the house or by
his son; priests, lawyers, and doctors who take advantage of their
women consultants; grooms who find their brides impure and seek
revenge or, being unable to consummate their marriages, commit suicide; the retarded, the maimed, the blind. Other stories deal with collective rape, homosexuality, women's incontinence. One of the most
successful stories, entitled "O Espião" ("The Spy"), describes condi-

tions in a school for abandoned girls run by Catholic sisters. Under the pretext of doing good, they often do incredible harm, for the strict discipline finally delivers the girls from "this hell," an event lightly dismissed by the nuns with the words, "they will go to heaven."

These multiple descriptions of human degradation are finally surmised in *Desastres de Amor* under a global vision of foreboding doom:

Woe to Curitiba, thy people perish and my heart breaks, for today is the day of the Lord's visitation. People will ask: 'your arrogance, your treasures, your titles, where are they now?' . . . Cursed be the day human beings first inhabited you; the day in which it was said that a city was born may it be forgotten; why did you not always remain a desert, instead of surrounded by walls to be once again deserted? . . . Oh Curitiba Curitiba Curitiba hear the cry of the Lord like a hammer driving down the nails. Your very name shall become a proverb, a curse, an eternal shame. . . . The sword came upon Curitiba, and Curitiba was, it is no more.

Other short-story writers of the sixties describe the Babylonian qualities of the modern city, none, however, with the unremitting pungency, the humorless detail of Trevisan's vision of apocalyptical evil.

Samuel Rawet's collection of short stories entitled *Os Sete Sonhos (The Seven Dreams, 1967),* introduces the modern city to the short story of the sixties. Unlike Dalton Trevisan's vision of arrant human knavery amid provincial surroundings, Rawet's fictional world harbors the "creatures of disenchantment," outcasts from a machine civilization, gravitating between receding rural traditional values and modern society's overemphasis on technology, methodical efficiency, and minute detail. Since the author, following the decade's general literary tendencies, is more concerned with individual characterization than with the description of social ills, the above traits are not treated directly but are implied through ironic portrayals of an egotistical bureaucrat, a beautiful elocutionist, and a cold philosopher.

In contrast to these inhuman types, by-products of a machine civilization impervious to sentiments or feelings, Rawet's collective protagonist emerges as a modern picaresque antihero. He is the wanderer in "Crônica de um Vagabundo" ("A Vagabond's Story"), through whose critical eyes and unusual personal experiences we are led into the world of the dejected. Like the picaresque antihero, the wanderer is without a family, social status, or purposeful objective, except immediate survival. Attesting the protagonist's modernity, however, these basic picaresque traits are complemented with others related to the present-day human predicament. Realizing the absurd-ity of human existence, he disowns all tradition and eradicates the recollection of his own past, whereas in picaresque literature, socially more conscious, the antihero's humble or obscure beginnings were emphasized. His struggle for survival is instinctive, immediate, it concerns the present moment only, since he has also disavowed the future. Besides being physically estranged from society, the modern picaresque antihero is, in addition, isolated in the soul: "What should we say to a man walled in his cell who insists on staying there saying: 'Is there anything else besides what you call a cell?' "

In his wanderings throughout the city, Rawet's protagonist pica-resquely disregards his earthly possessions and renounces all interested motives. He sells his watch, agrees to help bathe a paralyzed old lady, reacts indifferently and ironically to being robbed, refuses to yield to a pitiful young homosexual but fraternizes with him (not out of sym-pathy, but obeying he knows not what hidden impulse), gives all his money to an aging prostitute. For these are the "creatures of disen-chantment," as lonely as he, alienated from an impersonal machine civilization. In such a world, man must circumscribe his life to the pur-suit of immediate, base, elemental needs.

Love, or the lack of it, a constant theme in the contemporary urban short story, is beyond the disaffected protagonist's considera-tion. He renounces all feeling—for self, for man, for the world, for God. All critical faculties are to be surrendered. Man is to become an object only—every action is to be freed from its accompanying thought:

If only we could do away with the word in our speech as well as in our
thought! Then we would be objects merely, we'd live in a world of facts,
those strictly necessary. Then we'd be able to wrest intelligence from deeds.
Our reasoning, devoid of its thought-provoking faculty, would then be
implicitly tied to our actions.

This is a partially developed code of loneliness, for even norms of conduct seem strangely out of place in the incoherent, fragmented, chaotic world portrayed by Samuel Rawet in Os Sete Sonhos.

Contemporary Brazilian society has been interpreted most effec-tively by Rubem Fonseca (born, 1926), a young American-educated business executive, born in the State of Minas Gerais but living in Rio de Janeiro from the time he was four. A popular short-story writer in Brazil today, Rubem Fonseca has had published three short-story volumes to date: *Os Prisioneiros (The Prisioners*, 1963), *A Coleira do Cão (The Dog's Collar*, 1965), and *Lúcia McCartney* (1969). In 1969, he was awarded the coveted Curitiba Prize for the Short Story. Reported to be at work on a novel, Rubem Fonseca's literary production has so far been confined to the short story.

The reason for the author's popularity may be found in his unusually competent assimilation of middle-class, fairly educated, everyday speech patterns—a blend of sophisticated speech intermingled with foreign phrases and the current, youth-inspired *carioca* slang—as well as in the immediacy of his social themes depicting disaffected man in the midst of relative affluence. For Rubem Fonseca's protagonist is a hero rather than an antihero. He is a full-fledged member of the new society. He knows no other. Well-endowed physically, intelligent, articulate, he has been sieved from lesser competitors and proven himself a worthy representative of the new social order. As a result, he has status—money, position, and, outwardly at least, a family. He has been nurtured in an industrialized, competitive society and has partaken of its cultural and material advantages.

Having so generously treated contemporary urban society and its human byproducts, Rubem Fonseca, investing himself in the role of the detached, scientific observer, pours an additional element into his human formula—he endows the protagonist with feeling. The result is disastrous. Isolation, loneliness, lack of love come to the fore, perilously engulfing the hero. Sometimes isolation takes the form of a sudden, drastic falling out with society's *modus operandi.* "O Conformista Incorrigível" ("The Incorrigible Conformist") takes place during a psychiatric examination. The protagonist's gregariousness is interpreted as a sign of insanity by society's mental wardens, thriving on Erich Fromm and Norman Mailer (pictures of the two adorn the clinic's walls). In "Os Prisioneiros," the first volume's title story, human and scientific values clash. Set clinical psychiatric procedures, intent on comparting and labeling human behavior, are unsuccessfully challenged by the protagonist. Loneliness hides itself behind a telephone and a tape recorder, impersonal symbols of our age of cybernetics, in the story entitled "O Gravador" ("The Tape-Recorder"). A hurried, thorough, census-taker in "O Agente" ("The Agent"), is momentarily baffled by the intended suicide of a successful business executive but moves on, zealous of his time, insensitive to the approaching tragedy.

In addition to stories depicting the estrangement of man from the society that made him, there are those that deal with man's falling out with himself. "We are prisoners of ourselves, don't forget that. There's no possible escape." The author has inserted this percept, taken from Lao Tse, in an epigraph placed before his first book. Surfeited with material goods, the character gropes for the one further element in his life that might bring him fulfillment to meet, instead, with disappointment and sorrow. Love is his supreme test, the lack of it the reminder of human insufficiency: "Everyman is an island, the rest is poetry."

Influences of Ernest Hemingway's work have been traced in this particular phase of Rubem Fonseca's short story output by Brazilian literary critics. True enough, the powerful athlete's spiritual pangs in "A Força Humana" ("Human Strength") seem to remind us of Hemingway's stereotyped hero whose outward toughness concealed a damaged soul. Rubem Fonseca's protagonist is, however, quite different from the Hemingway hero, since his problems arise out of an over-all metaphysical insufficiency and not from a specific social cause: "The worst of the world I hadn't seen as yet, but I was close, pretty close to that." Equally sensitive, he is in addition to the Hemingway hero, urbane, sophisticated, affluent, and unconcerned with the broad issues of social violence or war. Rather than shield his feelings stoically from the world, Rubem Fonseca's modern hero, when he "cries in the night," is aware that he is interpreting man's generalized anguish:

Suddenly I began to cry. I hadn't cried for thirty years. It's something so strange, I must tell it in detail. After a while (if you're alone), the eyes close; you feel the tears slowly coming down your face and a sense of relief like you had been poisoned and a vein had opened oozing forth all the bad blood and with each drop of blood you were feeling better—lighter, purer, more deserving, happier in your self-pity.

The awareness of man's metaphysical insufficiency is more evident in Luis Vilela's short stories. In "Tremor de Terra" ("The Earthquake"), which merited Luis Vilela the aforementioned Curitiba Prize, a young man's innocent love for his happily married school teacher is set within an atmosphere of pungent sorrow and disenchantment. The protagonist's intense feelings, "like an earthquake," remind the reader of all the things life has chosen not to permit. The hero becomes more mature while life loses some of its magic:

I am going home to sleep and pray and tomorrow I'll go out, find myself a girl, Sônia, Lúcia, Marta or Regina or Bia or Mariza, and I am going to call

her honey and she will call me honey, and I'm going to give her presents and
she is going to give me presents, we'll go to the movies, and kiss each other
and get married and have children and put on weight and get old and get
grandchildren and die to be buried in the earth where we shall rest in peace.

Although inhabiting the same opaque, fragmented, chaotic
world, a world without God or apparent ultimate purpose, the next
group of short-story writers react more affirmatively. Devoid of ideals
or preconceived notions regarding the modern human condition—out
of place in the modern world's context—these writers attempt to find
in the most insignificant events of their daily lives a private vision of
endurable truth wrested from the wasteland of their day to day existence. Setting is incidental only to their stories. Although taking place
in the city, the stories develop within a very personal literary vision
impervious to time and space. Neither is there an attempt on the part
of these writers to bestow on their characters the present-day nuances
of Brazilian speech. They control language and content, juxtaposing
them in a simultaneity indispensable to the communication of their
complex vision. Given the multiplicity of their themes, the boldness
of their technical innovations, and the originality of their experience,
the work of these writers represents the most distinguished, noteworthy contribution to the contemporary Brazilian short story.

Like some of her fellow short-story writers—Guimarães Rosa
served in several world capitals as a diplomat, Samuel Rawet came
from Poland as a young man, Rubem Fonseca studied in the United
States for four years—Clarice Lispector has lived outside of Brazil for
long periods of time. She was born in Tchetchelnik, Ukraine, came to
Brazil as a two-month-old Russian immigrant, and later, after her
marriage to a Brazilian diplomat, she lived, from 1945 to 1959, in
Europe and in the United States. "O Mistério do Coelho Pensante"
("The Mystery of the Thinking Rabbit), one of her children's stories,
was first written in English while the author resided in the United
States. The universality of her themes, the distinctive peculiarities of
her style—the simple, allusive vocabulary with which she expresses
the inexpressible—may have originated out of a long acquaintance
with European and American culture and the acknowledged experience in using English creatively.

Clarice Lispector's two volumes of short stories were published
in the sixties: Laços de Família (Family Ties, 1960), and A Legião
Estrangeira (The Foreign Legion, 1964). The stories explore, from

multiple perspectives—each story represents an aggregate composite of a larger fictional vision—the underlying essence of being. While Rubem Fonseca's characters yearn for the one further element that would make them whole as human beings, Clarice Lispector's, confronted with their human possibilities, turn away from them. Like Rubem Fonseca's, the characters in Clarice's short stories are well-adjusted, intelligent, sensitive, middle-class people. Through a trivial, but to them terribly important incident, the protagonists are led into a perilous human adventure which momentarily disrupts their daily routine. Yearnings after love, freedom, hope bring the abrupt awareness of the metaphysical insufficiency of life. Anguish, inebriation, nausea set in until the characters' return, gladly and consciously, to the drudgery of their daily existence. By refraining from human fulfillment, they withdraw into their fundamental role as beings—women, wives, mothers—unconsciously attuned to the incomprehensible, eternal flow of life.

"Devaneios de uma Rapariga" ("A Girl's Reveries"), the first short story in *Laços de Família*, is the account of such an adventure experienced by a happily married, young, plump, somewhat earthy Portuguese girl living in Rio de Janeiro. The sudden confrontation with her body and heretofore repressed multifaceted personality: "the unlaced robe reflected in the mirrors the half-revealed breasts of several girls," together with the late afternoon noises hailing from the street below—a package falling out of an upstairs window, the passing streetcar, the newspaper-boy's haunting cry—unspool into the young wife's mental reveries a catapult of freedom metaphors: "Who saw the little sparrow . . . went out the window . . . flew beyond the Minho."

The state of being versus being human are juxtaposed throughout the narrative. On one hand, a woman suddenly aware of her human potential; on the other hand, a woman sleeping, "open-mouthed, the spittle slowly dampening the pillow." On one hand, the deepened sensitivity, the flirtatious mood, the sudden inebriation with life. On the other hand, the gradual affirmation of her role as woman, mother, wife. While in the restaurant, she gazes at a young girl sitting across from the table: "All aglow under a new hat, modestly proud of her small waist. She couldn't even, probably, give birth to a child." She feels secure, respected as a married woman, but the memories of those wild reveries linger:

How well you could see the moon on these summer nights. She bent herself

forward a little, unconcerned, resigned. The moon. How well you could see
it. The high, yellow moon wandering through the sky, poor moon!
Wandering, wandering. High, high. The moon. Then her coarseness exploded
in sudden love; bitch, she said, smiling.

To accept the fundamental condition of being is to accept the
end of innocence. "Preciosidade" ("Preciousness"), the institution
of marriage "Devaneios de uma Rapariga," motherhood, "Amor"
("Love"), and finally death. The old woman in "Feliz Aniversário"
("Happy Birthday"), is contrasted to the other members of her family, gathered together to celebrate the birthday, by the calm acceptance of death: "With her fist clinched firmly upon the table, she
would never again be just what her thoughts were. Her appearance
transcended her; surpassing her, it had become serenely gigantic. . . .
Life is short, life is short, she seemed to be saying . . . death was her
mystery."
Guided by primitive, basic instincts, animals are closer to the
essence of being than humans. Several of Clarice Lispector's short
stories have animals as their principal characters. Humans lose sight
of life's basic goals through emotions. "Uma Galinha" ("A Hen"), a
much anthologized short story from *Laços de Família*, treats the
"short, happy life" of a Sunday-dinner hen. Before noon, the hen
escapes onto a rooftop. Like the girl in "Devaneios de uma Rapariga,"
the chicken yearns for freedom: "then she looked so free." Finally
caught, the chicken lays an egg, a characteristic event, innate to her
being. The whole family becomes suddenly concerned over the hen,
taking the egg-laying spree as a sign of generous affection. "The
chicken had become queen of the household. Everyone knew it except
her. She continued wandering to and fro, between the back porch
and the kitchen, relying on her two capacities: apathy and fear." For
a brief, glorious moment she had escaped, "silhouetted against the
sky ready to annunciate." But chickens do not annunciate: "It was
just a chicken's head—the same that had been designed in the beginning of time." To contribute toward the preservation of the species
is all important to Clarice Lispector's characters. There is enough
heroism in doing just that. There is heroism enough in being.

While Clarice Lispector strips man of all soul-begotten, superflu-
ous, meddling emotions in order to bring him closer to the fundamental issues of being, Osman Lins relates the human being's fragmented,
chaotic state affirmatively to the order and geometrical symmetry of

the cosmos in an attempt to achieve a global explanation for contemporary man's absurd condition.

Born in the Northeastern state of Pernambuco, Osman Lins, who presently resides in São Paulo, has chosen the region of his birth as the appropriate setting for most of his short stories. His fictional vision, however, like that of Clarice Lispector, transcends mere regionalism to include universal portrayals of man everywhere. Local color is definitely not an important aspect in the broad context of Osman Lins's realm of fiction.

Osman Lins is the author of several novels as well as volumes of short fiction. In 1966, he had published a collection of short stories —he prefers to call them "narratives"—entitled *Nove, Novena (Nine, Novena)*. The volume includes nine interrelated tales loosely grouped together to form an organic whole.

Multiplicity and fragmentation characterize these stories, both thematically and in their technical aspects. Several narratives comprehend three or more short stories, which criss-cross one another but are narrated simultaneously. At times, a larger narrative will include one or two short stories complete in themselves. The thematic incidents are narrated by several protagonists from multiple points of view. In order to identify the speaker, the author has introduced into the text small, geometrical signs preceding each new, changing voice. Sometimes, when two characters speak simultaneously, the larger sign includes a smaller one—for example, a triangle inside of a circle. Normally, the thematic incident becomes interwoven into the world's substance through its diffusion in the whirlpool-like, interior monologue emanating from the point of view of each of the several protagonists. Sometimes the diffused incident is spiralled onto the cosmos through what the author calls ornaments—intensely poetic, verbal decorations, which appear to glorify the world's body.

In "Perdidos e Achados" ("Lost and Found"), the incident revolves around a father's tragic search for his son possibly lost at sea. The father's anguish is transmitted to the witnessing protagonists and becomes part of their thoughts—they had also been physically and mentally victimized by the sea. Anguish becomes, through this process, an abstract, all-absorbing human condition and not just the father's particularized emotion. The conflict is now between the sea and humanity, the characters' anguish having become part of the larger context. The people gathering at the scene, whose incantational voices (the ornaments), sing both of the voraciousness of the sea and human frailty appear to leave no doubt as to the outcome.

In the face of disaster, humanity will endure: Then one day, "some tools, domesticated animals and fire are brought back by an escaping couple."

The political upheavals that assailed Brazilian society in the beginning of the decade are scarcely represented within the context of the contemporary short story. Since the political turmoils in the sixties are treated in previous chapters, we will refrain from enumerating them here. Suffice it to say that social protest is not the overt concern of the short-story writers in the sixties. As previously mentioned, after 1946, Guimarães Rosa, Dalton Trevisan, and Clarice Lispector began to portray the hopeless condition of man in an alien world. This trend was well launched before revolutionary ideals began to take hold in the Brazilian cumulative consciousness. Rather than deviating from their path, short-story authors chose to remain silent during the early sixties to emerge again in the old familiar line, that is, to depict human despair in the light of an incoherent universe. The defeated social struggle, however, now became incorporated into the over-all human predicament. The fall of ideals is defined by these authors as being synonymous with political defeat. They return to the country, fleeing from the city, the source of their misfortunes, to reflect on the human social condition among quieter surroundings, gathering strength for future retaliation.

Wander Piroli's volume of short stories *A Mãe e o Filho da Mãe* (*Mother and Son*, 1966), opens with a quotation from Fernando Pessôa: "The river runs into the sea/and its waters are the same as they always were." Piroli's stories take place in an interim between revolutions. It is a period of self-assertion, of evaluation, where the ideals have fallen only momentarily. The characters in the stories are all possessed of the same human indestructibility, which will, the author seems to be saying, eventually win out. The streetcar conductor who foils the owner's attempt to fire him—he is soon to attain stability for having worked more than ten years—by proving with the help of an understanding passenger that he has counted the fares properly is a good example. The story is entitled "A Manhã Seguinte" ("The Next Morning"), since the day before the conductor's son had passed away. The owners, the *gordos*, assumed he wouldn't come to work and intended to get rid of him. The *gordos* are contrasted by *os nossos*, symbolized by the conductor, the driver, and the passenger himself. In "Festa," a Negro and two small boys eat their "feast" heartily—a beer, two bottles of *guaraná* and some bread dipped in the gravy provided free by the waiter—one of the *nossos*. It is this contentment with the small pleasures of life, the discipline over want, their human solidarity that will eventually win the battle with the rich. In a trip to Ouro Preto, a city symbolizing Brazil's traditions, the protagonist ("Passeio a Sabará"), refuses to look for the "golden museum" to fraternize in a bar with os nossos—victims, such as he, of the existing social order. Tradition has nothing to teach for the revolution ahead. Human solidarity is far more important.

At times, the protagonists are shown as painstaking learners of the skills that will lead to a successful revolution. In "Rio de Dentro" ("The Inner River")—the title recalls Pessoa's poem quoted in the epigraph—there is a juxtaposition between the character's methodical preparation for fishing "out of season" and the guerrilla-type expedition taking place moments later up the river. The protagonist's skilled approach to fishing foretells the success of the guerrilla venture, for the exterior expertise is a reflection of the human stamina, endurance beyond defeat, stemming from man's unceasing resourcefulness. "Out of season" alludes to the aforementioned period between revolutions.

Love, marriage, fatherhood are impossible under the present circumstances. "Até Amanhã" ("Till Tomorrow") depicts true love between a rich girl and a middle-class boy. The latter forsakes the girl, since their union would not be feasible in a world aware of class distinctions. He decides to renounce her, in spite of his love, in order to commit himself to the revolution. The same disheartening renouncement takes place in "Um Entre Dois" ("One Between Two") and "Par or Impar" ("Even Number, Odd Number"), in relation to men's acceptance of fatherhood. "Trabalhadores do Brasil" ("Brazil's Workers"), is a story that tells what happens when love and fatherhood do take place. The protagonist's family is devoted to him and together they form the same human solidarity that characterized the nossos. The title is ironically derived from the standard opening lines with which Getúlio Vargas began his speeches promising a better lot to the workers. The character is out of work. He subsists by drawing Getúlio's face in the public square. Besides the miserable lot of the man, his condition is made more pathetic by his wasting away a talent that could have been fostered under different social circumstances.

All these short stories take place in the aftermath of the fallen ideals represented by the military takeover. At the same time, they take place in the beginning of a new dawn charged with great human energy, between the night of defeat and the coming of the inevitable social liberation of the masses. It is the time to take account of human resources for the big forward thrust—the river must ultimately lead to the sea.

Clarice Lispector, who in *A Legião Estrangeira* had already dealt with her inability to refer artistically to the problems of social injustice: "they are so innate to my being that I am unable to treat them in my work. I can't write about what is evident to me," reaffirmed her views in a recent interview. When asked how she felt in regard to the war in Viet Nam, she answered: "I feel pain and a sense of frustration." Similarly, Guimarães Rosa declined to comment, during an international writers' conference, on whether literature may serve as a proper vehicle for the dissemination of social issues without losing its aesthetic value. Wander Piroli's short stories notwithstanding, the critics' clamor for more militant writing in the sixties has gone unheeded. In the decade just ending, Brazilian literature has not been characterized by a concern for sociopolitical themes. The fallen ideals, that is, political defeat, are just another source—an overwhelming one in Wander Piroli's case—for Brazilian man's over-all human predicament as portrayed by the most representative short-story writers in the sixties.

REFERENCES

Works

Coelho, Nelson. *O Inventor de Deus.* São Paulo:Editôra Paulo de Azevedo Ltda., 1962.

Fonseca, Rubem. *Os Prisioneiros.* Rio de Janeiro:Edições GRD, 1963.

———. *A Coleira do Cão.* Rio:Edições GRD, 1965.

———. *Lúcia McCartney.* Rio:Olivé Editor, 1969.

Gomes, José Edson. *As Sementes de Deus.* Rio:Editôra Leitura, 1965.

———. *Os Ossos Rotulados.* Rio:Editôra Leitura, 1966.

———. *O Ôvo no Teto.* Rio:Editôra Leitura. S.A., 1967.

Lins, Osman. *Nove, Novena:Narrativas.* São Paulo:Editôra Martins, 1966.

Lispector, Clarice. *A Legião Estrangeira.* Rio:Editôra do Autor, 1964.

———. *Laços de Família.* 2a.ed., Rio:Editôra do Autor, 1965.

Piñon, Nélida. *Tempo de Frutas.* Rio:José Alvaro, Editor, 1966.

Piroli, Wander. *A Mãe e o Filho da Mãe,* Belo Horizonte, 1966.

Ramos, Ricardo. *Os Desertos.* São Paulo:Edições Melhoramentos, s/d.

Rosa, João Guimarães, *Sagarana.* Rio:Livraria José Olympio Editôra, 1946.

———. *Primeiras Estórias.* Rio:José Olympio, 1963.

———. *Tutaméia:Terceiras Estórias.* Rio:José Olympio, 1967.

———. *Estas Estorias.* Rio:Livraria José Olympio, 1969.

Sant'Anna, Sérgio. *O Sobrevivente.* Belo Horizonte:Edições Estória, 1969.

Rawet, Samuel. *Diálogo.* Rio:Edições GRD, 1963.

———. *Os Sete Sonhos.* Rio: Orfeu, 1967.

Trevisan, Dalton. *Novelas Nada Exemplares.* Rio:Livraria José Olympio Editôra, 1959.

———. *Morte na Praça.* Rio:Editôra do Autor, 1964.

———. *Cemitério de Elefantes.* Rio:Editôra Civilização Brasileira, 1964.

———. *O Vampiro de Curitiba.* Rio:Editôra Civilização Brasileira, 1965.

———. *Desastres do Amor.* Rio:Editôra Civilização Brasileira, 1968.

———. *Guerra Conjugal.* Editôra Civilização Brasileira, 1969.

Vieira, José J. *Os Cavalinhos do Platiplanto.* Rio:Editôra Nítida Ltda., 1969.

———. *A Máquina Extraviada.* Rio:Editôra Prelo, 1968.

Vilela, Luís. *Tremor de Terra.* Belo Horizonte, 1967.

———. *No Bar.* Rio:1969.

English Translations

Rosa, João Guimarães. *Sagarana: A Cycle of Stories,* transl. by Harriet de Onís. New York: Alfred A. Knopf, 1966.

———. *The Third Bank of the River and Other Stories,* translated with an introduction by Barbara Shelby. New York: Alfred A. Knopf, 1968.

Veiga, José J. *The Misplaced Machine and Other Stories,* transl. by Pamela Bird. New York: Alfred A. Knopf, 1970.

Criticism

Araújo, Zilah C. "Rubem Fonseca", "Suplemento Literário" *Minas Gerais* (March 23, 1969).

Brasil, Assis. *Clarice Lispector.* Rio:Organizações Simões, 1969.

———. *Guimarães Rosa.* Rio:Organização Simões, 1969.

Cândido, Antônio. *Tese e Antítese.* São Paulo:Editôra Nacional, 1964.

———. "Movimento Geral da Literatura Contemporânea", *O Tempo e o Modo no Brasil* (special issue), 50:82-88.

Cavalheiro, Edgard. *Evolução do Conto Brasileiro. Boletim Bibliográfico.* São Paulo, viii (July-September, 1945), pp. 101-120.

Dohman, Barbara and Harss, Luís. *Into the Mainstream.* New York: Harper and Row, 1967.

Daniel, Mary Lou. *João Guimarães Rosa:Travessia Literária.* Rio:Livraria José Olympio Editôra, 1968.

Filho, Adonias. *Modernos Ficcionistas Brasileiros* (.1st and 2nd. series). Rio:O Cruzeiro, 1958, 1965.

Herman, Rita. "Existence in *Laços de Família*" . *Luso-Brazilian Review,* IV, 1 (June, 1967).

Studies in Short Fiction (Special issue on Latin American Short Fiction published in April 1971).

Lepeckni, Maria Lúcia. "O Conto de Rubem Fonseca". In "Suplemento Literário" *Minas Gerais*. Ano III, Nº100 (July 27, 1968), p. 2.

Lima, Herman. *Variações Sôbre o Conto*. Rio:Ministério de Educação e Saúde, 1952.

Lima, Luiz Costa. "A Mística ao Revés de Clarice Lispector," in *Por Que Literatura*. Petrópolis:Vozes, 1966.

Lucas, Fábio. "Cultural Aspects of Brazilian Literature," *Triquarterly* 14-15, 1968.

———. *O Caráter Social da Literatura Brasileira*. Rio:Editôra Paz e Terra, 1970.

Martins, Wilson. "Brazilian Literature: The Task of the Next Twenty Years," in *Portugal and Brazil in Transition*, Raymond S. Sayers, ed. Minneapolis: University of Minnesota Press, 1968.

Merquior, José Guilherme. "As Fronteiras da Arte," in "Suplemento Literário" *Minas Gerais*, Ano V,Nº185 (March 14, 1970).

Montello, Josué. *O Conto Brasileiro:de Machado de Assis a Monteiro Lobato*. Rio:Edições de Ouro, 1967.

Mourão, Rui. "Cão Sem Coleira," in "Suplemento Literário" *Estado de São Paulo* (June 14, 1969), p. 3.

Nunes, Benedito. *O Dorso do Tigre*. São Paulo:Edições Perspectiva, 1969.

Pequeno Dicionário de Literatura Brasileira. Massaud Moisés & José Paulo Paes, eds. São Paulo:Editôra Cultrix, 1967.

Pontual, Roberto. "Tutaméia," in *Revista de Civilização Brasileira*, III, 16 (Nov.-Dec., 1967), 252.

Reis, Fernando G. "Quem Tem Mêdo de Clarice Lispector," in *Revista de Civilização Brasileira*, IV, 17 (Jan.-Feb., 1968) 225-34.

Rodrigues, Urbano Tavares. "Pontos Altos da Novela Brasileira," in "Suplemento Literário," *Estado de São Paulo* (Oct. 26, 1968), p. 5.

Siebenmann, Gustavo. "O Romance Hispano-Americano Como Reflexão na Situação Social," in "Suplemento Literário" *Minas Gerais*, V, 184 (March 7, 1970), 1-3.

"Symposium on the Short Story," *The Kenyon Review*, XXX,XXXI,121,123, 126, (1968, 1969).

Zagury, E. "O Que Clarice Diz de Clarice," in *Cadernos Brasileiros*, X,50 (Nov.-Dec., 1968), 69-79.

12 EARL W. THOMAS

Protest in the Novel and Theater

A GREAT part of literature through the ages has an element of protest. The authors inveighed against the wrongs of society, against the injustices of man, against the political or social structure in which they had to live. The Brazilian is likely to have a high degree of theoretical idealism, along with a pronounced tendency toward pessimism: if he is a writer, he is quite likely to express the contrast between his ideals for society and government and the actual state of affairs. Thus, protest in Brazilian literature is as old as the poetry of Gregório de Matos, who left us an unflattering picture of society and government in the colonial Northeast in the heyday of the sugar plantations.

Protest in the Novel

Social protest in the novel of Brazil has a long and illustrious history. It gained particular prominence in the works of the "Generation of 1930," which was largely socially oriented. In some of the authors of that group, the principal concern was simply an accurate presentation of social situations, without involving a primary purpose of suggesting remedies or of protesting against any one class or group. The novels of José Lins do Rêgo and those of Rachel de Queiroz, for example, can hardly be considered as overt expressions of protest, although the situations they presented obviously required urgent remedy. In the novels of Graciliano Ramos, however, the note

397

of protest is clear, and the remedy he would apply is suggested, if never clearly expressed. Jorge Amado, in several early works, expresses both protest and the remedy he would apply to the situation.

There is a specifically political novel in Brazil, the main purpose of which is to expose the defects of the political system and especially of those who engage in politics. It is found mostly in the state of Minas Gerais, where politics is a preoccupation of more people than in any other state. It has dealt with the periods other than the present and for that reason has not drawn the fire of the present regime, although frequently the same objections could be made today. On the surface, it seems to support the thesis of the military government, according to which the corruption of the democratic regime required a strong hand to save the country from the politicians.

As examples of the political novels, we will consider briefly two by Mário Palmério and one by Oscar Dias Corrêa.

The works of Palmério are primarily concerned with the politics of Minas Gerais at their worst. *Vila dos Confins* (1957) precedes the decade of 1960; *Chapadão do Bugre* (1965), while it was published more than a year after the Revolution of 1964, was almost complete by that date and has no connection with conditions under the military government which followed. Both novels are laid in the interior, in small towns and districts far from the centers of politics and of power. Both make it clear to the reader, however, that a great deal of the corruption of politics in those areas, possibly the worst abuses, have their origin in the capital of the state.

The earlier novel presents an election campaign in a new district in a distant part of the state. The political process includes the use of influence, threats, bribes, substitution of ballots, tricks of every kind. The author is even more concerned, however, with the social conditions which produce politics of this sort than with politics as such. The result is a great novel which will maintain its interest long after the changing times have transformed completely the political situation.

If in *Vila dos Confins* Palmério was able to write of politics with humor and compassion, in *Chapadão do Bugre* his mood has changed to dark pessimism and revulsion. Here we have little reference to the actual political institutions, and the local elections are merely the pretext for the intervention of the Special Police of the state in the frontier region. The intervention is brought about by one of the feuding groups in the locality, through its influence in the state capital, and brings into focus one of the prime subjects of protest in literature over the past forty years—police brutality.

The Special Police have been recruited among criminal elements who have been forgiven their crimes on the condition of joining the police. It is evident that this system is followed partly with the intention of organizing a body of men who will carry out any order of their superiors and who will have no compunction about killing or torturing their prisoners. The author is again less concerned with the police as such than with the social and cultural conditions which bring about this situation. Where other authors frequently blame their political or ideological opponents for similar situations, and consequently excuse or ignore similar brutalities committed by members of their own groups, Palmério is concerned with the deep underlying causes. He is no partisan.

Oscar Dias Corrêa, the author of *Brasílio* (1968), states, "Any resemblance to facts or personages of real life is simple coincidence." Throughout the novel, however, the coincidences are so numerous and so obvious that no one could possibly take this statement seriously. His protagonist, who becomes governor of the state of Minas Gerais, and the president of the country at the time, are called respectively Brasílio Val-verde and Genésio Vasques. Even if the coincidence of the initials and the similarity of the names were not enough, the allusions to anecdotes current at the time would point clearly to Benedito Valadares and Getúlio Vargas. In any case, the two *were* the men who occupied these two positions during the years in question, as millions of persons know perfectly well. Of course, the facts are not all history.

Brasílio is, at first glance, a biting satire of the politicians in the period of Vargas and of his assumption of the dictatorship through the clever use of not-so-brilliant stooges. Brasílio is lazy, of very mediocre intelligence but very clever at taking advantage of circumstances for his own ends. He manages to get a degree in pharmacy at a mediocre school, largely by cheating and by persuading others to do his work. Through clever maneuvers, he manages to get himself chosen mayor of his small town. Before his disastrous administration catches up with him, he uses friends' influence to get elected to the state legislature. While in this position, he meets the president. The latter immediately senses in Brasílio a useful tool, encourages him, and forces him on the party as candidate for governor. During this period the chicaneries of state and national politics are exposed by the author with the authority of one who was fully acquainted with the situation of that period.

The author gives examples of the alliance of corrupt politics with other social institutions, as well as of other social situations not directly connected with the political scene. There is, for example, a certain Colonel Ribas who holds the controlling interest in a business. He uses the funds of the business for all his own expenses, as well as for political contributions. There is Padre João, who fancies himself a political power. He gives his support to the candidate who has made the greatest monetary contribution to his church and denounces from the pulpit the immorality of this man's opponent. Then there is the school of law in which Brasílio is enrolled but never attends. At the end of four years he receives his degree.

In its main lines, as can be seen from this brief exposition, this book is a satire of the politics of another period. But there are a number of indications of the interest of the author in the present day and strong hints that the existing situation is similar.

One of the more brilliant feats of Brasílio is the invention of the "rotation" of political leaders. He uses this to get rid of politicians who are not loyal to him and to replace them with his own creatures. This device is later copied by the president. The rotation of political leaders is one of the favorite devices of the present government, adopted supposedly to replace the old-style politicians with new and more honest and efficient ones.

The period during which Brasílio and the president were establishing the dictatorial government "was when there was discovered a leftist plan for the subversion of order. Extreme measures were taken —imprisonment, suspension of guarantees, retirement of military officers, etc."

"It was enough to say: 'so-and-so is an extremist' and Wham! to the police station, incommunicado, with no possible proof to the contrary—not even a certificate from the Holy See." This practice is now known as *dedo-durismo*, pointing the "hard finger" at one's opponent, in or out of politics.

"Finally, it was announced that democratic principles were in danger, because of the ineptness of those who represented them." This is, of course, the justification of the present regime.

The novel of Geraldo França de Lima, *Brejo Alegre* (1964), is basically concerned with a corrupt society. The relatively small mention of politics is incidental.

The scene is a small town in the interior, in a region which the author carefully avoids identifying, during World War II. The people are divided between the good and the evil, largely on class lines. The town is dominated by two families, one of rich landowners, the other headed by an ex-politician.

The rich—these two families, with their relatives and retainers—are presented in the darkest colors. They are incredibly corrupt, so stupid that the young ones must buy their college degrees, completely without scruples, hesitating at no crime in order to achieve their purposes. They are even represented as physically dirty.

On the other hand, the poor are examples of goodness, education, intelligence, and nobility of character. Curiously, the female protagonist, who has all the nobility of character of the poor, is a daughter of the wicked rich.

Here we have some of the principal themes of literature of protest: the wicked latifundiary who starves his laborers and abuses them in other ways; the corruptness of politics, allied to the wickedness of the industrialist and financier. On the other hand, and in contrast to these, we find nobility in the humble, and especially in the humble Negro, represented here in the person of an ex-slave who now sells lottery tickets. There is another theme, one of recent origin, which we will see repeated in much more expressive terms—the adoption of Getúlio Vargas as a hero of the Left. In this novel, the only expression of it is to be found in the fact that the shoemaker keeps flowers in front of the picture of Vargas. Questioned by his son, who is an opponent of Vargas, the father refers to the benefits granted to Labor—such as health insurance and retirement pay—by Vargas.

Another theme, presented in attenuated form without much insistence, is that of pacifism. This idea, dear to the Left in many countries in which it is an arm of opposition to the government, hardly appears in Brazil. The Brazilian Left often favors violence.

As a work of art, this book presents certain defects. In addition to the pure black and white of the characters, several of the main ones remain so undefined as personages as to make it difficult to follow the thread of the narrative. In spite of weaknesses, the author shows promise of outstanding qualities. The principal narrative thread, the love story of João and Rosa Maria, is a poetic tale, with an atmosphere somewhat mystical, with a slight suggestion of magic. The author dominates his linguistic medium with noteworthy skill. These qualities are more fully revealed in his second novel, *Branca Bela* (1965), which has no theme of protest.

Emissários do Diabo (1968), by the young writer Gilvan Lemos of Pernambuco, was not written as a novel of protest. It illustrates the fact, however, that certain social themes are so much a part of the present-day literature of Brazil that they occur almost automatically.

The story related is the struggle of a small landowner (one who operates a "family farm") to protect his property against an attempted takeover by his uncle, who is a powerful latifundiary. He is also quite dark, in contrast to his uncle and other unfriendly relatives who are fair-skinned and blond. Other than the protagonist, all the characters of the book who show sentiments of honesty and loyalty are Negroes —a widespread theme among many contemporary Brazilian writers.

Another Northeastern theme, that of the bandits, appears also. There is no hint of the developing legend of the famous bandit Lampião, however, who is beginning to take on the character of a folk hero, the defender of the oppressed against both landowners and government.

The style of the work is simple but adequate, without exaggeration of the defects of the language of the uneducated or touches of misplaced erudition. The analysis of the characters, especially of the protagonist, is excellent, concise in its expression, and thoroughly integrated into the continuity. The end of the story departs from the strictly realistic tone of the rest, with touches of poetic style in which the influence of Guimarães Rosa appears evident. This is only a small inconsistency in what is basically an excellent work.

In some of the novels written after the Revolution of 1964, the intention of protest directed at it is made very clear. The authors make no secret of their Marxist leanings and are particularly bitter because of the successful coup which was anti-Communist in its origin. The transformation of the movement into a continuing military dictatorship, with increasing suppression of democratic institutions and ever tighter control over freedom of expression, has given much greater force and popularity to such protests by legitimizing a great part of their complaints.

It should be emphasized that the nonfiction writings of this type are much more voluminous than the fiction. The commitment to Marxism is very widespread among Brazilian intellectuals, although often only partial. The repression of censorship is irregular, inconsistent, and often capricious. It is heaviest on those forms of expression which have a wide popular appeal. Musicians and comedians are the most closely watched. The theater seems to be the next most important on the list. The newspapers are of course, tightly controlled. Prose writers, whether of fiction or nonfiction, are still often able to get into print, since relatively few read them and they do not reach the masses. Such works have at times, however, been removed from the bookshelves and confiscated by the police.

Two recent novels which express clearly the Marxist point of view will be discussed here: *Roteiro da Agonia*, by Macedo Miranda, and *Quarup*, by Antônio Callado.

Roteiro da Agonia (1965) is placed in an unspecified rural region which might be in the state of Rio de Janeiro or southern Minas Gerais. The time extends from shortly before until shortly after the Revolution of 1964. The protagonist, Luiz Pacuera, is a simple and nearly illiterate farm laborer on an estate which had formerly belonged to a traditional "colonel." This land and surrounding estates have been taken over by a shadowy group known simply as "The Administration." These people are called "gringos," a term which may identify any foreigner. From time to time, however, they let slip a few words in English. They are suspected of being only agents of other gringos who are outside the country. Their purpose is not very clear at first. The local Communists believe that they are removing a special type of soil—possibly radioactive sand—for shipment abroad. It finally becomes clear, however, that they are only acting as agents for a Brazilian state electric company—a statement which makes it more difficult to fathom the point of the whole narrative.

In any case, the "gringos" of this story behave exactly like other villains of recent Brazilian literature of protest. They warn the poor laborer about contacts with Communists and summarily drive him off their land. They violate the daughter of one of the workers. They apparently have a worker killed after robbing him of his land and then have another one beaten until he is obliged to confess the murder. They maintain a police force recruited among criminal elements and give it a free hand to deal with suspected malcontents by any means it wishes.

The forces acting against him should have made the protagonist, in the logic of the story, an agent of Communism. But he is weak and vacillating, a heritage of the "colonel's" time. He has never known a situation in which he could take the initiative. The Communists realize this and state, "He is not our man." Pacuera typifies the dilemma of the Communists—how to get the peasant to become a fanatical guerrilla fighter.

Several themes of the Brazilian Marxist doctrine are clearly expressed in *Roteiro da Agonia*. The principal one is the alliance of foreigners—evidently Americans—with minority groups in Brazil who believe they profit from the alliance. These two groups actively prevent the progress of the country, according to this theory. One of the Communists of the story states that the reason the "Administration" can exist in Brazil is that the country does not have technicians. Why does not Brazil have technicians? "Because they don't allow us to."

Another theme is the straw man of Integralism, the long-extinct Brazilian party modeled on Nazism, set up as the opponent of Communism, with convenient disregard for democracy. The man who denounces the Communist connections of Pacuera, and later the Communists themselves, was apparently a friend. But he makes such statements as, "The Germany of Hitler was not so bad as is claimed." And later his connections with the Integralists are made clear.

The attitude toward religion is ambivalent, illustrating the divided opinion within the church. Two priests are mentioned, one of whom does not actually appear. He is a "hard-liner," an exponent of traditional Catholicism, an ally of the upper classes, and will have nothing to do with persons unacceptable to society. He is also partially responsible for making Pacuera useless as a Communist agent, since he has taught him that God forbids violence. The other priest is friendly to all, going so far as to scandalize society and risk his own position in the church by visiting a prostitute who has taken poison.

Quarup (An Indian Festival, 1966), by Antônio Callado, as a novel is weak, badly organized, diffuse. What purports to be love in it is almost solely sex. Of this there is a vast quantity—perhaps five hundred incidents of fornication or adultery. Between fornications, the lovers engage in pseudo-philosophical discussions which are both artificial and out of place. On the other hand, the author manages the language with a great deal of skill. The nonphilosophic dialogues are often excellent and in authentic language. This author has written much better works when he was less preoccupied with propaganda—at times even when he was.

As an expression of the Marxist wing of dissent, the book is one of the most complete and frank that can be found in Brazilian literature. The setting is Pernambuco, in and about the city of Recife. There is a long section in the middle laid in the Amazonian jungle that has little real connection with the rest of the book. Apparently it is a device to cover the years between his first and third sections. In Pernambuco, the situation is particularly suited to a work of this sort; the great division between the rich and the poor, the very considerable activity of Communists, and the mood of violence rampant there give a tone of authenticity and immediacy to this fictionalized account of the history of recent years.

The protagonist illustrates a situation of particular interest in recent years—the increasing approximation of Marxists and one wing of the church. He first appears as a priest, apparently sincere in his be-

liefs but with a wandering eye for female beauty. We learn that he is
scheduled to depart for the Amazon as a missionary but has held back.
He secretly fears not being able to resist the charms of nude Indian
women. He is cured of this complex by the wife of an English friend—
both of them leftist agents—who seduces him while her husband is
away on Marxist business. With his mind at rest, he departs for the
jungle, removes his priestly vestments, and finds enough white females
to keep his mind off the squaws. Before his return to Pernambuco he
abandons the priesthood completely. This break does not, however,
indicate any lack of sympathy between church and Marx. The mutual
liking continues to be revealed both by the ex-priest and by others
who have remained in the church.

At the end, the protagonist kills a policeman who is attempting
to take him to prison and escapes to the interior to take up guerrilla
warfare. The author states that his hero regards the corpse without remorse. Since the circumstances described are such that only a very
strict conscience could feel remorse, the meaning seems to be that the
ex-priest comes to accept violence as the only way to reform.

One of the themes most frequently expressed in the book is that
of the cruelty of the military police. It presents numerous cases of torture of prisoners, some innocent, some guilty of opposition to the regime, some guilty of what any civilized society accepts as crimes.
These tortures are revolting, and they are not the pure invention of the
author. Similar cases have been written into numerous works of fiction
and nonfiction and have been amply documented.[1] But an interesting
fact in this book is that the Marxists show the same tendency to destroy their opponents by the use of violence no more commendable
than that of the police. It is quite clear that if they came to power the
situation would change only in regard to the identity of the victims.

As happens so often in Marxist literature, the military officer who
is responsible for some of the worst tortures against the Marxists is
represented as an ex-Integralist—the well-known image of the Fascist
devil as the great source of evil.

To Callado, the really great source of evil, the devil behind practically all evils, is naturally the United States. Curiously, very few
specific acts of evil are mentioned in this book. But the hatred expressed by several characters is deep and bitter. One refuses to be res-
cued from the jungle by a boat sent by the Americans. Another goes

---

1. See, for example, the magazine *Veja*, December 10, 1969; also, Hermilo Borba
Filho, *Um Cavalheiro da Segunda Decadência*, vol. I.

so far as to destroy smallpox vaccine sent from the United States, even though it is to be used to check an epidemic which is killing off great numbers of the poor. The protagonist is not directly involved in this. He even expresses mild disapproval, but he does not act to prevent it.

Who are the heroes of the Marxists? Among foreigners the main ones are Fidel Castro, Ché Guevara, and their associates. In Brazil, they are Getúlio Vargas, João Goulart, and Miguel Arraes. The legend of Vargas has already been mentioned and will be shown more fully in the discussion of a play about him. Goulart merits only weak praise because of his indecision and weakness which permitted the Revolution against him. Arraes, governor of Pernambuco during the time of Goulart, is a favorite. His support of causes dear to the left brought about his downfall along with that of Goulart.

Of the other political figures of recent years, only Carlos Lacerda receives mention. He is the object of the intense hate of the left. A reason for this is the memory of his battle with Vargas which drove the latter from the presidency and to commit suicide. Another is Lacerda's supposed close relationship with the United States.

The justification for the activities of the Marxists in Pernambuco is clearly expressed as the defense of the peasants. Several of the characters are actively engaged in organizing the farm workers, defending their rights according to existing laws, helping some who have been banished from the land or otherwise mistreated, or even giving them arms. The situation is real, of course, and little or no better than Callado paints it. Unlike Macedo Miranda, Callado has hopes that the farm worker can be aroused to fight. His protagonist flees to the *sertão* to become a leader in guerrilla warfare. Most of his fellow ideologists had already given up that solution by 1968, after several failures of similar attempts.

A work of considerable interest in connection with these questions is the tetralogy of Hermilo Borba Filho, *Um Cavalheiro da Segunda Decadência* (Vol. I, 1966; Vol. II, 1968; Vol. III, 1969; Vol. IV, not yet published). Autobiographical in form, and doubtless to a large extent in content, it cannot properly be considered a novel, and it is not directly concerned with protest. It is not evidently Marxist in orientation, although there are points of agreement in ideas. It is a very interesting document of the times in Pernambuco and in São Paulo from about 1930 to the present. It contains revealing pictures of social corruption, dishonest politics, prison tortures, and military violence, along with interesting inside views of the Brazilian movie industry, television, and the dramatic arts. Many of the personages of the time appear, with only slight efforts to conceal their identities.

Protest in the Theater

Dramatic literature is plentiful in Brazil. In the past, much of it has not been of very high quality, although the art of presentation on the stage has been remarkably good. There has been great improvement in writing for the stage in relatively recent times, along with considerable experimentation with varying results. The change of themes and preoccupation with serious problems has been a positive contribution. Some of the experimentation has given good results, and other features may well do so with further development.

The play is more effective than the novel in the rapid transmission of ideas. The histrionic ability of the actors, the emotional content of their expression, and the closer attention of the spectators caused by the circumstances of the presentation tend to bring about a rapport between the actors and the public which leaves a strong impression on the latter. For these reasons, the play is a better vehicle of protest than the novel. It is also more obvious to the watchful eye of the censor and much more likely to be forbidden.

Dias Gomes opened the cycle of the protest play of the sixties with the very successful *Pagador de Promessas (Keeper of Promises,* first presented, 1960), later made into an excellent film. The question involved here is religious, but with emphasis on the social rather than the theological aspect of religion. The protagonist, known as Donkey Joe because of his fondness for the animal which is his partner in work, has made a vow to carry a cross "as heavy as that of Jesus" to place it before the altar of the church of Santa Barbara if his sick animal recovers. But, not having a proper place to pray to Santa Barbara, he has done it in the Afro-Brazilian rite, to the African deity who is equated with Santa Barbara.

In carrying out his vow, Donkey Joe meets with a complete lack of understanding and sympathy from everyone he encounters, especially from the priests, but also from his wife and friends. Some persons want to use him for commercial purposes, some for political propaganda.

Joe is a very simple person, of course. As a symbol of the common man, he is perhaps not very accurate; for the common man, while often ignorant, is little more likely to lack intelligence than is the man of another class. But his steadfastness of purpose and his unshakable faith contrast to the venality and fear of ridicule of the priests. Through his death, he and the common man he represents triumph over the opposition. Laying his body on the cross he had carried, the

common people pass through the doors of the church and lay it before the altar. The revolution represented is not against the church; it
is within the church in the largest sense of the word—a revolution of
the people against the authorities.

The theme of religion continues to interest Dias Gomes, who is
hardly a religious man. *A Revolução dos Beatos* (1962) deals with an
incident in the career of Padre Cícero Romão, the religious leader of the
sertão. For our present purposes, it is of less interest than *O Santo
Inquérito* (1966). In this play, based on a case of the Inquisition which
occurred in Paraíba in 1750, he clearly reveals the intention of drawing a parallel with the present situation.

The characters are New Christians, the son and granddaughter of
a Jew converted by force, and the fiancé of the granddaughter. A Jesuit
priest is saved from drowning by the girl, Branca, and revived when
she forces her own breath into his lungs. The priest is caught up in
passion for the girl, although he becomes aware of it only gradually.
In his talks with her, he learns details and hears expressions that seem
to him to indicate heresy. Partly impelled by his efforts to resist his
passion, the priest denounces her to the Inquisition. As in the case of
O Pagador de Promessas, her simple expressions of faith only serve to
condemn her. Her inquisitors twist the meaning of her words, finding
guilt where all is innocence.

The father, in an attempt to save something from his ruined life,
agrees to confess his guilt. The fiancé refuses to confess an untruth
even under torture that finally kills him. Branca herself is filled with
fear, totally unable to understand what is happening. She agrees to
sign a confession but at the last moment, inspired by the example of
her fiancé, refuses to sign and is led off to the stake.

The author is very careful to emphasize his intention of drawing
a parallel with the present day, so that the spectator or reader will not
fail to understand. During the trial, the inquisitor says to Branca, "It
is not just you; there are thousands who, like you, consciously or unconsciously, propagate revolutionary doctrines and subversive practices." The words "revolutionary" and "subversive" are hardly appropriate for the eighteenth-century religious context and indicate clearly
the intention.

After her condemnation, Branca indicates the audience and says,
"They, too, think that they can do nothing and that none of this has
anything to do with them. And within a little while they will leave
here at peace with their consciences, in their beautiful cars, and will go
to dine."

The author himself, in the preface which he wrote for the printed edition, seizes the opportunity to remove any possible doubts. Referring to the historical evidence concerning Branca, he indicates that there is some doubt as to whether she was actually burned or whether she "died in bed, like the generals." Later he relates another historical case of an *auto-da-fé*, saying, "Someone (an ancestor of the modern 'hard-fingers') had heard her and denounced her."

Dias Gomes was unable to restrain himself from bringing the Americans into the case in his preface. He compares "McCarthyism" and the Committee on Un-American Activities to the Inquisition.

The same author's play, *A Invasão (The Invasion,* 1962), was written before the Revolution of 1964 and is therefore less pessimistic than *O Santo Inquérito.* The title refers to an "invasion" of a partially finished building by a group of slum-dwellers whose rude shelters had been carried away by a flood. The main theme is the struggle of these people to remain in the building, which they are occupying illegally. Since the laws protect the private property of the rich, there is no suggestion of support for legality, nor is there any thought expressed by anyone that there might be another solution, such as providing shelter for these people elsewhere.

The invaders are surrounded by exploiters who do not even trouble themselves to pose as defenders of the law. There is Manuel the Gorilla, who sells wood for hovels at a high price and rents to slum-dwellers land he does not own. He can do this only because he is protected by the Congressman, whom he aids in turn by rounding up votes. The Congressman is a demagogue, "the friend of the poor." He sends the police to evict the invaders so that he can appear at the strategic moment and grant them a reprieve. Meanwhile, he seduces the daughter of one of the invaders. The police are eager to act against these people, whom they consider Communists. They are especially eager to capture a certain Rafael, an "organizer" (we never learn what he organizes), who does not appear but who gives advice to the invaders.

In spite of the atmosphere of conspiracy against the poor which the author presents, he allows them to win their case in court on grounds that are never made clear. One can only surmise that someone who is sympathetic to their point of view decides arbitrarily in their favor. If the play had been written after March 1964, it is unlikely that he would have given this solution.

O Berço do Herói (The Hero's Home Town, 1965), by the same author, was never presented on the stage. It is one of the most savage attacks in Brazilian literature upon certain social, political, and military institutions. It is evident that, given the existence of a political-military censorship, this work would be suppressed. The author tells us in an article in the *Revista Civilização Brasileira*[2] how the showing was stopped just before it was to go on the stage. He accuses Carlos Lacerda, the bête noire of the far left, although it is difficult to understand why Lacerda would be concerned.

The story concerns a certain Corporal George, who had died a hero in Italy. His native town has taken his name, erected a statue to him, and is exploiting his glory in every way. His uncle has become the local political boss, has his mistress pass for George's widow, and celebrates festivals in honor of George in which everybody makes a profit, including the church.

Ten years later, George appears in the town, ignorant of everything. He had been no hero but had simply gone out of his mind during the battle. He had fled from the field and remained in Italy until a crime committed there threatened to catch up with him. He is simply a "modern" who wants to do only what suits his immediate needs. He claims that he has learned a great deal and can be useful to his native town, but we never get an inkling of what it is he has learned.

His return in these circumstances can only be a disaster to many citizens of the town, if not all. He threatens the political setup, the livelihood of numerous citizens and, worst of all, the veracity and wisdom of the military, which had declared him a hero. He must be eliminated. All forces unite against him, from the bordello to the church, passing through the military and the politicians.

This play presents a very gloomy picture of society. The political boss uses his nephew's fame to gain advantages both for the town he controls and for himself. The mayor is his creature, with no will but to enjoy the prerogatives of his office. The priest preaches drastic sermons against the bordello but accepts money from it through a third person. The religious women of the town are raging fanatics who go out to stone the bordello. The general who is called in to settle the problem of Corporal George's return is both stupid and vicious. Corporal George himself is not a very prepossessing character, having committed robbery and murder in Italy.

In this, as in most of the plays of Dias Gomes, there are qualities of excellence and numerous defects. The final scene, in which the judge

2. Dias Gomes, "*O Berço do Herói* e as armas do Carlos," Revista Civilização Brasileira, Ano I, No. 4 (September 1965), pp. 257-268.

spies through the keyhole while the mayor "inaugurates" the new bordello, is not only in extremely bad taste in itself, but also detracts from the dramatic unity of the play.

Dr. Getúlio, sua Vida e sua Glória (Getúlio Vargas, His Life and His Glory, 1968) is a product of the collaboration of Dias Gomes and Ferreira Gullar. It illustrates, and probably contributes to, a curious and growing legend, the fantastic glorification of Vargas as a hero of the Left.

The technique the authors use is a new and interesting device. A "samba school," one of the groups organized to perform during Carnival, decides to present the story of Vargas in the next Carnival and is rehearsing the story. There is also within the school a struggle for power which parallels to a considerable degree the story they are telling. At times we see the *sambistas* as themselves, at others in the roles they assume in the story. This technique may have been suggested by the cinema, which has better resources to exploit it than exist in the theater.

The story told here is that of the election of Vargas as president in 1950 and of his government and death. His previous period of fifteen years of dictatorship is largely ignored. He is represented as the great friend of the poor and a defender of Brazilian nationalism against the Americans. The latter are represented by an insolent ambassador, while three birds of prey hover in the background.

The specific works for which Vargas is praised are the creation of Petrobrás, the government oil monopoly; the creation of Volta Redonda, the government steel plant; and the law limiting the remission of profits back to the investors' country.

The main opponent attacked here is the United States. The Americans are accused of sending back excessive profits (up to 500 percent in one year), of cutting off purchases of coffee, of the attack by gunmen on Lacerda in which Lacerda was wounded and an officer killed. There is even an anachronistic mention of the "invasion" of the Dominican Republic to be carried out thirteen years in the future.

The second most important target is Carlos Lacerda. He is made to speak to a group of admiring women on the subject, "How to depose a president." The formula is as follows: raise the banner of morality, accusing the government of corruption; use the Communist threat, saying the government is filled with them; accuse the government of planning to carry out the coup which you yourself plan to carry out. The hatred of Lacerda, which is common among laborers, is based mostly on his opposition to Vargas.

As a play, this one is quite weak. The technique of using a school of samba to represent the story has the advantage of presenting Vargas's case as the feeling of the humble people. More skill in organizing the complex structure is needed, however, to bring out the greatest possibilities.

As a thesis, the story of Vargas is not likely to convince those who do not already hold a favorable opinion—not just the enemies of Vargas or of the left, but the impartial spectator. The authors are well aware of the other side of the coin, the other interpretations given to Vargas's acts, and make some feeble attempts to rebut them. They make Tucão, the opponent of the president of the school of samba, object, "This nice Getúlio that you are showing never existed in fact. It is a Getúlio invented to hoodwink the people. Go ask the Congressman what the New State was like. It was people in jail, it was fellows tortured."[3] To this and other criticisms, the principal reply is that Vargas was a nationalist.

Dias Gomes is undoubtedly one of the outstanding dramatic authors of contemporary Brazil. From a literary point of view, his plays are often weakened by the intent of indoctrination carried out to the point of insisting on the obvious. His attempts to renovate the theater and bring it closer to the people have been only partially successful. With further work, he may perfect these techniques and produce superior drama.

A play that deals with social corruption, with only indirect political implications, is *Senhora na Boca do Lixo (Lady in the Police Station,* 1968), by Jorge Andrade. The author of numerous plays concerned with problems of individuals and the relations of one person to another, Andrade here attempts a work of criticism of Brazilian society and produces one of the best Brazilian plays.

The subject is the practice of bringing contraband goods into the country without payment of customs duties, used by persons of the upper classes. The "lady" of the title is an impoverished aristocrat. In spite of her poverty, she travels abroad frequently, financing her trip through the sale of expensive goods she brings back. She has friends among the rich and powerful who encourage her in this practice and who apparently also profit in this way.

The lady has a daughter who accepts her poverty, works to earn her living, and has a high sense of honesty. Her fiancé, equally honest

3. For an account of the treatment the Vargas dictatorship gave to leftists, read Graciliano Ramos's *Memórias do Cárcere.*

and idealistic, is employed in the police, attached to the group which combats smuggling. The lady herself is a basically good person, true to her aristocratic upbringing, serene in her feeling that she has done nothing inconsistent with it.

Horácio, the fiancé, is placed in the difficult position of arresting his future mother-in-law but is compelled to do so by his sense of duty. The daughter, with an equal sense of duty, supports him. Both suffer from the conflicting claims upon them. Only the lady herself accepts the arrest with calmness and the confidence of one who has no fear of the result. Taken to the police station (the name of which is "Boca do Lixo" and gives the title to the play), she remembers how she danced there when it was an aristocratic residence and calls on powerful friends who effect her release.

It becomes clear that this case was given to Horácio with the purpose of getting rid of an honest police agent who has made it difficult for others to engage in dishonest practices. As one of his colleagues says to him, "What is the use of believing in justice if you can't practice it?"

While the lady is waiting in the police station, a poor woman is also there, trying to help her imprisoned son. With her customary affability and kindness, the lady strikes up a conversation. The author employs this device to bring out the contrast between the upper classes who escape without punishment and the humble people who are severely punished for small offenses.

The political implications are not directly aimed at the present regime, although the time of the play is stated to be the present. In fact, the audience in São Paulo doubtless remembered a certain prominent former official of the state who was publicly implicated in a similar situation. The play clearly presumes, however, that corruption in high places, and in the police, continues. It is also probably significant that the lady of the play is protected by a general.

There have been a number of recent plays in which the motifs, and even the forms, of folk literature have been adopted. The purpose may be purely artistic, but in several cases folklore has been used for the expression of protest.

Joaquim Cardozo, a poet since the days of the Modernist Movement, is the author of *O Coronel de Macambira* (1963). It is constructed in the pattern of the *bumba-meu-boi*, a dramatic folk form of the Northeast with roots lost in the distant past. In this form there are certain traditional personages—the Captain, the Colonel (landowner), various slaves, along with any number of other type characters, animals, and supernatural or fantastic folk creations. The dialogue is humorous, often coarse, interrupted frequently by songs and dances. The title is derived from the ox, a central character who always dies but in the older forms of the story is resuscitated.

In the work of Cardozo, the characters have symbolic value which goes beyond the meaning of the traditional *bumbas*. The ox seems to represent the wealth, or potential wealth, of Brazil. He is owned by the small farmer, coveted by the Colonel (latifundiary), protected by the Captain (who probably represents the Brazilian people, rather than the army). The ox is killed by a mysterious shot. The doctor (apparently the government), called on to save it, discusses learnedly and absurdly its anatomy, miraculous cures, etc., while the ox dies.

The satire is light, more amusing than biting. A "producer," who appears and boasts of his productivity, admits that he produces largely *cachaça* (the native rum), for that is what brings him most money. Unmasked, he turns out to be the latifundiary.

The "economist" wishes to get possession of the ox, "using a policy of the best of neighborhoods." He, too, is unmasked, and is revealed as the tax-collector.

The priest is willing to marry two young people, but only at a very high price, "because of the high cost of wine, oil, wax candles, etc." He offers them credit financing, however.

The satire is typical of the real *bumba-meu-boi*. It is generally directed at types found in the interior, sometimes at specific individuals. Only the symbolism gives this one a more immediate note of protest. The author explains in an epilogue that his main purpose was to create an artistic work based on the folk theme of the *bumba-meu-boi* and using an actual one as a model. In this he was eminently successful, aided by his considerable poetic talent.

In *Forró no Engenho Cananéia (Big Stir at the Cananeia Planta-tion,* 1964), Antônio Callado had a much clearer intention of protest or, more accurately, of arousing his public to action. The play takes place on a sugar plantation in the Northeast owned by the usual "colonel" and concerns the attempt of the landowner to destroy the cemetery his workers use in order to plant it in cane.

The colonel had been tricked into promising not to take the land, but he uses his influence to persuade the government agency against droughts to do so. There is no drought, but one is declared by the bureaucrats, who then proceed to combat it. A popular singer, Zé Gato, is considered the most refractory of the peasants, so two assassins are hired to dispatch him. He escapes with a slight wound and takes refuge in the house of his mistress, whose father sells coffins and collects antiques. The mistress locks him in a room without his clothes so that he will not face danger again. He finds a suit of armor to cover him until he can get home to put on clothes and escapes by the window.

In the street is an old hermit who haunts the place. He had been at Canudos with Antônio Conselheiro as a child and later with the famous bandit Lampião. He is a religious fanatic, believing firmly in the legend of King Sebastian and that he will return to save the world. Seeing a figure in armor walking in the village, he believes that Sebastian has returned. Hurrying to his cave, he brings out weapons and ammunition left over from the time of Lampião. These weapons enable the peasants to defeat their opponents.

The evident purpose of the author is to suggest the use of armed force against the latifundiaries. For this purpose, three things are necessary: organization of the peasants, arms with which to resist, and the will to fight. None of these has yet been much in evidence among the farm workers, although none is completely absent.

Nelson Werneck Sodré considered, in an article in the *Revista Civilização Brasileira*[4], the problem of persuading the Brazilian peasant to fight. He contrasted the "fanatical valor" of the Vietnamese peasant to the passive attitude of most Brazilian peasants. His conclusion was that only religious fanaticism has ever led the Brazilian to fight vigorously, citing Canudos and other incidents in the history of the Northeast. In religious fanaticism he saw a possible key to release the fighting ability of the Northeasterner. It is interesting that Callado had used religious fanaticism in this play four years earlier, although the fanaticism is found in only one person. But with an Antônio Conselheiro or a Padre Cícero to urge them on, could these people be persuaded to fight?

Two theatrical groups have in recent years been in the forefront of both theatrical innovation and protest theater. These are the *Grupo Opinião* of Rio de Janeiro and the *Teatro de Arena* of São Paulo. They have used history, folklore, and legend with great freedom of interpretation and made a great deal of use of music derived from the folk music of the country.

The important launching point of this movement was the *Show Opinião* (1965), in which the two groups co-operated. This was not a

4. Nos. 19-20 (maio-agosto 1968), p. 198.

play in the usual sense of the word. The artists (original group—Nara Leão, Zé Keti, and Jõao do Vale) sometimes addressed the public in monologues, sometimes carried on dialogue but, above all, they sang. The main theme was hunger—the perennial hunger of a large part of the population of Brazil. It was not an attack on any political group or ideology nor was it directed at any social class or group; it was an exposition of the suffering of the lower classes—an expression of opinion. Its resounding success was in large part because of its songs, several of which immediately became national favorites.

The *Grupo Opinião* has devoted a great deal of its activity in recent years to the preservation of the traditional forms of popular music, especially the samba. But some of its members have also written plays in which the themes of protest are expressed.

Oduvaldo Vianna Filho and Ferreira Gullar are the co-authors of *Se Correr o Bicho Pega, se Ficar o Bicho Come (If You Run the Bogey Will Catch You, if You Stay the Bogey will Eat You, 1966)*. It is a diffuse and somewhat chaotic piece which attempts to cover a great part of the life of the Northeast, with an unusually large cast of characters. They include the usual "colonel," numerous tenants, many politicians, judges, jailers, policemen, a professional killer, a priest, a seller of images, a "little informer," refugees from drought, newspapermen, sugar-mill workers, soldiers, and even two donkeys.

The prologue, signed by the Grupo Opinião, proclaims unhesitatingly the purpose of the play: "a political answer to the situation in which we live."

"The philosophy of the government," states the preface, "is based on a vote of lack of confidence in the capacity for political discernment of the Brazilian people. *O Bicho* is a vote of confidence in the Brazilian people."

The play is written in verse, with numerous musical interludes. The whole is presented as a farce. As the authors explain, "We made it amusing because . . . it would be extremely cruel, even unendurably so, if it were not done in a key of comedy."

The farce is carried to an extreme: a man recovers immediately from several "mortal wounds"; there is a seduction in a privy; two prominent politicians dispute ridiculously for the favors of a boarding-housekeeper; the hero is jailed and released repeatedly; numerous characters, important or not, are again and again placed in ridiculous circumstances. The motive may be that alleged by the authors, but the reader cannot escape the thought that a serious play on the subject might not have eluded the censor. Throughout the play there are seri-

ous short scenes and expositions of the impasse of the poor which it
might not have been possible to deal with in a serious play without its
being forbidden. Examples of this are the use of fugitives from the
drought who are willing to work for mere sustenance to replace paid
workers at the sugar mill and the candidate who does not appear, but
whose platform is the redistribution of the land. In order to make
amply clear the solution proposed, the farce closes with three alternate
endings. The first, the "happy ending," shows the "hero" as the new
landowner, expelling a tenant just as he himself had been expelled; the
second, the "juridical ending," shows him dividing the land with the
peasants; the third, or "Brazilian ending" announces that he has been
called by the new governor to help carry out the agrarian reform.

As a play, *O Bicho* is extremely weak. The excess of farce is tir-
ing, and the mixture of farce and serious propaganda weakens the effect of both. Its length and complexity make it difficult to follow the
thread of the action.

The *Teatro de Arena* has attempted to create a new dramatic form,
the *Arena Conta . . .* later called the *Coringa*. This type took definite
shape first with *Arena Conta Zumbi (Arena Tells the Story of Zumbi*,
first performed in 1965), by Gianfrancesco Guarnieri and Augusto
Boal, music by Edu Lobo. This play was followed by various others of
similar mold, the most important being *Arena Conta Tiradentes*
(1967), by the same authors.

The *Coringa* (the word means "joker" at cards) usually takes a
character from history or legend, someone who can represent the principles the authors wish to express. These may be nationalism and love
of liberty, as in the case of Tiradentes. In *Zumbi*, they present love of
liberty, willingness to defend one's rights with arms and, possibly in-
cidentally, the dignity of the Negro. The story is told with considerable liberty of interpretation by a group of only a few actors who take
numerous rôles, interchange places, and make little attempt to represent the personages to the eye of the spectator. Only the outstanding
characteristics of the main characters are kept to identify them—the
bravery and anger of Zumbi, the idealism of Tiradentes, etc. This is
termed by the *Teatro de Arena* "collective interpretation."

Zumbi narrates the story of Palmares, where escaped slaves took
refuge in colonial times, formed a viable community, and for many
years resisted all efforts to dislodge them. The scenes selected to tell
the story cover a considerable number of years, include a rather large
number of characters, and are of different moods—comic, melodramat-
ic, tragic. While the scenes follow the main outlines of the story as it

is known to history, the interpretation of the characters, and even of the incidents, is quite free. In order for this type of story to be intelligible to the audience, it requires a narrator (Coringa), who fills in between scenes and introduces the next scene, placing it in the context of the entire story. The mood of the individual scenes is set in part by the narration and in part by the music that accompanies it.

The authors of *Zumbi* use the story from the past in order to express ideas about the present. The Negroes of Palmares took up arms in defense of their liberty, fleeing from the slavery of the plantations. The speech of the Portuguese governor concerning the runaways is quite modern in the expression of the principle of authority—most of it was taken from recent newspapers. The governor is presented as both tyrannical and ridiculous. The fact that a Negro is the hero of the story is possibly incidental but more probably is quite intentional. Negroes form a disproportionate part of the poorest classes and have been protagonists in a great many recent works that deal with the lower classes.

The technique represents a fairly radical change in the theater, forming what amounts to a new type of dramatic work. It will doubtless not replace the traditional theater but may continue alongside it. The weaknesses that exist in this and other plays of this type are more in the conception of the story itself than in the structure of the *coringa.*

The Principles of Protest

What are the principles and ideas held by the protesters? They vary with the individual and with his philosophical and political orientation. Some of the main ideas often expressed are the following:

—Politicians in general are dishonest, inefficient, completely corrupt, often capable of committing crimes in order to get rich or to keep or acquire power. They are generally connected with the wealthier classes, whom they help get rich at the expense of the poor. One can get legitimate help from a politician only by doing him some important favor or by using the influence of other powerful persons. Few Brazilians will name more than one or two prominent politicians whom they believe to be honest and sincere.

—Large estates are ruled by unscrupulous persons who not only exploit the poor but mistreat them personally. They dismiss summarily the poor worker who offends them in any way, leaving him suddenly without means of support. If any worker wishes to protest his lot or demand those rights which the law theoretically guarantees to him, he is labeled a dangerous radical and turned over to the corrupt police, or may even be killed. The wives and daughters of the workers are at the mercy of the landowners, who feel no concern that these women are then driven from their families and fall into prostitution.

—The large estates should be broken up and divided among those who work on them. This idea is widespread and persistent and has been ratified by several governments, but with very little result.

—Freedom of the press and of speech should be restored. This is one of the most important points for the intellectuals, but the humble people are naturally much less concerned with this than with their economic difficulties.

—The intellectuals protest the control and closing of congress, the general domination of state and local officials by the federal government, and the "elections" of new presidents by a rubber-stamp-controlled Congress. The people, while they express some concern for this, are more directly affected by the treatment given to leaders whom they consider to be friends of the poor. The followers of such leaders as Kubitschek, Goulart, Arraes, and Lacerda are particularly bitter against the military government.

—The Armed Forces should get out of politics and control of education, business, and government. Frankly military in nature, with officers in control of most departments of government, in government monopolies in industry and business, of the police, and less directly in education, this government has brought down on the military an unprecedented dislike of a great part of the people.

—The government causes or allows political prisoners and others to be tortured. These accusations have appeared from time to time in the press and are found in numerous works of fiction and nonfiction. Some attempts to document them have been made.[5] The present administration has stated that it will not tolerate such practices, but few have been convinced.

—The Americans are an evil influence. This is naturally a fixed idea with the Marxist wing, but it is also widely accepted among others. The arguments presented to support it range from the reasonable to the fantastic, the second type perhaps more often believed than the first. The most frequently expressed anti-American arguments might be summed up as follows:

—The United States is an imperialist power that wants to and does dominate Brazil, but especially covets the Amazon Valley.

5. See footnote 2.

(missing)

—The American government is the tool of big business (or, just as frequently, the contrary). It wishes to prevent Brazil from industrializing, buy its raw products cheap, sell industrial products high. It particularly wants to get control of oil, iron, manganese, and similar products of importance to industry.

—The Americans support the rightist elements in Brazil—the military, the landowners, the rich in general. These in turn are pro-American because they make money through the Americans, at the expense of Brazil.

It is interesting to note that the Catholic Church is almost never the object of attack in protest literature. One might expect the Marxists, at least, to attack religion. A few individual churchmen are subjected to attack, but the general attitude is friendly. The reason is to be found in recent events within the church in Brazil. A considerable part of it, at least, is on the side of the protesters. Some churchmen are concerned with social ills but try to promote reform while avoiding departure from the traditional principles of their church. Others, fairly numerous, go so far as to give active aid to the partisans of violent revolution[6] or even to become spokesmen for it. There is, of course, a wing of the church that is vigorously opposed.[7]

REFERENCES

Andrade, Jorge, *Senhora na Boca do Lixo*. Rio de Janeiro: Editôra Civilização Brasileira, 1968.

Boal, Augusto, and Gianfrancesco Guarnieri, *Arena Conta Tiradentes*. São Paulo: Livraria Editôra Sagarana, 1967.

Borba Filho, Hermilo, *Um Cavalheiro da Segunda Decadência*, 4 vols. Rio de Janeiro, Editôra Civilização Brasileira, vol. I, 1966; vol. II, 1968; vol. III, 1969; vol. IV, not yet published.

Callado, Antônio, *Forró no Engenho Cananéia*. Rio de Janeiro: Editôra Civilização Brasileira, 1964.

———, *Quarup*. Rio de Janeiro: Editôra Civilização Brasileira, 1966.

Cardozo, Joaquim, *O Coronel de Macambira*. Rio de Janeiro: Editôra Civilização Brasileira, 1963.

Corrêa, Oscar Dias, *Brasílio*. Rio de Janeiro: Gráfica Record Editôra, 1968.

Costa, Armando, Oduvaldo Vianna Filho, and Paulo Pontes, *Show Opinião*.

6. See *Veja*, No. 63, November 19, 1969.
7. See the article mentioned in footnote 5.

Rio de Janeiro: Edições do Val, 1965.

Gomes, Alfredo Dias, *O Berço do Herói*. Rio de Janeiro: Editôra Civilização Brasileira, 1965.

———, *A Invasão e A Revolução dos Beatos*. Rio de Janeiro: Editôra Civilização Brasileira, 1962.

———, *O Santo Inquérito*. Rio de Janeiro: Editôra Civilização Brasileira, 1966.

———, *O Pagador de Promessas*, 2nd Ed.; Rio de Janeiro: Livraria Agir Editôra, 1962.

———, and Ferreira Gullar (José Ribamar Ferreira), *Dr. Getúlio, sua Vida e sua Glória*. Rio de Janeiro: Editôra Civilização Brasileira, 1968.

Guarnieri, Gianfrancesco, *Êles não Usam Black-tie*. São Paulo: Editôra Brasiliense, 1966.

———, and Augusto Boal, *Arena Conta Zumbi* (presented in 1965).

Lemos, Gilvan, *Emissários do Diabo*. Rio de Janeiro: Editôra Civilização Brasileira, 1968.

Lima, Geraldo França de, *Brejo Alegre*. Rio de Janeiro: Livraria São José, 1964.

———, *Branca Bela*. Rio de Janeiro: Livraria São José, 1965.

Miranda, Macedo, *Roteiro da Agonia*. Rio de Janeiro: Editôra Civilização Brasileira, 1965.

Palmério, Mário, *Vila dos Confins*. Rio de Janeiro: Livraria José Olympio Editôra, 1957.

———, *Chapadão do Bugre*. Rio de Janeiro: Livraria José Olympio Editôra, 1965.

Rangel, Flávio, and Millôr Fernandes, *Liberdade, Liberdade*. Rio de Janeiro: Editôra Civilização Brasileira, 1965.

Vianna Filho, Oduvaldo, and Ferreira Gullar, *Se Correr o Bicho Pega, se Ficar o Bicho Come*. Rio de Janeiro: Editôra Civilização Brasileira, 1966.

Index

In indexing Brazilian personal names, we have used the system followed at present in Brazilian libraries: the index entry is under the *final* name, whether that is the name by which the person is generally known or not. Thus, for example, Humberto Castello Branco is indexed under *Branco*, despite the fact that he is referred to in the text as *Castello Branco*; Joaquim Maria Machado de Assis is indexed under *Assis*, even though he is sometimes referred to simply as *Machado*.

All Brazilian personal names indexed under *final* name.

All Brazilian personal names indexed under *final* name.

All Brazilian personal names indexed under *final* name.

All Brazilian personal names indexed under *final* name.

All Brazilian personal names indexed under *final* name.

All Brazilian personal names indexed under *final* name.

All Brazilian personal names indexed under *final* name.

All Brazilian personal names indexed under *final* name.

All Brazilian personal names indexed under *final* name.

All Brazilian personal names indexed under *final* name.